ISBN 978-1-5278-6744-4
PIBN 10888933

FB &c Ltd, Dalton House, 60 Windsor Avenue, London, SW19 2RR.
Company number 08720141. Registered in England and Wales.

For support please visit www.forgottenbooks.com

agazine Devoted to History, Genealogy and Biography

THOMAS FRANKLIN WATERS, *Editor*. IPSWICH, MASS.

— ASSOCIATE AND ADVISORY EDITORS —

FRANK A. GARDNER, M.D. SALEM, MASS. CHARLES A. FLAGG WASHINGTON, D. C. JOHN N. MCCLINTOCK DORCHESTER, MASS. ALBERT W. DENNIS SALEM, MASS.

Issued in January, April, July and October. Subscription, $2.50 per year, Single copies 75c.

VOL. II **JANUARY, 1909** **NO. I**

Contents of this Issue.

THE "SCARLET LETTER" AND OLD KETTERIE — *Herbert M. Sylvester* 3

COLONEL EPHRAIM DOOLITTLE'S REGIMENT . . — *F. A. Gardner, M.D.* 11

THE REV. JAMES NOYES HOUSE IN NEWBURY — *Benj. L. Noyes, M.D.* 30

THE PATHFINDER AT MARIETTA, OHIO IN 1888 — *George Sheldon* . . 33

MASSACHUSETTS PIONEERS IN MICHIGAN . . . — *Charles A. Flagg* . 39

THE WILLIAMS HOUSE AT DEERFIELD 41

SOME ARTICLES CONCERNING MASSACHUSETTS IN RECENT MAGAZINES . . . . — *Charles A. Flagg* . 42

DEPARTMENT OF THE AMERICAN REVOLUTION — *F. A. Gardner, M.D.* 45

CRITICISM AND COMMENT 48

SOME MASSACHUSETTS HISTORICAL WRITERS 51

PILGRIMS AND PLANTERS . . . . — *Lucie M. Gardner* . 54

OUR EDITORIAL PAGES . . . . — *Thomas F. Waters* . 55

CORRESPONDENCE of a business nature should be sent to THE MASSACHUSETTS MAGAZINE, Salem, Mass.

CORRESPONDENCE in regard to contributions to the MAGAZINE may be sent to the editor, Rev. T. F. Waters, Ipswich, Mass., or to the office of publication, in Salem.

BOOKS for review may be sent to the office of publication in Salem. Books should not be sent to individual editors of the magazine, unless by previous correspondence the editor consents to review the book.

SUBSCRIPTION should be sent to THE MASSACHUSETTS MAGAZINE, Salem, Mass. Subscriptions are $2.50 payable in advance, post paid to any address in the United States or Canada. To foreign countries in the Postal Union $3.00. Single copies of back numbers 75 cents each.

REMITTANCES may be made in currency or two cent postage stamps; many subscriptions are sent through the mail in this way, and they are seldom lost, but such remittances must be at the risk of the sender. To avoid all danger of loss send by post-office money order, bank check, or express money order.

CHANGES OF ADDRESS. When a subscriber makes a change of address he should notify the publishers, giving both his old and new addresses. The publishers cannot be responsible for lost copies, if they are not notified of such changes.

ON SALE. Copies of this magazine are on sale in *Boston*, at W. B. Clark's & Co., 26 Tremont Street, Old Corner Book Store, 29 Bromfield Street. Geo. E. Littlefield, 67 Cornhill, Smith & McCance, 38 Bromfield Street; in *New York*, at John Wanamaker's, Broadway 4th, 9th and 10th Streets; in *Philadelphia*, Am. Baptist Pub. Society, 1630 Chestnut Street; in *Washington*, at Brentanos, F & 13th St.; in *Chicago*, at A. C. McClurg's & Co., 221 Wabash Ave.; in *London*, at B. F. Stevens & Brown, 4 Trafalgar Sq. Also on sale at principal stands of N. E. News Co.

Entered as second-class matter March 13, 1908, at the post office at Salem, Mass., under the act of Congress of March 3, 1879. Office of publication, 4 Central Street, Salem, Mass.

THE "SCARLET LETTER" AND OLD KETTERIE

By Herbert M. Sylvester

HAWTHORNE'S "Scarlet Letter" offers no suggestion of the source from which he drew the inspiration for his creation of the immortal Hester Prynne, or of the story of Mary Bachiller of old Ketterie; yet one may well assume the tale as not unknown to him whose brain teemed with quaint and curious New England happenings. Mary Bachiller's spirit may have looked over the shoulder of Hawthorne as he wrote this tragedy in prose which has become one of the choicest classics of New England literature.

Old Salem, as Hawthorne knew it, was conducive to the mood in which he must have been to have written as weirdly as he did at times; for he must have been under a "spell" to have wrought the characters so foreign to his own experiences. Be that as it may, his desk in the old Custom House was not so far from famous Kittery, which lay up the coast a day's drive on the east shore of the Piscataqua just opposite ancient Strawberry-bank, now historic Portsmouth, like olden Newcastle and Sagamore Creek, overlooked, by the many gabled manse of the New Hampshire Wentworths, whose rarest and most romantic memories are resolved into the tradition of the wooing and winning of Martha Hilton, the fairest flower of old Newcastle, and the whilom waiting-maid at "The Dolphin," who became Lady Benning Wentworth much to the astonishment of Mistress Stavers who kept that notable inn in old Queen street. Just down the bay were the wharves of old

Gosport which nestled against the side of Haley's Island, one of the seven islands that made up the Isles of Shoals where Parson Tucke in the middle of the 17th century had his little university, and where for years he taught the select youth of Massachusetts Bay their Greek, Latin and Mathematics to his own satisfaction if not to that of his pupils.

There is no more picturesque country than just here where New Hampshire and Maine touch elbows through the fogs of the Piscataqua. No part of the coast is possessed of more lively traditions or antiquarian lore; for

A GLIMPSE OF KITTERY POINT.

even in these days the shore of modern Kittery is lined with a score of roof-trees that date back to the beginning of things English on the Maine coast. Here are floors that have echoed to the tread of the first settlers, the Shapleighs, Hiltons, Gunnisons and the Pepperells and those who came along with them. The whole length of Kittery Point shore runs a country highway as unsuggestive of a summer resort as heart could desire, along which are strung like so many pearls the silvery roofs that were contemporary with the Palatinate of Sir Ferdinando Gorges.

The Parsonage dates back to 1629. The church was built the following year. Alexander Shapleigh built in 1635 and set up the first tavern. Fifteen years later William Hilton was using it as an "ordinary" as taverns were known in those days, and the Rev. Stephen Bachiller had taken up his residence among the Kittery folk. Bachiller was a character whose marital experiences might have suggested to Alexander Pope, who was born thirty-seven years later, to exploit in pungent verse the alliance of January and May. Moreover, he was a lively thorn in the flesh of the politic Winthrop and as well *persona non grata* to the Great and General Court.

Born in England in 1561, his Non-Conformist affiliations compelled him to take asylum in Holland. Some years later he had drifted back to London, and on March 9th, 1632 he set sail for Boston on the *William and Francis* to join his daughter Theodate who had preceded him New England-ward. Arriving safely in Boston he made his way to Lynn to the residence of his daughter, where he began at once to "hold forth," whereupon the General Court ordered him "To forbeare exercising his gifts as pastor or teacher publiquely in our Pattent." From Lynn, Bachiller went to Ipswich where he had a land-grant; but having in mind the establishment of a church at Yarmouth, he set out for that place afoot, in mid-winter, of 1637,—a hundred mile journey. Failing in this project, he went to Hampton. He was about eighty years of age at this time "when he committed a heinous offence, which he at first denied but finally acknowledged, and was excommunicated from the church therefor."

His disgrace was but temporary, as he was soon after admitted to Communion and invited to preach at Exeter; but the General Court would not permit him to accept the call. This was in 1644, and six years later he was in Portsmouth, where, at the extreme age of eighty-nine he determined to take unto himself a third wife. Hardly a novice in marital matters he decided that—

"A stale virgin with a wintry face,"

would not be to his taste, and likewise endowed with the fervent belief that

"A wife is the peculiar gift of Heaven,"

he forthwith married one Mary,—the surname is lost,—for his third spouse whose age is given as "twenty-three."

Unfortunately for the peace of the Kittery settlement, with or without provocation, Mary Bachiller became enamoured of a worthless fellow, one George Rogers, whose untimely and scandalous behaviour with the girlish, and no doubt charming, wife of this foolish old man was such that in October

of 1651 they were indicted under the Laws of Massachusetts Bay and brought summarily to book. It was a swift disillusionment for the poor wife; for upon their presentment to the Court, which was undoubtedly held in Hugh Gunnison's tavern, the same previously carried on by Shapleigh and afterward by Hilton, they were duly sentenced. The trial is given at length in "Book B" of the York Records. Rogers, after the fashion of the time, was let off with "forty stroakes save one at ye first Towne Meeting held at Kittery," which he could cover up with his coat; while the girl-wife was adjudged to receive "forty stroakes save one at ye first Towne Meeting held at Kittery 6 weekes after her delivery, & be branded with the letter A . . . two inches long, and proportionable bigness, cut out of cloath of a contrary color to her cloathes and sewed upon her upper garments on the outside of her arm or on her back in open view," and if by mischance or intent she should be found without her letter, she was to be "publiquely whipt."

The "Towne Meeting" was held in the old church now standing upon its original foundation just opposite the ancient burial-ground, and it was upon the Common, doubtless, in front of this historic edifice that the sentence was carried out upon the culprit.

Here was a Hester Prynne ready-made for Hawthorne, with the difference, that Mary Bachiller came by her "Letter" by due process of law and not under the magic wand of the romancer. Poor woman, forever disgraced and branded on that fateful day "six weekes after," her story, ghostlike, will never down!

Kittery is not a far-cry from old Salem, and it is not to be doubted for a moment but Hawthorne was aware of the circumstance. It was the only case of its kind east of the Piscataqua River, and in fact, the only one within the knowledge of the writer as having occurred within the purlieus of Massachusetts Bay, as it was then designated, so suggestive in its character.

If Hawthorne derived his inspiration from Mary Bachiller's misfortune, and it seems most likely that he did, she was fortunate in her interpreter; for I apprehend, taking into consideration the laxity of morals in those days, and lax they were, she was more sinned against than sinning,—nor is the stage-setting of her story less weird and lonely than the times were harsh and unmerciful to her sex. It is a great story, however, and worthy of New England's greatest romancer,—a wizard tale, by a veritable wizard.

What became of Mary Bachiller is unknown. The historian of that day is silent. Nothing exists by which her fate can be gleaned either by record or tradition. But for the musty records of old York her story would have been as much a myth as is that of Hester Prynne. As for her nonogenarian

consort, he sailed for England that same year, where, undivorced from his third wife, he married a fourth with whom he spent the remainder of his days which were terminated in 1660.

What a commentary on the times, the old times of the Colonies, this incident, or rather, tragedy, affords, when sentiment and merey were measured out with niggard hand; when everybody was bitted, and not a few saddled; when the right of way was hereditary; when the clergy carried the whip and held the reins; when the preacher went from his pulpit to the Bench, and when Precedent was good law and seldom called to halt! The superstitions that made the Salem witch-trials of 1690 a possibility, indicated cloudy skies and doubtful weather to such as exercised liberty of thought and action which were as likely to be pointed with tragedy as otherwise. Strange and soul-troubling vagaries were a common heritage, and wherever the law touched, whether the culprit went to the whipping-post, pillory, stocks, ducking-stool, or common gaol, it left a brutal scar for a genius like Hawthorne's to immortalize.

As for the tragedy of Mary Bachiller, for tragedy it was, it is one of the hideous things to keep one company along this oldest highway of Maine, with the gray worn roofs of a nondescript architecture strewn along its marge at uncertain intervals, the relics of a quaint and original people. As one goes, Witch of Endor-like, he conjures the past with many a spell of the imagination, or reads their stories in the original to translate as freely as a lively imagination will allow. For all that has been written, one sees as through a glass, darkly, wishing in vain for the Mormon's Goggles, where Time has set a wall as impassable as the Bridge of Al Araf. Yet, through it all, out of it all, comes the hopeless wail of Mary Bachiller as the lash falls upon her nude back at the whipping-post, and the gleam of a flame-like letter blisters and burns upon the vision. It is like the stain upon the hand of Lady Macbeth that will not out, this letter that perpetuated the degradation of a woman, settling in entail upon an innocent offspring a like degradation *in perpetuum*.

But what a setting, this riant landscape, for such a memory! Behind one is the ghost of the whipping-post, and before, the shimmer of the shales where the tide makes up, the glittering lustres of the micas, or the gray glooms of the massive granites, their feet sandalled in the emerald of the sea, snooded with bands of dusky kelp. Always as one looks over the low wall of the old burial-ground, with the old church at his back and its unchristian associations as well, the vision is filled with a medley of hooded capes dyed with the blue of the farthest waters or the purple of royalty. Along the broken shores the trees have been sculptured into fantastic shapes by the vagrant

winds. Sleep-distilling pine-laden odors haunt the zephyrs that steal with noiseless foot-fall across the golden floors of the marshes, or with hastened pace weave the salt grasses into webs of unmatchable color. Deep bays make spacious anchorages that might hold all the navies of the world, and numberless inlets and creeks make inlayings of silver amid the inland verte, that

KITTERY POINT MEETINGHOUSE.

This, the oldest church east of the Piscataqua, was built in 1630. The Parsonage which makes the background of the sketch, was erected a year earlier. Both are in a fine state of preservation. The first home of the Episcopalians in the Gorges jurisdiction, it was presented with a silver communion service by Sir William Pepperrell which is still in use. It was in this church undoubtedly that Mary Batchiller had her trial. Under the shadow of its low gable she stood in pillory, and had her "thirty-nine stroakes."

lay mostly fast asleep in the summer sun after a vagabondish fashion, where even the wildest gales are shorn of their tumult. No wonder men set up their easels along these ribs of sun-bleached sands to catch

"The tremulous shadow of the sea!"

For all the charm and beauty of these Kittery shores and the sea that lies beyond, look as I may, the glow of that "Scarlet Letter" marks the uneasy spirit of Mary Bachiller, whose noiseless footfall keeps loitering pace with my own, even as the rift in the cloud-smothered horizon at set of sun betrays the ruddy stain of a day that is dead.

There is a flavor of brutality to this story that makes the blood mount in temperature. While its meagreness of detail throws something of a shadow over this swift meting out of justice,—and justice was younger then than now,—that in itself reflects the rough indifference of the times. One cringes as if Norton's lash were whistling about one's ears: and it would be incredible altogether, except that forty years later alleged witches were swirling from Gallows-trees on the top of Witch's Hill. Lest in these days of imaginative writing, any doubt should be left, the original relation burnt into the time-yellowed page of the ancient York Records is here quoted. Mary Bachiller's first appearance in Court was in October of 1651. (O. S.). The Record has this entry,—

> The Court boulden at Kittery the 14th of this P^r sent Month of Octob : 1651. & Election mad as Follows
> P^r sent. m^r Edward Godfrey Govr
> m^r Richard Leader ma'estrat
> m^r Nicolas Shaply ma'estrat
> m^r Abraham Preble ma'estrat
> m^r Tho. Weathers ma'estrat
> m^r Edward Rishworth w^th *Unius Amicus* Consent chosen an Assistant ma'estrat & Recorder
> Actions knowne to be entered, somoneses granted out Recogniscences payrtys bound to appere as delinquent & others to give evadence against them; in regard of Late decease of the Recorder, we call y^m to remembrance as followeth
> Actions or sommones granted :
> x x x x x x
> P^r sentments mayd by the Grand inquest houlden at Pischa : Octob : 16 : 1651
> We do p^r sent George Rodgers for, & mary Batcheller the wife of m^r Steven Batcheller minis^tr for adultery. It is ordered by ye Court y^t George Rodgers for his adultery with mis batcheller shall forthwith have fourty stripes save one upon the bare skinne given him : It is ordered y^t mis Batcheller for her adultery shall receave 40 stroakes save one at ye First Towne meeting held at Kittery, 6 weekes after her delivery & be branded with the letter A:
> Execution Done.
> p^r. Ed : Rishworth Record"

Five months later, Mrs. Bachiller was again presented, and suffered the delayed penalty.

> "P^r sentments given in by the Grand inQuest: Held at Gorgeana March : 18 : 1651
> We p^rsent mis Bacheller for adultery
> mis Batcheller is to be whipped at the next town-meeting & m^r Norton is to be sent for"

From this entry it is evident that the gossip over the affairs of Mary Bachiller had achieved a culminating point. Kittery society had called a halt by giving her over to Norton for discipline. There is no mention of the evidence taken in the case,—only the bare finality, the stripping off the

garb of womanhood to brand the remnant a moral leper, an outcast among her kind, whose distinguishing mark never to be thereafter hidden from the eyes of men, was the initial letter of her offense. There is no accent of regret, extenuation, or apology on the part of the Court,—only the coarse cry of the lash and the taunt of the Scarlet Woman.

The following year we find another entry in the Court record. It is a part and parcel of the spirit of the times. Norton and his whipping-post, the pillory and the "brand" had not proved efficacious. In this record we have Mary Bachiller's final appearance, and one wonders if she were so very much the worse than those who sat in judgement upon her. The same record lets in a side light as to George Rogers, who appears to have had a family of his own, and with the disposition of whose children the tale of old Kittery's scandal is closed. Here is the record, —

> "P^{r} sentments brought in by the Grand inQuest at a Court houlden at Agament^{s} Oct 14 1652
>
> For the Province
>
> "We p^{r} sent mis Batcheller for entertayneing Idle people on the sabbath day
>
> "It^{s} ordered y^{t} George Rogers, his children, shall be desposed of as followeth, The one child is to be desposed of to Daniell Hard & m^{r} Shapleigh or m^{r} Withers are to see the indenters drawne betwixt them Ed Rishworth is to despose of another Girls at hangst^{o}. Anthony Emrey is to have another & m^{r} Shapleigh & m^{r} Withers are to be putt out as is specifyd & y^{n} indentars drawne."

The hand that wrote this story in the original is stilled. The chirography is labored and hieroglyphic. Words touch elbows, and the lines are jammed into irregular parallels, but the ink, like the blood on the hand of Lady Macbeth is of the indelible sort, and the paper sewed into its vellum covers is unmatchable. 1651–2, the decadence of the Gorges Palatinate had not been consummated; but the ancient records remain, and so far as Mary Bachiller is concerned, a stain upon the times and an indictment of those who had a part in the making. And the people,— how rough and uncouth, who could so outrage common decency, much less leer at helpless Mary Bachiller where the sunlight beat most fiercely upon her degradation.

Hawthorne felt all this. His resentment found its highest expression when he had impelled Arthur Dimmesdale to creep through the shadows of the night to where Hester Prynne, with an unnamable terror had shivered and quailed at the hoots and jeers of the Puritan purists. It remained for Hawthorne to rechristen Mary Bachiller and to make her the heroine of New England's greatest tragedy in prose.

COLONEL EPHRAIM DOOLITTLE'S REGIMENT

Colonel Ephraim Doolittle's Minute-Men's Regiment. 1775.

Twenty-fourth Regiment, Army of the United Colonies. 1775.

By Frank A. Gardner, M. D.

This regiment was composed largely of men from the central part of the state. It was one of the first to be equipped and ready for active service, and had an honorable record all through the opening year of the war, at the close of which it disbanded.

The following document gives us an interesting insight into the character of the command and the difficulties which Colonel Doolittle encountered at the beginning of the conflict.

"To the Honble John Hancock, Prefident of the Honble Provential Congrefs to be holden by adjiournment at Concord on the 22nd Day of March Inftant Sr Pleafe to communicate the following To your Body haveing Rec^{d} a Requifition for the Hon^{le} Congrefs Directing of me To make Return of my Regiment, their Numbers and acquipments for war I have accordingly appli'd my self to the Bufinefs but have not as yet obtained a Return of But Two or three Companys and if I Can obtain a full account before the Congrefs Rifes Shall forward it Emediately—but we are in a moft Lamentable Scituation for want of a Sanction of Government on our Establifhments our Tory Enemies ufing all their Secret machenations to divide us and Break us to pieces ad to this the Deficulties that arife by ambitious men who are Indeavouring to Break our Companys to pieces in order to get Promotion for as there is no Eftablifhment but what aRifes in the Breafts of Individuals we are Continually Breaking to Peases and a Number of Companys in my Regiment are now in such Circumftances and I fear if we are not soon Called to action we shall be Like a Rope of Sand and have no more Strength—if it may be Rec^{d} with Candour I should be

Exceeding Glad if our Continental Committee might be Instructed to Lay the Deficulties which we Labour under for want of a Civil Conftitution before that Body and that they Indeavour to obtain their voice in Justification of this Provinces Eftablishing one. God Give you all Grace and Wifdom to Direct you in the Important afair of American Liberty. Remain your and the Publicks well wisher and Humble Ser[t]

Ephr[m] Doolittle

Petersham March 31-1775"

Colonel Doolittle demonstrated his untiring patriotic zeal and executive ability during the few weeks following, for he had a regiment of eight companies, properly officered when the Lexington Alarm was sounded on the 19th of April. These officers were as follows:—

Colonel, Ephraim Doolittle.
Lieut. Colonel, Benjamin Holden.
Major, Willard Moore.
Adjutant, William Bridge.

Holden Company.
Captain, James Davis.
First Lieutenant, Samuel Thompson.
Second Lieutenant, Samuel Hubbard.
2 sergeants, 4 corporals, 1 fifer and 29 men.

Athol Company.
Captain, Ichabod Dexter.
First Lieutenant, Ephraim Stockwell.
Second Lieutenant, Abner Graves.
4 sergeants, 4 corporals and 21 men.

Royalston Company.
Captain, Jonas Allen.
Lieutenant, Daniel Pike.
4 sergeants, 2 corporals and 16 men.

Templeton Company.
Captain, Joel Fletcher.
First Lieutenant, Paul Kendall.
Second Lieutenant, John Wilder.
4 sergeants, 4 corporals, 1 drummer and 31 men.

Hubbardston Company.
Captain, William Marean.
Lieutenant, Adam Wheeler.
Ensign, William Mussey.
4 sergeants, 4 corporals and 25 men.

Princeton Company.
Captain, Boaz Moore.
First Lieutenant, John Jones.
Second Lieutenant, Adonijah How.
3 sergeants, 4 corporals, 1 fifer, 1 drummer, 27 men.

Paxton Company.
Captain, Phineas Moore.
First Lieutenant, Josiah Newton.
Second Lieutenant, Seth Snow.
2 sergeants, 1 fifer and 28 men.

Winchendon Company.
Captain, Abel Wilder.
First Lieutenant, John Boynton.
Second Lieutenant, Dudley Parley.
4 sergeants, 4 corporals and 30 privates.

Petersham Company.
Captain, John Wheeler.
Lieutenant, Edward Barker.
Ensign, John Bowker.

When the regiment was reorganized a few days later the following officers were appointed:—

Colonel Ephraim Doolittle,	engaged April 24.
Lieut. Colonel Benjamin Holden,	" " "
Major Willard Moore,	" " "
Adjutant John Woodward,	" " "
Surgeon Barnit Wait,	" " "
Surgeon's Mate Enoch Dole,	" " "

"On the 3d of May, a party of two hundred privates and officers, under Colonel Doolittle, were ordered on fatigue; the directions for the work to be done were to be given by Mr. Charwick, engineer."

The following report shows the strength of the regiment at the date appended:—

Epharaim Doolittle Coll°
Benj[n] Holden Lieut. Coll°
Willard Moore Major

"Cap[t] Abel Wilder	51	men.
Cap[t] Adam Wheeler	59	"
Cap[t] Joel Fletcher	59	"
Cap[t] Eben Millet	45	"
Cap[t] Ichabod Dexter	38	"
Cap[t] Jon[a] Holman	59	"
Cap[t] Robert Oliver	59	"
Cap[t] John Woods	59	"
Cap[t] Abijah Moore	59	"
Cap[t] Hezekiah Stowell	59	"
	547	

Oliver Holman, Adj't.
May 20, 1775."

"To the Hon[le] Prefedent of the Colony Congrefs S[r] if you will Deliver the Commifsions for my Reg[t] to my Major Willard Moore you will oblige your moft obedient Humble Ser[t]

Eph[m] Doolittle Coll°

May 23, 1775."

A number of men petitioned the Colonial Congress, June 10, 1775, stating that "when they Ingeaged had an Expectation that Cap[t] Ichabod Dexter would have been their Cap[t] and that they underftood at the same Time that they were to be of Co[ll] Ephraim Doolittle's Reg[t] and further say that we have Done Duty and Draw[d] Provetions for a Considerable Time in his Reg[t] until of Late we have underftood that Cap[t] Dexter had Returned his Company in Col[l] Woodbridge's Regiment without Confulting his Company thereon we would further Reprefent that our Company is not full as there is Still an opening in Col[l] Doolittle's Reg[t] whereby our Company may be Compleat by Joyning Cap[t] Abijah More who is willing to Receive us with the men he has Inlifted whereby we may be Emediately Muftered and Receive our Pay Therefore we Humbly Petetion that we may Emediately be alow[d] to Joyn the Company of Abijah More aforesaid and the Reg[t] of which Eph[m] Doolittle is Collonel and not be Joyned to any other Reg[t]

June 10. 1775
Abner Graves L[t]" (and 16 others.)

The records show that this petition was not granted.

"A Lift of the Company officers in Coll Doolittle's Reg't Ready to be Commifsioned June 12, 1775.

Capt Joel Fletcher.
Lt John Wheeler.
Enf^n^ Jonas Proctor.

Capt Robert Oliver.
Lt Thos Grover.
Enf^n^ Abraham Pennel.

Capt Adam Wheeler.
Lt Elijah Stearns.
Enf^n^ Adam Maynard.

Capt Able Wilder.
Lt Jonas Allin.
Enf^n^ Daniel Pike.

Capt Jon^a^ Holman.
Lt John Bowker.
Enf^n^ David Poor.

Capt John Lealand.
Lt Saml Burbank.

Capt John Jones.
Lt Saml Thomfon...

Frothingham in his account of the Battle of Bunker Hill mentions this regiment as follows:—"The colonel and lieutenant-colonel were absent on the day of the battle, and Major Willard Moore led on, it is stated, three hundred of its men. Few details are preserved of the service of this regiment, or the conduct of its officers. The depositions speak in glowing terms of the good qualities of Major Moore. He was a firm patriot and chivalrous soldier. On the second attack he received a ball in the thigh, and while his men were carrying him to the rear another ball went through his body. He called for water, but none could be obtained nearer than the Neck. He lingered until the time of the retreat, when feeling his wounds to be mortal, he requested his attendants to lay him down, leave him, and take care of themselves. He met a soldier's death . . . . . . Few notices appear of individuals of this regiment. Robert Steele, a drummer, stated in 1825, that he 'beat Yankee Doodle when he mustered for Bunker Hill on the morning of the 17th of June, 1775' "

The same authority in his "Battle of Bunker Hill," tells us that Captain Wheeler's Company of this regiment, Captain Crosby's Company of Colonel James Reed's (N. H.) Regiment, and a Company from Colonel B. Ruggles Woodbridge's Regiment, were stationed in Main Street, at the base of Breed's Hill and constituted the extreme right of the American line. Six men of this regiment were killed or missing and nine wounded, in the battle.

The following changes in the field and staff officers occurred during May and June:—

Major Jacob Miller, promoted June 18, to succeed Major Willard Moore who was killed in the battle of Bunker Hill.

Quartermaster Benjamin Haywood, appointed May 26.

Surgeon Enoch Dole, promoted from Surgeon's Mate, June 18.

Surgeon's Mate Absolom Russell, appointed June 21.

"A Regimental Return of the Number of Commifsioners & Soldiers, June 29, 1775," gave the same list of officers as the above list of June 12th, except that the name of "Enfign Frances Wilfon," was added to Captain John Jones Company.

The following comprises a list of company commanders in this regiment in June-July 1775, with the list of towns in which the companies were raised:

Captains.

"Robert Oliver, Conway, Montague, Colraine, Deerfield.
Josiah Stearns, Lunenburg, Edgecomb, Pownalsboro, Georgetown, Ashby, &c.
Oliver Capron, Richmond, Winchester, &c. &c.
Abel Wilder, Royalston, Winchendon, Lunenburg, &c. &c.
Joel Fletcher, Templeton, Petersham, Westford, &c.
John Jones, Princeton, Holden, Lancaster, Hubbardston, &c.
Jona. Holman, Templeton, Petersham, Winchendon, Hubbardston, &c.
James Hubbard, Wells, Arundel, Sanford.
Jacob Miller, Holliston, Dublin, Medway, &c.
Adam Wheeler, Hubbardston, Rutland, Princeton, Paxton."

Ten small arms were delivered to Colonel Doolittle, for the use of his regiment, amounting "as by appraisement, to twenty-two pounds, eighteen shillings, for which a receipt was taken in the minute book." We know from the returns that the regiment was stationed on Prospect Hill during the first three weeks of July. On the 16th Captain Robert Oliver was appointed recruiting officer. This regiment was assigned to Brigadier General Sullivan's Brigade, on the 22nd. and formed a part of the left wing of the army under Major General Lee. It was stationed on Winter Hill.

The following letter of three days later explains itself:—

"To The Gen^{tm} of the Committee of Supplies my Reg^{t} have unanimously agreed not to Drink any more of the Beer from the Brewers that have Laitly Supply^{d} us to be so Cheated out of our Rights and helth is unfufferable I have Converfed with Mr Capt Benj^{a} Hall of Medford who has ingeaged to Brew it according to my Direction and if you have any Inclination to Continew to us our Beer please to give him orders to Brew our Beer and Allow him the fully Quantity the Province allows for that purpofe I doubt not of your Readynefs to do us Justice otherways I should Emmediately have made application to aneother Quarter this from your moft obedient homble Ser^{t} July 25, 1775.

Eph^{m} Doolittle Coll^{o}"

This complaint was withdrawn two days later.

Returns made to August 1, show that the officers remained the same as given in the list above in the companies of Captains Fletcher, Holman, Jones, Oliver and Wilder. The other companies in the regiment were as follows:—

Capt. Oliver Capron, Richmond.
Lieut. David Barney, "
4 sergeants, 4 corporals, 1 drummer and 34 men.
Capt. Jacob Miller, Holliston. (Promoted Major June 18.)
Lt. Saml Burbank "
Ensign Oliv^{r} Work "
4 sergeants, 4 corporals, 1 drummer, 1 fifer, and 42 men.
Capt. Josiah Stearns, Lunenburgh.
Lieut. Nath'n P. Smith, Pownelsborough.
Ensign Wm Thurlo, Fitchburg.
3 sergeants, 4 corporals, 1 drummer and 40 men.
Capt. James Hubbard, Wells. (Report of this company dated Oct. 10.)
1st Lt. Joseph Churchill, "
2nd Lt. Nathan Cousins. "
4 sergeants, 4 corporals, 1 fifer, 1 drummer and 39 privates.

We know from the rolls and records of the regiment that it was still stationed on Winter Hill late in October, and probably remained there until disbanded at the end of the year.

The strength of this regiment at various periods through the year is shown by the following table:—

1775.	Com. Off.*	Staff	Non Com.	Rank & File†	Total
June 9,	21		36	330	344
July	19	3	42	333	397
Aug. 18,	28	4	48	369	449
Sept. 23,	31	4	58	458	551
Oct. 17,	19	5	43	382	449
Nov. 18,	24	5	47	393	469
Dec. 30,	26	4	40	378	448

COLONEL EPHRAIM DOOLITTLE was Captain of a company on the Crown Point Expedition, according to a muster roll bearing date of March 5, 1756. His expenses for guns, blankets, etc. lost, amounted to £8:10:06.

He was a member of the Petersham committee of correspondence in 1772. He represented that town and was moderator of the town meeting held there, January 4, 1773. In August he was a member of the Worcester Convention, and served on a committee to prepare resolves on the "state of public affairs." (Aug. 30.) October, 1774, he was a member of the Provincial Congress from Petersham and was appointed on a committee to wait on Governor Gage. He also served on a committee "to report a resolve recommending total disuse of India teas," and on a committee to prepare a non-consumption agreement. November 26, he was appointed on a committee to "devise some means of keeping up a correspondence between this province, Montreal, and Quebec, and of gaining very frequent intelligence from thence of their movements."

The account of his service as Colonel of the Minute Men's Regiment and the 24th Regiment, Army of the United Colonies, we have given above. He may have been and very likely was the Ephraim Doolittle who served as a private in Captain John Oliver's Company, in Colonel Nathan Sparhawk's Regiment, from September 28, to October 18, 1777, in the Northern Army as reinforcements against Burgoyne.

LIEUT. COLONEL BENJAMIN HOLDEN was born in Dedham. He was a Lieutenant in the French and Indian War and at that time resided in Roxbury. February 18, 1767, he was Captain in the 3d. Regi-

*Sergeants, fifers and drummers. †Corporals and privates.

ment of Worcester County Militia. The records show that he served as Captain of the "Prince town" Company in Colonel John Murray's Regiment, in the year 1767. He served as Lieut. Colonel in Colonel Ephraim Doolittle's Minute Men's Regiment in 1775 and the 24th Regiment to the end of the year. He was Lieut. Colonel of Colonel Israel Hutchinson's 27th. Continental Regiment, through 1776. His name appears on the pay accounts as Lieut. Colonel of the (late) Colonel Hutchinson's Regiment from January 1, 1777 to May 25, 1778. As Colonel Hutchinson's Regiment disbanded at the end of 1776, this pay was undoubtedly given to Lieut. Colonel Holden as a prisoner of war, for we know that he was captured at Long Island and held by the enemy.

MAJOR WILLARD MOORE came from Paxton. He took a prominent part in the Worcester Convention in September 1774. He was an Ensign in Captain Paul How's (Paxton) Company in Colonel John Chandler's Regiment. (Year not given.) He also served as Lieutenant in Captain Ralph Earl's (Paxton) Company, in Colonel John Chandler's 1st. Regiment Worcester County Militia in 1771. He was chosen Captain of a company of minute men in January, 1775. He was Major of Colonel Ephraim Doolittle's Minute Men's Regiment and marched for Cambridge on the Lexington Alarm. The story of his gallant service and death on the field of Bunker Hill have been given in the account of the exploits of the regiment. He was a brave officer and a loss to the patriot army.

MAJOR JACOB MILLER of Holliston, was called Major, and reported as field officer of the guard. May 9, 1775. He was a Captain in Colonel Doolittle's Regiment, appointed in the place of Captain John Lealand, resigned. Major Willard Moore was killed at the Battle of Bunker Hill and on the following day Captain Jacob Miller was engaged as Major of the regiment. He was, however, to retain command of his company. He served in the regiment through the year. May 10, 1776, he was engaged as Major of Colonel Josiah Whitney's 2nd. Worcester County Regiment.

ADJUTANT WILLIAM BRIDGE, held that office in Colonel Ephraim Doolittle's Minute Men's Regiment from April 19 to 26, 1775. He served as Adjutant of the 7th. Middlesex County Regiment in 1778. (Elected June 20.)

ADJUTANT JOHN WOODWARD was engaged April 24 (or 27), 1775, and served in Colonel Doolittle's Regiment through the year. He

was 2nd. Lieutenant and Adjutant of Colonel Loammi Baldwin's 26th. Regiment in the Continental Army through 1776, and was appointed Lieutenant and Paymaster of the 9th. Regiment, Massachusetts Line, January 1, 1777. He died October 17, 1778.

ADJUTANT OLIVER HOLMAN was mentioned in an order of the day dated May 16, 1775, as Adjutant of Colonel Doolittle's Regiment. Another order dated June 8, was signed by him. His name, however, does not appear in a list of staff officers of this regiment dated August 1, 1775, which was intended to include all who had served between April 24 and the above mentioned date.

QUARTERMASTER BENJAMIN HAYWOOD was engaged May 26, 1775. He may have been the "Benjamin Haywood" who was Paymaster of Colonel Nixon's 6th. Regiment, Massachusetts Line, in 1777 and a Captain in the same regiment later.

SURGEON BARNIT WAIT was engaged April 27, 1775, and served 1 month and 25 days. No further record of service is given.

SURGEON ENOCH DOLE of Lancaster was engaged April 24 (or 27) as Surgeon's Mate in this regiment and served until June 18, when he was promoted Surgeon. He served in that office through the year. He was Surgeon's Mate in Colonel Whitney's Regiment in 1776.

SURGEON'S MATE ABSOLOM RUSSELL was engaged June 21, 1775, and served at least 1 month and 13 days. No further record of service is given.

CAPTAIN JONAS ALLEN of Royalston, commanded a company in Colonel Doolittle's Minute Men's Regiment. He was probably the Captain Jonas Allen who was in charge of guard detail under Major Baldwin May 15, 1775. He served as Lieutenant in Captain Able Wilder's Company in the 24th. Regiment under the same commander through the year.

CAPTAIN OLIVER CAPRON of Richmond was engaged April 30, 1775. A muster roll dated August 1, showed that he had served 3 months, 9 days. He was recommended for a commission in a petition signed by Colonel Ephraim Doolittle. He was the son of Banfield and Hannah (Jencks) Capron. He was born in July, 1736. He lived in Cumberland a few years and then moved to Richmond, N. H. In the French war he served in two campaigns near Crown Point. He is described in the "Capron Genealogy" as "a stout, spry and active man, well built, rather more than middling stature, light complexion and reddish hair."

CAPTAIN JAMES DAVIS of Holden was a company commander in Colonel Doolittle's Regiment of Minute Men, April 19, 1775. His service lasted 19 1-2 days. He also served for 5 days as a Captain in Colonel Benjamin Flagg's (Worcester County) Regiment, in April, 1777.

CAPTAIN ICHABOD DEXTER of Athol commanded a company in Coonel Doolittle's Minute Men's Regiment, April 19, 1775. He was engaged as a Captain in Colonel Benjamin Ruggles Woodbridge's 25th. Regiment, April 24, and served in that regiment many months, probably through the year. He was the son of Samuel and Mary (Clark) Dexter, and was born in Athol 24 June, 1737. The statement is made that he and his brother were in the French and Indian war at the taking of Ticonderoga. They were taken captive by the Indians but awoke in the night, killed their captors and escaped. He was a selectman in Athol in 1768. In 1780 he removed to Hardwick and was a selectman there in 1781-2 and 1785 and a Representative in 1782-3.

CAPTAIN JOEL FLETCHER of Templeton served as Captain in a company in Colonel Doolittle's Minute Men's Regiment, April 19, 1775. He "Loft in the Battle of Chelfea,* one Blanket, one Pair of Shoes, one Pair of Plated Buckels, one Bayonet." He was in the Battle of Bunker Hill and lost at that time, "three Guns, Blankets three, three Cartuch boxs, 1 Powder Horn." "Capt Fletcher left in Mornin Battle his wearing Aperil his gun & Accutements and four Dollers of Cash Whofe Family is very needy." He served through the year in the 24th Regiment, Army of the United Colonies under the same commander.

CAPTAIN JONATHAN HOLMAN of Templeton was a lieutenant in Captain Ezekiel Knowlton's Company, in Colonel Nathan Sparhawk's Regiment, April 19, 1775. He was engaged April 24, as Captain in Colonel Doolittle's Regiment. At the Battle of Bunker Hill, he lost "one Coat. one Blanket, one Gun." He served through the year in the 24th. Regiment, Army of the United Colonies, under Colonel Doolittle.

CAPTAIN JAMES HUBBARD of Wells (now Maine) joined the regiment with his company in the last of June or early part of July and served into October. He died in that month while in the service at Cambridge. The "History of Wells" (Me.) states that "He was a worthy citizen, firm and resolute in his adhesion to the principles which were the

*May 27, 1775. See Massachusetts Magazine, v. I, p. 164.

moving cause of the Revolution, and ready to offer himself on the altar of liberty. He was one of the selectmen of the town; was also one of the committee of correspondence chosen to consult with the friends of liberty."

CAPTAIN JOHN JONES of Princeton was a Lieutenant in Captain Boaz Moore's Company, in Colonel Ephraim Doolittle's Regiment of Minute Men, April 19, 1775. He was engaged April 24th as Captain in Colonel Doolittle's Regiment. At the Battle of Bunker Hill he lost "one gun, two Blankets, two Coats, one Cutlafs, one fine Shirt. He served through the year under the same commander.

CAPTAIN JOHN LEALAND of Holliston was Captain of a Company of Minute Men in Colonel Abijah Pierce's Regiment, April 19, 1775. June 12th he commanded a company in Colonel Doolittle's Regiment. He resigned (probably in June or July) and Captain Jacob Miller was appointed in his place. He was the son of John Lealand and was born in Holliston, January 12, 1744. He was a farmer and schoolmaster before the war but afterward became a minister and settled in Partridgefield. He served there successfully for nearly forty years and died at the age of eighty.

CAPTAIN WILLIAM MAREAN of Hubbardston lived first in Newton, later in Barre and went to the first named town in 1768. He was Captain of a Company of Minute Men in Colonel Doolittle's Regiment, April 19, 1775, serving 17 days. He was chosen March 24, 1776, a Captain in Colonel Nathan Sparhawk's 7th. Worcester County Regiment. He also served as Captain in Colonel Jonathan Reed's 1st. Regiment of Guards in 1778 and in Colonel Stearns's Regiment of Guards in the same year. In 1779 he was First Major in Colonel Jonathan Grout's 7th. Worcester County Regiment. He died May 10, 1826, aged 83.

CAPTAIN EBENEZER MILLET of Holden served first as Quartermaster of Captain Davis's Company of Minute Men, April 19, 1775. He was a Captain in Colonel Doolittle's Regiment in May, 1775, but left the organization before June 12th.

CAPTAIN ABIJAH MOORE of Putney was Captain of a Company of Minute Men, April 19, 1775. In May he was Captain of a Company in Colonel Doolittle's Regiment but he left before June 12th. A man of the same name from the same town was a private in Captain Benjamin Hastings' Company in Colonel Asa Whitcomb's Regiment, in August and October, 1775.

CAPTAIN BOAZ MOORE of Princeton commanded a Company in Colonel Ephraim Doolittle's Regiment of Minute Men, April 19, 1775. He served for 13 days.

CAPTAIN PHINEAS MOORE of Paxton had command of a Company in Colonel Ephraim Doolittle's Regiment of Minute Men, April 19 1775. Service 10 days.

CAPTAIN ROBERT OLIVER of Conway was born near Boston in 1738. He commanded a Company of Minute Men which marched in Colonel Samuel Williams' Regiment, in response to the Lexington Alarm. He was engaged May 1, as Captain in Colonel Doolittle's Regiment and served through the year. He was in the Battle of Bunker Hill and lost "one Gun, one Piftol, one Gun Lock, four Pair of Leather Breeches, four Shirts, Trouser two Pair, Stockine four Pair, Shoes three pair, one Handkerchief." He was a Captain in Colonel John Greaton's 24th. Continental Regiment in 1776, and in the 3d. Regiment Massachusetts Line (2nd. in White Plains numbering) in 1777. He was promoted Major November 1, 1777, and served until January 1, 1783. On the latter date he was transferred to Lieut. Colonel Ebenezer Sprout's 2nd. Regiment, Massachusetts Line, and on the 30th of September was made Lieut. Colonel by brevet. He served to November 3, 1783. He was celebrated as a disciplinarian and for a time acted as Adjutant General of the Northern Division of the Army. He served as a volunteer in Shay's Rebellion and was a founder of Marietta, Ohio in 1788. He represented Washington County in the Territorial Legislature in 1798 and was President of the Territorial Council in 1800-3. He also served as Colonel of the 2nd. Territorial Regiment and Judge of the Court of Common Pleas. He was a Member of the Society of the Cincinnati.

CAPTAIN JOSIAH STEARNS of Lunenburg commanded a Company in Colonel Doolittle's Regiment as early as July 10, 1775, and served through the year. He was the son of Thomas and Abigail (Reed) Stearns of Littleton, and was born July 18, 1747. He moved to Lunenburg. In 1776 he was a member of the "Committee of Correspondence" and in the years following often served as assessor and selectman. He was Town Treasurer for eight years and Town Clerk from 1817 to 1822. He was a Representative for three years and a member of the Governor's Council fom 1797 to 1799. He died August 7, 1822.

CAPTAIN HEZEKIAH STOWELL was in command of a Company in Colonel Doolittle's Regiment, according to a general return dated May 20, 1775. He served only a short time.

CAPTAIN ADAM WHEELER of Hubbardston went there from Rutland about 1766. He served first as a Lieutenant in Captain William Marean's Company, in Colonel Ephraim Doolittle's Regiment of Minute Men, April 19, 1775. He was made a Captain soon after in the same regiment. In the Battle of Bunker Hill he lost "three Guns and one Coat." He served to the end of the year in Doolittle's 24th. Regiment and in 1776 was a Captain in Colonel John Nixon's 4th. Regiment, Continental Army. In 1777 and 1778 he was a Captain in Colonel Thomas Nixon's 6th. Regiment, Massachusetts Line. A receipt was given to Benjamin Heywood, dated Shrewsbury, June 21, 1779, signed by said Wheeler, Captain, for "$120 and a State note of £100 in full for the gratuity and first moiety granted him by the General Court for his service as a Captain in the Continental Army." Retired October 15, 1778. He commanded a company of men in sympathy with Daniel Shays in Shays's Rebellion. He fled to Canada where he remained four years until the proclamation of amnesty.

CAPTAIN JOHN WHEELER of Petersham was commander of a Company in Colonel Ephraim Doolittle's Regiment of Minute Men, April 19, 1775. On the 27th. of that month he was engaged as a Lieutenant in Captain Joel Fletcher's Company, in Colonel Doolittle's Regiment, and served through the year. He was commissioned an Ensign in Captain Ezekiel Knowlton's Company, in Colonel Nicholas Dike's Regiment, in October, 1776, and engaged as First Lieutenant on the 1st. of December in the same year. He with other officers agreed to tarry until March 1, 1777.

CAPTAIN ABEL WILDER of Winchendon served in that rank in Colonel Ephraim Doolittle's Regiment of Minute Men, April 19, 1775. He was at Bunker Hill and lost "three Coats, Shirts three, three Pair of Stockine, three Guns, one Drum, one Blanket." He was the son of Thomas and Mary (Wheeler) Wilder, and was one of the first settlers of Winchendon. He was the first Town Clerk and was annually elected for twenty-seven years, and was often moderator and selectman. It is said that he was plowing in the field when called on the Lexington Alarm. He served as a member of the State Constitutional Convention and was a representative in the first Legislature in 1781. He was a senator from Worcester County for

six consecutive years, and a presidential elector in 1792. "He was of stout build and had a pleasant countenance and a commanding presence. . . . . He filled the largest place in the history of the town. He was pre-eminently useful in life, cheerful and prepared for death and universally lamented."

CAPTAIN JOHN WOODS is given as a company commander in a list of officers of Colonel Doolittle's Regiment, May 20, 1775.

LIEUTENANT DAVID BARNEY of Richmond was a Lieutenant in Captain Oliver Capron's Company, in Colonel Doolittle's Regiment. He enlisted April 30, 1775, and served through the year.

LIEUTENANT JOHN BOWKER of Petersham served first as Ensign in Captain John Wheeler's Company, in Colonel Ephraim Doolittle's Regiment of Minute Men, April 19, 1775. Five days later he enlisted as a Lieutenant in Captain Jonathan Holman's Company in the same regiment. Reported deserted September 8, 1775 He was in Captain Nathan Hamilton's Company, in Colonel Samuel Brewer's Regiment, in February, 1777. In August of that year he was 2nd. Lieutenant in Captain Wing Spooner's Company, Colonel Nathan Sparhawk's Regiment.

LIEUTENANT JOHN BOYNTON of Winchendon held that rank in Captain Abel Wilder's Company, in Colonel Ephraim Doolittle's Regiment of Minute Men, April 19, 1775. He was commissioned, April 6, 1776, Captain of the 8th. Company in Colonel Nathan Sparhawk's (7th. Worcester Co.) Regiment. In 1777 he had two short terms of service in the same regiment, one at Bennington and the other in the Northern Army.

LIEUTENANT SAMUEL BURBANK of Holliston was an Ensign in Captain John Lealand's Company of Minute Men in Colonel Abijah Pierce's Regiment, April 19, 1775. June 12th. he was commissioned a Lieutenant in the same company. He continued to serve in this company under Captain Jacob Miller, through the year. July 27, 1777, he was commissioned Captain in Colonel Samuel Bullard's (5th. Middlesex Co.) Regiment, chosen in place of Benjamin Marshall, deceased. He was the son of Samuel Burbank and was born in Woburn in 1735. He settled in Holliston and later resided in Fitchburg, where he died February 6. 1828.

LIEUTENANT JOSEPH CHURCHILL of Wells held that rank in Captain James Hubbard's Company in Colonel Doolittle's Regiment. from August, through the year.

LIEUTENANT THOMAS GROVER of Montague was a Captain in Colonel Samuel Williams Regiment of Minute Men, April 19, 1775. May 1, he was engaged as a Lieutenant in Captain Robert Oliver's Company, Colonel Doolittle's Regiment, and served through the year. He was engaged July 20, 1779, as First Lieutenant in Captain Elisha Lyman's Company, Colonel Elisha Porter's (4th. Hampshire County) Regiment. Service 1 mo. 14 days. He also served in Captain Samuel Merriman's Company in Colonel Israel Chapin's 3d. Hampshire in 1779 and in Captain Oliver Shattuck's Company in Lieut. Colonel Barnabas Sears's Hampshire County Regiment, in 1781.

LIEUTENANT PAUL KENDALL held the rank of First Lieutenant in Captain Joel Fletcher's Company of Minute Men in Colonel Doolittle's Regiment, April 19, 1775. He was commissioned, June 26, 1777, Second Lieutenant in Captain Josiah Wilder's (3d.) Company, in Colonel Nathan Sparhawk's (7th. Worcester County) Regiment. From August 31 to November 29, 1777, he was a Second Lieutenant in Captain David Bent's Company, Colonel Job Cushing's Regiment.

LIEUTENANT JOSIAH NEWTON of Paxton served as a First Lieutenant in Captain Phineas Moore's Company, in Colonel Ephraim Doolittle's Regiment of Minute Men, April 19, 1775.

LIEUTENANT DANIEL PIKE of Royalston was Lieutenant of Captain Jonas Allen's Company in Colonel Doolittle's Regiment of Minute Men, April 19, 1775. He was Ensign in Captain Abel Wilder's Company in the same Regiment, commissioned June 12, 1775, and he served through the year.

LIEUTENANT DAVID POOR of Winchendon was a First Lieutenant in Captain Moses Hale's Company in Colonel Nathan Sparhawk's Regiment, which marched on the alarm, April 19, 1775. April 24, he was engaged as Ensign in Captain Jonathan Holman's Company, in Colonel Doolittle's Regiment. He was a Lieutenant in the same company in October. In 1776 he was a Lieutenant in Colonel Israel Hutchinson's 27th. Regiment, Continental Army, and was taken prisoner at Fort Washington, November 16, 1776. He was confined on Long Island for over four years, and was exchanged December 17, 1780.

LIEUTENANT NATHAN SMITH of Pownalsboro was engaged, April 26, 1775, to serve in Captain Josiah Stearns's Company, in Colonel

Doolittle's Regiment. In a company return given October 6, he was called First Lieutenant.

LIEUTENANT ELIJAH STEARNS of Rutland was in Captain Adam Wheeler's Company, Colonel Doolittle's Regiment, as early as June 12, 1775. Company returns show that he continued in that organization through the year.

LIEUTENANT EPHRAIM STOCKWELL of Athol served in that rank in Captain Ichabod Dexter's Company, Colonel Doolittle's Regiment of Minute Men, April 19, 1775. In April, 1776, he was commissioned First Lieutenant in Captain John Oliver's Company, in Colonel Nathan Sparhawk's (7th. Worcester County) Regiment. He was engaged July 28. 1777, as a Captain in Colonel Job Cushing's Regiment.

LIEUTENANT SAMUEL THOMSON of Holden held the rank of First Lieutenant in Captain James Davis's Company, Colonel Doolittle's Regiment of Minute Men, April 19, 1775. Five days later he was engaged as Lieutenant in Captain John Jones's Company in the same Regiment and served through the year. January 1, 1776, he was engaged as First Lieutenant in Colonel Loammi Baldwin's 26th. Regiment, Continental Army. September 26, 1777, he was engaged as Captain in Major Asa Baldwin's Division of Colonel Samuel Denny's Regiment. He served one month in the Northern department.

SECOND LIEUTENANT NATHANIEL COUSINS of Wells had served under General Abercrombie at Fort Niagara in 1758 and also at Lake George held that rank in Captain James Hubbard's Company. in Colonel Doolittle's 24th. Regiment, Army of the United Colonies, in October, 1775. A Nathaniel Cousens, probably the same man, was a Lieutenant in Captain Tobias Lord's (Seacoast) Company, which marched January 1. 1776, and served 11 months at Falmouth, Cumberland County. January 29, 1779, he was commissioned Captain in Colonel Thomas Cutts. 3d. York County Regiment. Later in that year he served as Captain in (late) Major Daniel Littlefield's detachment of York County Militia, and August 1. served as Major in the same command on the Penobscot expedition. He was a selectman of Wells. He died in 1832 aged 95 years.

SECOND LIEUTENANT ABNER GRAVES of Athol served first as an officer in Captain Ichabod Dexter's Company in Colonel Doolittle's Regiment of Minute Men, April 19, 1775. He was a Lieutenant in Captain

John Blanchard's Company, Colonel James Wesson's 9th. Regiment, Massachusetts Line, from January 1, 1777, to June 17, 1778.

SECOND LIEUTENANT ADONIJAH HOW of Princeton was an officer in Captain Boaz Moore's Company, in Colonel Doolittle's Regiment of Minute Men, April 19, 1775. He served 18 days.

SECOND LIEUTENANT SAMUEL HUBBARD of Holden held that rank in Captain James Davis's Company, in Colonel Doolittle's Regiment of Minute Men, April 19, 1775, service 5 1-2 days. April 5, 1776, he was commissioned First Lieutenant in Captain Nathan Harrington's Company, in Colonel Samuel Denny's 1st. Worcester County Regiment. He marched, July 27, 1777, as a Lieutenant in Captain Jesse Stone's Company, Colonel Job Cushing's Regiment, in General Warner's Brigade at Bennington. He was a Captain in the same Regiment from September 3 to November 29, 1777. March 5, 1779, he was commissioned Captain of the 3d. Company in Colonel Samuel Denny's 1st. Worcester County Regiment.

SECOND LIEUTENANT DUDLEY PARLEY of Winchendon served for 16 days in that rank in Captain Abel Wilder's Company, in Colonel Doolittle's Regiment of Minute Men, in response to the alarm call April 19, 1775.

SECOND LIEUTENANT SETH SNOW of Paxton was one of the officers in Captain Phineas Moore's Company in Colonel Doolittle's Minute Men's Regiment, April 19, 1775; service, 19 days.

SECOND LIEUTENANT JOHN WILDER of Templeton was an officer in Captain Joel Fletcher's Company in Colonel Doolittle's Regiment of Minute Men, April 19, 1775.

ENSIGN ADAM MAYNARD of Paxton served first as Sergeant in Captain Phineas Moore's (Paxton) Company in Colonel Doolittle's Minute Men's Regiment, April 19, 1775. He was an Ensign in Captain Adam Wheeler's Company, in Colonel Doolittle's Regiment, June 12, 1775. At Bennington in 1777, he was Second Lieutenant in Captain Loring Lincoln's Company, under Lieut. Colonel Flagg; and April 28, 1778, was commissioned Captain in the 1st. Regiment, Worcester County Militia.

ENSIGN WILLIAM MUSSEY of Hubbardston was an Ensign in Captain William Marean's Company, in Colonel Doolittle's Regiment of Minute Men, April 19, 1775; service, 17 days.

ENSIGN ABRAHAM PENNEL of Colrain served first as a Second Lieutenant in Captain Hugh McClellan's Company of Minute Men, in Colonel Samuel William's Regiment, which marched in response to the alarm of April 19, 1775. He was an Ensign in Captain Robert Oliver's Company, in Colonel Doolittle's Regiment, from May, through the year.

ENSIGN JONAS PROCTER of Westford was a Corporal in Captain Timothy Underwood's Company, in Colonel William Prescott's Regiment of Minute Men, April 19, 1775. He was engaged May 2, as an Ensign in Captain Joel Fletcher's Company, in Colonel Ephraim Doolittle's Regiment, and served through the year.

ENSIGN WILLIAM THURLO of Fitchburg was a Lieutenant in Captain Ebenezer Bridge's Company, in Colonel John Whitcomb's Regiment of Minute Men, April 19, 1775. He served as an Ensign in Captain Josiah Stearns's Company, in Colonel Ephraim Doolittle's Regiment; engaged July 13, 1775. He was a Lieutenant in the same company later in the year. In 1776 he was Captain in the 8th. Regiment, Worcester County Militia. In August, 1777, he was Captain of a company which marched under command of Major Ebenezer Bridge, to reinforce the troops at Bennington. In the following year he served under the same commander, and in July-September of that year was Captain of a company in Colonel Josiah Whitney's Regiment.

ENSIGN FRANCIS WILSON of Holden held that rank in Captain John Jones's Company, in Colonel Ephraim Doolittle's Regiment; engaged April 24, 1775. The Colonel and others, in a communication to General Washington, stated that he "behaved most valiantly in the Charlestown fight". He was a Captain in Colonel Danforth Keyes' Regiment; engaged June 27, 1777, and elected Major in the same regiment, then under Colonel Nathaniel Wade, February 27, 1778. He served as a Captain in Colonel Samuel Denny's Regiment from October 21 to November 23, 1779.

ENSIGN OLIVER WORK of Holliston was an Ensign in Captain Jacob Miller's Company, from April, through 1775.

THE REV. JAMES NOYES HOUSE IN NEWBURY

By Benjamin Lake Noyes, M. D.

Robert Noyes, of Cholderton, County of Wilts, England, through a negotiation with John Thornburg, in 1596, secured the "advowsan" or right of presentation of the rectory of his parish in such a way as to place William, one of his three sons, as pastor in that church. This Rev. William was born in 1568 and died in Cholderton shortly before 1622, after serving as rector about twenty years. He m. Anne Parker about 1595, and of their six children, the third and fourth, James and Nicholas Noyes, together with their cousin, Rev. Thomas Parker, in March, 1633, embarked for New England in the ship "Mary and John," of London, and were among the first settlers of Newbury, Mass., May, 1635. They first settled at the "Lower Green" on the Parker River, but in a very few years, upon the removal of the meeting house, in 1646, to the "Upper Green," Rev. James transferred his abode to a palatial (for the times) residence which he built near the church, and the same is yet found standing on what is now known as Parker street, Newbury, where he lived until death. He served as teacher in the Newbury church over which the Rev. Thomas Parker was pastor.

In the "Proprietors Book" it is recorded that, "In consideration of Mr. James Noyes his resigning up unto the towns hands four acres by the river (Parker) side, Two acres in Richard Kents Island & four acres in the Neck behind the great Swamp, they granted him eight acres by the New Pond at the New Town to continue in his and his heyrs for ever."

There is no date to this record, but it is probable that the grant did not take effect until 1646, as the commissioners appointed, in 1642, to lay out the new town, ordered "that in respect of the time for the inhabitants removing from the place they now inhabit, to that which is laid out and appointed for their new habitations, each inhabitant shall have their house lotte foure years from the day of the date of the commission."

The house was built about this time (1646) and the two cousins, minister and teacher, lived therein in pleasant companionship for nearly

ten years, when Mr. Noyes died, Oct. 22, 1656, aged forty-eight. Mr. Parker, writing of him, says "He was much honored and esteemed in the Country, and his death was much bewailed. I think he may be reckoned among the greatest worthies of the age."

The will of the Rev. James Noyes, dated Oct. 16, 1656, gave all his real estate and personal property to his wife, Sarah, who was the eldest daughter of Joseph Brown, of Southampton, England. In the inventory, filed in the Probate Office, in Salem, mention is made of a house with seven acres of land adjoining and an orchard all valued at 100 pounds. The enclosure described as an orchard will account for the additional acre named in the original proprietors grant. The house, orchard, and premises covered by this will are fairly well shown by the accompanying photograph taken by the author about the year 1902.

The widow and children, of Rev. James Noyes, continued to live in the house, with the Rev. Thomas Parker as an honored member of the family, and here Mr. Parker died, unmarried, April 24, 1677. Mrs. Noyes died ten or twelve years later and the house passed into the possession of her son Thomas, who was twice married and had thirteen children, and whose further offspring, for several successive generations, resided therein; the last occupant being Miss Mary Coffin Noyes (of the sixth generation from the Rev. James Noyes), who died Jan. 2, 1895.

The old house is still in a fine state of preservation as is readily attested to by a glance at the photographic view, and it, no doubt, is the oldest one in town. The heavy oak frame shows no signs of decay and occasional repairs have kept the exterior walls in excellent condition. The chimney was formerly about four yards square at the base, and extended nearly to the rear wall of the house. About the year 1881 it became necessary to somewhat reduce its size and in doing so, the existence of a secret closet was discovered. There was no entrance to it from either the first or second story and the only way of access was from the cellar. It was evidently constructed to serve as a safe hiding-place or deposit vault for gold and silver and other valuables that might require absolute security from fire or other destructive agencies that existed then, more so than today—especially Indian raids.

The main house was originally of four rooms, each about 18 by 22 feet. The west part was added on by Silas Noyes over one hundred years ago—or about 1803. The southeast room, down stairs, is now 18 by 21 feet and contains many articles associated with old bygone days. The northeast

side has the old table and chair of Rev. James Noyes, brought from England. In the hall, by the stairs is an old fashioned table, very oddly designed so as to fold up, if necessary. This is called an "eight legged table" and, together with an old oak arm chair, very heavy and clumsy, and some other articles, was also brought from England. The arrangement of the rooms is after the style of the times and the addition of the wing at the back gives the house the shape of the letter L. The small front entry with doors opening on either side, and the narrow staircase, making two square turns in an ascent of less than a dozen steps, has never been altered. The slender balusters are very quaint and seem very fragile to one not accustomed to the "old fashioned ways". The cellar door opens under the stairs and it is here that one first realizes the great bulk of the chimney, sufficient of which was removed to allow for the establishment of a small kitchen between the two large rooms in the main part of the house. The bricks falling out at the back of the chimney, owing to an excessive amount of sand in the mortar, was one incentive prompting the reducing of the chimney and of bricks and mortar taken away there were 20 wagon loads. Much of the plastering on the ceilings is over 250 years old and is as firm as ever. To enumerate the articles of antique furniture and heirlooms which this house contains would require more space than can be devoted to the purpose.

The northeast chamber has been divided into three ample apartments and the southeast chamber into two, each as large as the average room in a dwelling of our time.

In the rough, unfinished attic, which extends the whole length of the house, are many of the relics of the Noyeses of each generation. a clutter of most everything. Here we find three old guns, nearly six feet long and falling into pieces from extreme age. There we discover two swords. one an army weapon of antique pattern and the other a gentleman's rapier. such as dangled by the side of the gallants of old, ready to spring forth in a flash to defend an honored name, to resent an insult. or to strike a blow for church and country. May these things continue to be cherished for as many centuries and years to come! The elm trees shown in the pictures were undoubtedly planted about the time of the house's construction.

Without grimace or complaint. this treasured abode—a cherished memento—has combated the storms and tempests of over two and a half centuries; but it still stands a memorial of the past, closely identified with the pioneer history of Newbury and the domestic and sacred lives of two of its eminent divines, these first occupants both sleeping in the same cemetery close by.

The highway shown in the photograph is called "Parker Street" in honor to him who lived so nigh.

33

THE PATHFINDER AT MARIETTA, OHIO, IN 1888.

By George Sheldon.

The public is always responsive to "personal recollections" of distinguished people. Aside from its interest in the tale I have to tell, it seems fitting that an incident in the career of Mrs. Mary A. Livermore, to which I was knowing, should have a permanent record as of historic value in the annals of woman's achievement.

The third week of July, 1888, was a gala time in Marietta, Ohio. The five states carved out of the great Northwest Territory, had sent their most eminent citizens back to Marietta, the maternal hive, to celebrate the centennial of her birth. Governor Foraker and his stirring wife, kept open house during that week, in a fine mansion vacated for the occasion by the public-spirited owner. Tents were pitched upon the spacious lawn, for the governor's staff, and high officers of the state militia. Sentinels in showy uniforms guarded the grounds, day and night. Here were made welcome the distinguished visitors. There were representatives from the states of the great Northwest Territory, and men from the grandmother states, men of national fame who took part in the ceremonies of the week. Senator Evarts of New York, the eloquent but cold and philosophic orator; Senator Daniels the ardent, still Virginia's favorite son; the stately and polished Senator Sherman; General Ewing, the popular idol of Ohio; Professor Butler, the traveler and oriental scholar; Professor Hinsdale, the historian; Bishop Gilmore, Governor Smith, Senator Palmer, and a host of other leading men of the great Northwest. Busy among them all was Mrs. Martha J. Lamb, taking notes for the "Magazine of American History."

Apart and apparently aloof from them all, was the calm and dignified Mrs. Mary Livermore. For it had been decreed in the councils of the high-bred women of the city, who were several rounds of the ladder in advance of the men, that the work done by the pioneer women could be represented more fittingly by a woman; and for this office they selected Mrs. Livermore.

MARIETTA.

ections" of distinguished
to tell, it seems fitting
vernore, to which I was
toric value in the annals

[arietta, Ohio. The five
ad sent their most emi-
celebrate the centennial
kept open house during
n by the public-spirited

How far this step was in defiance of the "Lords of Creation," does not appear. Marietta was said to be "the richest and slowest of Ohio cities," and this was a radical advance for the place and event. The women had in view Mrs. Livermore's advanced position as a leader in demanding the rights of woman, and they were walking on thin ice; for the woman suffragists had so far, no standing in that stronghold of conservatism. There is no outside word as to this work of the committee of arrangements, but to show the inside object of inviting Mrs. Livermore, I will quote from a letter by one who was apparently on the committee.

"In arranging a program which should properly celebrate the work of the Settlers it was recognized by the Committee that a part of the work done by the pioneer women must be presented by a woman speaker, and an invitation was sent to Mrs. Livermore to fill that honored place. In our correspondence we used the arguments most likely to touch Mrs. Livermore's principles and opinions, as well as to overbalance the penalty of fatigue in a long July journey. To win her consent stress was laid on the fact that at no previous Centennial Celebration of this character, had woman been accorded such prominence as was now intended. It was an advance movement which as a Suffragist, she would, or should, value at its full worth. She would be able to emphasize the work of women, not as mothers only, but as co-workers in founding, nursing and developing the great communities of the Northwest. Of course such a review would be a tribute to woman's power of endurance, and to her preservation, even in hardships, of those gentler forms of life, all too apt to sink from sight in the camps of soldier or pioneer. This was almost too obvious to call for oratory, but experience shows that the obvious was not recognized at all by a large per cent of the history makers."

Through a fortuitous chain of circumstances I had been introduced to the managers of the celebration; had been invited to attend, and been assigned to the hospitality of Mr. W. H. B——, and his charming wife, who were among the leaders of the Committee of One Hundred. Thus I had an opportunity to see some of the inside workings of the machine. The exercises of the celebration were opened on Sunday.

Mrs. Livermore had been advertized in the printed program to appear on the platform on Monday morning. This was changed to Monday evening. An enterprising newspaper man printed an abstract of the address on Tuesday, as having been delivered Monday evening, and said she had a large and interested audience. But through some influence unknown to me, another party was put in her place for Monday evening. This was not an unusual,

nor was it the only break by the reporters. The small office force at command had more matter than it could digest. Frequent and sudden changes in the program occurred, and the contemporary newspaper reports cannot always be depended upon as to the order of events. As has been said, Mrs. Livermore's address had been put off; after the heavy artillery had been discharged, as they supposed, another date was fixed upon. It was to be in the evening, the third meeting of the day. On the morning of that day, my hostess appeared to be much disturbed in her mind. Her face was clouded, and she was seen occasionally gazing into vacancy. Presuming on my intimacy in the family, I ventured to inquire the reason of this apparent trouble. What was going amiss? Mrs. B—— frankly told me that she was worrying as to what kind of a reception Mrs. Livermore would receive in Marietta, the stronghold of conservatism. No woman had yet appeared on her public platform. Would anybody go to hear her? Would she be interrupted? abused? allowed to go on? Would she be insulted on the street when recognized? What did I think she could do to help matters along smoothly. Mrs. B—— had evidently been instrumental in bringing this radical woman to Marietta, and the responsibility was weighing heavily. The crucial hour was near. She was in torturing uncertainty as to the outcome. She was slightly relieved when assured that from my knowledge of Mrs. Livermore she need not have the slightest fear as to how the orator would be received by the audience. Regarding the number of hearers, we had no right to expect a large meeting after the gatherings and orations of morning and afternoon, for there was a limit to human endurance and capacity for listening. But get any audience, small or large, face to face with Mrs. Livermore, you need have no doubt whatever of a satisfactory result. There will be no insult, and no interruption, you may be sure of that. Mrs. B—— was grateful for this assurance, but she did not so fully rely upon it as I could wish. She had as little faith in my assurance, as I had sympathy in her troublous fear; she was also very skeptical about getting any audience at all. It may be supposed that Mrs. B—— represented the general feelings of the women, and it was decided, during the day, to open the evening with a procession of the Marietta women in carriages. This was a shrewd scheme, worthy the sharpest wits. The women would all be thus committed to the cause, would give Mrs. Livermore open support, and backing; they would become, at least, the nucleus of an audience, and above all, if worst came to worst, in case of any disturbance, the men of Marietta must rally to the rescue of their wives and daughters.

So at the appointed time a long array of carriages filled with women was drawn up on the street where Mrs. Livermore had been entertained by Mr. and Mrs. L——, ready for the parade. I was among the men who crowded the sidewalk, and noticed some shifting of the occupants. Suddenly I was seized by two marshals, resplendent with the insignia of office, who conducted me to the leading carriage in which Mrs. Livermore was seated, and asked me to enter. I positively refused; told them there was some mistake; that I knew all the arrangements of the affair; not a man but the coachmen was to be in the procession. A moment later, the marshals appeared again with smiling faces, saying, "Well, we have orders to put the gentleman from Massachusetts into this carriage."

Perhaps the hearts of the management had failed at the last moment; they could not take the risk of letting Mrs. Livermore go out of sight into unknown hazzards without a Massachusetts body guard. So, they may have reasoned, the responsibility will be divided. This was only twenty years ago. With our present light, all these performances seem almost incredible.

The signal given, the procession moved. With the rattle of drums, the braying of brass, the flashing lights and waving flags, we paraded the principal streets. The crowds were orderly, respectful. There were no signs of disturbance. But there was no cheering, no appearance whatever of approval. Doubts must needs arise. What is the meaning of all this machinery? What means this crowd, this silence? Does it bode ill or good? What will the harvest be?

Calm as a mountain lake in the moonlight, sat Mrs. Livermore utterly innocent of anything unusual in the air; not indifferent to the supposed honor paid her, but not having the most distant idea of ill or mischance. She had long been accustomed to the lime light.

She had also been accustomed to crowded houses in the East, and I felt it my duty to prepare her against a sudden disappointment. I dwelt upon the fact of the great meetings day after day, of the two meetings that very day, of a limit to the listening power, and said "we have no right to expect more than a small audience to-night." "How many do you predict?" she at length asked. "You will have just twelve hundred," was the positive reply.

"If I have twelve hundred," she said,"I shall be entirely satisfied. When Senator Evarts closed his eloquent oration he had only —— for I counted them." (Mrs. L—— gave the exact number which I cannot recall, but it was about six or seven hundred).

When the procession reached the front of the great Memorial Auditorium

on the bank of the Muskingum it turned down by one side to reach the platform by the rear entrance. As we passed the first and second of the great tall side doors, there was to be seen within a wide and dreary expanse of empty seats, and I trembled for my reputation as aprophet. But the lower door revealed a compact semicircle of men and women seated before the platform.

"Look there, Mrs. Livermore, there is your twelve hundred I promised," said the prophet. "Yes, there is, just about that, and I am entirely satisfied."

The face of Mrs. B ——, which had reminded one of the last quarter of the waning moon, now brightened up a trifle. We passed round to the rear where were men in plenty to help the women up the steps to the waiting room back of the platform. All parties looked pleased, the experiment was so far a success. The women were safe and sound, and an audience was waiting, twelve hundred strong. After a delay of four or five minutes for the women to preen themselves, we passed in to the platform. A wonderful transformation met the eye. We almost ceased to breathe with amazement. Every seat in that vast auditorium was filled, every door was crowded with faces, and on the great platform stood hundreds of the leading men of the Centennial Celebration. Governors crowded United States Senators, Senators elbowed Judges of the Supreme Court and officers of the several states. There even seemed scant room for the women escort. Mrs. B —— and the prophet exchanged swift glances. Her face glowed with the light of a double full moon, if such there could be. Together we looked on an audience of nearly six thousand people, awaiting the speaker in perfect silence. Together we looked upon the quiet but glowing face of Mrs. Livermore. Grand and queenly she stood, apparently the least surprised of us all, as if her feet were now on her native heath.

The silence was not for long. Mrs. Livermore had hardly taken the stand when see seemed to be caught up on the wings of a great enthusiasm, far beyond what I had ever before witnessed. She fully realized the situation; she felt the call to the uttermost, she saw the flood tide of opportunity, and responded magnificently. For an hour and a half she held that vast mass of humanity in the hollow of her hand, and swayed it at her will, as she might wave a silken banner. History, patriotism, reverence for woman, duty, service and sacrifice in the civil and social life of man and the nation, all took on a new form and meaning from her inspired lips. Cold indifference and the chain armor of fortified conservatism were alike melted in her elo-

quent and fervid pleadings for the right. Her strong but musical voice reached every ear in that rapt assembly, and applause from platform and floor filled the air as her eloquent periods enriched her lofty themes. Not one foot-print pointed outward during that long oration; but those standing without pressed steadily in, until every one of the long aisles was packed solidly to the platform, and every inch of standing room about the side doors was but a compact mass of faces with every eye fixed steadfastly on the speaker.

By unquestioned assent Mrs. Livermore's spontaneous outpouring was the event of the week. That night, as all agreed, she stormed the heart and head of Marietta. The backbone of conservatism was damaged beyond repair. Progress in civil and social life succeeded indifference and sloth, and the century-old Marietta entered on a new era of vital thought and action.

The uppermost reason for the invitation of Mrs. Livermore to Marietta has been given in an extract from a correspondent's offering. Another extract from the same source will show the result, as measured by her discerning mind, of the immediate and ultimate effect of this address of Mrs. Livermore. She says: — "The majestic appearance of Mrs. Livermore, her voice and personal presence, were fully equal to the large audience and the spacious platform. From the first word to the last, she held her audience with an ease which implied strength and eloquence hardly drawn upon, — a remarkable exhibition of physical vitality and mental resource. Perhaps," she continues, "it may be asked how much of that spell she worked over the gathered throng, was due to what met the eye, and how much the ear. The indirect influences of Mrs. Livermore's presence on this occasion should not be ignored, however impossible to trace them. So far as the town of Marietta is a measure, while public opinion was fairly ready for speaking by women in the churches and the City Hall, it was a jar to many conservatives, that a woman should be asked to address delegates from five states, and an audience up in the thousands. When the event came to hand, when the woman filled her part victoriously, and the people 'cried for more,' one more nail had been driven in the coffin of medievalism. Whatever advance in woman's share of civic and national life takes form in this great Middle West, while few may appreciate the pathfinder, certain it is that a wide and upward way began, and continues from Mrs. Livermore's address at Marietta in 1888."

CARPENTER, Harriet, b. 1805; m. Elijah Kingsley of Mich. Berrien Port., 426.

—— John E., soldier of 1812; set. N. Y. Berrien Port., 512.

—— Josiah, b. Adams, 1801; set. N. Y., 1826, Mich., 1836. Lenawee Hist. II, 460; Lenawee Port., 612.

—— Julius, b. Worcester, 1836; set. Mich., 1836. Oakland Port., 628.

—— Powell, b. 1771; set. N. Y., 1800? Oakland Biog., 423.

—— R., b. 1806; set. Mich., 1844. Washtenaw Hist., 495.

—— Sidney, b. Worcester Co., 1810; set. N. Y., 1824, Mich., 1836. St. Joseph, 188.

—— William, b. Charlestown, 1752; set. N. H., N. Y., 1808. Lenawee Illus., 120; Lenawee Port., 1202.

CARRIER, Elijah, b. 1798; set Ct., N. Y. Hillsdale Port., 582.

CARROLL, Deborah of Rowe; m. 1845 Josiah Upton of Mass. and Mich. Clinton Past., 422.

CARRUTH, Thomas, b. Marlborough, 1849; set. Mich., 1883. Monroe, appendix 36.

CARTER, Ira F., set. Wis., 1840? Saginaw Hist., 840.

—— Nathaniel, b. Leominster, 1806; set. Mich., 1831. Macomb Hist., 226, 245, 691.

CARY, Martha A., m. 1869 T. C. Bishop of Mich. Jackson Hist., 1064.

—— Selden P., b. Williamstown, 1819; set. Mich., 1853. Detroit, 1453.

CASE, Ezekiel, b. Washington; set. N. Y., 1810? Mich. Hillsdale Port., 233.

—— James, set. N. Y., 1800? Oakland Port., 347.

—— Sarah B., b. 1831; set. Mich. Washtenaw Hist., 495.

CASEY, Samuel, b. Lanesboro, 1803; set. N. Y., Mich., 1826. Washtenaw Hist., 1075.

CASSADA, James, set. N. Y., d. 1836. Gratiot, 560.

CASTLE, Melissa, m. 1825 Ashley Parks of N.Y. and Mich. Washtenaw Hist., 1310.

CASWELL, Solomon, b. Belchertown, 1796; set. N. Y., 1805, O., 1817. Mich., 1821. Oakland Hist., 286.

CATLIN, Jane, b. 1813; m. Daniel Hull of O. and Mich. Ionia Port., 318.

CAULKINS, Betsey, m. 1815? Horace Hovey of O. and Mich. Clinton Port., 480.

CAWKINS, Priscilla, m. 1825? Frederick Prior of Mass. and Mich. Oakland Biog., 577.

CAZAR, Jane, m. 1805? Elijah Moore of N.Y. Isabella, 477.

CHACE, Jonathan, b. Worcester Co., set. Vt., 1800? Saginaw Hist., 820.

CHADWICK, Benjamin F., set. N. Y., Mich. Berrien Hist., 479.

—— Lewis, b. 1799; set. Vt., 1800, Mich., 1834. St. Clair, 308.

CHALKER, Nathaniel, b. 1780; set. Vt., N. Y., Mich., 1837. Clinton Port., 890.

CHAMBERLAIN, Benjamin, set. N. Y., 1815? Kent, 702.

—— C. Cloa, of Dudley; m. 1805 Moses Curtis of N.Y. Kalamazoo Hist. facing 476.

—— Eliza M., b. Petersham, 1809; m. 1st, Jesse Rogers of Mass. and Mich., m. 2d, Robert J. Street of Mich. Lenawee Hist. I, 471.

—— Luther, b. Westford, 1795; set. Vt., N. Y., Mich., 1839. Kalamazoo Hist., 403.

—— Milton, set. Mich.; d. 1859. Genesee Port., 511.

—— Moses, b. Hopkinton, 1757; set. N. H., Vt. Berrien Port., 885.

—— Nicholas, set. N. Y., 1790? Kalamazoo Port., 381.

—— Samuel, b. Chelsea, 1734; set. N. H., Vt. Berrien Port., 885.

CHAMBERLIN, Benjamin, b. Bedford, 1806; set. N. Y., Mich., 1836. Calhoun, 175.

—— John M., b. Springfield, 1809; set. N. Y., Mich., 1828. Oakland Port., 672.

—— Nancy, of Dalton, m. 1805? Harry Day of N. Y. Macomb Hist., 695.

—— Porter, set. Mich., 1829. St. Clair, 721.

(To be continued.)

THE WILLIAMS HOUSE, AT DEERFIELD.

THE WILLIAMS HOUSE AT DEERFIELD

In its association with the eventful past, this venerable house is one of foremost interest among the many historic houses still standing in the old frontier town of Deerfield.

It was in a house occupying this same site that Parson John Williams and his family were sleeping on the occasion of that murderous Indian raid in 1704 when he and his family were dragged away to captivity, after two of his children and a negro nurse had been slain.

His wife was also killed the next day but he escaped death, and wrote a narrative of his dreadful experiences, which was published and forms one of the important contributions to the history of the Indian wars in the Massachusetts colony.

After a long captivity his release was secured. He left behind him his daughter Eunice, 7 years old, who married an Indian, 1713, and relapsed into their barbarous ways. He returned to Deerfield, and his home was rebuilt for him by the town, which is the house standing today.

He married again in 1707, and died in 1729, but his widow continued to live here until 1754.

Ownership in the house succeeded to one of Parson Williams' children, Maj. Elijah Williams (son by his second wife), who made extensive repairs to the house in 1756. But Mr. George Sheldon, Deerfield's historian, has given careful investigation to the subject, and concludes that there is no doubt but that the original frame of the old house is still preserved.

The following is a brief description of the house from Mr. Sheldon's pen. It is an extract from a public appeal made in 1879 which saved the house from destruction:

> The house stands fronting the east, is two stories high, the main part 47x21 feet, a gambrel-roofed ell 40x23 projects from the southwest rear, and a "lean-to" 20x10 from the northwest rear, the whole covered with rived or cleft clap-boards, nicely joined. There are nine windows in front and five at each end, and they are rather narrow. The upper tier are set close under the cornice, the lower ones are finished with handsome pointed pediments. There are three doors—one in front, one in the southwest cornor of the main building, and one in the ell. The front entrance is quite an elaborate affair; the door is double or folding, each divided into three parts, the upper finished with oblong, the center with square panels, and the lower with a sort of crusaders' cross. In the top of the door is a window, and a fine old brass knocker invites entrance.
>
> Entering, on the right and left are doors opening to the front rooms. These are finished with fine chimney-pieces, rich panels, and a heavy cornice, while the massive summer-tree across the centre cuts the ceiling into two large, deep panels. Both rooms have barred wooden shutters, and deep, cosy window-seats, suggesting security and comfort.
>
> In the south end of the garret is a finished room, and from this room a flight of stairs goes down into a mysterious room in the second story which is entirely isolated from the rest of the chambers. Adjoining this room is another, some eight feet square, near the center of the house, in the floor of which is a trap-door. This being raised discloses a very narrow and crooked stair-case landing in a small, dark closet on the lower floor, and with a trap-door in this, the cellar might be reached, thus affording communication between the garret and cellar secluded from observation and entirely distinct from the hall stairs or the back stairs in the ell.

SOME ARTICLES CONCERNING MASSACHUSETTS IN RECENT MAGAZINES

GENERAL. English notes about early settlers in New England. Communicated by Lothrop Withington. (Essex Institute. Historical collections, Oct., 1908. v. 44, p. 371–374).

—— How Mass. utilizes waste and neglected lands. (Outlook, 1 Aug., 1908. v. 89. p. 735–736).

—— Irish names in colonial military history. By P. O. Larkin. (American Catholic quarterly review, July, 1908. v. 33, p. 471–485).

—— Legal qualifications of voters in Mass. (Essex antiquarian, Oct., 1908. v. 12, p. 145–151).

BARNSTABLE. Barnstable vital records. Transcribed by G. E. Bowman. (Mayflower descendant, Oct., 1908. v. 10, p. 249–250).

Part 12; began in Oct., 1900. v. 2, p. 212.

BARNSTABLE COUNTY. Cape C d canal. By W. B. Parsons. (Annals of the American academy of political and social science, Jan., 1908. v. 31, p. 81–91).

—— Knocking about Cape Cod. By T. F. Day. (Outing, Aug., 1908. v. 52, p. 578–588).

—— Unrecorded Barnstable County deeds. Collected by G. E. Bowman. (Mayflower descendant, Oct., 1908. v. 10, p. 238–241.)

Part 3; began in July, 1906. v. 8, p. 155.

BOSTON. The battle for free speech. The police adopt Russian methods in Boston. By B. O. Flower. (Arena, Oct., 1908. v. 40, p. 345–350).

On the refusal by the authorities to allow a public meeting of Letts, Aug. 3, 1908, to protest against police methods.

—— Fenway district and its notable buildings. (Inland architect, July, 1908. v. 52, p. 3–4).

BOXFORD. Ancient Pearl house, West Boxford. (Essex antiquarian, Oct., 1908. v. 12, p. 175 and frontispiece.

BREWSTER see HARWICH.

BRISTOL COUNTY. Abstracts from the first book of Bristol County probate records. Copied by Mrs. L. H. Greenlaw. (New England historical and genealogical register, Oct., 1908. v. 62, p. 345–352).

Part 5; (first three instalments appeared in Genealogical advertiser, Dec., 1900–Dec., 1901 and the fourth in the Register, July, 1908.)

BROOKLINE. The wealthiest town in the world and the best governed. By T. F. Anderson. (New England magazine, Nov., 1908. v. 39, p. 265–277).

CAPE COD see BARNSTABLE COUNTY.

CHARLES RIVER. Boating on the Charles River. By A. S. Pier. (Outing, Aug., 1908. v. 52, p. 543–555).

CHATHAM. Deaths in Chatham, 1836. (New England historical and genealogical register, Oct., 1908. v. 62, p. 382–383.

—— Chatham vital records. Transcribed by G. E. Bowman. (Mayflower descendant, Oct., 1908. v. 10, p. 194–198).

Part 9; began in July, 1902. v. 4, p. 182.

CONCORD. A river that binds today with yesterday. [Concord River] By Perry Walton. (New England magazine, Nov., 1908. v. 39, p. 311–315).

—— Tarry at home travel, 1889. By E. E. Hale. III. (New England magazine, Nov., 1908. v. 39, p. 376–384).

DENNIS. Dennis vital records. transscribed by M. A. Baker. (Mayflower descendant, Oct., 1908. v. 10, p. 209–213.

Part 9; began in Jan., 1904. v. 6, p. 2.

DOUGLAS. Capt. Job Knapp chapter, D.A.R. East Douglas. By Mrs. Effie M. Jones, historian. (American monthly magazine, Oct., 1908. v. 33, p. 914).

EASTHAM. The records of Wellfleet, formerly the North precinct of Eastham. Transcribed by G. E. Bowman. (Mayflower descendant, Oct., 1908. v. 10, p. 221–225).

Part 7, (1739–1745); began Oct., 1902. v. 4, p. 227.

—— Records of the First church in Orleans, formerly the First church in

Eastham. (Mayflower descendant, Oct., 1908. v. 10, p. 230–233).
Part 2 (1772–1778); began July, 1908. v. 10, p. 165.

ESSEX COUNTY. Abstracts of all records in vol. 6 of the Suffolk County registry of deeds, relating to Essex County. (Essex antiquarian, Oct., 1908. v. 12, p. 167).
Part 6; began in July, 1905. v. 9, p. 97.

—— Essex County notarial records, 1697–1768. (Essex Institute. Historical collections, Oct., 1908. v. 44, p. 325–331).
Part 9 (1719–1721); began 1905. v. 41, p. 183.

—— Ipswich court records and files. (Essex antiquarian, Oct., 1908. v. 12, p. 168–172).
Part 6 (1658); began Jan., 1904. v. 8, p. 1.

—— Newspaper items relating to Essex County. (Essex Institute. Historical collections, Oct., 1908. v. 44, p. 338–347).
Part 5 (1757–1758); began 1906. v. 42, p. 214.

—— Soldiers and sailors of the Revolution. (Essex antiquarian, Oct., 1908. v. 12, p. 185–187).
Names Brimblecom to Brooks. From state records. Began in v. 1, Jan., 1897.

ESSEX COUNTY see also NORFOLK COUNTY, OLD.

FITCHBURG. An eastern city with western ideas. By D. C. O'Connor. (New England magazine, Oct., 1908. v. 39, p. 199–213).

GLOUCESTER. A sea lover's paradise. By S. T. Franklin. (New England magazine, Aug., 1908. v. 38, p. 689–696).

HARWICH. Records of the First parish in Brewster, formerly the First parish in Harwich. Transcribed by G. E. Bowman. (Mayflower descendant, Oct., 1908. v. 10, p. 251–253).
Part 13; began Oct., 1902. v. 4, p. 242.

HAVERHILL. Haverhill inscriptions prior to 1800. Greenwood cemetery. (Essex antiquarian, Oct., 1908. v. 12, p. 155).

—— Haverhill inscriptions prior to 1800. Walnut cemetery. (Essex antiquarian, Oct., 1908. v. 12, p. 152–155).

MANSFIELD. Mansfield, an economic study. By C. M. Rockwood. (New England magazine, Dec., 1908. v. 39, p. 493–499).

MARLBOROUGH. Colonial records of Marlborough. Copied by Miss M. E. Spalding and communicated by F. P. Rice. (New England historical and genealogical register, Oct., 1908. v. 62, p. 336–344).
Part 2 (1661–1662); began July, 1908. v. 62, p. 220.

MARSHFIELD. Gravestone records from the "Two mile" cemetery, Union street, North Marshfield. Communicated by J. W. Willard. (Mayflower descendant, Oct., 1908. v. 10, p. 246–249).

MEDFIELD. A private record of deaths in Medfield, 1746–1844. Kept by Thankful (Adams) Bullard, Amy Bullard and Elizabeth Bullard. (New England historical and genealogical register, Oct., 1908. v. 62, p. 368–372).

MEDFORD. Unpublished manuscripts: Washington in Medford, and List of schoolmasters, 1789–1821. (Medford historical register, Oct., 1908. v. 11, p. 94–96).

NANTUCKET. Nantucket Island. (Suburban life, Boston, July, 1908. v. 7, p. 15–16, 46–47).

—— The Spectator [on Nantucket]. (Outlook, 1 Aug., 1908. v. 89, p. 745–746).

—— Tales of an old whaling town. By R. P. Getty. (World to-day, Chicago, July, 1908. v. 15, p. 701–708).

NEWBURY see NEWBURYPORT.

NEWBURYPORT. The early church plate of Newburyport, Newbury, West Newbury and Rowley. By J. H. Buck. (Essex Institute. Historical collections, Oct., 1908. v. 44, p. 293–304).

—— Extracts from interleaved almanacs kept in Newburyport, probably by Joseph O'Brien. (Essex Institute. Historical collections, Oct., 1908. v. 44, p. 332–337).

—— Rev. John Murray. Reprint from Essex gazette, Sept. 5–12, 1769. (Essex antiquarian, Oct., 1908. v. 12, p. 173–175).

NORFOLK COUNTY, OLD. Old Norfolk County records. (Essex antiquarian, Oct., 1908. v. 12, p. 178–184).
Began in v. 1, Feb., 1907. Not the present Norfolk County but a county, organized in 1643 to include the towns north of the Merrimack River.

ORLEANS see EASTHAM.

PEMBROKE. Gravestone records from the Cemetery at Pembroke Centre. Communicated by J. W. Willard. (Mayflower descendant, Oct., 1908. v. 10. p. 234–238).
Part 6 (Parris–Sturtevant); began in Jan., 1907 v. 9, p. 3.

PEPPERELL. Prudence Wright chapter D. A. R. Report by Lucy B. Page. (American monthly magazine, Dec., 1908. v. 33, p. 1135–1136).

PLYMOUTH COLONY. Plymouth Colony deeds. (Mayflower descendant, Oct., 1908. v, 10. p. 213–217).
1656–1657; series began in v. 1, Apr., 1899.

—— Plymouth Colony wills and inventories. (Mayflower descendant, Oct., 1908, v. 10, p. 198–203).
1651; series began in v. 1, Jan., 1899.

PLYMPTON. Gravestone records in the Old cemetery at Plympton. Communicated by J. W. Willard. (Mayflower descendant, Oct., 1908. v. 10, p. 217–221).
Part 6 (M.-Pratt); began in July, 1906. v. 8, p. 150.

ROWLEY see NEWBURYPORT.

SALEM. Notable paintings from old Salem. By J. R. Dexter. (New England magazine, Dec., 1908. v. 39, p. 419–422).

—— Revolutionary letters written to Colonel Timothy Pickering. By George Williams of Salem. (Essex Institute. Historical collections, Oct., 1908. v. 44, p. 313–324).
Part 4; began Oct., 1906. v. 42, p. 313.

—— Salem in 1700. By Sidney Perley. (Essex antiquarian, Oct., 1908. v. 12, p. 177–178).
No. 33; series began in Nov., 1898; each number has a plan showing old streets and boundary lines of estates.

SCITUATE. Records of the First church in Scituate. Transcribed by G. E. Bowman. (Mayflower descendant, Oct., 1908. v. 10, p. 225–230).
Part 2 (1716–1723); began in Apr., 1908, v. 10, p. 90.

SPRINGFIELD. An international Fourth of July. By Mary V. Clark. (Charities and The commons, N. Y., July 11, 1908. v. 20, p. 469–470).

—— Springfield, the model city of the Connecticut Valley. By E. N. Bagg. (New England magazine, Aug., 1908. v. 38, p. 711–721).

WELLFLEET. Records of the Duck Creek cemetery, Wellfleet. Communicated by S. W. Smith. (Mayflower descendant, Oct., 1908. v. 10, p. 204–208).
Part 2 (Cheever-Freeman); began July, 1908. v. 10, p. 180.

WELLFLEET see also EASTHAM.

WEST NEWBURY see NEWBURYPORT.

YARMOUTH. A Cape Cod Christmas gift. By C. H. Miller. (Country life in America, Dec., 1908. v. 15, p. 141–142, 204–206).
An old house in Yarmouthport and its contents.

—— Yarmouth vital records. Transcribed by G. E. Bowman. (Mayflower descendant, Oct., 1908. v. 10, p. 242–245).
Part 9 (1692–1746); began in Oct., 1900. v. 2, p. 207.

Department of the American Revolution
1775–1782
FRANK A. GARDNER, M. D. Editor.

State Brigantine Independence.

This vessel although ably commanded had the misfortune early to meet a superior force, and her career was shorter than that of many of her sister ships. The first legislation with reference to her construction was the following resolve;—

"In Council Decr 29th 1775 Whereas ſeveral of the united Colonies have of late thought it expedient and neceſsary, to fitt out armed Veſsells for the Defence of American Liberty, and it appears to this Court neceſsary that Meaſures be taken by this Colony for our further Protection by ſea therefore

Reſolved that Jno Adams & Joseph Palmer Esqrs with ſuch as the Honourable Houſe ſhall join be a Committee to conſider and report to this Court a Plan for fitting out one or more armed Veſsells, for the Defence of American Liberty.

ſent down for Concurrence

Perez Morton Depy Secy

In the Houſe of Repreſentatives

Read & concurred and Sent up Decr 30, 1775, Coll Orne, Mr Brown of Boſton & Coll. Otis are joined.

William Cooper,
Speaker Pro Tem."

A committee was appointed in the House of Representatives, December 29, 1775, to report on a plan for fitting out one or more armed vessels. This committee reported January 10, 1776. On the 6th of February, the following act was passed:

"Resolved, That there be built at public Expense of this Colony, for the Defence of American Liberty Ten Sloops of War of one hundred & ten Tons or fifteen Tons each suitable to Carry from fourteen to Sixteen Carriage Guns of Six & four pounders." Four days later the "Comtee for fitting out ten veſsells" had a grant of £2000. On the 17th a resolve was passed directing the committee to suspend contract for more than five. The committee on armed vessels was ordered, March 14th, to revise the act relative to fitting them out.

A report was made as follows: "To the Honble the Council & House of Representatives in Genl Court aſsembled at Watertown, March 26, 1776.

The Memorial of William Sever & Thomas Durfey.

That your Memorialists were by the Honl Court with others appointed on a committee for building & equipping Sundry armed veſsels which were proposed to be rigged Sloops, that your Memorialists are of the opinion the two veſsels they are now building for that purpose are of such size that it will be very Inexpedient to rig them as Sloops, they therefore request that they may be authorized & directed by yr honors to rig & fix the sd Veſsells as Brigantines.

yr Memorialists would also represent to yr honors that they are unable to purchase Duck for sails for the said Veſsells & if your honors think proper they pray that the Comiſsary Genl be directed to Supply them with Eighteen Bolts of duck out of the Colony Stores for each of the said veſsels & yr memorialists shall ever pray.

Wm Stover
Thomas Durfee"

Permission to make the change was granted and 36 bolts of Duck were allowed for use in the two vessels, April 3, 1776. Two days later the commissary was directed to supply the duck required.

"The Houſe, according to the Order of the Day, made choice by Ballot, of Simeon Sampson, as a Captain to command the armed Brigantine, building at Kingston, for the Service of the Colony, under the Direction of the honorable William Sever Esq.

Sent up for Concurrence"

April 17, 1776.

"In the Houſe of Repreſentatives, April 19, 1776.

The Committee appointed to report ſuitable Names for the five armed Veſ-

sels now building by this Colony, reported that the Brigantine building at Kingston be called the *Independence* that the Brigantine building at Dartmouth be called the *Rifing Empire* that the Sloop building at Salifbury be called the *Tyrannicide* that one of the Sloops building as Swanzey be called the *Republic* and the other the *Freedom*.

Read and Accepted,

April 19, 1776.

Sent up for Concurrence,

J. Warren."

"In the House of Representatives, April 24, 1776.

Resolved that the Commisary General be & he is hereby directed to procure Eight Duble fortified Cannon Suitable for Ships use that will Carry a Ball of 6[lb] w[t] each, one hundred & Twenty Swivel Guns & Twenty Cohorns. also Ten Tons of Round Shott, five Tons of Chain & Duble headed Shott, Three Tons Grape Shott, Three Tons of Powder and one Ton of hand Grenadoes, as Soon as Pofsible, and deliver the Same or any part thereof to the Hon W[m] Seiver y[e] Hon Rich[d] Derby the Hon Jerethmeel Bowers & Thomas Durfey Esq[r] and Cap[t] Josiah Batchelder J[r] or to either of their Orders to be by them applied for the use of the armed Vefsels, now Building &c for the Service of this Colony.

Sent up for Concurrence

J. Warren Spkr

April 24, 1776."

The officers of the "Independence" on her first cruise were as follows;—

Simeon Samson, Commander. Entered service, April 17, 1776.

Daniel Adams, First Lieutenant, Entered service, April 30, 1776.

Solomon Higgins, Second Lieutenant, Entered service, May 2, 1776.

Walter Hatch, Master, Entered service, April, 30, 1776.

Samuel Nutting, Surgeon, Entered service, May 10, 1776.

Samuel Gilbert, Surgeon's Mate, Entered service, May 10, 1776.

CAPTAIN SIMEON SAMSON'S full record has already been published in this magazine in v. I. pp. 195–8. The Independence was the first naval vessel commanded by him.

Captain Samson and Surgeon's Mate Gilbert were from Plymouth, Master Walter Hatch from Hingham, and Surgeon Samuel Nutting from Danvers. No record is found of previous naval service of any of the officers in the above list.

SECOND LIEUTENANT SOLOMON HIGGINS resigned September 22nd, 1776, and Charles Dyer of Plymouth was appointed to that office in his stead.

MASTER WALTER HATCH was commissioned commander of the privateer schooner "Hope" September 26, 1776, his service in the "Independence," ending four days before that date. He later served in the State brigantine, "Hazard," and a full account of said service will be found in the Massachusetts Magazine, v. I. pp. 195–7. He was succeeded in the "Independence" by Theophilus Cotton, of Plymouth, who had served as Prizemaster from July 1st.

The officers of the "Independence" were then as follows; Simeon Samson, Captain; Daniel Adams, First Lieutenant; Charles Dyer, Second Lieutenant; Theophilus Cotton, Master; Samuel Nutting, Surgeon and Samuel Gilbert, Surgeon's Mate.

In January 1777, the brigantine, "Nancy," prize of the brigantine "Independence" arrived in Plymouth, under the command of First Lieutenant Daniel Adams, manned with 17 seamen and one boy from the "Independence."

FIRST LIEUTENANT DANIEL ADAMS left the "Independence" at this time and was engaged January 20, 1777, to go on board the State brigantine "Freedom" as First Lieutenant, under Captain John Clouston. He served in the last named vessel until captured some time between August and October, 1777. He was exchanged in the following year for Richard Emmes. His commission as commander of the sloop "Lively" was approved April 22, 1782. His name is erroneously given as "David" Adams in some of the documents.

MASTER THEOPHILUS COTTON left the vessel March 25, 1777. He was commissioned November 15, 1777, Master's Mate of the brigantine "Hazard," having been engaged August 20, 1777. He served until April 13, 1778. Reported deceased.

SURGEON'S MATE SAMUEL GILBERT also left the "Independence" March 25, 1777. He was commissioned Surgeon of the state brigantine "Hazard" November 15, of the same year, serving until March 24, 1778. He was reported sick at Martinico.

The "Independence" was captured in the spring of 1777. Captain Samson's name appears in a list of prisoners sent from Halifax by Sir George Collier, June 28, 1777, to be exchanged for British prisoners. August 9, he was chosen Commander of the vessel then building which was later called the "Hazard." A record of his service in this state vessel and the state ship "Mars" has already been given in the Massachusetts Magazine, v. 1, pp. 195–8.

SECOND LIEUTENANT DYER was also in the "Independence" when she was captured. He was sent from Halifax June 28, to be exchanged. He was engaged August 20, to serve as First Lieutenant on the state brigantine "Hazard." His service on that vessel has already been given in the above mentioned reference.

SURGEON SAMUEL NUTTING was exchanged at the same time as his commander. He was serving as Surgeon of the ship "Rhodes," commanded by Captain Nehemiah Buffington, August 14, 1780. His description being as follows: "Age 38; stature, 5 ft. 8 in.; complexion, light; residence, Danvers." In the following year he served from August 16, to December 2, as Surgeon, Lieut. Col. Joseph Webb's Regiment, said regiment being stationed at Peekskill.

"State of Massachusetts Bay.

Council Chamber Aug[t] 12, 1777.

You are hereby directed to pay out of the public Treafury of this State to Capt Simeon Sampson for the Use of the men borne on the annexed Roll for Services on Board Brig Independence & during their captivity from Jany 1777 to the 5th. July 1777 the Sum of One Hundred & Eighty nine pounds & 2[d] in full discharge of said Roll.

for which this shall be your fufficient Warrant

By Advice of Council,

£1089:00:02 Jn[o] Avery, Dy Secr'y

Hon[ble] Henry Gardner Esq[r] Treasurer."

"A List of the Small Arms & other Warlik Implements taken in the Brigantine Independence belonging to the Officers & Men taken with said Brigantine under the Command of Cap[t] Simeon Samfon

Simeon Samfon Cap[t] 1 Fuzee Compleat & Small fword neetly mounted."

Charles Dyer first Lieu[t] I Fuzee & Ranger (and 21 petty officers and men who lost 1 gun each.)

This list was accompanied by a petition from Captain Samson and Lieutenant Dyer in which they state that, "Your Petitioners flatter themselves, that their conduct was fuch as has fecured to them the approbation of their Countrymen, and they cannot suppofe your Honors will oblige them to fustain the lofs of weapons, which they employed in defence of the United States, and for the particular advantage of this. They therefore request your Honors to grant them fuch a compenfation, as will enable them to replace the Arms & accoutrements which they loft as aforefaid. And your Petitioners as in duty bound shall ever pray

Sim[n] Samson

Charles Dyer."

"The Committe on the Petition of Simion Sampson Charles Dyer & others report by way of Refolve—

State of Mafsachufetts Bay In the Houfe of Reprefentatives December 15, 1777.

Refolved that the Board of War Deliver to Cap[t] Simion Sampson Lef[t] Charles Dyer (and 21 others) to each of them a Gun or Firelock to Replace thofe Loft by them in the Capture of the Brig[t] Independence.

Sent up for Concurrence,

J. Warren, Spk[r]"

February 11, 1778, Henry Goodwin petitioned for back pay as clerk to Captain Simeon Samson, commander of the "Independence." The General Court resolved that the "Comifsary of Stores of this State be and he is hereby Directed to the Said Henry Goodwin two hundred and Seventeen Days Rations being the whole now Due to him.

Sent up for Concurrence

J. Pitt, Spk[r] P. Tem."

Criticism & Comment

on Books and Other Subjects

Dedication of the Massachusetts Monument at Newbern, N. C.

On Nov. 11 there was dedicated at Newbern, N. C., the monument erected by Massachusetts in memory of 600 of our soldiers who lost their lives in the Civil War and are there interred. In the absence of the Governor, the state was represented by Hon. W. D. Chapple, president of the Senate. Various Confederate patriotic organizations took a prominent part in the ceremonies, while representatives of no less than 16 North Carolina regiments of the Confederate army, it is said, were present.

This was by no means the first of such occasions on which men of the Bay State have met as brethren those who were once their foes. Such events as these are indicative, far more than the speech of politicians or newspaper editorials, that rabid sectionalism has nearly spent itself. No better confirmation is needed than has lately been given in the agitation regarding the Wirz monument at Andersonville. On the one hand we of the North have seen little of that vehement and angry protest which such a proposal would have called out a decade ago, while the intemperate Southern spirit which would have insisted on an inscription laudatory and defiant beyond reason, was overcome by wiser counsels.

It is well to bear in mind that large numbers of able bodied men confined in idleness are not easy to control, so that commandants of military prisons are seldom beloved by their enforced guests, as one can as easily see who cares to read the experiences of southern men in northern prisons. It is also true that men of large heroic nature will not commonly be found, in war time, guarding prisoners in the rear. C. A. F.

The name "Massachusetts Magazine."

It may be unknown to many of our readers that ours is not the first periodical to be called the "Massachusetts Magazine." At least two earlier publications have borne that title.

I. The Massachusetts Magazine; or Monthly Museum of Knowledge and Rational Entertainment. This was a general or literary monthly, containing fiction, poetry, essays, comment, etc., with a department of current news and each number embellished with a fine engraving as frontispiece. Eight volumes were published, 1789 to 1796, regularly except for the fact that vol. 7 began in April instead of Jan. and so had 9 nos. only. The editor was Thaddeus Mason Harris, who however withdrew in the middle of the last year, the last 6 nos. of vol. 8 being edited by William Biglow. The printers of vols. 1–5 were Isaiah Thomas and E. T. Andrews, Boston; vol. 6, Weld and Greenough, Boston, vol. 7, W. Greenough (nos. 1–6) and Alexander Marten (nos. 7–9), vol. 8, James Cutler, Boston.

II. The Bay State Monthly (predecessor of the present New England Magazine) was started in Jan. 1884 under the editorship of our present associate editor John N. McClintock who was also its publisher. Two volumes and part of a third were issued down to vol. III, no. 2, May, 1885, when there was litigation resulting in the proprietor losing his interest, the Bay State Monthly being continued in other hands. Mr. McClintock at once began the publication of a new periodical, to be known as the Massachusetts Magazine, vol. I, no. 1 appearing in Aug., 1885, with the imprint of J. A. Cline & Co., Boston.

It was very similar to the Bay State Monthly consisting for the most part of historical articles with an admixture of purely literary features, poetry, stories, etc.

The next number, dated Nov., 1885, was called vol. II, no. 4, certain changes having meanwhile been decided on: reissuing the Oct. and Nov., 1884 nos. of the Bay State Monthly (vol. II, nos. 1 & 2) with new covers as vol. II, no. 1 and 2 of the Massachusetts

usetts in

diers who lost their lives in the Civil War and are there interred. In the absence of the Governor, the state was represented by Hon. W. D. Ch pie, president of the Senate. Various Confederate patriotic organizations took a prominent part in the ceremonies, while representatives of no less than 16 North C regiments of the Confederate army is said, present.

This was by no means the first of such occasions on which men of the Bay State have met as brethren those who were once their foes. Such events as these are indicative, far more than the speech of politicians or newspaper editorials, that rabid sectionalism has greatly spent itself. No better confirmation is needed than has lately been given in the agitation regarding the Wirz monument at Andersonville. On the one hand we of the North have seen little of that vehement and angry protest which such a proposal would have called out a decade ago, while the intemperate Southern spirit which would have insisted on an inscription laudatory and defiant beyond reason, was overcome by wiser counsels.

It is well to bear in mind that large numbers of able bodied men confined in idleness are not easy to control, so that commandants of military prisons are seldom beloved by their enforced guests, as one can as easily see who cares to read the experiences of southern men in northern prisons. It is also true that men of fame heroic will not commonly be found in war guarding prisoners in the rear. C. A.

The name "Massachusetts Magazine,"

It may unknown many of

Magazine, the Aug., 1885 number thenceforth being known as vol. II, no. 3 (instead of vol. I, no. 1.) Vol. II, no. 5 appeared in April, 1886, with no publisher named and the periodical was concluded with vol. II, no. 6, Jan., 1886, that issue, as well as the title page and index for the volume bearing imprint, Cupples, Upham & Co., Boston.

Some Massachusetts books of 1908.

As this magazine has, during the past year, endeavored to list important magazine articles on Massachusetts, it may not be uninteresting to our readers to barely mention the more notable 1908 books on state and local history that have come to our attention. Some of them may be found critically reviewed in the literary or historical periodicals, while a good proportion will be listed in the trade bibliographies; but nowhere grouped for the convenience of Massachusetts users.

I GENERAL.

Bradford's history of Plymouth Plantation 1606–1646. New edition by W. T. Davis, in the series of Original narratives of early American history. 437 p.

John Harvard's life in America, or Social and political life in New England 1637–1638. By A. M. Davis. 45 p.

Heads of families at the first census of the U. S. taken in the year 1790. Massachusetts volume. Pub. by the Bureau of the census. 363 p.

Early New England towns; a comparative study of their development. By Anne B. MacLear. Being v. 29, no. 1, of studies in history, economics and pubic law of Columbia University, 181 p. (Cambridge, Dorchester, Roxbury, Salem and Watertown are considered).

History of the 45th regiment, Massachusetts Volunteer Militia. By A. W. Mann. 562 p.

New England historical and genealogical register. Index of subjects for volumes 1–50. (Being vol. 4, of the full index of which v. 1–3 comprise the Index of names). 296 p.

Thomas Pownall, by C. A. W. Pownall. 488 p.

Sons of the Puritans, a group of brief biographies reprinted from the Harvard graduate's magazine. 244 p.

Winthrop's Journal "History of New England." New edition by J. K. Hosmer in the series of Original narratives of early American history. 2 vols.

II. LOCAL.

ANDOVER. Old Andover days by S. S. Robbins. 189 p.

BILLERICA. Vital records of Billerica. 405 p.

BOSTON. A volume of records ... containing Minutes of the selectmen's meetings 1811 to 1817. (Record commissioner's report v. 38). 378 p.

—— St. Botolph's town. By M. C. Crawford. 365 p.

—— Boston's story in inscriptions. By State street trust co. 37 p.

CAMBRIDGE. see "Early New England towns" in section I.

CHELSEA. Documentary history of Chelsea. 1624–1824. By M. Chamberlain. 2 vols.

—— The burning of Chelsea. By W. M. Pratt. 149 p.

DORCHESTER. see "Early New England towns" in section I.

DOVER. Dedication of the Sawin Memorial Building. By the Dover Historical and Natural History Society, 24 p.

—— The founders of the First Parish. By F. Smith. 24 p.

—— Vital records of Dover. 107. p.

DUDLEY. Vital records of Dudley. 288 p.

ESSEX. Vital records of Essex. 86 p.

HAMILTON. Vital records of Hamilton. 112 p.

HATFIELD. The Hatfield book. By C. A. Wight. 59 p.

HOLLISTON. Vital records of Holliston. 358 p.

LINCOLN. Vital records of Lincoln. 179 p.

MARBLEHEAD. Vital records of Marblehead. Vol. III containing supplementary records collected by J. W. Chapman. 43 p.

MARLBOROUGH. Marlborough, Mass., burial ground inscriptions. By F. P. Rice. 218 p.

MARTHA'S VINEYARD. The story of Martha's Vineyard. By C. G. Hine. 224 p.

MIDDLESEX COUNTY. Historic homes and places and genealogical and personal memoirs relating to the families of Middlesex County. By W. R. Cutter. 4 vols.

MILTON. The first four meeting houses of Milton. By J. A. Tucker. 5 p. with places.

NEW BEDFORD. Commemorative exercises held in City hall, Mar. 30, 1908. Pub. by the Free Public Library. 20 p.

ROXBURY. History of the First Church in Roxbury. By W. E. Thwing. 428 p.
—— see also "Early New England towns" in section I.

SALEM. see "Early New England towns" in section I.

SHARON. The church records of Rev. Philip Curtis of Sharon 1742–1797. J. G. Phillips, editor. Being no. 5 of Pub. of Sharon Historical Society. 64 p.

WATERTOWN. see "Early New England town" in section I.

WESTMINSTER. Vital records of Westminster.

Pioneers of Maine and New Hampshire.

"The Pioneers of Maine and New Hampshire 1623 to 1660; a descriptive list, drawn from records of the colonies, towns, churches, courts and other contemporary sources. By Charles Henry Pope. . . . With foreword by James Phinney Baxter. Boston, published by Charles H. Pope, 221 Columbus Avenue, 1908." xi, 252 pages. $5.

The author, already well known to the genealogical world through his connection with several important family histories and especially since the publication of his "Pioneers of Massachusetts" has here given us the result of his researches in a new field. While the last named work dealt with Massachusetts colonists for 30 years following the first permanent settlement of 1620; the present one starting at the date of the grant to Gorges and Mason, includes the settlers north and east of the Merrimac River down to the period of the Restoration, that date marking at once the close of the great English emigration to the colonies and the complete absorption of the eastern plantations under the Mass. provincial government (Maine to there continue down to 1820 while New Hampshire was to begin its independent colonial existence in 1679). As justifying the initial date of 1623, it should be noted that the settlements of an earlier period, such as the Popham colony of 1607 and the French in eastern Maine, had no connection with the subsequent development of the region.

A score of plantations and towns are mentioned in the introduction, whose records together with sundry contemporary memoirs and manuscript collections comprise the sources drawn upon.

In the body of the work the arrangement follows the alphabetical order, giving under each name, chronologically, such mention as is found in town, church and probate records, deeds and courts files. Vital records of the immediate family of each settler are appended in each case, and at the end follows the only index needed, one of names incidentally mentioned. A rather elaborate system of abbreviations allows the condensation of much in small space. There are inserted some admirable special studies, as under Hilton, Wheelwright, etc. The work seems admirably done and one can feel pretty confident that the records extant have been carefully gleaned.

As brought into comparison with the old standard "Savage" it should be noted that the earlier work covers all New England, all immigrants before 1700 and not only children, but grandchildren of each settler; but in view of the many additional sources of informations now available, the "Pioneers of Maine and New Hampshire" must entirely supersede it in the field covered.

So involved and perplexing is the early history of these trans-Merrimac settlements, distinct, confederated or quarrelsome as they were, that we could wish the author had chosen to give a concise introductory essay in a few pages, covering their history down to 1660, with perhaps a chart showing the various and conflicting grants, or at least indicated where such account may be found. Delving for this information in the pages of Bancroft, Palfrey, Osgood or the various other colonial or state histories requires considerable effort.

A few minor points might be criticized: Under Authorities quoted, it would have been well to indicate which are manuscript and where such are to be consulted, as Lygonia Assembly, Records; and in case of printed books, fuller titles, with at least date of issue would be helpful. Essex Historical Society Collections doubtless is an error for Essex Institute Historical Collections.

Either in the list on page vii or elsewhere explanation should be given of such obsolete terms as Spurwink, Oyster River, etc. which occur in the text. Frequent references have been made from varying spellings of surnames to the form chosen for entry, but still others would be useful, as from Hurd to Heard, from Leighton to Layton, etc. C. A. F.

SOME MASSACHUSETTS HISTORICAL WRITERS

[Under this heading in each issue we shall give concise biographical sketches of town historians, family genealogists, and writers on other historical subjects pertaining to Massachusetts.]

BODGE, GEORGE MADISON, clergyman; born Windham, Me., February 14, 1841; son of Rev. John Anderson Bodge, and Esther A. Harmon Bodge. He lived on a farm in his native town and attended the district school until the age of fourteen, when he removed with his father's family, to Naples, Me., and there continued school in the winter, studying the higher branches under the instruction of Dr. H. D. Torrey, M. D., for several years; then attended Bridgton Academy, in the Fall and Spring terms, teaching school in the winters, and working in the summers, at whatever offered. Obliged to "work his way," he was partially fitted for College in 1861, when the war broke out, and he was in the army till the fall of 1862, when he resumed study at the Academy; entered Bowdoin College in 1864, and graduated from that institution in 1868. He was successively, Principal of Hallowell Academy, Gould's Academy, Bethel, Me., Gorham Seminary, and Westbrook Seminary. He graduated at Harvard Divinity School in 1878, and entered the Unitarian Ministry, being immediately settled at Dorchester, Mass., and afterwards held continuous pastorates, at East Boston, Leominster, and Westwood, Mass., till 1905, when in broken health, he was obliged to retire.

Mr. Bodge enlisted in the Seventh Maine Regiment in July, 1861, was appointed Fife-Major of the regiment in August, and served until June, 1862, when, prostrated by malarial fever, in the Chicahominy swamps, he was sent home to Maine, and discharged in August following.

He became a member of the Grand Army of the Republic, Post "Cuvier Grover," Bethel, Me., and was elected Commander, in 1871. He was made a Free Mason, in Bethel Lodge, in 1868, took Royal Arch degrees, in Oxford Chapter, in 1869, and has been Prelate of William Parkman Commandery, Knight Templars, of East Boston, since 1885. Was a Charter member of Columbia Lodge, Knights of Pythias, in 1893, was elected Grand Prelate of the

Rev. George M. Bodge.

Grand Lodge of Massachusetts, in 1895, and served until 1905; Chaplain of the Massachusetts Society of Colonial Wars from 1894 to 1905; Member of the Sons of the American Revolution; Member of the Society of Mayflower Descendants; an

active member, since 1875, of the New England Historic Genealogical Society.

Historical work has been: The History of Windham, Maine, to the close of the French and Indian wars, with the history of the Churches down to 1850, published in the Maine Genealogical Recorder, also "Soldiers in King Philip's War," published for the author, in Boston, now in the third edition. Numerous sketches and memoirs of members of the N. E. H. & Gen. Society in the Register. Editor and colleague—compiler of the "Churchill Family in America." Has now in preparation, Windham Maine Genealogies, and also genealogies of the Bodge, Plummer, and Harmon families and allied lines.

The title page to Mr. Bodge's great work reads as follows: "Soldiers in King Philip's War, being a critical account of that war, with a concise history of the Indian wars of New England from 1620 to 1677; official lists of the soldiers of Massachusetts Colony serving in Philip's war, and sketches of the principal officers, copies of the ancient documents and records relating to the war; also lists of the Narraganset grantees of the United Colonies Massachusetts, Plymouth and Connecticut; with an appendix." The first edition was published in 1892, a second edition was called for in 1896, and a third edition issued in 1906. The author's plan in presenting the history of the war is to give the experiences of individual companies, in separate chapters as follows: Beginning of hostilities, Capt. Henchman's company; Capt. Samuel Mosely and his company; Cavalry companies, or "Troops," of Capt. Prentice, Lieut. Oakes, and Capt. Nicholas Paige; Major Thomas Savage, his forces and operations; Capt. Thomas Wheeler and Edward Hutchinson at Brookfield; Major Simon Willard, his military operations and men; Capts. Richard Beers, Thomas Lathrop and their companies; Major Samuel Appleton, his operations and men; Capt. Isaac Johnson and his company; Capt. Joseph Gardiner and his company; Capt Nathaniel Davenport and his company; Capt. James Oliver and his company; Narraganset campaign, the Swamp Fort Battle; close of the Narraganset campaign, the hungry march; Capt. Brocklebank's company, Marlboro garrison; Capt. Samuel Wadsworth, the Sudbury fight; Capt. William Turner, the Falls Fight; Capts. Jonathan Poole, Thomas Brattle, and companies; Capt. Joseph Sill and his company; Various officers and companies; Major Richard Walderne's operations and men; Capt. William Hathorne and his men; Capt. Joshua Scottow and his Black Point garrison; Capts. Benjamin Swett and Michael Peirse; Lancaster and other garrisons, assignment of wages; Philip, Canonchet, and other hostile Indians; the Christian Indians of New England; Narragansett townships, additional credits, etc.

In the fore part of the third edition Mr. Bodge has introduced a long chapter of forty-three pages giving a concise history of the Indian wars of New Elngand from 1620 to 1677. There is also an appendix containing lists of governors, deputy governors and others; additional matter relating to the three colonies. At the end of the book is given a personal-names index, and a place-names index.

Mr. Bodge married Margaret E. Wentworth, a lineal descendant of Elder William Wentworth, of Wills, Me. They had three daughters: May Alice, died at Leominster, 1896; Clare J., married Russell H. Damon, of Leominster, and lives there; and Margaret W., who married George A. Littlefield, of Boston and lives at West Roxbury.

Mr. Bodge's address is "11 Meredith Street, West Roxbury, Mass.

SYLVESTER, HERBERT MILTON, lawyer and author, born Feb. 20, 1849, at Lowell, Mass.; son of Ezekiel J. and Miriam T. (Sargent) Sylvester; attended Bridgeton Academy. Married August 5, 1872, Clara Marie Elder, at Portland, Me., and has one son, Robert E. Sylvester, aged 34. Congregational in religion. Republican in politics. Admitted to the Cumberland bar in 1872 and practiced law in Portland for 13 years; admitted to Suffolk bar in 1885, and practiced law in Boston for 14 years; returned to Otisfield, Me., in 1899 retiring from active practice, has since devoted his time to literary work; trial justice of Cumberland County. He is a Sir Knight and a thirty-second degree Mason.

Historical Works: Romance of Casco Bay, in five historical sketches in New England Magazine, 1890; "The Romance of the Maine Coast," a five-volume historical work upon the period of earliest discovery of the Maine Coast, the five volumes being entitled: Casco Bay, Old York, Sokoki Trail, Olde Pemaquid, Land of St. Castin;

Herbert M. Sylvester.

also a sixth supplemental volume entitled The Wawennock (four volumes issued; the fifth and sixth in press): a History of Maine, in five volumes; Ancient Burial Grounds of Maine; Ancient Roof-Trees of Maine in preparation.

Mr. Sylvester's greatest published work is his projected five volumes entitled "Maine Coast Romance," four of which have already been published, under the sub-titles or individual titles: "Ye Romance of Casco Bay," "Ye Romance of Old York," "The Sokoki Trail," "Ye Romance of Olde Pemaquid." Each volume contains upwards of 400 pages and is profusely illustrated with first-hand pen-and-ink sketches from the author's own pen of old houses, ancient land-marks and bits of scenery associated with the history and traditions of these old places. There are as many as 150 of these sketches in one volume. With Sir Walter Scott as an ideal, the writer's aim has been to bring out and preserve the romance and history of these shore towns along the Maine coast. The first volume on Casco Bay contains the following chapters; Cascoe; Stogummor; A relic; Harrow House; A Wayside Inn; An Old Fish-Yard; Mountjoy's Island; The Wizard of Casco; The Troll of Richmon's Island; The Passing of Bagnall. The second volume on Old York has chapters on The Voyagers; Accomenticus; The Bells of York; Saddle-bag Days; Old Ketterie; Back-log Stories; The Pleiads of the Piscataqua. The third volume: The Forerunners; The Winter Harbor Settlement; The Isle of Bacchus; The Story of A Broken Tytle; The Romance of Black Point; The Sokoki Trail. The fourth volume: Early Explorers at Sagadahoc; Fort St. George; Pemaquid; Monhegan; Sheepscot; The Priest of Nanrantsouak. The fifth volume of the series is to be entitled The Land of St. Castin.

Other literary works: Prose Pastorals, published by Ticknor in 1887; Homestead Highways, published by Ticknor in 1888; A series of nature stories in Donahue's magazine in 1891; in preparation three historical readers for public schools of Maine.

Mr. Sylvester is an illustrator as well as author, his Maine Coast Romance containing between seven and eight hundred of his pen drawings.

Residence, Otisfield, Me.; business address, Harrison, Me.

Pilgrims and Planters

1620–1630

LUCIE M. GARDNER, A.B., Editor.

Societies

MAYFLOWER SOCIETY.

Membership, Confined to Descendants of the Mayflower Passengers.

GOVERNOR—ASA P. FRENCH.
DEPUTY GOVERNOR—JOHN MASON LITTLE.
CAPTAIN—EDWIN S. CRANDON.
ELDER—REV. GEORGE HODGES, D. D.
SECRETARY—GEORGE ERNEST BOWMAN.
TREASURER—ARTHUR I. NASH.
HISTORIAN—STANLEY W. SMITH.
SURGEON—WILLIAM H. PRESCOTT, M. D.
ASSISTANTS—EDWARD H. WHORF.
MRS. LESLIE C. WEAD.
HENRY D. FORBES.
MRS. ANNIE QUINCY EMERY.
LORENZO D. BAKER, JR.
MISS MARY E. WOOD.
MISS MARY F. EDSON.

THE OLD PLANTERS SOCIETY,
INCORPORATED.

Membership Confined to Descendants of Settlers in New England prior to the Transfer of the Charter to New England in 1630.

PRESIDENT—COL. THOMAS WENTWORTH HIGGINSON, CAMBRIDGE
VICE PRES.—FRANK A. GARDNER, M. D., SALEM.
SECRETARY—LUCIE M. GARDNER, SALEM.
TREASURER—FRANK V. WRIGHT, SALEM.
REGISTRAR—MRS. LORA A. W. UNDERHILL, BRIGHTON.
COUNCILLORS—WM. PRESCOTT GREENLAW, BOSTON.
R. W. SPRAGUE, M. D., BOSTON.
HON. A. P. GARDNER, HAMILTON.
NATHANIEL CONANT, BROOKLINE.
FRANCIS H. LEE, SALEM.
COL. J. GRANVILLE LEACH, PHILA.
FRANCIS N. BALCH, JAMAICA PLAIN.
JOSEPH A. TORREY, MANCHESTER.
EDWARD O. SKELTON, ROXBURY.

The Society held its fall meeting in Ellis Hall, in the Massachusetts Historical Society building, Thursday, November 19th. The paper of the afternoon was on "The Settlers about Boston Bay prior to 1630," by Miss Lucie Marion Gardner, Secretary of the society. The first part of the paper consisted of a brief sketch of the various temporary and scattered settlements at Wessagusset, Wollaston, Shawmut, etc., etc., up to the arrival of Governor Winthrop's fleet in June 1630. The second part included a biographical list of nearly fifty men who resided along the shores of Boston Bay between 1622 and 1630.

Dr. Frank A. Gardner Vice-President of the society, presided in the absence of the President, Colonel Thomas Wentworth Higginson. He congratulated the members upon the fact that satisfactory arrangements had been made with the publishers of the Massachusetts Magazine, whereby all members of the society will be regularly supplied with copies of the magazine. He outlined the society's plans for the coming season and spoke of the increase of interest in historical matters in general and of the growth in numbers as well as interest of "The Old Planters."

The address of the afternoon will be published in the April number of the Massachusetts Magazine.

The Annual Meeting of the Old Planters Society will be held in Salem, March 24, at the parlors of the Young Men's Christian Association. A meeting of the Council will be held at 2.30 P. M., to be followed by the general meeting at 3 o'clock. The annual reports will be read and officers elected for the ensuing year.

The annual address will be delivered by Dr. C. J. H. Woodbury, of Lynn, upon "John Woodbury, Planter." This biographical address will be one of a series delivered before the society. Similar contributions have been given concerning Roger Conant, Thomas Gardner, William Jeffery and in the end it is hoped to include all of the men who came to New England before 1630. Many of these men lived to an advanced age and were very prominent in the affairs of the Colony. What they accomplished is a matter of deep interest not only to their many descendants but to all students of early American history. This will be followed by an informal reception to the guests and their friends and light refreshments will be served. A cordial invitation is extended to all who are interested in New England History.

Our Editorial Pages

REV. THOMAS FRANKLIN WATERS.

LOWELL'S acute essay on "a certain condescension of foreigners" might be followed, if the genial but critical essayist were still with us, by another on "the presumption of genealogists." The time is ripe. The dimensions of the genealogical quest have expanded within a few years by leaps and bounds. Ancestor hunting is already a close second in popularity to the hunting of game with gun or fishing tackle. It has become a fine art with some, and is recognized as a professional employment, which entitles its practitioner to an ample fee. As for the amateur searcher of pedigrees his name is legion.

No pursuit, perhaps, involves a greater dependence on the help of others. The investigator is constantly finding that he has need of data, which he cannot obtain except by journeying hither and thither to consult public records or interview individuals, who are regarded as treasure-houses of information. But he has no time to spare, and the pecuniary expense is prohibitive. It is vastly easier and cheaper to presume on the good nature of a town clerk, or the keeper of a city record, or the local antiquarian or town historian, and forthwith a letter is written, not always couched in gracious speech, requesting the desired data.

Just here the trouble begins. There is a perfectly innocent forgetfulness on the part of some inquirers that there may be as real a trespass upon a man's time, or good nature, as upon his domicile, that inquiries of this kind may be so frequent that they become burdensome, and that it is wholly unreasonable to expect a town official or an expert student in local lore to feel the personal interest, which animates the writer. It would be a matter of genuine surprise to many an investigator, if he could know the experience of the town clerk or the historian. He could tell of many letters received, which enclosed not even a return stamp, of courteous replies which he has made, containing transcripts of records, which did not elicit a word of thanks, and of extended researches, undertaken with the promise of due compensation, for which not a cent was ever paid.

The natural consequence of this easy make-shift on the part of the genealogical inquirer, is that the individuals in every community, who have become their target, have become case-hardened. They are neither impolite, nor rude, as many affirm. Our own experience is that nobody could be more helpful and kindly when any reasonable service is asked.

But in self defence, they refuse to listen to the appeal of the stranger and cast the letter into the waste basket. With perfect justice, they regard the service which is asked, as a professional service, which may not be asked gratuitously, any more than the service of a lawyer or a physician. No one is offended, when the carpenter, who has stopped a leak, or the plumber, who has thawed the frozen pipe sends in his bill, and the custodian of records, or the student of local history, has equal right to set some value on his time and skill and his reserves of knowledge, and equal right not to be called crabbed or mercenary if he insists on his perquisite.

The passion for genealogical pursuits and kindred studies must not be allowed to make its enthusiasts intolerable bores. The rules of good breeding and the square deal, which is fundamental in business transactions, must be observed. Gratuitous favors must not be taken for granted. Let the easy-going ancestor hunter, sparing himself the toil and expense of original research, inclose a modest fee for a small service, and a proportionately larger for a larger demand, which will be a pledge of good faith in ultimate settlement, and he will relieve himself of the just reproach of presumption, and will greatly facilitate his quest.

AT THE recent Convention of the Modern Language Association of America at Princeton, discussion arose as to the attitude of the Carnegie Institute at Washington in failing, as it was declared, to further scientific researches in literature and art, as well as in the field of science. Resolutions were adopted looking toward a closer cooperation with the Institute for the publication of historical, archaeological, philosophical, linguistic, literary and artistic researches. It may be that the extremely broad scheme proposed would overtax even the splendid resources of the Carnegie foundation, but it commends itself as wise and timely. Scientific research is alluring and is crowned with results of the profoundest value to humankind. The enthusiastic investigator in chemistry, in physiology, in bacteriology, and in many other departments of exact science, deserves all the help and all the honor that may come to him. But the student in literature, in history, in archaeology, though he fails to achieve results as sharply defined and materially valuable, as the scientific investigator, is doing much for the welfare of humanity. His labors tend to enlarge the field of knowledge, to create an atmosphere of culture, and make life increasingly interesting. His contribution to the general well being is direct and generous. He may claim with good reason the same financial support as the student of science.

This is specially obvious in the research of the historical student. His realm may seem narrow and insignificant. He may be delving in the records of a single State, or only a single community. But prolonged and accurate research in the many records of even a small village or town inevitably contributes at once to the bettering of the life of that community, when published in readable and attractive form. The patient, sturdy life, the hard toil, the intense devotion to high spiritual ideals, the heroism in time of danger, the stern laws and cruel penalties of by-gone generations, are a stimulating tonic to the life of to-day. Every present day dweller in the community, which has been taught the story of its past, is helped to become a broader minded and better citizen.

But the local history is the unit in the compiling of general history. The history of a State is the collective history of its cities, towns, and villages. In our own Commonwealth, the history of Plymouth, Salem and Boston, of Deerfield, Lexington and Concord, are part and parcel of the history of Massachusetts, and America, and of the human race. In less striking ways, the history of every community is part of the history of the nation and of the world.

THE student of history is engaged, then, in a large and distinguished work. He needs just the help and encouragement, which the Carnegie foundation offers. The history of no community can be completely investigated within its own limits. Resort must be made to large libraries, to various depositories of records, and to the archives of the State, and the expense incident to long-continued study is not inconsiderable. The thoroughgoing examination of the many sources of information requires months and years. The collaboration of the material thus derived is tedious, and the final work of writing is slow and even painful. The financial question involved in all this is a very serious one. Many a would-be student finds the expense of travel, and of temporary residence within easy reach of the material he needs, prohibitive. Many an investigator, diligent, acute, enthusiastic, is obliged to earn his bread and butter by long hours of work at his vocation, and steal what time he can for his hobby. Even with rich material all gathered, publication is an impossibility, for the writer must bear the heavy expense, and the limited sale which only can be anticipated, will reimburse him in small degree for his outlay. Can not the Carnegie fund or a similar one in every State in our land, be so administered that the pecuniary obstacles to wise, thorough, and productive investigation and research in this realm may be removed, wholly or in large degree? With a State Commission to administer such a trust, selecting worthy and promising investigators for its benefaction, and directing perhaps the work of research, great impetus might be given to the search for new material, and to the publication of many volumes of standard and enduring value.

THE MASSACHVSETTS MAGAZINE

The Massachusetts Magazine

Published Quarterly

e y Magazine Devoted to History, Genealogy and Biography

THOMAS FRANKLIN WATERS, *Editor.* IPSWICH, MASS.

— *ASSOCIATE AND ADVISORY EDITORS* —

FRANK A. GARDNER, M.D. SALEM, MASS. | CHARLES A. FLAGG WASHINGTON, D. C. | JOHN N. MCCLINTOCK DORCHESTER, MASS. | ALBERT W. DENNIS SALEM, MASS.

Issued in January, April, July and October. Subscription, $2.50 per year, Single copies 75c.

VOL. II **APRIL, 1909** **NO. 2**

Contents of this Issue.

CHARLES WILLIAM ELIOT, *Edward J. James, Booker T. Washington, Daniel Starr Jordan, Cyrus Northrop* 59
MASSACHUSETTS PIONEERS IN MICHIGAN . . . *Charles A. Flagg* . 66
COLONEL TIMOTHY DANIELSON'S REGIMENT . . *F. A. Gardner, M.D.* 69
LOCAL HISTORICAL SOCIETIES IN MASSACHUSETTS *Charles A. Flagg* . 84
THE OLD MERRIAM HOUSE . . . . *Charles A. Flagg* . 98
SOME ARTICLES CONCERNING MASSACHUSETTS IN RECENT MAGAZINES . . . . *Charles A. Flagg* . 99
DEPARTMENT OF THE AMERICAN REVOLUTION *F. A. Gardner, M.D.* 101
CRITICISM AND COMMENT 107
PERSONAL DIARY OF ASHLEY BOWEN OF MARBLEHEAD 109
PILGRIMS AND PLANTERS . . . . *Lucie M. Gardner* . 115
OUR EDITORIAL PAGES . . . . *Thomas F. Waters* . 118

CORRESPONDENCE of a business nature should be sent to THE MASSACHUSETTS MAGAZINE, Salem, Mass.

CORRESPONDENCE in regard to contributions to the MAGAZINE may be sent to the editor, Rev. T. F. Waters, Ipswich, Mass., or to the office of publication, in Salem.

BOOKS for review may be sent to the office of publication in Salem. Books should not be sent to individual editors of the magazine, unless by previous correspondence the editor consents to review the book.

SUBSCRIPTION should be sent to THE MASSACHUSETTS MAGAZINE, Salem, Mass. Subscriptions are $2.50 payable in advance, post-paid to any address in the United States or Canada. To foreign countries in the Postal Union $3.00. Single copies of back numbers 75 cents each.

REMITTANCES may be made in currency or two cent postage stamps; many subscriptions are sent through the mail in this way, and they are seldom lost, but such remittances must be at the risk of the sender. To avoid all danger of loss send by post-office money order, bank check, or express money order.

CHANGES OF ADDRESS. When a subscriber makes a change of address he should notify the publishers giving both his old and new addresses. The publishers cannot be responsible for lost copies, if they are not notified of such changes.

ON SALE. Copies of this magazine are on sale in *Boston*, at W. B. Clark's & Co., 26 Tremont Street, Old Corner Book Store, 29 Bromfield Street. Geo. E. Littlefield, 67 Cornhill, Smith & McCance, 38 Bromfield Street; in *New York*, at John Wanamaker's, Broadway 4th, 9th and 10th Streets; in *Philadelphia*, Am. Baptist Pub. Society, 1630 Chestnut Street; in *Washington*, at Brentanos, F & 13th St.; in *Chicago*, at A. C. McClurg's & Co., 221 Wabash Ave.; in *London*, at B. F. Stevens & Brown, 4 Trafalgar Sq. Also on sale at principal stands of N. E. News Co.

Entered as second-class matter March 13, 1908, at the post office at Salem, Mass., under the act of Congress of March 3, 1879. Office of publication, 4 Central Street, Salem, Mass.

CHARLES WILLIAM ELIOT.

TRIBUTES BY PRESIDENT EDWARD J. JAMES OF THE UNIVERSITY OF ILLINOIS, PRINCIPAL BOOKER T. WASHINGTON OF TUSKEEGEE INSTITUTE, PRESIDENT DAVID STARR JORDAN OF LELAND STANIFORD JR. UNIVERSITY, PRESIDENT CYRUS NORTHROP OF UNIVERSITY OF MINNESOTA.

HARLES WILLIAM ELIOT will retire from the presidency of Harvard University on May 17th, 1909, when he will have completed forty years of service in this position. His personal character and the success of his administration of this great educational institution, make him one of the most admired and most influential men in American life today. He is often referred to as our first American citizen. Barring the president of the United States and the exceptional popularity of our one living ex-president, there is probably no one to contest him this title. As Booker T. Washington says in the article which follows: "Certainly there is no citizen in this country who has exerted a larger or more lasting influence during recent years."

Nothing is more significant of his position in the public mind today than the fact that since the announcement of his retirement, made several months ago, but two of the many American magazines of prominence has attempted to tell the story of his life and work.

His influence is too far-reaching and his greatness too obvious to allow of a careful study of his career at the present time, but the accompanying personal tributes from four American leading educators, will give some idea of the esteem of his compeers.

The simple facts of Doctor Eliot's life are these: Born March 20, 1834.

His father was Samuel Atkins Eliot, a prosperous Boston merchant. His mother was Mary Lyman. He was fitted for college at the Boston Latin School; was graduated from Harvard in 1853; was Instructor in mathematics at Harvard and student in chemistry with Prof. Josiah P. Cooke, 1854-8; Assistant professor of mathematics and chemistry at Lawrence Scientific School, Harvard, 1858-63; studied chemistry and investigated educational methods in Europe, 1863-5; Professor of analytical chemistry at the Massachusetts Institute of Technology, 1865-9; elected President of Harvard in 1869. Married twice: first October 27, 1858, Ellen D. Peabody; second October 30, 1877, Grace M. Hopkinson.

It will be thirty-five years next autumn, November first, 1874, when I saw President Eliot for the first time. I remember the occasion as well as if it were yesterday. I had been employed during the summer season just passed on the U. S. Lake Survey. The party was not disbanded until the last week in October and consequently I arrived late at Cambridge to begin my work as Freshman in Harvard College.

As it was against the rules to admit students except at the regular times for opening the college year, I was obliged to seek a special dispensation from the President of the University. This took me to President Eliot's house. The interview was brief and confined chiefly to the necessary inquiries as to why I had arrived late, and what my previous preparation had been. The President gave me no advice, did not indulge in any exhortation to be industrious, avoid bad habits, or any of the usual lectures to incoming Freshmen. But I left his presence with a conscious sense of increased power and determination. I felt that virtue had come into me, and I experienced an unexpressed but deep feeling that there was a man whom I would wish to be like.

This sense of looking up to President Eliot as a leader has remained with me during all these years and I am delighted to have this opportunity to give public expression to it.

I have been for more than twenty-five years a member of university faculties, first at Pennsylvania, then at Chicago, and Northwestern and the University of Illinois. I do not think it is too much to say that no large question of University policy has ever been discussed in any of the numerous faculty meetings I have attended in the quarter of a century without bringing to the surface one or another of the issues which President Eliot has made in American higher education. In fact I should sum up his work

in a word as that of issue-maker and if we add to that, pace-maker in educational progress, we sum up in a general way his career.

A distinguished college professor in one of the smaller New England Colleges said to me on one occasion, many years ago, with a touch of bitterness in his voice: "President Eliot has been dragging the New England Colleges around at his chariot wheels now for ten years as Achilles dragged the dead body of Hector around the walls of Troy, and it is time to stop it." Of course, it was not stopped since President Eliot was heading the party of progress and the day of old things was passing away.

It is not too much to say that President Eliot has been the most prominent figure and I believe the most potent single influence in the reorganization of American higher education in the great historical institutions of the country. No other man was in a position to do so much as he, owing to his native ability and educational experience and insight and above all his dauntless courage. Nor could he have done his work in any other institution than Harvard. It was a combination of time, place and the man such as does not often occur. The result has been a unique career in the history of education not only in this country but in the world—a career of which every American may well be proud, since it represents the possibilities of world wide influence open to American brains, courage and character.

EDWARD J. JAMES.

UNIVERSITY OF ILLINOIS.

I have noted that when distinguished men come to this country from abroad they frequently express their surprise that the people of all classes in this country take as much interest as they do in the subject of education.

These strangers had heard and seen so much of the business energy and material progress of this country that they imagined, before they came here, that the ideals of the American people must be low and that as a people Americans were not interested in spiritual things. Nothing shows so clearly that this is not true as the fact that outside of the President, the most influential citizen of the United States is the president of a University, Doctor Charles W. Eliot, of Harvard. Certainly there is no citizen in this country who has exerted a larger or more lasting influence, during recent years, and this fact but illustrates again the enormous power which the Universities, largely under the influence of Dr. Eliot's example, have attained in this country.

While I do not feel myself competent to define the character or extent of Dr. Eliot's influence, it seems to me he derives a large part of his power from his ability to state simply, incisively, and in a few words, the ideas

which he has gathered from a wide and deep knowledge of men and events. He has been able to lend a kind of distinction to the most familiar and homely truth from the manner in which he utters it. On the other hand he has frequently expressed original ideas and profound truths, with such directness, force, and simplicity that they have seemed to us who heard or read them as convincing and familiar, as if we had always known them.

Few men of wide learning and deep knowledge, I venture to say, have known how to express themselves so clearly and so impressively. President Eliot's ability in this direction is, in my opinion not merely a large source of his power as an educator and an administrator, but it is at the same time the expression of his great and sane mind. In fact it often seemed to me that in the case of Doctor Eliot it is almost possible to say that sanity has amounted to genius.

I have had several opportunities for meeting and knowing President Eliot in a personal way, but I have never met him that I have not been singularly impressed with his dignity and with his scholarly bearing. The thing that emphasized this impression was that in him dignity was combined with simplicity ; scholarship had not put him out of touch with plain and practical interests of life.

It has been my fortune at different times to ask assistance of Dr. Eliot in matters that I appreciated would make some rather severe demands upon his time and attention. In every case, he has readily and without hesitation, granted what I asked. I remember at one time, when we were arranging for a large public meeting in Boston, in the interest of Tuskegee Institute that I went to him in order to try to induce him to deliver one of the principal addresses. I had never met him before, and I naturally had some fear, that he would not be able to grant my request, but I told him plainly and frankly what I wanted, and without hesitation he consented to assist us in the way I had suggested.

Later, when we celebrated our twenty-fifth anniversary at Tuskeegee Institute, I went to him and told him that I wanted him to represent Harvard University and be one of the speakers on that occasion. Again he consented without hesitation and with apparent willingness to do anything he could to lend importance to our celebration.

To me, the most interesting occasion upon which I met Dr. Eliot was when I was invited, by the trustees of Harvard University, to receive an honorary degree. Throughout the day, I was thrown in frequent contact with him, and on eaoh occasion, he was most kind in his bearing toward me and left nothing undone to make me feel welcome at Harvard.

One other thing that has impressed itself upon me, in regard to Dr. Eliot is his ability to keep himself in touch with the latest and best things that are taking place in the world. Usually, we expect a man at his age to become very set in his ways and in his manner of thinking and doing things. After men reach a certain age, we know that they are disposed to live in the past. Dr. Lyman Abbott and President Eliot, in this regard, are two striking exceptions. These two men live just as much in the present as men of twenty-five or thirty years of age. In this respect, President Eliot sets a great example, in my opinion, to all Americans.

BOOKER T. WASHINGTON.

TUSKEEGEE INSTITUTE,
ALABAMA.

It is easy to say that for forty years President Eliot has been the leader of our leaders in higher education, the man all the rest have looked up to and by the side of whom the oldest and most experienced of the others have seemed hopelessly young.

It is also clear that this leadership has been due mainly to three things — his sure mastery of business affairs, his untiring industry, and his courage in setting aside the present to deal with the future, which he knows will come.

As a result of this, Harvard College—Harvard University—has never been a fact accomplished. It has been a continuous struggle, a movement towards the future, a struggle for greater means, better methods, stronger men and higher ideals. Because Harvard has thus been a continuous struggle, all other American institutions have become such. This is their chief distinction as compared with the universities of other nations. American universities are never completed. They are still being born.

In the forty years of rebuilding Harvard, Dr. Elliot has led the race, and the long procession of institutions representing higher education in America, have followed near or far in his trail. The various impulses of originality in other institutions, notably those originating with White at Cornell and Gilman at Johns Hopkins, have been absorbed and carried forward by Harvard. To Cornell we owe originally the doctrine of democracy of studies, the idea that no one shall say which study or which discipline is best until one knows the man who administers the discipline and the man on whom it is to be tried. To Johns Hopkins we owe the idea that advanced work in any subject has a greater culture value than elementary work in the same or

other subjects. The one great educational idea which Harvard has not assimilated is that which finds its best representative in the University of Wisconsin. This is the idea that the state university, as the centre of intelligence and force should recreate the state, advancing and strengthening all its varied interests.

The greatest single achievement of Dr. Eliot has been the establishment of the elective system in higher education. The rival systems have passed away never to return, and our real problem is that of adjusting checks and balances in such a way as to best develop the individual student.

In many lines, courses are prescribed in the nature of things, one subject following another with which it is linked and on which it depends. But there is no longer any place for prescribed courses of mixed science, literature, art and philosophy, so many units of one, so many of another, disjointed members brought together in the name of culture. These results of the pulling and hauling of college faculties have passed away for good.

The checks needed in the elective system must, for the most part, come from the student himself. He must train himself to guard against premature specialization or rather against advanced work on inadequate foundation on the one hand, and from the greater danger of limp diffuseness on the other. Specialization is but another name for thoroughness. "The mind is made strong by the thorough possession of something."

The writer once heard President Eliot disclaim any unusual degree of prophetic vision, allowing for himself only an honest industry, attacking one problem after another, as it arose with such solution of each as might be within the range of practical action.

One of Dr. Eliot's predecessors in Harvard was once complimented on the logical coherence of his sermons. He disclaimed all special excellence in this regard "I write one sentence," he said, "then I thank God and write another." President Eliot has himself accepted this definition of his method. One thing done, he turns to and does the next, and this is the essence of his educational foresight. He does the next and the next, never stopping with the first result or the first achievement.

It is this doing what is needed, not for today, but for the unseen tomorrow and the oncoming years to follow, which has made the history of Harvard, a history of unending endeavor, of continuous struggle. On the continuance of this struggle by men never satisfied with what is already achieved, the hope of higher education in America depends.

David Starr Jordan.

The forty years of President Charles W. Eliot's administration as head of Harvard University have been remarkable for the changes in educational methods introduced into Harvard and widely copied by other institutions. For these changes President Eliot has himself been mainly responsible. Believing that men will work best when they like their work and that students will study best when they are interested in the subject studied, and that mental discipline can be cultivated as well in the investigation of things that are important as of things that are not important but are only difficult, he took away the barriers that confined students to a very limited number of subjects for study, and gave to every student the liberty of choosing whatever he pleased from the whole field of knowledge. It was a sad blow to old ideas and old methods. But he made a success of it at Harvard, and though subjected to much criticism he is as confident to-day that his plan is right as he has ever been; and judging from the number of colleges which are to-day conducted according to his ideas as far as their resources will permit, it is safe to say that the opinion of the educational world is practically a unit in favor of his essential idea. Undoubtedly the tremendous increase in the number of college students in the last twenty years may be attributed in some considerable degree to the enlarged curriculum and greater freedom of choice offered to students. President Eliot has clearly vindicated his right to be considered the leading educator of the last half century.

But his fame does not by any means rest exclusively upon his work in Harvard. He has been a careful student of our national, political and industrial life, and of the civic administration of government in cities, and of the administration of boards of education throughout the country. A profound thinker he has contributed much to the clear understanding of many vital questions. Always having the courage of his convictions he has spoken frankly whether in the presence of friends or foes to his ideas, and his courageous expression of opinions has always commanded respect for the man even among those who were not convinced by his arguments. The interest which he has manifested in the various conditions of human life and the suggestions which he has made to remedy evils and promote the civic welfare have given him a very high place as a citizen, so that he is hardly more honored as the great educator than he is as the great citizen. With an acute intellect, deep interest in human welfare, profound study of great problems, and a readiness to give the whole country the benefit of his best thoughts, he has achieved greatness in more than one field of labor, and he is to-day a mighty force in moulding public sentiment on many vital questions. Less militant than he once was, but not less earnest, the sweetness and fruitfulness of his closing years are making his last days his best days; and honor awaits him wherever he goes—at home or abroad.

CYRUS NORTHROP.

[This is the fifth instalment of a series of articles on Massachusetts Pioneers to other states, to be published by The Massachusetts Magazine.]

MASSACHUSETTS PIONEERS. MICHIGAN SERIES.

By Charles A. Flagg

Besides the abbreviations of book titles, (explained on pages 76, 77, 78 and 79 of April issue) the following are used: b. for born; d. for died; m. for married; set. for settled in.

Chamberlin, Wells, set. N. Y., 1820? Washtenaw Port., 344.

Chandler, Jonathan, b. Concord? set. Vt., N. Y., Mich. Branch Port., 484.

Chaney, Hannah, m. Nathaniel Parmeter of Mass. and N. Y. Newaygo, 328.

Chapel, Annis L., m. 1840? Luke L. Dennison of Mass. Midland, 197.

Chapin, Almno M., b. Chicopee, 1810; set. N. Y., Mich., 1843. Ingham Hist., 313, 316; St. Clair, 122.

—— Gad, set. Vt.; Revolutionary soldier; set. N. Y., 1879. Washtenaw Hist., 284.

—— Hannah, b. Franklin Co.; d. 1833; m. Zadock Hale of Vt. Kalamazoo Port., 407.

—— Henry A., b. Leyden, 1813 or 14; set. Mich., 1836. Cass Hist., 146; Cass Twent., 60, 357.

—— James set. Mich., 1840? Mecosta, 479.

—— Jane, m. 1835? Joseph L. Beebe of N. Y. Jackson Hist., 587.

—— Joseph, b. Pamsa(?); set. N. Y., Pa., 1832. Kalamazoo Port., 824.

—— Levi, b. Chicopee, 1787; set. N. Y., 1818, Mich., 1844. Ingham Hist., 316.

—— Marshall, b. Bernardston, 1798; set. N. Y., Mich., 1819. Detroit, 1033; Wayne Chron., 202.

—— Noah J., b. 1814; set., N. Y. 1815? Mich., 1854. Traverse, 287.

—— Rachel, m. Paul Davis, Revolutionary soldier, of Mass. and N. Y. Branch Port., 459.

Chapman, Alcott C., of Pittsfield, b. 1793; set. Mich., 1816? Monroe, 140.

—— Edmond, set. N. Y., 1810? Mich., 1836. Branch Twent., 500.

Chapman, George W., b. Belchertown, 1815; set. Mich, 1841. Saginaw Hist., 816; Saginaw Port., 815.

—— Jane, m. 1830? Jarrah Sherman of N. Y. Jackson Port., 753.

—— Lucius W., b. Franklin Co., 1820; set. Mich., 1870. Saginaw Port., 251, 899.

—— Nina, m. 1840? Lyman West of O. and Mich. Clinton Past., 238.

—— Wellington, b. Hampshire Co., 1814; set. Mich., 1841. Saginaw Hist., 818; Saginaw Port., 855.

—— William H. H., b. Berkshire Co., 1841; set. Mich., 1841. Saginaw Port., 815.

Chappell, William, set. N. Y., 1800? Clinton Past. 193.

Chase, Alanson, b. 1806; set. Mich., 1830? Washtenaw Hist., 1076.

—— Benjamin, set. N. Y., 1815? Washtenaw Hist., 973.

——Clark, set. N. Y., 1800? d. 1821. Kalamazoo Hist., facing 423.

—— Mrs. J. M., b. 1822; set. Mich., 1847. Washtenaw Hist., 496.

Chesebrough, Elisha, set. N. Y., 1820? Jackson Port., 697.

—— Maria, m. 1820? Milton Holmes of Mass. and N. Y. Jackson Port., 698.

—— Sarah, b. 1793; m. 1815? Warner I. Hodge of Mass. and Mich. Jackson Hist., 831; Jackson Port., 697.

Child, Alpha, b. Boston, 1836; set. Wis., Mich., 1872. Kent, 422.

Childs, Clarissa, b. 1790? m. 1810 Shubael Atherton of N. Y. and Mich. Genesee Hist., 348; Genesee Port., 815.

—— Daniel, b. 1779; set. N. Y., 1819. Hillsdale Port., 266.

CHILDS, Henry B., b. Shelburne, 1814; set. Mich., 1846. Grand Rapids City, 604; Kent, 263.

—— Sarah, m. 1819 Shubael Atherton of N. Y. Genesee Hist., 349.

—— Sophia, b. Pittsfield, 1789; m. 1816 Samuel Ledyard of N. Y. Branch Port., 615.

CHITTENDEN, Elizabeth, b. 1783; set. Mich. Washtenaw Hist., 590.

CHUBB, Franklin, set. Mich., 1830? Clinton Port., 335.

CHURCH, Chandler M., b. Berkshire Co., 1804; set. N. Y., Mich. Calhoun, 145.

—— Jesse, set. N. Y., 1807. Calhoun, 145.

—— Lucy, m. 1810? Appolos Baker of Mass. and N. Y. Lenawee Port., 594.

—— Nathan, b. 1847; set. Mich., 1869. Kent, 429.

—— Thomas B., b. Dighton, 1813 or 21; set. Mich., 1838. Grand Rapids Hist., 725; Grand Rapids Lowell, 753; Kent, 971.

CLAGHORN, Elizabeth, b. Williamsburg; m. 1800? Joseph Beal of N. Y. and Mich. Ionia Port., 457; Lenawee Hist. II, 175.

—— Sarah, b. Williamsburg, 1776; m. 1800 Ephraim Green of N. Y. Lenawee Hist. I, 484.

CLAPP, James H., set. N. Y., 1850, O. Grand Rapids City, 436.

—— Luther, b. Hampshire Co., set. O. 1840. Gratiot, 362.

—— Stephen, b. Northampton, 1750; set. N. Y., 1780. Lenawee Hist. I, 492.

CLARK, Albert, b. Northampton; set. O., Mich., 1863. Berrien Port., 583.

—— Aurilla, m. 1820? Justus Stiles of N.Y. and Mich. Muskegon Port., 322.

—— Calvin, b. Westhampton, 1805; set. Mich., 1835. St. Clair, 122.

—— Climene, b. Westhampton; m. 1839 Erastus Hopkins of Mich. Oakland Hist., 189.

—— Enos, set. N. Y., 1820? Mich., 1839. Allegan Twent., 455.

—— Ethan A., set. N. Y., 1820? Oakland Port., 269.

—— Hannah, of Greenwich, m. 1804 Bradford Newcomb of Vt. Lenawee Hist. I, 309.

—— James M., set. O., 1840? Osceola, 240.

CLARK, Jason, b. 1791; set. N. Y., Mich., 1823. Ingham Port., 761.

—— John, b. 1770; set. Vt., 1777, Mich., 1833. Shiawassee, 442.

—— Lucius L., b. Hawley, 1816; set. Mich., 1839. St. Clair, 122.

—— Lydia, b. Hampshire Co., 1803? m. Alvah Whitmarsh of Mass., N. Y., and Ill. Lenawee Port., 1136.

—— Mary, m. 1815? Nathaniel Macumber of N. Y. and Mich. Newaygo, 267.

—— Mary A., of Northampton; m. 1835 Watson Loud of Mass. and Mich. Macomb Hist., 663.

—— Miles D., set. O., 1838. Washtenaw Hist., 1261.

—— Nancy, b. Somerset, 1773; m. 1796 Henry Weatherwax of N. Y. and Mich. Lenawee Hist. II, 234.

—— Orange, b. Berkshire Co., set. N. Y., O., 1831, Mich., 1854. Berrien Twent., 579.

—— Polly, b. Colerain, 1792; m. 1811 Daniel Jennings of N. Y., Hillsdale Port, 222; Lenawee Hist. I, 272; Lenawee Port., 395.

—— Rhoda, b. Sharon; m. 1820? Fisher Bullard of N. H. Kent, 1392.

—— Robert W., from near Pelham; set. N. Y.; d. 1839. Ingham Port., 750.

—— Sophronia, b. Southwick, 1803; m. Henry W. Clapp of O. and Mich. Jackson Hist., 1010.

—— William A., b. Pittsfield; set. N. Y., 1820? Saginaw Port., 455.

—— William H., b. Hopkinton, 1805; set. Mich., 1845. Macomb Hist., 693.

CLARKE, Archibald S., set. N. Y., 1810? Jackson Hist., 968.

—— Franklin S., b. Berkshire Co., 1812; set. N. Y., Mich., 1843. Jackson Hist., 611.

—— John, Jr., b. Brewster, 1824; set. N.Y. Cal., Mich., 1860. Hillsdale Port., 263.

—— Linus, set. N. Y., 1825. Jackson Hist., 611.

—— Robert M., b. Brewster, 1825; set. Cal. Hillsdale Port., 263.

—— William B., set. N. Y., 1820? Saginaw Hist., 744.

CLEAVES, William S., b. Lowell, 1851; set. Mich., 1860. Upper P., 277.

CLEGG, Alice, b. Taunton, 1852; m. Asa L. Crane of Mich. Hillsdale Port., 842.

CLEMANS, Asa, b. Worcester, 1804? set. Mich., 1837. Hillsdale Port., 372.

CLEMENS, Jonathan, Revolutionary soldier; set. N. Y. Jackson Port., 341.

CLOUGH, Elijah, set. Mich., 1839. Oakland Port., 765.

COBB, John, set. Mich., 1834; d. 1875. Jackson Hist., 880.

COBURN, Jeptha, set. Mich., 1830. Oakland Port., 488.

—— Sallie, m. 1820? Daniel Stearns of N. Y. Newaygo, 274.

CODDING, Abiah, set. Vt., 1812 soldier. Berrien Port., 481.

CODY, Rufus, set. N. Y., 1800. Hillsdale Port., 715.

COFFIN, Lydia, b. Nantucket, 1780; m. 1797 Obed Macy of Mass., N. Y. and Mich. Lenawee Hist. II, 326.

COGSWELL, Asahel, set. N. Y., 1800? Saginaw Hist., 755.

COLE, Dyer, b. 1799; set. Mich. Lansing, 182.

—— Luther, set. N. Y., 1785. Monroe, 152.

—— Nathaniel, b. Rehoboth, 1794; set. N. Y., Mich., 1837. Macomb Hist., 650.

COLEMAN, Almeda, m. 1820? John Russell of N. Y. and Mich. Jackson Hist., 955.

COLES, Columbus, b. Williamsburg, 1828; set. O., Mich., 1854. Isabella, 353.

—— Horace, set. O., 1839; d. 1882. Isabella, 353.

—— Oliver, b. Belchertown, 1790? set. N. Y. and Mich. Osceola, 255.

COLLIER, Charles S., b. Charlestown, 1803; set. N. Y., 1840, Mich, 1853. Oakland Biog., 76.

—— Susan, m. 1830? Samuel Andrews of Mich. Bay Gansser, 486.

COLLINS, Angeline, b. 1811; m. Alanson Flower of Mich. Oakland Port., 421.

—— Benjamin, from Cape Cod; set. N. Y., 1802. Berrien Hist., 326.

—— George, b. Wilbraham; set. Mich., 1830? Washtenaw Past, 165.

—— John, b. Hampshire Co., 1816; set. Mich. Genesee Port., 500.

COLLINS, Jonah S., b. Cape Cod, 1769; set. Mich. Genesee Port., 500.

—— Nathaniel, set. N. Y., 1825? Newaygo, 278.

COLT, Clara or Clarissa, m. 1825 Elnathan Phelps of Mass. and Mich. Oakland Biog., 607; Oakland Port., 640.

—— George, b. Pittsfield, 1807; set. Fla., 1828, Cuba, 1836, Mich., 1853. Clinton Port., 385.

—— Sylvia E., b. Pittsfield, 1796; m. 1813 Charles Larned of Mich. Wayne Chron., 325.

COLTON, John B., b. Conway, 1827; set. Mich., 1844. Kent, 264.

COLVER, Calvin, b. 1788; set. Mich. Washtenaw Hist., 590.

COMAN, Samuel, set. N. Y., 1800; Mich., 1835. Hillsdale Port., 700.

COMINGS, Chester, from Worcester County, set. Mich., 1837. Allegan Hist., 219, 253.

COMSTOCK, John, b. 1774; set. N. Y., 1788, Mich., 1830. Lenawee Hist. I, 497. Lenawee Port., 648.

—— Nathan, set. N. Y., 1788. Lenawee Hist. I, 497.

—— William, set. Mich., 1850? Muskegon Port., 434.

CONANT, Charles R., b. Franklin Co., 1814; set. Vt., 1823, Mich., 1851. Jackson Port., 594.

CONE, Obed, b. 1792; set. N. Y., 1825? Mich., 1853. Lenawee Hist. II, 130.

CONGDON, William T., b. near Boston; set. N. Y., 1830? Ingham Port., 246.

CONKLIN, Ebenezer H., b. Lenox 1790; set. N. Y., 1806, Mich., 1831. Washtenaw Hist., 1336.

CONN, George, set. N. H., 1795? N. Y. Clinton Port., 719.

CONNABLE, Abbie, b. Bernardston; m. 1830? James C. Bontecou of R. I., Mass. and O. Northern M., 474.

CONVERSE, Benjamin, b. Belchertown, 1813; set. Mich., 1834. Lenawee Port., 1207.

—— Ephraim, b. Brookfield, 1779; res. Belchertown; set. Mich., 1851. Lenawee Port., 1207.

(To be continued.)

[This is the fourth of a series of articles, giving the organization and history of all the Massachusetts regiments which took part in the war of the Revolution.]

COLONEL TIMOTHY DANIELSON'S REGIMENT

COLONEL TIMOTHY DANIELSON'S MINUTE MEN'S REGIMENT, 1775.
18TH REGIMENT ARMY OF THE UNITED COLONIES, 1775.

BY FRANK A. GARDNER, M. D.

The southern division of Hampshire County, which has been known as Hampden county since the division in 1812, furnished nearly all of the men for this regiment. The snug farmhouses which nestled in these fertile valleys or withstood the gales on the green hillsides of this attractive region were the homes from which went hundreds of sturdy fighters in the cause of liberty.

Colonel Danielson in response to the Lexington alarm of April 19, 1775, assembled a regiment of eight companies with the following officers:—

"Colonel Timothy Danielson, of Brimfield.
Lieut. Colonel William Shepard, of Westfield.
Major David Leonard, of West Springfield.

Springfield Company.
Captain, Gideon Burt.
First Lieutenant, Walter Pynchon.
Second Lieutenant, Aaron Steele.
61 men.

Westfield Company.
Captain, Warham Parks.
First Lieutenant, John Shepard.
Second Lieutenant, Richard Falley.
70 men.

West Springfield Company.
Captain, Enoch Chapin.
First Lieutenant, Samuel Flower.
Second Lieutenant, Luke Day.
53 men.

Blandford and Murrayfield Company.
Captain, John Ferguson.
First Lieutenant, David Hamilton.
(No Second Lieutenant)
36 men.

Granville Company.
Captain, Lebbeus Ball.
First Lieutenant, Lemuel Bancroft.
(No Second Lieutenant)
60 men.

Southwick Company.
Captain, Silas Fowler.
First Lieutenant, George Grainger.
Second Lieutenant, John Keent.
22 men.

Monson Company.
Captain, Freeborn Moulton.
First Lieutenant, Asa Fisk.
Second Lieutenant, Abel Allen.

Brimfield Company.
Captain, Joseph Thompson.
First Lieutenant, Aaron Mighill.
Second Lieutenant, Joseph Hoar.
45 men.

The long distance covered in the march to Cambridge made the regiment late in arriving at headquarters. It was assigned upon arrival to the fortifications at Roxbury. The following note on the roll of Captain Fowler's Company is of interest:—"Captain Silas Fowler's Co. of Southwick left there Apr. 21, 1775, marched 110 miles to Roxbury arrived there Apr. 29 & joined Col. Danielson's Regt."

May 22d, the regiment was made up as follows:

"Joseph Thompson	1	2	4	2	52	61	Caleb Keep John Carpenter
Enoch Cheapin	1	2	4	1	43	51	Sam'l Flower Luke Day Jr.
Warhum Parks	1	2	4	1	52	60	John Shepard Jun Richard Falley

Lebbeus Ball	1	2	4	2	48	57	Lemuel Bencraft Levy Dunham
Gideon Burt	1		4	2	50	57	
Paul Langdon	1	1			37	39	Dan'l Cadwell
John Ferguson	1	1			26	28	Dav[d] Hambilton
Sylvanus Walker	1	1	3	1	35	41	
	8	11	23	9	343	399	

David Shepard, Surgeon; John Miller, Surgeon's Mate; William Toogood, Adjutant.

Signed, William Shepard."

The field officers at this time were the same as in the Minute Men's Regiment. William Young of Hatfield was made Quartermaster May 15th. On the 16th of June the total membership of the regiment was 463, with 9 "not yet joined." They had in their possession 423 guns and 168 bayonets. The regiment was numbered the "Eighth" in the Provincial Army under General Artemas Ward and contained, about July 1, 1775, 579 men in all, wanting only 1 sergeant, 5 drummers, and fifers, and 57 men to complete. The following list gives the names of the company commanders about this time, with a list of the towns in which the companies were raised:

Captains.

Sylvanus Walker, Palmer, Brookfield, Sturbridge, Brimfield, Western, Ware etc.

Daniel Egrey, Dartmouth, Rochester, Middleboro.

Lebbeus Ball, Granville, Southwick, Loudon, Roxbury.

Thomas Plympton,* Dartmouth, Rochester, Westerly, R. I.

John Fergueson, Blanford, Murrayfield, Brimfield.

Joseph Thompson, Brimfield, Marion, South Brimfield, Palmer.

Warham Parks, Westfield.

Enoch Chapin, West Springfield, Watertown, Suffield, Ct.

Gideon Burt, Springfield, Marblehead, Ludlow.

Paul Langdon, Wilbraham, Ludlow, Belchertown, Somers and Windsor, Ct.

Nathan Peters, Stonington, Preston, Norwich and Suffield, Ct.

General Washington took command of the forces on July 4th, and in the formation of the Army of the United Colonies this regiment became the "Eighteenth" and was in Brigadier General Thomas's Brigade, "Major General Artemas Ward's Division. It was stationed at Roxbury as it had been

* Mistake in the original. It should be "Kempton."

in May and June in the Provincial Army. The regiment continued to serve in these fortifications through the year.

The strength of the company each month is shown in the following table:

1775	Com. Off.	Staff.	Non.-com.	Rank & File.	Total
Aug. 18,	32	3	60	491	586
Sept. 23,	33	4	61	481	579
Oct. 17,	33	4	59	466	562
Nov. 18,	31	4	59	454	548
Dec. 30,	27	2	57	453	539

COLONEL TIMOTHY DANIELSON, the third son of John and Margaret (Mughill) Danielson, was born December 6, 1733. His father intended him for the ministry. He graduated from Yale in 1756 and later received the degree of A. M. from the same college. He never became a preacher, however, but taught school, and in 1771 was one of the two traders in Brimfield. He represented the town in General Court from 1766 to 1773.

September 26, 1768, he was chosen by the citizens of Brimfield to attend a convention in Boston, "in order that such measures may be consulted and advised, as his Majesty's service and the peace and safety of his subjects may require." In September 1774, "Mr. Timothy Danielson of Brimfield" was chairman of a "Congress of committees, from every town and district within the County of Hampshire, and province of the Massachusetts Bay, excepting Charlemont and Southwick, held at the courthouse in Northampton." He was a member of the First Provincial Congress which met at Salem in October 1774, serving on several important committees, including the one, appointed October 21st, "to report a non-consumption agreement relative to British and India teas." December 7, 1774, he was appointed on a committee with "John Adams, Esq., and Mr. Samuel Adams," to bring in a resolve directing the Hon. James Russell Esq., import officer, to pay the moneys now in his hands to Henry Gardner, Esq. and not to Harrison Gray, Esq."

February 1, 1775, he was chosen a member of the Second Provincial Congress, from Brimfield and Monson. March 22, he was made chairman of the committee "to receive the returns of the several officers of militia, of their numbers and equipments." In April he served on a committee to consider a letter from the "Committee of Correspondence of Boston," was chosen "a gentleman to be added to the delegates appointed to repair to Connecticut," and appointed on a county committee of five for Hampshire. He served as a committeeman in May on a letter from General Ward, on a committee "to

consider a false account of the excursion of the King's troops to Concord" and one on "an application to the Continental Congress for leave to take up civil government." He was chosen May 31, to represent the same two towns in the Third Provincial Congress, and was speaker pro tem. of the House of Representatives June 17, 1776. He commanded a regiment of Minute Men, April 19, 1775, and led them to Cambridge. This body of men was reorganized, later in the month, as the 8th Regiment of the Provincial Army under General Artemas Ward, and in July, into the 18th Regiment of the Army of the United Colonies under General Washington. The command was stationed through the year in the defences at Roxbury.

He was chosen Brigadier General for Hampshire County, January 30, 1776 and commissioned February 8th. A distinguished honor was conferred upon him Oct. 19th, 1776, when he was appointed chairman of a committee of five, the other members being "Jonathan Gardner, Jun. Esq., George Partridge, Esq., Colonel Josiah Sartell and Capt. Seth Washburn," "to repair without delay to the camp at or near New York; and there, after gaining the best intelligence they can get, and after advising with his Excellency General Washington, the Commander-in Chief in that department respecting the character of the officers belonging to this state now in the Army proceed to appoint from the officers now in the Army, or others, the Field and Staff officers for seven Battalions; and also the Captains and Subalterns for the Companies of seven Battalions,"etc., etc. He made reports in November concerning the condition of the Army at White Plains and in December upon the regimental officers.

Another committee was to repair to Ticonderoga and after consulting with General Gates, do the same acts in the formation of five battalions. He made returns of a detachment of Hampshire County militia in the spring of 1777, which marched to reinforce the army at Ticonderoga, and commanded a secret expedition in September of the same year. He was chosen Major General by a ballot in the Senate dated May 8, 1781, and the House concurred. He was commended by General Gates for his efficiency in raising recruits and forwarding supplies to the army.

He was a member of the Massachusetts Constitutional Convention in 1779-80, and a Fellow of the American Academy. In 1779 the degree of A. M. was conferred upon him by Harvard College. He died at Brimfield Sept. 19, 1791, aged 58 years and was buried with high military honors. According to tradition he "possessed a Herculean frame, united with Herculean strength. He was bold, energetic and combined in an eminent degree many of the qualities of a popular leader."

LIEUT. COLONEL WILLIAM SHEPARD was born in Westfield, December 1, 1737, and received the common school education of those days. He enlisted in the French and Indian War, serving as Sergeant in Captain Jonathan Bull's Company, Colonel William William's regiment from April 13 to Nov. 3, (probably 1758, year not given in the original document.) He served as Captain from February 22, to December 1, in 1761 and also held the same rank in 1762 and 3. April 20, 1775, he was engaged as Lieut. Colonel of Colonel Timothy Danielson's Minute Men's Regiment, which responded to the call of the Lexington Alarm. He served in the same rank under Colonel Danielson through the year and was commissioned Lieut. Colonel in Colonel Ebenezer Learned's 3d Regiment in the Continental Army, January 1, 1776. Colonel Learned petitioned, May 2, 1776, to be relieved on account of sickness, and William Shepard served as Lieut. Colonel in command until Oct. 2, when he was commissioned Colonel to rank from May 4, 1776. He served through the year and Jan. 1, 1777 was appointed commander of the 4th Regiment, Massachusetts Line, which he commanded until January 1st, 1783, when he retired. He commanded the 1st Massachusetts Brigade, December 1781, and January 1782. May 20, 1782 he was granted a furlough at West Point by order of the Commander. The following account of his military service appeared in the biographical notices of the members of the Massachusetts Society of the Cincinnati.

"He was present at the siege of Boston; the evacuation of Long Island; was wounded at Frog's Point, N. Y., 18 Oct. 1776, by a musket-ball through the neck; was in the campaign ending in Burgoyne's surrender; commanded a brigade in the battle of Monmouth; and established a high character for bravery, sound judgment and humanity. As Major General of the Hampshire County militia, he protected the U. S. arsenal at Springfield when threatened by insurgents under Shays in January, 1787. Upon the advance of the latter on the afternoon of the 25th to attack him, General Shepard, after twice ordering them to retire, and warning them of their danger if they proceeded, discharged his canon on the centre of the rebel column, which immediately broke and fled in confusion, leaving three of their number dead and a fourth mortally wounded. This was the only hostile collision during the rebellion, and its effect was such as to effectually pave the way for General Lincoln's subsequent successful operations, by which this apparently formidable movement was in a short time entirely subdued. General Shepard was a member of Congress in 1797-1803, a member of the Executive Council in 1788-90, and held other public trusts."

MAJOR DAVID LEONARD, of West Springfield, held that rank in Colonel Danielson's Minute Men's Regiment in April 1775, and continued under the same commander through the year. He was commissioned 2d Major of Colonel Daniel Moseley's 3d Hampshire County Regiment, February 8, 1776, and on June 25th was chosen Lieut. Colonel of Colonel B. Ruggles Woodbridge's Hampshire County Regiment raised for service " at Quebec and New York." In February 1777, he was Colonel of a regiment of volunteers raised in Hampshire County for service at Ticonderoga.

ADJUTANT WILLIAM TOOGOOD was engaged April 28, 1775, in Colonel Timothy Danielson's Regiment in the Provincial Army, and served through the year. He was First Lieutenant in Captain Joseph Thompson's Company in Colonel Thomas Nixon's 4th Continental Regiment through 1776. January 1, 1777 he was commissioned Captain in Colonel Thomas Nixon's 6th Regiment Massachusetts Line. "Omitted" June, 1779.

SURGEON DAVID SHEPARD, of Ludlow, served as a volunteer Surgeon at Concord and Lexington, April 19, 1775. He was Captain of a company in Col. Seth Pomeroy's Minute Men's Regiment which marched April 22nd in response to the Lexington alarm. On the 28th of the same month he was appointed Surgeon of Colonel Danielson's Regiment and served through the year. He was a Surgeon of Militia at Bennington in August 1777.

SURGEON'S MATE JOHN MILLER held that rank in Colonel Danielson's Regiment as shown by a return, dated Roxbury May 22, 1775.

QUARTERMASTER WILLIAM YOUNG, of Hatfield, served in the regiment from about May 15th to the end of the year. A William Young of Hatfield, (probably the same man) was a private in Captain Israel Chapin's Company, in Colonel John Fellow's Regiment of Minute Men, April 20, 1775.

CAPTAIN LIBBEUS BALL, of Granville, served under Captain Benjamin Day in the South Regiment of Hampshire County, 25 days in October, 1756. He was Captain of an independent company of Minute Men, which marched April 20, 1775, in response to the Lexington alarm, serving nine days. On the 29th of April, he was engaged as a Captain in Colonel Danielson's Regiment and served through the year. During 1776 he was a Captain in Col. Ebenezer Learned's 3d Continental Regiment. January 1, 1777 he was commissioned Captain in Colonel William Shepard's 4th Regiment Massachusett's Line, and on November 1st was promoted to the rank of Major, holding that office until he retired January 1, 1781. He served

seven days in June 1782, as Major in Colonel David Moseley's 3d Hampshire County Regiment.

CAPTAIN JONATHAN BARDWELL was probably the man of that name who served in May, 1747, under Ensign Obediah Dickinson. He served as a Captain in Colonel Jonathan Warner's Minute Men's Regiment, April 19, 1775. May 27, he was commissioned a Captain in Colonel Timothy Danielson's Regiment, and June 12, 1775 he was recommended for commission as Captain in Col. David Brewer's Regiment and he continued to serve in that organization through the year. In September and October, 1777, he served for a short time in Colonel Elisha Porter's 4th Hampshire County Regiment and on Jan. 9, 1778, he was commissioned Captain in that command.

CAPTAIN GIDEON BURT of Springfield was a descendant of Nathaniel in the 5th generation. He was born July 30, 1743. He responded to the Lexington alarm as First Lieutenant of Major Andrew Colton's Company of Minute Men. May 27, he was commissioned Captain in Colonel Timothy Danielson's Regiment in which he continued to serve through the year. June 13, 1776, he was commissioned Captain in Colonel Charles Pynchon's 1st Hampshire County Regiment, In March and April, 1777, he served as a company commander in Colonel David Leonard's Regiment, organized to reinforce the garrison at Ticonderoga. He was commissioned Oct. 7, 1777, 1st Major of Colonel John Bliss's 1st Hampshire County Regiment. Later he became Colonel of the same command and did tours of duty June 12 and 16, 1782, and Sept. 28, 1784. He died June 12, 1825.

CAPTAIN ENOCH CHAPIN, of West Springfield, did duty as "Centinel" at Fort Massachusetts from Dec. 1st, 1753, to September 22, 1754, under Captain Elisha Chapin; from that date to March 29, 1755, under Captain Ephraim Williams; and from the 29th of that month to June 26, 1757, under Capt. Isaac Wyman. He commanded an independent company of Minute Men, which marched from West Springfield April 20, 1775. He enlisted in Col. Timothy Danielson's Regiment, April 28, 1775 and served in command of a company through the year. July 6, 1778, he was commissioned Captain in a Hampshire County Regiment of Guards under Col. Jacob Gerrish and was in command of guards at Springfield until December 31, of that year.

CAPTAIN DANIEL EGREY, of Dartmouth, was a Lieutenant in Captain Benjamin Terrey's 2nd Dartmouth company, in Colonel Thomas Gilbert's 2nd Bristol County Regiment, July, 1771. He was Captain of an indepen-

dent company of Minute Men which marched from Dartmouth, April 21, 1775. He was engaged May 4, 1775, as Captain in Colonel Timothy Danielson's Regiment and served through the year. The records show that for a short time in June he was in Colonel David Brewer's Regiment. January 1, 1776, he was commissioned Captain in Colonel William Bond's 25th Continental Regiment and served at least as late as July 23d.

CAPTAIN JOHN FERGUSON, of Blandford, was a private in Lieutenant David Black's Company, in Colonel John Worthington's Regiment, in the French and Indian War, and a statement that a bayonet was issued to him was sworn to December 30, 1758. He was also a private in Captain Jonathan Ball's Company, Colonel William William's Regiment, April 13 to November 3, probably 1758. He served as a Sergeant in Captain William Shepard's Company. (Endorsed 1760) He was Captain of a Company in Colonel Timothy Danielson's Minute Men's Regiment, April 20, 1775, and continued to serve under the same commander through the year. He was a Captain in Colonel Samuel Brewer's Regiment at Ticonderoga in 1776.

CAPTAIN SILAS FOWLER of Southwick, commanded a company of Minute Men from that town which marched in response to the Lexington alarm on April 19, 1775, and joined Colonel Timothy Danielson's Regiment and served 21 days. He was commissioned a Captain in Colonel John Mosely's 3d Hampshire County Regiment, April 26, 1776. He held various terms of service in this regiment under different commanders, the last service ending June 17, 1782.

CAPTAIN THOMAS KEMPTON, of Dartmouth, may have been the man of that name who was a private in Captain James Andrews's Company, Colonel Thomas Doty's Regiment, from April 10 to October 19, 1758, at that time of Plymouth. He was Captain of an independent company of Minute Men which marched from Dartmouth, April 21, 1775. May 4, 1775, he was engaged as a Captain in Colonel Timothy Danielson's Regiment and served through the year. He was in Colonel David Brewer's Regiment a short time in June. He was commissioned Lieut. Colonel of Col. Jacob French's Regiment in March, 1776.

CAPTAIN PAUL LANGDON, of Wilbraham, was the son of Lieutenant Paul and Mary Langdon. He was a "Centinel" in 1747 and 8 under Lieutenant John Catlin and also under Maj. Israel Williams in the latter year. He was in Capt. Samuel Day's Company in the South Hampshire Regiment, " within two years of 1756." From April 19 to Dec. 9, (1755?) he

was a Sergeant in Capt. Luke Hitchcock's Company, Colonel John Worthington's Regiment serving in the Crown Point expedition. He was captain of an Independent company of Minute Men which marched from Wilbraham, April 20, 1775. May 27, 1775, he was ordered commissioned a Captain in Colonel Timothy Danielson's Regiment in which command he served through the year. He died June 23, 1804.

CAPTAIN FREEBORN MOULTON commanded a company from Monson, in Colonel Timothy Danielson's Minute Men's Regiment, April 19, 1775. Service 21 days.

CAPTAIN WARHAM PARKS was engaged in that rank in Colonel Timothy Danielson's Regiment, April 24, 1775. He was commissioned a Captain in Colonel Ebenezer Learned's 3d Continental Regiment, January 1, 1776, and served through the year. He was Major of Colonel William Shepard's 4th Continental Regiment from January 1, 1777 to July of the following year.

CAPTAIN NATHAN PETERS, of Preston, Conn., was the son of William and Hannah (Chenery) Peters. He was born in Medfield August 26, 1747. He was a private in Colonel Well's Connecticut Regiment which responded to the Lexington alarm. April 26, 1775, he was an Ensign in the 7th Company of the 6th Connecticut Regiment. He was engaged on the following day as Captain in Colonel Timothy Danielson's Regiment, serving through the year. He was Brigade Major in the Rhode Island Campaign under General Tyler. In 1780 he engaged in privateering from New London, Conn. He died February 7, 1824.

CAPTAIN THOMAS PLYMPTON'S name is given in one of the lists of company commanders in the records but it is evidently a mistake, "Kempton" being intended.

CAPTAIN JOSEPH THOMPSON, of Brimfield, was the son of James and Mary (Hancock) Thompson, and was born in Brimfield, March 25, 1733. He was an ensign in Captain Timothy Hamant's Company from May 26 to December 16, 1759. In the following year he was a 2nd Lieutenant in Captain "Trustum" Davis's Company in "his majesty's service" from February 14th to December 16, 1760. He was also a Lieutenant in Capt. Moses Hart's Company from April 18 to December 5 (1761?). In March 1775, he "was desired to raise a minute company of fifty men, to be paid one shilling every half day they shall train, and to train one half day each week." This company marched as a part of Colonel Timothy Danielson's Regiment on the

Lexington alarm. Captain Thompson served under the same commander through the year and in 1776 was a Captain in Col. Nixon's 4th Continental Regiment. From January 1 to Dec. 19, 1777, he was Major of Col. Thomas Nixon's 6th Regiment Massachusetts line, and from that date to the end of 1779 was Lieut. Colonel of the same regiment. Through 1780 he was Lieut. Colonel of Col. Thomas Marshall's 10th Regiment Massachusetts Line. He was taken prisoner Febuary 3d of that year and exchanged on the 8th of the December following. He was retired January 1, 1781. After the war he went to live in Partridgefield, Berkshire County, (Peru and Hinsdale now). He removed later to Ohio where he had a landed estate. He died in Marietta, Ohio.

CAPTAIN SYLVANUS WALKER, of Palmer, was a Corporal in Captain Solomon Keyes's Company from April 11 to December 11, 1755, on the Crown Point expedition. He was Ensign of Capt. John Moseley's Company from Feb. 18 to Nov. 28, 1756, on another expedition to the same place. In the following year he was commissioned 1st Lieutenant in Col. Ebenezer Learned's Regiment, and was a Captain from May 15 to December 23, (1759?) He was engaged April 24, 1775 as a Captain in Colonel Timothy Danielson's Regiment, and served (probably) through the year. He was a Member of the Committee of Safety, March 21, 1780.

LIEUTENANT ABEL ALLEN was in Captain Freeborn Moulton's Company in Colonel Timothy Danielson's Minute Men's Regiment. He was credited with 21 days service and was reported "left Cambridge" May 6, 1775.

FIRST LIEUTENANT LEMUEL BANCROFT of Granville, held that rank in Captain Lebbeus Ball's Company of Minute Men, which marched April 20, 1775. He served through the year in Colonel Timothy Danielson's Regiment.

FIRST LIEUTENANT DANIEL CADWELL, of Wilbraham, held that rank in Captain Paul Langdon's Company of Minute Men which marched April 20, 1775. He continued to serve under the same company and regimental commanders through the year. He was a Captain in Col. Charles Pynchon's 1st Hampshire County Regiment in 1776, and December 25th of that year entered service as Captain in Colonel Timothy Robinson's detachment of Hampshire County militia at Ticonderoga. He died of small pox March 27, 1777.

FIRST LIEUTENANT ASA COBURN, of Sturbridge, enlisted April 24, 1775, in Captain Sylvanus Walker's Company in Colonel Timothy Danielson's

Regiment in the above rank and served through the year. He held the same rank in the 5th Continental Regiment through 1776. January 1, 1777, he was commissioned Captain in the 7th Regiment Massachusetts and served until June 1783 in that command, under Colonel Ichabod Alden and Lieut. Colonel Commanding John Brooks. He removed to Ohio.

FIRST LIEUTENANT SAMUEL FLOWER, of West Springfield, was called Lieutenant in Captain Chapin's Company in Colonel Timothy Danielson's Regiment as early as May 22, 1775. Later in the year his rank is given specifically as "First" Lieutenant. He served through the year. January 1, 1777, he was commissioned Captain in Col. John Greaton's 3d Regiment Massachusetts line. He served until March 31, 1780, when he resigned. In June 1782, he served as Major of Col. David Moseley's 3d Hampshire County Regiment, on duty in support of the government at Northampton.

FIRST LIEUTENANT WILLIAM GILMORE, of Ware, served first in Captain Jonathan Bardwell's Company in Colonel Timothy Danielson's Regiment, in May and part of June 1775. When Captain Bardwell was transferred to Col. David Brewer's 9th Regiment, Army of the United Colonies, Lieutenant Gilmore went with him and served through the year.

FIRST LIEUTENANT GEORGE GRAINGER of Southwick, marched from that town April 21, 1775, in Captain Silas Fowler's Company of Minute Men. He arrived at Roxbury April 29, and joined Colonel Timothy Danielson's Regiment. He was dismissed at Roxbury and returned home after 21 days service.

FIRST LIEUTENANT DAVID HAMILTON, of Blandford, held that rank in Captain John Ferguson's Company, Colonel Timothy Danielson's Minute Mens Regiment, April 20, 1775. He served under the same officers through the year. In September, 1776, he was a Lieutenant in Captain Reuben Munn's Company, Colonel Nicholas Dike's Regiment, May 31, 1779, he was commissioned First Lieutenant in Captain Samuel Sloper's Company, Colonel John Moseley's 3d Hampshire County Regiment. He served with them again in June, 1782.

FIRST LIEUTENANT CALEB KEEP, of Monson, served first as a Sergeant in Captain Freeborn Moulton's Company in Colonel Timothy Danielson's Regiment of Minute Men, April 19, 1775. He was a Lieutenant in Captain Enoch Chapin's Company, and still later a First Lieutenant in Captain Joseph Thompson's Company, both companies being in Colonel Timothy Danielson's Regiment. He was a Captain in Colonel William Shep-

ard's 4th Regiment Massachusetts Line, from Jannary 1, 1777, to April 13, 1778, when he resigned. January 14, 1779, he was commissioned Captain in the 1st Hampshire County Regiment, and Oct. 15th was engaged as Captain in Colonel Israel Chapin's Regiment. He was discharged November 21, 1779.

FIRST LIEUTENANT AARON MIGHILL, of Brimfield, was in Captain "Trustum's" Davis's Company from February 14, to December 16, 1760, in the French and Indian war. He was a Lieutenant in Captain Joseph Thompson's Company in Colonel Timothy Danielson's Minute Men s Regiment, April 19, 1775, and served to April 29th. He was a Lieutenant in Captain John Morgan's Company, detached from the militia to guard stores at Springfield and Brookfield between December 26, 1777 and July 1, 1778. October 2, 1778, he was commissioned Second Lieutenant in Captain Joseph Browning's Company in the 1st Hampshire County Regiment under Colonel John Bliss.

FIRST LIEUTENANT JOHN PICKENS, OF DARTMOUTH, was engaged May 4, 1775, in Captain Daniel Egrey's Company, in Colonel Timothy Danielson's Regiment, and served through the year.

FIRST LIEUTENANT WALTER PYNCHON, of Springfield, was second Lieutenant of Major Andrew Colton's Company of Minute Men, April 19, 1775. On the 28th of April he was engaged as First Lieutenant of Captain Gideon Burt's Company in Colonel Timothy Danielson's Regiment and he served through the year. May 21, 1776, he became a Captain in the 1st Hampshire County Regiment and was Commissioned June 13, 1776.

FIRST LIEUTENANT JOHN SHEPARD JR., of Westfield, held that rank in Captain Warham Park's Company in Colonel Timothy Danielson's Regiment from April 28, to August 1. 1775, and probably through the year.

FIRST LIEUTENANT AMASA SOPER, of Dartmouth, held that rank in Captain Thomas Kempton's Company of Minute Men, April 21, 1775. He continued under the same Captain through the year, although credited to Colonel David Brewer's Regiment for a time in June. He was named as Captain in a list proposed for Colonel Joseph Henshaw's Regiment, probably in 1775. February 27, 1776, he was First Lieutenant in Colonel Jacob French's Regiment, and on July 5th was commissioned a Captain in Colonel Thomas Marshall's Boston Regiment. He continued to serve under the same commander in the 10th Regiment Massachusetts Line until he resigned Oct. 30 (31 or Nov. 2),1780.

LIEUTENANT JOHN CARPENTER, of Brimfield, was a Sergeant in Captain James Sherman's Company, Colonel Pynchon's Regiment, which marched on the alarm of April 19, 1775. He was commissioned a Lieutenant in Captain Joseph Thompson's Company, Colonel Timothy Danielson's Regiment, May 27, 1775. He was evidently an Ensign during a part of his term of service in this regiment. June 27, 1777, he was engaged as First Lieutenant in Captain Joseph Sibley's Company, Colonel Danforth Keyes's Regiment, and served in Rhode Island until January 4, 1778. He was a Captain in Col. Ezra Wood's 3d Worcester County Regiment from the following May until February 2, 1779. He was engaged as Captain of a Company of guards, March 5, 1779, and continued in such service to March 31, 1783.

SECOND LIEUTENANT JOHN CHADWICK, of Dartmouth, was a Sergeant in Captain Thomas Kempton's Company of Minute Men, April 21, 1775. He enlisted May 4, 1775, as a Second Lieutenant in Colonel Timothy Danielson's Regiment, and served through the year

SECOND LIEUTENANT LUKE DAY, of West Springfield, served in that rank in Captain Enoch Chapin's Company of Minute Men, April 20, 1775. He was an Ensign in Captain Chapin's Company in Colonel Timothy Danielson's Regiment, and May 22nd his name appears on the roll as Lieutenant. In a company return dated October 6, he was reported as "on command at Quebec." He was commissioned January 1, 1777, Captain in the 7th Regiment Massachusetts Line and served in that command under Colonels Alden and Brooks until June 3, 1783. He became a prominent leader with Shays in the rebellion of 1786-7.

SECOND LIEUTENANT LEVI DUNHAM, of Southwick, was a Sergeant in Captain Silas Fowler's Company of Minute Men, April 21, 1775. He became an Ensign in Captain Lebbeus Ball's Company in Colonel Timothy Danielson's Regiment, and later a Second Lieutenant in the same command, serving through the year.

SECOND LIEUTENANT RICHARD FALLEY, of Westfield, served first as Ensign and then as Second Lieutenant in Captain Warham Park's Company in Colonel Timothy Danielson's Regiment. He was engaged first May 4, 1775, and later was appointed armorer and allowed "20 per month in addition to his pay as Ensign" as he was "a complete master of the business." In 1776, he was a First Lieutenant in Captain Jedediah Southworth's Company, Colonel Lemuel Robinson's Regiment. He was granted beating orders for Hampshire County, April 11, 1776, as a member of Captain Josiah Smith's Company.

SECOND LIEUTENANT JOSEPH HOAR, of Brimfield, held that rank in Captain Joseph Thompson's Company in Colonel Timothy Danielson's Minute Men's Regiment, April 19, 1775. June 13, 1776, he was commissioned First Lieutenant in Captain Aaron Charles's Company in Colonel

Charles Pynchon's 1st Hampshire County Regiment. He was engaged March 1, 1777, as a First Lieutenant in Captain Reuben Munn's Company, (late) Colonel David Leonard's Regiment, to reinforce the army at Ticonderoga. August 14 of that year he was engaged to serve in the same rank in Captain Daniel Winchester's Company, Colonel B. Ruggles Woodbridge's Regiment, He was engaged as Captain in Colonel Gideon Burt's Regiment, June 16, 1782.

LIEUTENANT MOSES HOW, of Captain Jonathan Bardwell's Company in Colonel Timothy Danielson's Regiment, was in camp at Roxbury May 27, 1775. June 12th, it was recommended that he be given a commission as Ensign under the same Captain Bardwell who was then in Colonel David Brewer's Regiment.

SECOND LIEUTENANT JOHN KEENT of Southwick, held that rank in Captain Silas Fowler's (Southwick) Company of Minute Men. This company marched in response to the Lexington alarm and arrived at Roxbury April 29, 1775. He joined Colonel Timothy Danielson's Regiment and served in it 21 days.

SECOND LIEUTENANT AVERY PARKER, of Dartmonth, was an officer in Captain Daniel Egery's Company of Minute Men which marched April 21, 1775, in response to the Lexington alarm. He served through the year under the same commanders except for a short time in June, when the company was in Colonel David Brewer's Regiment. He was a Second Lieutenant in Captain Benjamin Dillingham's Company, Colonel Jacob French's Regiment at Winter Hill in February and March, 1776. In August, 1780, he served for a few days as Captain in Colonel John Hathaway's 2d Bristol County Regiment.

SECOND LIEUTENANT SETH SMITH of Suffield, was an Ensign in Captain Nathan Peter's Company, Colonel Timothy Danielson's Regiment, and later served to the end of the year as Second Lieutenant in the same company. He held the same rank in Colonel Ebenezer Learned's 3d Continental Regiment through 1776. He died July 6, 1830.

SECOND LIEUTENANT AARON STEEL, of Springfield, was a Sergeant in Major Andrew Colton's Company of Minute Men which marched April 20, 1775. He was engaged April 28, as a Second Lieutenant in Captain Gideon Burt's Company, Colonel Timothy Danielson's Regiment. January 1, 1777, he was appointed First Lieutenant in Captain Asa Coburn's Company in Colonel Ichabod Alden's 7th Regiment Massachusetts Line. He served in that regiment until he died November 24, 1777. Half pay was allowed his family to November 25, 1784.

SECOND LIEUTENANT JOSIAH WINTER held that rank in Colonel Timothy Danielson's Regiment from May to December, 1775.

LOCAL HISTORICAL SOCIETIES IN MASSACHUSETTS

By Chas. A. Flagg

The purpose of the Massachusetts Magazine being to gather and preserve the history of the state, it is appropriate that it should notice some of the other agencies engaged in the same work. Probably there is no other state with anywhere near the number of historical societies found here, and yet there is no list of them even approaching completeness.

This list has been compiled from replies sent in by officers of the societies themselves, in nearly every case.

Societies are entered under the name of city or town where they are located. Reference is made from other towns covered, except for county societies (which are indicated in the last part of the list.)

The following particulars are given: 1, Corporate name; 2, Date of organization (abbreviated by O.); 3, Incorporation (abbreviated by I.); 4, Number of members (abbreviated by M.); 5, Frequency of meetings (+ indicating that besides the regular meetings mentioned, there are special ones subject to call; 6, Names of president, secretary and treasurer, address being given when differing from place of society's headquarters.

There are also added notes of territory covered by local societies, if broader than a single town, and titles of *serial* publications issued, if any, etc. No mention is made of single or special publications, nor of the printing of local records undertaken by several of our societies.*

Extinct societies are also noted with such information as could be obtained about them.

It can hardly be expected that the list will be found free from errors or omissions. Any such, however trifling, should be reported, and correction will appear in the next number of the magazine.

* Those who wish full lists of society publications are referred to "Bibliography of American historical societies," by A. P. C. Griffin, 2d edition, 1907.

No attempt is made to include the denominational historical societies, of which there are a number with varying fields of activity; nor the national patriotic-hereditary societies with their state organizations and local chapters. These last named bodies are often found doing very valuable work in local history; but through their numerous registers and other publications it is comparatively easy to follow their activities.

Of the 356 cities and towns in the commonwealth 87 have active societies and 31 more are represented in the list by references.

There are 10 towns represented only by societies which are dead or inactive.

Acton.
Acton Historical Society. Inactive.

Acushnet, see under **New Bedford.**

Amesbury. Amesbury Improvement Association. O. 1886. I. 1897. M. 80. Monthly. *Pres.* Cyrus W. Rowell; *Sec.* Mrs. Emily B. Smith, 6 Pleasant St.; *Treas.* Fred W. Merrill.
"Transactions," vol. I, 1901.

Amherst. Amherst Historical Society. O. 1899. I. 1903. M. about 50. Four each year. *Pres.* Mrs. Mabel L. Todd; *Sec.* William I. Fletcher; *Treas.* George Cutler.

Andover. Andover Natural History Society. O. 1904. M. 40. Monthly. *Pres.* William G. Goldsmith; *Sec.* and *Treas.* Myron E. Gutterson.
Devoted to civil as well as natural history.

Arlington. Arlington Historical Society. O. 1897. I. 1898. M. 134. Monthly, Sept. to Apr. *Pres.* Hon. James P. Parmenter; *Sec.* Frederick E. Fowle, 430 Massachusetts Ave.; *Treas.* Warren A. Peirce.

Ashby. Ashby Historical Society. O. 1898. M. 25. Three each year+. *Pres.* Henry A. Lawrence; *Sec.* Miss Sophia E. Lawrence; *Treas.* Mrs. Mary E. Shaw.

Ashland.
There is now being organized a historical society under direction of a committee of three ladies, appointed four years ago by the Ashland Home Study Club.

Ayer, see under **Groton.**

Bedford. Bedford Historical Society. O. 1893 as an adjunct to the Bedford Free Public Library Corporation. M. 20. Irregular. *Pres.* George R. Blinn; *Sec.* Abram E. Brown; *Treas.* Charles W. Jenks.

Belchertown. Belchertown Historical Association. O. 1903. M. 44. Annual+. *Pres.* Dwight P. Clapp; *Recording Sec.* Marion, Bartlett; *Corresponding Sec.* Daniel D. Hazen; *Treas.* Mrs. William Bridgeman.

Bellingham, see under **Mendon.**

Belmont, see under **Watertown.**

Beverly. Beverly Historical Society. O. 1901. I. 1901. M. 87. Quarterly. *Pres.* George E. Woodbury; *Sec.* Annie March Kilham; *Treas.* Roland W. Boyden.

Billerica. Billerica Historical Society. O. 1894. I. 1896. M. 42. Annual. *Pres.* Charles E. Hosmer, M. D., South Billerica; *Sec.* Miss Martha A. Dodge; *Treas.* T. Frank Lyons.

Blackstone, see under **Mendon.**

Boston. Bostonian Society. O. 1881 (as successor of Boston Antiquarian Club 1879–81.) I. 1881. M. about 1125. Monthly, Oct. to May. *Pres.* James F. Hunnewell; *Clerk* and *Treas.* Charles F. Read.
"Proceedings," annual since 1882; "Publications," vol. I–V, 1886–1908.

Bunker Hill Monument Association. O. 1823. I. 1823. M. about 700. Annual. *Pres.* John C. Warren, M. D.; *Sec.* Francis H. Brown, M. D. *Treas.* Francis H. Lincoln, Hingham.
"Proceedings," annual since 1861.

Dorchester Historical Society. O. 1891. I. 1893. M. 125. Monthly. *Pres.* Richard C. Humphreys; *Sec.* and *Treas.* John A. Fowle, Columbia Road.
There was an earlier society, "The Dorchester Antiquarian and Historical Society" in existence 1843–93, which published "Collections," no. 1–3, 1844–50.

Old South Historical Society. O. 1891. I. 1901. M. about 80. Monthly *Pres.* J. C. S. Andrew, Beachmont; *Sec.* Nellie I. Simpson, 23 Franklin St., Charlestown; *Treas.* Jessie G. Paine, Cambridge.

Roxbury Historical Society. O. 1891 (as Roxbury Military Historical Society.) I. 1901, under present name. M 400. Quarterly. *Pres.* John E. Gilman; *Sec.* Henry A. May, 98 Moreland St., Roxbury; *Treas.* William S. Rumrill.

Society of Mayflower Descendants (The parent or N. Y. Society. O. 1894.) Mass. society O. 1896. I. 1896. *Governor,* Asa P. French; *Sec.* George E. Bowman, 53 Mt. Vernon St., Boston; *Treas.* Arthur I. Nash.
"Mayflower Descendant," quarterly, vol. 1–10, 1899–1908.

South Boston Historical Society. Such a society was reported O. 1896, but seems to be no longer in existence.

Bridgewater. Old Bridgewater Historical Society. O. 1894. I. 1895. M. 300. Quarterly. *Pres.* Robert O. Harris, East Bridgewater; *Recording Sec.* Edward B. Maglathlin, West Bridgewater; *Corresponding Sec.* Joshua E. Crane, Bridgewater; *Treas.* Fred A. Hunting, East Bridgewater.
For the old town of Bridgewater, including present Bridgewater, Brockton, East Bridgewater and West Bridgewater.

Brockton, see under **Bridgewater.**

Brookfield. Quaboag Historical Society. O. 1895. I. 1895. M. about 350. Two each year. *Pres.* Robert Batchelder, Boston: *Sec.* John S. Cooke, North Brookfield; *Treas.* Philander Holmes, Brookfield.

For the original town of Brookfield, from which the following towns were formed, wholly or in part: Brookfield, New Braintree, North Brookfield, Warren and West Brookfield.

Brookline. Brookline Historical Society. O. 1891. I. 1901. M. 180. Monthly, Oct. to May. *Pres.* Rufus G. F. Candage; *Sec.* and *Treas.* Edward W. Baker.

"Proceedings," annually 1902–06; "Publications," no. 1–3, 1903–04.
1895–1900 there was in existence a society with name Brookline Historical Publication Society, which issued 2 volumes of "Publications."

Cambridge. Cambridge Historical Society. O. 1905. I. 1905. M. about 185. Three a year. *Pres.* Richard H. Dana; *Sec.* Frank G. Cook, 44 Garden St.; *Treas.* Henry H. Edes.

"Publications;" no. I–III, 1906–08.

Harvard Memorial Society. O. 1895. M. 40 from each college class. Irregular. *Pres.* William C. Lane; *Sec.* George Gund, 21 Russell Hall; *Treas.* J. M. Groton.

There was an earlier Harvard Historical Society in the "eighties."

Shepard Historical Society O. 1889. M. about 100. Annual +. *Pres.* Alexander McKenzie, D. D.; *Sec.* Hewitt G. Fletcher, 375 Harvard St.; *Treas.* Edwin S. Chapin.

History of First Church in Cambridge, and parish and town in which it is situated.

Canton. Canton Historical Society. O. 1871. I. 1893. M. 69. Five each year. *Pres.* Winthrop Packard, Canton Corner; *Clerk,* William A. Tucker, Randolph St., Ponkapoag; *Treas.* A. Herman Gill, Canton Corner.

Charlemont. Old Folks' Association of Charlemont and Vicinity. O. 1870. Annual. *Pres.* Ansel L. Tyler; *Sec.* and *Treas.* Edward P. Smead.

Charlestown, see **Boston.**

Charlton, see under **Southbridge.**

Clinton. Clinton Historical Society. O. 1894. I. 1903. M. 105. Monthly, Sept. to June. *Pres.* Jonathan Smith; *Sec.* W. Irving Jenkins, 256 Chestnut St.; *Treas.* William O. Johnson.

Concord. Concord Antiquarian Society. O. 1886. I. 1886. M. 160. Monthly, Sept. to June. *Pres.* Adams Tolman; *Sec.* Henry F. Smith, Jr.; *Treas.* Thomas Todd.

[Publications] 11 nos. 1902–03.

Danvers. Danvers Historical Society. O. 1889. I. 1893. M. 250. Annual and quarterly+. *Pres.* Ezra D. Hines; *Sec.* Andrew Nichols, Hathorne, Mass.; *Treas.* Loring B. Goodale.

Dartmouth, see under **New Bedford.**

Dedham. Dedham Historical Society. O. 1859. I. 1862. M. 142. Monthly, Oct. to June. *Pres.* Julius H. Tuttle; *Sec.* Frank E. Morse, Franklin Square, Dedham; *Treas.* George W. Humphrey.

"Annual report" 1889–92; "Dedham Historical Register," quarterly, vol. 1–14. 1890–1903.

Deerfield. Pocumtuck Valley Memorial Association. O. 1870. I. 1870. M. not given. Annual. *Pres.* George Sheldon; *Corresponding Sec.* Mrs. M. Elizabeth Stebbins; *Recording Sec.* Rev. Richard E. Birks; *Treas.* John Sheldon, Greenfield.

"History and Proceedings" vol. 1–4, 1890–1905.

Dorchester, see **Boston.**

Dover. Dover Historical and Natural History Society. O. 1895. I. 1900. M. 65. Quarterly. *Pres.* Frank Smith; *Sec.* and *Treas.* Mrs. Sarah A. Higgins.

Dudley, see under **Southbridge.**

Dunstable, see under **Groton.**

East Bridgewater, see under **Bridgewater.**

Fairhaven, see under **New Bedford.**

Falmouth. Falmouth Historical Society. O. 1900. I. 1905. M. 42. Quarterly. *Pres.* Henry H. Smythe; *Sec.* Seba A. Holton; William H. Hewins.

Fitchburg. Fitchburg Historical Society. O. 1892. I. 1896. M. 63. Monthly, Oct. to May. *Pres.* Frederick F. Woodward; *Sec.* Ebenezer Bailey, 39 High St.; *Treas.* Frederick A. Currier.

"Proceedings" vol. 1–4, 1895–1908.

Foxborough. Foxborough Historical Society. O. 1898. I. 1898. M. 31, Quarterly. *Pres.* William E. Horton; *Sec.* Mrs. Alice M. Horton; *Treas.* William H. Carpenter.

Framingham. Framingham Historical and Natural History Society. O. 1888. I. 1892. M. 110. Annual +. *Pres.* John H. Temple, South Framingham; *Sec.* Constantine C. Esty, Framingham; *Treas.* George H. Eames, South Framingham.

Gloucester. Cape Ann Scientific and Literary Association. O. 1875. I. 1892. M. 229. Several meetings a month except in summer. *Pres.* Dr. William Hale; *Sec.* Alfred E. Presson, 6 Liberty St.; *Treas.* George W. Woodbury.

Greenfield. Greenfield Historical Society. O. 1907. I. 1907. M. 89; Monthly during winter. *Pres.* Judge John A. Aiken; *Sec.* Albert L. Wing, Church St.; *Treas.* Charles Nims.

Groton. Groton Historical Society. O. 1894. I. 1894. M. 100. Four each year. *Pres.* Dr. Samuel A. Green, Boston; *Sec.* Thomas L. Motley; *Treas.* Lillian W. Kane.

For the towns wholly or partly included within the limits of old Groton: Groton, Pepperell, Shirley, Ayer, Littleton, Harvard, Westford and Dunstable.

Harvard. Harvard Historical Society. O. 1897. I. 1900. M. 64. Quarterly. *Pres.* Dr. H. B. Royal; *Sec.* Miss S. E. Pollard; *Treas.* Albert H. Bigelow.
See also under **Groton.**

Haverhill. Haverhill Historical Society. O. 1897. I. 1898. M. 400. Quarterly +. *Pres.* Edward G. Frothingham; *Sec.* Stanley D. Gray, 9 Dustin St.; *Treas.* Raymond Noyes.

Heath. Heath Historical Society. O. 1900. I. 1902. M. 73. Annual. *Pres.* William A. Dickinson; *Sec.* Mamie E. Maxwell; *Treas.* Hugh Maxwell.

Holbrook. Holbrook Historical Society. O. 1897. I. 1897. M. about 25. Irregular. *Pres.* Lewis Alden; *Sec.* Mrs. Abbie H. French; *Treas.* Mrs. Annie M. Southworth.

Hopedale. See under **Mendon.**

Hyde Park. Hyde Park Historical Society. O. 1887. I. 1890. M. about 125. Quarterly +. *Pres.* Charles G. Chick; *Recording Sec.* Fred L. Johnson; *Corresponding Sec.* Henry B. Carrington, Summer St.; *Treas.* Henry B. Humphrey.

"Hyde Park Historical Record," vol. I–VI, 1892–1908.

Ipswich. Ipswich Historical Society. O. 1890. I. 1898. M. 267. Annual +. *Pres.* T. Frank Waters; *Recording Sec.* John W. Goodhue; *Corresponding Sec. and Treas.* T. Frank Waters.

"Publications," I–XV, 1894–1907.

Lawrence. Lawrence Society of Natural History and Archaeology. O. 1887. I. 1895. M. 106. Monthly. *Pres.* Richard H. Barlow; *Sec.* Mrs. Elizabeth Schneider, 36 Summer St.; *Treas.* Miss Helen M. Church.

Leominster. Leominster Historical Society. O. 1906. I. 1907. M. 40. Monthly, Sept. to June. *Pres.* Perley M. Russell; *Sec.* Charles S. Houghton, 61 Orchard St.; *Treas.* Fred B. Hills.

Lexington. Lexington Historical Society. O. 1886. I. 1886. M. about 200. Five each year. *Pres.* George O. Whiting; *Recording Sec.* Irving P. Fox; *Corresponding Sec.* Mary E. Hudson; *Treas.* Charles F. Prince.

"Proceedings and Papers," vol. 1–3, 1890–1905.

Littleton. Littleton Historical Society. O. 1896. I. 1896. M. 16. Quarterly. *Pres.* Herbert J. Harwood; *Sec. and Treas.* Miss S. F. White.
See also under **Groton.**

Longmeadow. Longmeadow Historical Society. O. 1899. I. 1900. M. about 100. Annual +. *Pres.* Capt. Simon B. Parker; *Sec.* Water P. Sherman; *Treas.* Frank S. Burt.

Lowell. Lowell Historical Society. O. 1902. I. 1902. M. about 150. Four each year. *Pres.* Solon W. Stevens; *Recording Sec.* Horace S. Bacon; *Corresponding Sec.* Alfred P. Seaver, 45 Merrimack St.; *Treas.* Albert L. Bacheller.

Successor of Old Residents' Historical Society of Lowell, O, 1868, which published 6 volumes of "Contributions," 1873–1904.
"Contributions of Lowell Historical Society," vol. I, no. 1, 1907.

Lunenburg. Lunenburg Historical Society. O. 1897. M. 50. Annual +. *Pres.* James Hildreth; *Sec.* office vacant; *Treas.* George E. Jones.

Lynn. Lynn Historical Society. O. 1897. I. 1897. M. 550. Monthly. *Pres.* Benjamin N. Johnson; *Sec.* John Albree, Swampscott; *Treas.* Everett H. Black.

"Register," 1898–1905, 7 vols.

Malden. Malden Historical Society. O. 1886. I. 1887. M. 100. Four each year. *Pres.* Deloraine P. Corey; *Sec.* Frank E. Woodward, 93 Rockland Ave.; *Treas.* office vacant.

Manchester.
Manchester Historical Society. O. 1886. I. 1896. M. 75. Quarterly. (Inactive since July, 1907.) *Pres.* office vacant; *Sec. and Treas.* Alfred S. Jewett.

Marblehead. Marblehead Historical Society. O. 1898. I. 1902. M. 160. Monthly. *Pres.* Nathan P. Sanborn; *Sec.* Richard Tutt, Maverick St.; *Treas.* William D. T. Trefry.

Medfield. Medfield Historical Society. O. 1891. I. 1891. M. 43. Two each year +. *Pres.* John M. Richardson; *Sec.* Harriet A. Fowle, 69 Main St.; *Treas.* William S. Tilden.

Medford. Medford Historical Society. O. 1896. I. 1896. M. 275. Two each month, Oct. to Apr. *Pres.* Will C. Eddy; *Recording Sec.* Miss Alice E. Curtis; *Corresponding Sec.*, George S. T. Fuller, 7 Alfred St.; *Treas.* Alfred R. Winter.

"Medford Historical Register," vol. I–XI, 1898–1908.

Medway. Medway Historical Society. O. 1901. I. 1902. M. 52. Monthly except in summer. *Pres.* Herbert N. Hixon, West Medway; *Sec.* Orion T. Mason, School St., Medway; *Treas.* W. Irving Kelsey, West Medway.

Mendon. Mendon Historical Society. O. 1896. M. 186. Two each year, one in Mendon and one in Bellingham. *Pres.* Marcus M. Aldrich; *Sec.* Horace C. Adams; *Treas.* Mrs. Herbert J. George.

Old Mendon and her daughter towns: Bellingham, Uxbridge, Upton, Northbridge, Milford, Blackstone and Hopedale.

Methuen. Methuen Historical Society. O. 1895. I. 1895. M. 120.

Monthly, Oct. to June. *Pres.* Hon. Joseph S. Howe; *Sec.* Elizabeth B. Currier, 59 Hampshire St.; *Treas.* Dr. George E. Woodbury.
"Publications," no. 1–2, 1896. The society has issued other later "Publications," but not in the numbered series.

Milford, see under **Mendon.**

Milton. Milton Historical Society. O. 1905. I. 1905. M. 220. Three each year. *Pres.* Nathaniel T. Kidder; *Corresponding Sec.* Mrs. Caleb L. Cunningham, 401 Adams St., East Milton; *Recording Sec.* Charles E. Churchill; *Treas.* Arthur H. Tucker.
"Annual Report," 1st–3d, 1906–08.

Monson.
Monson Historical Society. I. 1895. M. about 30. Has been inactive for a number of years. *Treas.* Geo. C. Flynt.

Nantucket. Nantucket Historical Association O. 1894. I. 1894. M. 318. Annual. *Pres.* Alexander Starbuck; *Sec.* Mrs. Elizabeth C. Bennett; *Treas.* Henry S. Wyer.
"Bulletin," vol. I, no. 1–2; vol. II, no. 1–5; vol. III. no. 1, 1898–1906. "Proceedings in. of 4th–14th annual meeting 1898–1908. (Proceedings of 1st–3d meetings 1895–97, pub one pamphlet 1907.)

Natick. Historical, Natural History and Library Society of South Natick. O. 1873. I. 1873. M. 136. Quarterly. *Pres.* Gustavus Smith, South Natick; *Sec.* Isabelle R. Heinlein, South Natick; *Treas.* Morton V. B. Bartlett.
Successor of the Historical and Natural History Society of Eliot, O. 1870.

New Bedford. Old Dartmouth Historical Society. O. 1903. I. 1903. M. about 1000. Quarterly. *Pres.* Edmund Wood; *Sec.* William A. Wing, 20 South 6th St.; *Treas.* William A. Mackie.
Old Dartmouth and her daughter towns; Dartmouth, New Bedford, Westport, Fairhaven, Acushnet.

New Braintree, see under **Brookfield.**

Newbury, see under **Newburyport.**

Newburyport. Historical Society of Old Newbury. O. 1879, as Antiquarian and Historical Society of Old Newbury; name changed 1882. I. 1896. M. 300. Monthly, Sept. to June. *Pres.* Rev. Herbert E. Lombard, Byfield Parish, Newbury; *Sec.* Miss Harriet E. Jones, Newburyport; *Treas.* Arthur W. Moody, Newbury.
Old Newbury included the modern Newbury, Newburyport and West Newbury.

Newton. Newton Historical Society. O. 1902. I. 1902. M. 11. Annual +. *Pres.* Hon. Thomas Weston; *Sec.* Alfred W. Fuller; *Treas.* Frank A. Mason, 107 Homer Street.

North Adams. Fort Massachusetts Historical Society. O. 1895. I. 1895. M. 150. Annual. *Pres.* Junius B. Temple; *Sec.* Willard E. Whitaker; *Treas.* Mrs. Hannah B. Richmond.

North Brookfield.
North Brookfield Historical Society. O. 1864. Probably lived but a short time.
See also under **Brookfield.**

Northborough. Northborough Historical Society. O. 1906. M. 70. Monthly, Oct. to Apr. *Pres.* Gilman B. Howe; *Sec.* Rev. Josiah C. Kent; *Treas.* Ezra H. Bigelow.

Northbridge, see under **Mendon.**

Norwood. Norwood Historical Society. O. 1907. I. 1907. M. 33. Monthly Sept. to June. *Pres.* Milton H. Howard; *Sec.* Walter J. Berwick, 24 Cottage St.; *Treas.* Emily C. Fisher.

Orange. Orange Historical and Antiquarian Society. O. 1898. I. 1898. M. 21. Quarterly. *Pres.* Arthur F. Slate; *Sec.* Caroline M. Mayo, 24 Winter St.; *Treas.* Matilda Slate.

Oxford.
Huguenot Memorial Association, I 1881. Composed of descendants of the early Huguenot settlers; it bought a piece of land and erected a monument in 1884. Since then has been inactive.

Palmer. Palmer Historical Society. O. 1900. I. 1900. M. 50. Monthly, Oct. to May. *Pres.* James B. Stone; *Sec.* Mrs. Lucy A. Hitchcook, 15 Squier St.; *Treas.* Mrs. L. E. Carpenter.

Peabody. Peabody Historical Society. O. 1896. I. 1896. M. about 160. Quarterly +. *Pres.* William Armstrong; *Sec.* Mrs. Elizabeth C. Osborn, 55 Central St.; *Treas.* Sylvanus L. Newhall.
"Annual Report," 1st–11th, 1896–1907.

Pepperell. see under **Groton.**

Pittsfield. Berkshire Historical and Scientific Society. O. 1878. M. 150. Quarterly. *Pres.* Joseph Peirson; *Sec. and Treas.* H. H. Ballard.
"Collections" (early nos. have varying titles,) 1886–1900.

Plymouth. Pilgrim Society. O. 1819. I. 1820. M. not given. Two each year. *Pres.* Arthur Lord; *Sec.* William W. Brewster; *Treas.* Charles B. Stoddard.

Provincetown. Cape Cod Pilgrim Memorial Association. I. 1892. M. not given. *Pres.* J. Henry Sears, Brewster; *Sec.* Osborne Nickerson, Chathamport; *Treas.* Howard F. Hopkins, Provincetown.
Formed for the purpose of erecting a monument to commemorate the first landing of the Pilgrims at Provincetown.

Quincy. Quincy Historical Society. O. 1893. I. 1893. M. about 120. Four each year. *Pres.* Brooks Adams; *Sec.* Emery L. Crane; *Treas.* James L. Edwards.

Rehoboth. Rehoboth Antiquarian Society. O. 1884. I. 1885. M. about 100. Annual +. *Pres.* Hon. George N. Goff; *Sec.* Ellery L. Goff, Elm Square; *Treas.* Henry T. Horton.

Rockport, see under **Gloucester.**

Roxbury, see **Boston.**

Salem. Essex Institute. O. 1848. I. 1848. M. 664. Monthly +. *Pres.* Francis H. Appleton, Peabody; *Sec.* George F. Dow, Topsfield; *Treas.* William O. Chapman, Salem.

Founded by union of Essex Historical Society (I. 1821) with Essex County Natural History Society.
"Proceedings," vol. I–VI, 1856–70; "Historical Collections," vol. I–XLIV, 1859–1908; "Bulletin," vol. I–XXX, 1870–98; "Annual Report," 1899–1908.

Old Planter's Society. O. 1899. I. 1908. Annual +. *Pres.* Col. T. W. Higginson, Cambridge; *Sec.* Miss Lucie Marion Gardner, 4 Lynde St., Salem; *Treas.* Frank V. Wright, Salem.

Sandwich. Sandwich Historical Society. O. 1907. I. 1907. M. 52. Quarterly. *Pres.* William L. Nye; *Sec.* Charles M. Thompson; *Treas.* George E. Burbank.

Sharon. Sharon Historical Society. O. 1903. I. 1903. M. 154. Quarterly. *Pres.* Edmund H. Talbot, Boston; *Corresponding Sec.* George Kempton; *Treas.* W. Winthrop Capen.

Continues the work of the Sharon Antiquarian Committee, established by the town in 1888 and reorganized in 1895.
"Publications," no. 1–5, 1904–08.

Shirley, see under **Groton.**

Shrewsbury. Shrewsbury Historical Society. O. 1898. I. 1902. M. 72. Five each year. *Pres.* Alfred H. Knight; *Sec.* Mrs. Jessie Prairie; *Treas.* George W. Cogswell.

Somerville. Somerville Historical Society. O. 1897. I. 1897. M. 206. Two each month. *Pres.* Frank M. Hawes; *Sec.* Ella R. Hurd, 458a Medford St.; *Treas.* William B. Holmes.

"Publications," no. 1, 1901; "Historic leaves," quarterly, vol. 1–VI, 1902–1908.

South Natick, see **Natick.**

Southbridge. Quinabaug Historical Society. O. 1899 as Southbridge Historical Society. I. 1899, under present name. M. 135. Monthly, Oct. to Apr. +. *Pres.* John M. Cochran; *Corresponding Sec.* Miss Mary E. Clemence; *Recording Sec.* Mrs. Newton E. Putney; *Treas.* Alvah L. Hyde.

For territory comprising towns of Sturbridge, Southbridge, Dudley and Charlton.
"Leaflets," vol. 1, 25 nos. (1902–07); vol. 2, no. 1–6.

Springfield. Connecticut Valley Historical Society. O. 1876. M. about 220. Five each year. *Pres.* William F. Adams; *Sec.* Henry A. Booth; *Treas.* William C. Stone.

"Papers and proceedings," vol. 1–2, 1881–1904.

Stoughton. Stoughton Historical Society. O. 1895. I. 1903. M. about 80. Monthly, Oct. to Apr. *Pres.* Henri L. Johnson; *Sec.* Amelia M. Clifton; *Treas.* Richard B. Ward.

Sturbridge, see under **Southbridge.**

Swampscott.
Swampscott Historical Society. Has been inactive for some time.

Taunton. Old Colony Historical Society. I. 1853. M. 680. Four each year. *Pres.* Henry M. Lovering; *Sec.* James E. Seaver; *Treas.* George A. King.
"Collections," no. 1-6, 1879-99.

Topsfield. Topsfield Historical Society. O. 1894. M. 261. Five each year. *Pres.* Charles J. Peabody; *Sec. and Treas.* George F. Dow.
"Historical Collections," vol. 1-13, 1895-1908.

Townsend.
Townsend Historical Society. O. 1896. I. 1896. M. 37. Inactive since 1897.

Upton, see under **Mendon.**

Uxbridge, see under **Mendon.**

Wakefield. Wakefield Historical Society. O. 1890. I. 1893. M. not given. Annual. *Pres.* Ashton H. Thayer; *Corresponding Sec.* Charles F. Mansfield, Avon St.; *Recording Sec.* F. W. Young; *Treas.* A. A. Hawkes.

Walpole.
Walpole Historical Society. O. 1898. I. 1898. M. about 45. No meetings for about two years.
Pres. J. Edward Plimpton; *Recording Sec.* Gilman F. Allen.

Waltham, see under **Watertown.**

Warren, see under **Brookfield.**

Watertown. Historical Society of Watertown. O. 1888. I. 1891. M. about 50. Five each year. *Pres.* Dr. Bennett F. Davenport; *Sec.* Alberto F. Haynes, 8 Marshall St.; *Treas.* Charles F. Mason.
Original town of Watertown, covering present towns of Watertown, Weston, Waltham and Belmont.

West Bridgewater, see under **Bridgewater.**

West Brookfield, see under **Brookfield.**

West Newbury. West Newbury Natural History Club. O. 1876 as West Newbury Botanical Club. Name changed 1882. I. 1901. M. about 40. Meetings irregular. *Pres.* George E. Noyes; *Sec.* William Merrill; *Treas.* Miss Marion H. Warren.
Incorporated "for the purpose of promoting the knowledge of natural science and local history."

See also under **Newburyport.**

West Springfield. Ramapogue Historical Society. O. 1903. I. 1903. M. about 150. Annual. *Pres.* Ethan Brooks; *Sec.* Mrs. Howard K. Regal, 181 Park Ave.; *Treas.* Robert D. White.

Westborough. Westborough Historical Society. O. 1889. I. 1889. M. 142. Six each year. *Pres.* S. Ingersoll Briant; *Sec.* Mrs. Abby K. Harvey, 52 West Main St.; *Treas.* Dr. G. B. Gibson.

Westfield. Western Hampden Historical Society. O. 1901. M. not given. Annual. *Pres.* Hon. Milton B. Whitney; *Sec.* Louis M. Dewey, 279 Elm St.; *Treas.* Edwin L. Sanford.

Westford, see under **Groton.**

Weston, see under **Watertown.**

Westport, see under **New Bedford.**

Weymouth. Weymouth Historical Society. O. 1879. I. 1886. M. not given. Monthly, Aug. to May. *Pres.* John J. Loud; *Sec.* Rev. William Hyde; *Treas.* Francis H. Cowing.
"Publications," no. 1–3, 1881–1905.

Winchester.
Winchester Historical and Genealogical Society. O. 1884. Issued "Winchester record" vol. 1–3, 1885–87. Inactive for a number of years.

Woburn. Rumford Historical Association. O. 1877. I. 1877. M. 194. Annual. *Pres.* Hon. Edward F. Johnson; *Sec.* Andrew R. Linscott; *Treas.* Samuel A. Thompson.
Organized to secure and hold the birthplace of Count Rumford, and to maintain a library, museum and reading room.

Worcester. Worcester Society of Antiquity. O. 1875. I. 1877. M. about 300. Monthly, except Aug. *Pres.* Mander A. Maynard; *Sec.* Walter Davidson; *Treas.* Frank E. Williamson.
"Collections," vol. 1–15, 1881–97; "Bulletin" no. 1–14, 1897–99; Proceedings, vol. 16–23, 1898–1908.
There was an earlier Worcester County Historical Society, I. 1831 which lived only 5 or 6 years.

Yarmouth.
Cape Cod Historical Society. O. 1882. I. 1883. M. not given. No meeting since 1906. *Pres.* Frederick C. Swift; *Sec.* Charles W. Swift; *Treas.* Samuel Snow, Brockton.

CONDITIONS IN THE COUNTIES

Barnstable County. 15 towns, of which 3 have societies. There is no county society. The Cape Cod Historical Society, Yarmouth (now inactive) may have attempetd to cover the field. This territory, however, is within that belonging to the Old Colony Historical Society, Taunton, the Pilgrim Society, Plymouth, and the Society of Mayflower Descendants, Boston, the last named in particular, collecting and publishing much in the way of local records. The Cape Cod Pilgrim Memorial Society, Provincetown, is also virtually a county organization.

Berkshire County. 32 cities and towns, of which 2 have societies. The Berkshire Historical and Scientific Society, Pittsfield, is the county society.

Bristol County. 20 cities and towns, of which 3 have societies. No county society. The Old Colony Historical Society, Taunton, includes all southeastern Mass. as its field, and the Society of Mayflower Descendants,

Boston, collects and publishes material on the county. The Old Dartmouth Historical Society, New Bedford, covers a group of towns.

Dukes County. 7 towns. No historical society, local or general.

Essex County. 34 cities and towns, of which 16 have societies. Essex Institute, Salem, is the county society. The Old Planters Society, Salem, is also particularly interested in this county. Gloucester and Newburyport have societies covering groups of towns.

Franklin County. 26 towns, of which 5 have societies. No county society in the strict sense, but the Pocumtuck Valley Memorial Association, Deerfield has largely assumed the function of one, while this territory is also included in that covered by the Connecticut Valley Historical Society, Springfield.

Hampden County. 23 cities and towns, of which 5 have societies. No county society but the Connecticut Valley Historical Society, Springfield, is specially interested in this county. The Western Hampden Historical Society, Westfield, is concerned with that portion of the county.

Hampshire County. 23 cities and towns, of which 2 have societies. No county society, but this county also is in the region covered by the Connecticut Valley Historical Society.

Middlesex County. 54 cities and towns, of which 19 have societies. No county society. Groton and Watertown have societies covering groups of towns.

Nantucket County. Only one town in this county, so the Nantucket Historical Association is both general and local.

Norfolk County. 29 cities and towns, of which 15 have societies. No county society.

Plymouth County. 27 cities and towns, of which 2 have societies. No county society. The Pilgrim Society, Plymouth, and Old Colony Historical Society, Taunton, include it in their field; and the Society of Mayflower Descendants, Boston, is collecting and publishing much in the line of local records. The Old Bridgewater Historical Society, Bridgewater, covers a group of towns.

Suffolk County. 4 cities and towns, of which 1 (Boston) has a number of historical societies. No county society. The Old Planters Society, Salem, covers this region, also.

Worcester County, 59 cities and towns, of which 12 have societies. The county society is the Worcester Society of Antiquity. The Systematic History Fund (F. P. Rice, trustee) of Worcester, though not a society, is publishing much in the line of local records in this county. Brookfield, Mendon and Southbridge have societies covering groups of towns.

GENERAL OR STATE SOCIETIES IN MASSACHUSETTS

Though hardly within the scope of this paper, it may not be uninteresting to mention briefly certain important general historical societies in the state.

American Antiquarian Society, Worcester. O. 1812. I. 1812. Two meetings a year.
Antiquities of the country at large, with special attention to history of Mass.

Bay State Historical League. O. 1903. *Pres.* Will C. Eddy, Medford; *Sec.* John F. Ayer, Somerville; *Treas.* Howard M. Newhall, Lynn.
A league of the local historical societies of the state, at present including 34 such societies, largely in Essex and Middlesex counties. Meetings twice a year. Has issued 3 "Publications," 1903–08, no. III containing lists of papers read before each society, 1902–07.

Colonial Society of Massachusetts, Boston. O. 1892. I. 1892. Six meetings each year.
Colonial history, especially that of the Plymouth and Massachusetts Bay colonies.

Massachusetts Historical Society, Boston. O. 1791. I. 1794. Meetings monthly +.
Resident membership limited to 100, with additional Honorary and Corresponding members. For a number of years it has devoted most of its energies in the line of publication to selections from its own extensive and valuable manuscript collections.

Military Historical Society of Massachusetts, Boston. I. 1891. Meetings monthly Nov. to Apr.
Military history and especially that of the Civil war period.

New England Historic Genealogical Society, Boston. O. 1844. I. 1845. Meetings monthly, Oct. to May.
Genealogy, biography and local history of New England, especially Mass.

Prince Society, Boston. O. 1858. I. 1874. Meetings annually.
Publications of rare works in print or manuscript relating to early America.

THE OLD MERRIAM HOUSE, AT GRAFTON.

99

SOME ARTICLES CONCERNING MASSACHUSETTS IN RECENT MAGAZINES

By Charles A. Flagg

General. Report of the D. A. R. committee on patriotic education—Massachusetts. (American monthly magazine, Jan., 1909. v. 34, p. 91–93).

Bedford. Bedford intentions of marriage. Communicated by C. W. Jenks. (New England historical and genealogical register, Jan., 1909. v. 63, p. 73–76).
1748–1776; supplementing "Vital records of Bedford to the year 1850," 1903.

Boston. Boston—why it is and what? By M. A. DeWolfe Howe. (Harper's weekly, Nov. 21, 1808. v. 52, no. 2709, p. 8–11).

—— Boston's government. The proposed Boston charter. (The Outlook, 27 Feb., 1909. v. 91, p. 418–420.)

—— Modern Boston as contrasted with New York. (Harper's monthly magazine, Jan. 1909. v. 118, p. 317–320).

—— Old South Chapter, D. A. R., Boston. By Sarah R. Sturgis, historian. (American monthly magazine, Mar., 1909. v. 34, p. 283–284).

—— The playgrounds of greater Boston. By Mrs. Kate S. Bingham. (New England magazine, Apr., 1909. v. 39, p. 185–192).

—— Social Boston, past and present. By Julia Ward Howe. (Harper's bazaar, Feb., 1909. v. 43, p. 105–110).

Bristol County. Abstracts from the first book of Bristol County probate records. Copied by Mrs. Lucy H. Greenlaw. (New England historical and genealogical register, Jan., 1909. v. 63, p. 77–84).
Part 6; first three instalments appeared in Genealogical advertiser, Dec., 1900–Dec., 1901, and the 4th–5th in the Register, July–Oct., 1908.

Brockton. Deborah Sampson chapter, D. A. R., Brockton. By Mary E. Charles, historian. (American monthly magazine, Apr., 1909. v. 34, p. 389–390).

Brookfield. Great fights in early New England history. By H. A. Bruce. II. The siege of Brookfield. (New England magazine, Mar., 1909. v. 40, p. 31–37).

Essex County. Domestic animals in the early days. (Essex antiquarian, Apr., 1909. v. 13, p. 49–55).

—— Essex County notarial records, 1697–1768. (Essex Institute. Historical collections, Jan.–Apr., 1909. v. 45, p. 90–96, 130–136).
Parts 10 and 11 (1722–1732); series began Apr., 1905. v. 41, p. 183.

—— Newspaper items relating to Essex County. (Essex Institute. Historical collections. Apr., 1909. v. 45, p. 157–160).
Part 6 (1758); series began Apr., 1906. v. 42, p. 2[illegible].

—— Salem court records and files. (Essex antiquarian, Jan.–Apr., 1909. v. 13, p. 28–34, 88–93).
Parts 29 and 30 (1653–1660); series began June, 1899. v. 3, p. 81.

—— Suffolk County deeds, v. VII and VIII. (Essex antiquarian. Jan.–Apr., 1909. v. 13, p. 41–42, 83–85).
Abstracts of all records in "Suffolk deeds" libri VII and VIII, 1894–1896, relating to Essex County.
Parts 6–7; series began with liber I in July, 1905. v. 9. p. 97.

Framingham. The Framingham of today. By Thomas Fenwick. (New England magazine, Feb., 1909. v. 39, p. 739–753).

Hull. An old fashioned day at Nantasket. By Isabel A. Dame. (New England magazine, Apr., 1909. v. 39, p. 159–161).

Ipswich. Ipswich inscriptions before 1800. Ancient burying ground. (Essex antiquarian, Jan.–Apr., 1909. v. 13, p. 1–24, 58–80).

—— Notable American homes. By Barr Ferree. The house of C. P. Searle at Ipswich. (American homes and gardens, Feb., 1909. v. 6, p. 45–49).

LEOMINSTER. Leominster's lesson to the growing cities of Mass. By F. H. Pope. (New England magazine, Feb., 1909. v. 39, p. 709–721).

LEXINGTON. How the news of the battle of Lexington reached England. By E. L. Waitt. (New England magazine, Mar. 1909. v. 40, p. 92–97).

MARLBOROUGH. Colonial records of Marlborough. Copied by Mary E. Spalding and communicated by F. P. Rice. (New England historical and genealogical register, Jan., 1909. v. 43, p. 59–67).
Part 3 (1663–1664); series began July, 1908. v. 62, p. 220.

MARTHA'S VINEYARD. Martha's Vineyard, the gem of the North Atlantic. By Capt. G. W. Eldridge. (New England magazine, Apr., 1909. v. 39, p. 162–179).

MEDFORD. Medford advertising in 1776. (Medford historical register, Jan., 1909. v. 12, p. 22–24).

—— One of Medford's historic houses: Jonathan Watson's. Some old Medford fish stories. From the Caleb Swan MSS. (Medford historical register, Jan., 1909. v. 12, p. 20–21).

—— Wood's dam and the mill beyond the Mystic. By M. W. Mann. (Medford historical register, Jan., 1909. v. 12, p. 13–20).

MIDDLEBOROUGH. Nemasket chapter, D. A. R. Report by Charlotte E. Ellis, historian. (American monthly magazine, Jan., 1909. v. 34, p. 41–43).

NANTASKET, see HULL.

PEPPERELL. Prudence Wright chapter, D. A. R. Report by Lucy B. Page. (American monthly magazine, Jan., 1909. v. 34, p. 43–49).

—— Prudence Wright chapter, D. A. R. Erection of marker in Old burying ground to Prudence Wright. By Annetta S. Merrill. (American monthly magazine, Mar., 1909. v. 34, p. 284–288).

RUTLAND. Rutland—the cradle of Ohio. A little journey to the home of Rufus Putnam. By E. O. Randall. (Ohio archaeological and historical quarterly, Jan., 1909. v. 18, p. 54–78).

SALEM. The new Salem; remarkable evolution of the historic Mass. city from Puritanism to progressiveness. By Thomas Fenwick. (New England magazine, Mar., 1909. v. 40, p. 47–57).

—— Old Salem ships and sailors. By R. D. Paine. Parts VII–XIV. (Outing magazine, Aug.–Dec., 1908, Jan.–Feb. and Apr., 1909. v. 52, p. 607–615, 743–751; v. 53, p. 97–103, 226–234, 291–300, 413–425, 559–570; v. 54, p. 104–112).
Contents:—VII. The first American voyagers to Japan.—VIII. The famous clipper privateers of 1812.—IX. The voyages of Nathaniel Silsbee.—X. The last pirates of the Spanish Main.—XI. The first Yankee ship at Guam.—XII. How Sumatra pirates took the "Friendship."—XIII. Adventuring among the Fijis.—XIV. A port of vanished fleets.
Series began in Jan., 1908. v. 51, p. 385.

—— Revolutionary letters written to Colonel Timothy Pickering. (Essex Institute. Historical collections, Apr., 1909. v. 45, p. 119–129).
Part 5; series began in Oct., 1906. v. 42, p. 313.

—— Salem in 1700, nos. 34 and 35. By Sidney Perley. (Essex antiquarian, Jan.–Apr., 1909. v. 13, p. 35–37, 80–82).
Series began in Nov., 1898; each number has a plan showing old streets and boundary lines of estates.

—— Twenty-five largest ships registered in Salem. Compiled from Salem ship registers, 1789–1900. (Essex Institute. Historical collections, Apr., 1909. v. 45, p. 204).

SCITUATE. Chief Justice Cushing chapter, D. A. R. Scituate. (American monthly magazine, Mar, 1909. v. 34, p. 280–282).

SHIRLEY. Old Shirley chapter, D. A. R. Shirley. By Abbie J. Wells. (American monthly magazine, Apr., 1909. v. 34, p. 390–391).

Department of the American Revolution

1775–1782

FRANK A. GARDNER, M. D. Editor.

State Sloop* Freedom.

The House of Representatives, in February 1776, authorized the construction of five war vessels for the State and two of them, the "Freedom" and "Republic" were built at Swanzey, The following officers served on the "Freedom's" first cruise;

Captain, John Clouston.
First Lieutenant, James Scott.
Second Lieutenant, Timothy Tobey.
Master, David Bowers, Jun.
Surgeon, Daniel Parker.
Surgeon's Mate, Nathaniel Cook.

The full complement of the vessel consisted of twelve other officers and seventy men and boys.

CAPTAIN JOHN CLOUSTON was of Scotch descent. He married about 1760, Hannah Bowers, daughter of Colonel George and Abigail (Fisher) Bowers, and went to live in a house which is still standing on the "Old Bristol Roade" just below the Taunton line towards Dighton.

FIRST LIEUTENANT JAMES SCOTT was engaged to serve in that rank on the "Freedom," July 8, 1776.

SECOND LIEUTENANT TIMOTHY TOBEY was engaged to serve as an officer on the "Freedom," June 22, 1776.

MASTER DAVID BOWERS JUN. was engaged to serve on this vessel June 22, 1776.

SURGEON DANIEL PARKER was engaged June 18. 1776. His commission was dated Sept 19, 1776.

SURGEON'S MATE, NATHANIEL COOK was chosen to that rank in Colonel Jacob Young's Regiment, stationed at Winter Hill, January 23, 1776. He was engaged for service on the "Freedom," June 18, 1776.

The following document relative to the fitting out of this vessel is of interest:

"Boston, September 1, 1776.

To Carpenter's Stores for the Sloop Freedom.

To 100 feet of oak Plank, 2 inch.
To 200 feet 2-inch pine Plank.
To 60 feet 4-inch Plank, oak.
To 50 weight Spikes, 6 inches long.
To 28 pounds Deck Nails.
To 1000 Drawing Nails.
To 1000 Shingle Nails.
To 1000 Clap-Board Nails.
To 10 pounds Pump Leather.
To 2000 Pump Nails.
To Jack Plane.
To one Smoothing Plane.
To 100 feet pine Boards.
To 2 hhds Rum.
To 2 bolts Duck.
To 1 Iron Tiller.

Watersail and Ringsale, and Gafftopsail, and Topmast Steeringsail (from the) Brig at Plymouth.

To 4 double blocks, Iron Pins & Brass Cogs.

To sundry Hooks and Thimbles and Bolts for deck and ring.

To 1 yawl 17 feet; 1 Iron hearth aboard the Brig at Plymouth.

To 2 tons of broken Cannon for ballast.

To 1 Anchor, about 200 pounds weight for Hawser of 6 inches.

To 1 Iron grappling aboard the Brig."

*Afterwards altered into a brigantine.

"For Sloop Freedom

100 double-headed Shot at Plymouth.
10 6-pound Cannon and Carriages at do.
11 Swivel Guns and 1 Cohorn.
The Brig's Spritsail Topsails.
30 Hammocks.
2 bolts Duck.
2 Studding-sails.
2 barrels Powder.

Captain John Clouston."

" Return of Officers on board the Armed Sloop called the Freedom, whereof John Clouston is Commander:

John Clouston, Captain.
James Scott, First Lieutenant.
Timothy Tobey, Second Lieutenant.

In Council September 4. 1776

Read and Ordered that the above Officers be commissioned agreeable to their respective ranks.
Samuel Adams, Secretary."

Richard Devens delivered to Captain John Clouston's order,

"Seven Cannon of 6-pound each, £50	£350 0 0
To Shell upwards of twenty tons at £20 per ton	400 0 0
To three ton Grape Shell £100	300 0 0
To freight and Iron, one ton	20 0 0
To 630 Pots 5s	157 10 0
To two tons of Shot to Closton, at £30 per ton	60 0 0
. . . .	
To carting 13 guns to Taunton .10s per Williams and Closton	6 10 0

Other stores were delivered to the "Freedom" September 19, 1776.

" State of Massachusetts-Bay to John Clouston, Commander of the Sloop Freedom, in the service of said State.

You are hereby directed and commanded to repair, with the vessel under your command, to the harbour of Boston, in company with the sloop Republick, commanded by Captain John Foster Williams, now in Dartmouth, and there to wait for the further orders of the Council.

By order of a major part of the Council, the 4th of September, 1776.

Samuel Adams, Secretary."

The following letter explains itself;

" Captain John Clouston;

The sloop *Freedom*, under your command, being in all respects equipped in warlike manner, and being also well and properly manned, so as to enable you to proceed on a cruise, you therefore are directed to range the eastern shore of this State laying between the River Piscataqua and Machias, in order to clear that coast of any of the enemy's cruisers that may be infesting the same, and from thence proceed to the mouth of the River St. Lawrence, and there cruise until the first of November in order to intercept any of the enemy's vessels that may be passing that way, and from thence you must proceed to the coast of *Newfoundland*, and there cruise until the middle of November aforesaid, in order to surprise and seize such vessels of the enemy as you meet upon that coast, or in any of the harbours of the same, after which you may proceed upon a cruise as far southward as latitude 38° north, and continue upon said cruise so long as you find it practicable or expedient; and then you are to return to the harbour of Boston, always using every necessary precaution to prevent the sloop under your command from falling into the hands of the enemy. You are to observe and follow such orders and directions as you shall from time to time receive from Captain Daniel Souther, provided they are consistent with the instructions now given you. And whereas you have received a commission by force of arms to attack, seize, and take on the high seas, all ships and other vessels belonging to the inhabitants of Great Britain or others infesting the sea-coast of this Continent, you are therefore punctually to follow the instructions already delivered you

for regulating your conduct in this matter, and in all things conduct yourself consistent with the trust reposed in you.

In Council, September 20, 1776.
In the name and by order of Council,
John Avery, Deputy Secretary."

"In Council, October 1, 1776.

Whereas Captain John Foster Williams of the sloop Republick and Captain John Clouston of the Sloop Freedom, both belonging to this State, are in want of some iron ballast that they may immediately proceed on their intended cruise; therefore the Committee for fortifying the Harbour of Boston be, and they are hereby directed to deliver the said Williams and Clouston, out of the row galley lying in Boston harbour, so much iron ballast, as they may stand in need of at this time for their several sloops."

"State of MASSACHUSETTS-BAY to Benjamin Austin, Dr. 1776, September 28. —To cash paid Captain *John Clouston* of the sloop Freedom, for one month's advance wages to the men on board the said Sloop at 40s each £14.

Errours excepted

Benj'n Austin.

In council, October 3, 1776.

Read and allowed, and ordered, That a warrant be drawn on the Treasury for £14, in full of the above acccount.

John Avery, Deputy Secretary.

Boston, 28 September, 1776.

Received of *Benjamin Austin*, Esquire, fourteen pounds being so much he paid me for one months advance wages to seven men inlisted on board the sloop *Freedom*, belonging to this State.

£14. Captain John Clouston."

The "Freedom" cruised in October and November and one of the vessels taken by her was the ship "La Soye Planter" which was recaptured before making an American port.

This cruise was interrupted as the following resolves will explain:

"Whereas the armed Sloop Freedom, Captain John Clouston, belonging to this state, has had the misfortune to have her mast split, and is thereby disabled from continuing on her cruise, and is now in the harbour of Plymouth; and whereas it will be much for the advantage of this State that the said Sloop should be altered into a Brigantine; and the masts, sails, and rigging of the Brigantine *Rising Empire*, belonging to this State, lately condemned, and now in said harbour, are every way suitable for that purpose.

Ordered, that *Ephraim Spooner* Esq. of *Plymouth*, be desired, and is hereby empowered, in conjunction with Captain *Clouston*, to see that the masts, sails and rigging belonging to the Brigantine *Rising Empire*, be taken out of her, and forthwith applied to equip the said sloop as a Brigantine, that she may be able, as soon as possible, to proceed on her cruise." Passed October 9, 1776.

"Whereas this Court on the 9th instant appointed Ephraim Spooner Esq., in connection with Captain Clouston, to see that the masts, sails, and rigging belonging to the Brigantine Rising Empire be taken out of her and forthwith applied to equip the said sloop as a brig: and whereas it appears to this Court necessary that some person acquainted with building and rigging vessels should be upon the said committee:

Therefore Resolved; that Willlam Drew Esq., be added to the Committee aforesaid, he to repair forthwith to Plymouth, and advise and direct in performing said business." October 14, 1776.

The term of service of the officers expired in December and none of them returned to serve under Captain Clouston on the next voyage. We have no further record of any service of First Lieutenant James Scott, Second Lieutenant Timothy

Tobey, Surgeon Daniel Parker, or Surgeon's Mate Nathaniel Cook. Surgeon Parker was reported "deserted."

MASTER DAVID BOWERS was sent on board the ship "La Soye Planter," with the prize crew and was captured in her by a British commander. His name appears in a list of prisoners brought in the first cartel from Rhode Island, as returned by John Ayers dated Providence January 18, 1777. He was discharged March 2, 1777, and was reported as sick with small pox to that date.

The following rather ambiguous note is found in some miscellaneous records of the Council:

"Voted that Capt. Clouston of Brig Freedom be fitted for sea."

It will be noticed that this vessel, which up to this time has been a sloop, is now referred to as "brig" or more correctly as in nearly all other references, brigantine. The same change had been made in her rig as was made in the "Tyrannicide" after she had been in service awhile.

The "Freedom" was officered and manned for the next cruise as follows;

John Clouston, Captain. Engaged January 2, 1777.

Daniel Adams, First Lieutenant.
John Hooper, Second Lieutenant.
John Proctor, Master.
John Haven, Surgeon.
Edward Carrell, Surgeon's Mate.

FIRST LIEUTENANT DANIEL ADAMS (called also in the records "David," by mistake) served first as First Lieutenant of the State brigantine "Independence" under Captain Simeon Samson, his commission bearing date of September 19, 1776. He was engaged to serve on the "Freedom" January 20, 1777, and his commission was altered to allow him to serve on her, February 18, 1777.

SECOND LIEUTENANT JOHN HOOPER held that rank first under Captain William Cole in the privateer schooner "True Blue." August 29, 1776. He shipped on the "Freedom" February 4, 1777, and was commissioned February 19th.

MASTER JOHN PROCTOR was engaged to serve on the "Freedom" February 4, 1777.

SURGEON JOHN HAVEN was commissioned January 14, 1777, to serve as Surgeon of the State brigantine "Massachusetts" under Capt. Williams. February 14th he was engaged to hold the same office on the "Freedom" and his commission was altered accordingly on the 18th.

SURGEON'S SECOND MATE EDWARD CARRELL was engaged February 4, 1777. In addition were 17 other officers, 57 men, 11 boys and 16 French men.

Sailing orders were issued to Captain Clouston in February and we know from the following bills that he went to France. One of the bills rendered by Morris Pliarne, Penet & Co., for ship supplies including medicines and surgical instruments, and money for the pay roll, amounted to £2149:05:08. This was made out to June 9th. A supplementary bill including items "omitted in J. Gruel & Co.'s General Account of Disbursements dated the 6th June, 1777" included the following interesting items:

"31 Cuttlafses @ 4:10	139:10: .
31 belts for do @ 2:00	62: : .
4 Pairs of fhip pistols a 10: 10	42 : . .
	243:10: .
Errors excepted. Commifsion a 5 p Ct	12: 3: 6.
Nantes 23d September 1778 Penet DaCosta freres & Co."	255:13: 6.
"Omitted in ye General Acct of 6 May last Vizt	
To the Butcher for 230 lb fresh meat at22 pr Ct	50.12:
Commision at 5 p. Ct	2:10:07.
	53:02:07.

Errors excepted
Nantes 11 May 1778
Penet Da Costa freres & Co."

Among the captures made on this cruise was the brigantine "Penelope," and the "William and Ann."

Master John Proctor, Surgeon John Haven and Surgeon's Mate Edward Carrell left the "Freedom" at the end of this cruise and we can find no further record of service.

SECOND LIEUTENANT JOHN HOOPER was evidently put on the "William and Ann" with a prize crew and was captured. He was paid to January 23, 1778, the time when his captivity ended. He was commissioned on the 12th of the following September, First Lieutenant of the privateer ship "Pilgrim" of Salem, Captain Hugh Hill, commander.

Captain John Clouston and First Lieutenant Daniel Adams re-engaged for the fall cruise of 1777. The following is a full list of the officers;

John Clouston, Captain.
Daniel Adams, First Lieutenant.
Thomas Doten, Second Lieutenant.
Caleb Dyer, Master.
Jacob Bacon, Surgeon.
John Samuel Phillips, Surgeon's Mate.

Second Lieutenant Thomas Doten was engaged July 23d; Master Caleb Dyer was engaged August 25th; Surgeon Jacob Bacon, September 4th; and Surgeon's Mate John Samuel Phillips August 1st. We have no record that any of them had previously seen service in an armed vessel.

The "Freedom" was captured some time in September or October, 1777. Negotiations were entered into in October 1777, to effect an exchange of prisoners.

CAPTAIN JOHN CLOUSTON'S name appears on a list of prisoners to be exchanged, said list bearing date of February 24, 1778. He was exchanged for Captain William Roome of the ship "Maesgwin," and the Surgeon of the "Freedom" SURGEON JACOB BACON was exchanged for the Surgeon of the "Maesgwin," Dr. Joseph Mills. Captain Clouston landed at Bristol March 7, 1778. Neither Captain Clouston or Surgeon Bacon have further records on board armed vessels.

FIRST LIEUTENANT DANIEL ADAMS was exchanged for Richard Emmes, mate of the "Maesgwin." Lieutenant Adams was commissioned April 22, 1782, commander of the sloop "Lively," and a petition dated November 18th of the same year asked that he might be commissioned commander of still another vessel.

SECOND LIEUTENANT DOTEN later commanded the ship "Russell" from Salem for Hispaniola, and was captured on the outward passage by the Halifax Packet and carried into New York. His exchange was advised in the Council, January 30, 1783.

MASTER CALEB DYER had wages allowed him to November 30, 1778. He was reported "detained in New York." December 5, 1778, he was engaged as Master of the sloop "Republic" in which he served until January 12, 1779. No further record of Surgeon's Mate Phillips is given.

"The Struggle for American Independence."

The last word in the Genesis of the Revolutionary War has not been spoken. Every teacher of the history of that period seems to find some new light or make some new interpretation. Professor Channing of Harvard is engaged upon a monumental work which will cover the whole field of American history. Every year brings some fresh volumes. The last that has caught our eye is Sidney George Fisher's "The Struggle for American Independence."

In presenting this work the author has performed a distinct service to the student of the formative era of the American na-

tion. His contention that the final outbreak was simply the logical culmination of an evolutionary movement which started in very early colonial times, is ably borne out. He proves how England dreaded to use any oppressive measures so long as France held Canada on our north, but having conquered the French there the repression of the colonists was considered an easier matter. Our ancestors having had greater freedom than any other British colonies had ever enjoyed either before or since, would not be restricted. The stamp act fanned the flame but the fire had been smouldering and growing hotter for generations.

The following paragraphs from his able and exhaustive review of the loyalists are characteristic:

"The fatal defect in the loyalist position was its unnaturalness. They gave their devotion not to the land they lived in, and the government and social system that would naturally grow from that soil. They loved and worshipped a country and a government three thousand miles away. They had vaguely magnificent ideas that the colonists should support and encourage the superiortiy of England, join her in vast schemes of conquest, and reap some enormous reward in the plunder of inferior peoples in Asia, Africa, and India. The desire of the patriot party to own America as their own country was, the loyalists said a mere 'sentiment of self importance,' too ridiculous to be mentioned in the presence of the power and splendor of Great Britain." All the loyalist writings and arguments are filled with this awe-struck admiration for the wonderful British constitution and the glorious British empire. Such devotion to a distant excellence, is both political and spiritual degeneration. In the long run nothing but contempt awaits the men who will not stand by their own, who weakly wish to be ruled by a foreign power for the sake of what they suppose to be a superior refinement or civilization." . . . "At the time of the Revolution a large part of the lower classes of our people were more or less on the loyalist side, because of the habit of dependence on England, fear of change or lack of conviction of any material advantage in Americanism. As William Wirt long ago pointed out in his 'Life of Patrick Henry,' the Revolution originated among the upper classes of Americans, among rich planters, merchants and lawyers, who led the masses into the movement often very much against their will.

The whole fabric and foundation of the Revolution, those long years of argumentation from 1764 to 1775, that basis of constitutional and legal reasoning, that application of the Reformation doctrines of the rights of man, could never have been wrought out in their perfection and finally expressed in effective language and drafted into state constitutions and governmental documents except by men of the highest education and training. No ignorant or untrained man, no upstart or mere popular demagogue can be found among the great leaders of the patriot party. It was the work of a Hamilton, a Jefferson, a Dickinson, the Adamses, the Lees, and the Rutledges, a Bland, a Mason, a Drayton, a Cushing, or a Laurens."

The author is to be especially commended for the careful and painstaking way in which he has cited authorities and given references in the footnotes. The work is certainly a valuable one for all students of American history.

2v: octavo, J. B. Lippincott Company, Philadelphia.

Criticism & Comment

on Books and Other Subjects

Historical Pageants.

We are pleased to announce that the movement in favor of the presentation this summer of a series of historical pageants, is being worked out by an able and efficient committee made up of representatives of the Copley Society, the state normal schools and the patriotic societies.

Some of the events which they expect to represent are the following:

1. The Indian home life and arrival of Norse Viking at "Vinland the Good" introducing Lief the Lucky.
2. A Pilgrim Sabbath service, introducing the Pilgrim characters.
3. The election at Cambridge in 1637 when Winthrop was elected over Vane.
4. The attack on Hadley. Introducing Phillip and Goffe the regicide.
5. The court of King George III, when he sent Gen. Gage, Lord Howe, Clinton, Andre, etc. to subdue Boston.
6. The impeachment of Chief Justice Oliver, introducing the Adamses, Otis, Paine, Cushing, Governor Hutchinson and prominent Tories.
7. The establishment of the Commonwealth and the inauguration of John Hancock.
8. Western migration at Rutland.
9. Visit of Lafayette in 1824, introducing Webster, Everett, Quincy, etc.
10. Return of battle flags to Governor Andrew and presentation of the key of Libby prison to Whittier, introducing anti-slavery leaders.

F. A. G.

Ancestors of Benjamin Clemens Witherell.

The following letter has been received at the office of the Massachusetts Magazine and in reply we give the appended list of names and dates from the records.

"Dear Sir:

Will you kindly inform me if you have any data or information in regard to the Witherell and Clemens Families of early Salem. They were there as early as 1715. I have been trying to trace the ancestors of Benjamin Clemens Witherell. I do not find them in the Norton Witherells, descended from William Witherell 1643, the first settler. They may be among the Salem families of that name I should deem it a favor if you could throw any light on the matter for me."

Salem Town Records.

Clemons. Births; Samuel 1687, William 1689, John 1690, Benjamin 1792. Marriages; Samuel 1709, John 1712, Philip 1725, Samuel 1739, Martha 1742, Samuel 1750. No Clemens deaths recorded before 1818.

Witherell. Births; William 1716, Joshua 1717-8, Samuel 1721. Marriages; Joshua 1715, Joshua 1739. No other Witherells before 1750.

Essex County Probate Records.

Clemens.

Abraham, Salisbury. Administration and Bond. 1716.
Fawn, Newbury. Will and Probate. 1740.
Job, Haverhill. Will. 1733.
John, Haverhill. Bond etc. 1693.
John, Beverly. Administration and Bond. 1750.
Joseph, Haverhill. Guardianship and Bond. 1736.
Mary, Salem. Will and Probate. 1741.

Nathaniel, Haverhill. Inventory. 1690.
Robert, Haverhill. Will and Inventory (on file). 1658.
Timothy, Beverly. Administration and Bond. 1731.

Witherell.

Susannah (Spinster,) Marblehead. 1772.
No other Witherells from 1638 to 1840.

Essex County Registry of Deeds.

Clemons, Clemens, etc., etc. Grantees
Abraham, 1693-6.
Anna (ux Timothy,) 1729.
Benjamin, 1745-1793.
Edward, 1720.
Elizabeth, 1694-1720.
Fawne, 1694-1732.
Hannah, 1760-5.
Jacob, 1754-1795.
Jeremiah, 1716.
Job, 1703-1736.
John, 1654-1798.
Jonathan, 1719-1765.
Joseph, 1733-1798.
Mary (alias Osgood), 1695.
Mary (ux Joseph), 1750.
Mehetable, 1736.
Moses, 1738-1787.
Nathaniel, 1731-1760.
Robert, 1694-1742.
Ruth (ux Samuel), 1709.
Samuel, 1689-1798.
Sarah, 1777-8.
Stephen, 1788-92.
Timothy, 1721-1757.
William, 1661.
No Witherell records given.

F. A. G.

(Continued from Vol. 1, No. 4.)

PERSONAL DIARY OF ASHLEY BOWEN OF MARBLEHEAD.*

X.

Memoranday of Coullax 1772

May ye 15 R H s g Brig Nancy	£0.6.8
Ditto	0.5.4
June y 22 R H s g Schooner Nancy	0.5.4
Septem R H s g 2 p pack 8	0.2.8
Decem 12 Brig Nancy	0.6.0
	1.6.0

XI.

Memorandam for a Schooner for Capt Philip Digings

Main mast 57 feet 7 ha 9 ha
fore mast 53 Ditto 7 D. 9 D
bowsprit 37 Ditto
Main Boom 55 Ditto
Main Topmast 25 hist fore 27 D
To 100 fathoms of Shrouding 6
To a Tigh Stay 11 fathoms 7 Inch
To a four Stay 8 fathoms 6 Inch
To 75 fathoms of 4 Inch
To 100 fathoms of 3 3-4 Inch
To 75 Ditto of 3 1-2 Inch
To 60 Ditto of 3 1-4 Ditto
To 120 Ditto of 3 — D
To 140 Ditto of 2 1-2 D
To 220 of 2 1-4 Inch
To 60 fat of 2
To 3 Coils of 12 Thread Ratline
To 3 Coils 3 yarn Spun
2 of 2

XII.

(A long list of charges to the town of Marblehead for milk, work on fences, and burial of the dead. The following persons were buried on the dates named.)

1773

Aug y^e 1 to Buriing Mrs Rodger	£0.6.0
Ditto ye 5 to Bury Ela Rodger	0.6.0
Ditto ye 9 to buring Mrs Cleark	0.6.0
Ditto ye 10 to bury Mrs Goold	0.6.0
Ditto ye 11 to burying T Dodd	0.6.0
ye 16 to buring Clearck Child	0.6.0
To Buring Thomas Goold	0.6.0

XIII.

Memerandum of Coll Orne &c New Brig July 1774 —

Main mast 50 feet 6 feet hd
fore mast 44 Ditto 6. ditto
Bowsprit 21 Ditto feet or Stem
M D four Topmast 27 feet 3:6
Four yard 37 X Tay 37 D
Main & four Top yard 27 D
Jibb boom 24 feet
Sprit Sail yard 27 Ditto
Top gall mast 17 Ditto 3 D
Top gall yards 18
Main Boom 44 Ditto

(Diary proper, June, 1773.)

About ye 1 Came in John Wooldread
y^e 3 Sailed pitt Packit Leech
y 12 Sailed Wittrong Barbudg
about y 15 Sarah Mathew poisend .
y^e 17 the Custom h Boatt Sunk weareby 7 women and 3 men was Drowned
5 women Prenent
19 Sailed adventure Fittel
24 Sailed Brig Gaspy Huntor

July

y 3 Saild Ben Boden for Eur
abut y 1 Sarah Hendly brok out with what was Said Poisen
16 Sail Richd Stacey for Europ
17 Sald Ben Cally for Europ
the 20 M[rs] Sarah Shaw broke out
22 Sailed Alex. Rows for Europ
23 Great Tolks of Small Pox in Town
the 24 M[rs] Mary Bowen Removed Sarah Goold Sarah Reef Rodge Ann Rodge Wido Marcy Brinto M[rs] Cheambers M[rs] Dodd all tacon Small Pox at the Same time and many more much Suspected to have it
the 28 Died M[rs] Sarah Shaw Ag 79
y 31 Son Nathan Sent to his mother

August

y[e] 1 Dd Sarah Reef Rodger 80
y 5 Dd Elishaw Rodgers 4 m
y 7 Dd Elisebth Arbucal fery
y 8 Dd Hannah Loveas fery
y 9 Dd M[rs] Cleark at y[e] Almshous
y 10 Dd Mrs Goold at y[e] Almshous
y 11 Dd Tho Dodd at y[e] Almshous
y 11 Dd Persiler Adley a ferry
y 16 a child of Clearks at Alm
y 16 Dd Thom Goold at Almho
y 22 Dd M[rs] Wodden at ferry
y 23 Dd Mrs Savage at ferry
y 25 my wife Returned home
y 27 Come in g Brews a boy Dd
y 31 a child of John Adams Dd ferry
11 Saild Stephen Bleano in Brigg
y 20 Sailed Brig Woodbridg Poatt
arived Wittron from St Martins
28 Saild Tho[m] Coller for Europe

September 1773

y 1 Dd M[rs] Abbott & Child at ferry
y 11 Dd M[rs] Stone at fery

y 11 Dd Lear a bacor at fery
y 12 Dd Ann mills a fery
13 Dd a child of J Northys
y 14 We hear John Dolly Dd a b
y 21 Dd Richd Mace at fery
y 30 Dd a Child of T Brays at fery
3 Saild Richd Hincley Capt White
4 Saild Capt Corbit W Indies
7 Sailed Ship Volture for Europe
Ditto Will Bleaner West Indies
16 Sailed R James & Wittrone W In
17 Mr John Tucker Drownded

Octob ye 1773

ye 5 Dd Mrs Sandy at fery
6 Dd Mary Pitman fery
8 Dd a boy Bacor fery
9 Dd Mary Bacor fery
22 Dd Elis Parsons fery
5 arved Bartlit & Phillyp Coners
15 Saild John Hooper and Burn
23 arived John Stephen
24 Sailed St Barbe
Ditto J Lee in Brodbay
28 Sailed Brig Tener Woolf Hill for verjenea
arived John Addams Europe
31 Arived St Paull H Gording

November

y 1 Dd a Child fery
2 Arivd Da Lee from Gibberalter
7 Arived Brig Patty Ballistor
y 12 Dd a Girl at Catt Island
25 Thanksgiving day
29 arivd Leech from Europe
y 17 Dd Mrs Cruff at fery
y 19 Alce Bray Dd At home
y 21 Dd a Boy Witham a fery
y 22 Joseph Abbitt Two Ser Drownd

y 19 Saild George Gording in Snow Gordoq for Europe
19 Saild Jones for Verjinea
21 Sailed Power for Europe
Ditto Dav Lee for Verjenea
24 Arivd Salsbury Roboson

December 1773

ye 1 Dd Benje Eaton Juner at Catt Is
ye 3 Dd Doctor Hump Deverax Do
y 4 Capt Lowel. Lost his Aamus Do
y 14 Dd a Child of W Courts Juner Do
Dd Will Allen at R Island
Dd Thos Dollebar June Dto
Dd a Child John Milzer
Dd a Child Dodd fery
Dd Mrs Beseunes at home
11 arived D Dennes W Indies
13 arived Sing dier from W Inds
16 arived Brig Ledia T Coller
and Tuck from W Indies
17 arived S Green Ed Lewis and W Tucker all from W Inds
16 Dd John Fowler at fery
18 arivd Capt Ben Calley and Stephen Bleaner from Cadis
21 Dd Mrs Aston fery
21 Arivd Capt John Grnshw
22 Saild Brig Brig Patty Basester
24 Arived Sch Adventure Titte
25 Arived R James W Indis
29 Saild Sahoone Rappall
30 Saild Jo Bubear for Europe
December 27 1773 a town meeting and voted the Boat Should not land at New Worf nor Neck Cove but on Peeches point or Read Stone Cove
31 Sam Reeds wife Like to Die at Ospital

1774

January

y 3 Sailed Brigg St Paul N Gord and Sloop Charlot J Reed Verjenear
y 5 arived Will Andrews W Indies

A Proklemation of King Georg ye 3 of England on October ye 7 1763 of granting Lands to Solders and Semen on the Expedishon Cannaday

y 10 Sarah Broodstreet Come from Catt Island Sick as Shee was

y 11 Sloop Ashley beet of from Nicks Cove obliged to go to Red Stone Cove with there Pashenjer

y 12 This Evening the Boatt was Burnt at Nick Cove

y 20 Granday Bredin Delap & Cleark Ware Tared and fetherd and halled to Salem and Back

y 26 this Night ye Essex Ospital took fier and was Confumed with Barn Litthous &c

14 Dd Hannah Bleaner

16 Capt Lowel arivd from Catt Island D Jack Disiered him not to Snowball any Body

21 Sailed Ambros James

Ditto John Gaile wind W N W

Ditto Arivd Absalem Dupee

26 Dd a Child Tomson a fery

29 Dd Mr Dorrell s Pox

30 Dd Clem How wife a fery

Pilgrims and Planters

1620–1630

LUCIE M. GARDNER, A. B., Editor.

Settlers About Boston Bay Prior to 1630.

LUCIE M. GARDNER.

In the first number of the Massachusetts Magazine we considered the early settlers of the Cape Ann-Salem colony and paid homage to those noble men who labored and struggled to lay the foundations of our beloved Commonwealth.

In this article we present the names of the men who settled about the shores of Boston Bay, prior to the coming of Gov. Winthrop in 1630. The limit of the pioneer period is an open question but we will confine ourselves to those men who were, to that locality, what Conant, Gardner, Woodbury, Balch and their associates were to Cape Ann;—the first to till the soil, to make new homes and to lay the foundations of that settlement which was to become Boston.

The casual reader is content to follow the teaching of several writers of history who begin the story of Boston with the arrival of the Winthrop party in 1630, entirely disregarding the pioneer work which preceded that event. The several settlements which were made and in turn abandoned, all contributed their shares toward founding this great city, and we naturally desire to know all that we can about those isolated homes established by Blackstone and Maverick in the wilderness. Captain John Smith and Governor Bradford have left valuable accounts of these very early days and even the rambling descriptions of Thomas Morton make a vivid picture of the early struggles of the settlers of Boston Bay. We will consider in the first place the various settlements about the shores of what is now Boston harbor, which were made or attempted before the coming of Winthrop; and then give brief biographical sketches of the forty-three men concerning whom the writer has found sufficient proof of residence before May, 1630.

In 1614 Captain John Smith undoubtedly entered and, to some extent explored Boston Bay, especially the southern portions. His map on which Quincy and Weymouth bays are very clearly indicated is sufficient evidence of this. In the years 1616 and 1617 that dreadful pestilence raged which killed off so many of the Massachussetts Indians, "clearing the woods of those pernicious creatures to make room for a better growth" as Rev. Cotton Mather stated eighty years later. On a September afternoon in 1621, Miles Standish in command of a party composed of 10 Europeans and 3 savages, cast anchor off what is now Thompson's Island and named it Trevour in honor of William Trevour, one of their number. Under the leadership of the Indian guide Squanto, they explored the shore, seeking out the scattered remnant of the Indian tribe who were hiding in fear. In the afternoon they crossed to the Charlestown or Chelsea shore near the Mystic. The next day they landed and pushed inland in the direction of Medford and Winchester. They found the deserted home of Nanepashemet and traded with a few squaws. They returned to Plymouth after an absence of four days, having seen Boston harbor with its islands and beautiful surroundings during the finest season of the New England year. Small wonder then. that the Plymouth shore seemed flat and tame and that they spoke regretfully of the broad harbor and beautiful region they had just left. Smith had been impressed in the same way seven years before and had pronounced the vicinity of Boston Bay "the paradise of all these parts."

Some localities about Boston harbor still bear the names given by the Plymouth visitors—Point Allerton, was named for Isaac Allerton who was for many years deputy-governor under Bradford, the Brewsters, for Elder Brewster. Trevour's Island soon lost the name given it by Miles Standish and since 1626 has been called Thompson's Island, but the peninsula opposite has always retained its original name, Squantum, perpetuating the memory of the Indian interpreter who guided the first party of Europeans that ever set foot upon it. Squanto has not had his due place in New England history. He was for a time

the most essential factor perhaps in prolonging the existence of the Plymouth colony, for it was he who showed them how to plant and tend the maize without which they could not have survived.

We may pass over the unfortunate experiences of Weston and his "fellows" of Wessagusset. Suffice it to say that they reflected little glory on their friends and themselves. The settlement was but temporary at best. Their houses which Bradford had cautioned the savages not to destroy, were unoccupied but a few months, for Captain Robert Gorges took possession in the September following that memorable April, 1623. Weston was a man of the city, an adventurer and a trader. Gorges was a gentleman adventurer, a man of the court and a soldier. So far as jurisdiction was concerned the powers civil and criminal intrusted to young Gorges were of the amplest description, for he was authorized to arrest, imprison and punish even capitally. The following spring Gorges was glad to return to England. Besides the hardships of the season, he had found his official position one of little consideration and no encouragement. His one attempt at authority had resulted in a miserable wrangle with Weston and he had been powerless to control the fishermen and traders. As a settlement, it had resulted in so little that it failed completely to influence the course of subsequent events and has been deemed worthy of scant notice in history; yet it was an organized attempt replete with possibilities.

The few who lingered there after Gorges left, were in the care of Reverend Mr. Morrell. For the year following there is no record of them. In the spring of 1625 Morrell also returned to England. Those whom he left behind began to reach out to more favored points in Boston Bay. Blackstone moved across to the north shore and finally established himself where, five years later, Winthrop found him on the western slope of the peninsula of Shawmut opposite the mouth of the Charles river. Thomas Walford, an English blacksmith, who probably came as a mechanic with Robert Gorges, presently went over, with his wife, and built him a house near the mouth of the Mystic, and was there in what is now Charlestown when the Spragues and others went there in 1629. This place was first known a Mishawam. Samuel Maverick, a youug man of 22, came over in 1624, bringing with him his wife, Amias, and built at Winnissimet or Chelsea, a house which 35 years later was still standing.

About the time Morrell left Wessagusset, a Captain Wollaston sailed into Boston Bay with a little company of adventurers, some three or four men of substance and between thirty and forty servants. Of this man we know little. He came from English obscurity, rested for a brief time on a hillock overlooking Boston Bay, giving to it his name, and then disappeared into oblivion. Thomas Morton is the only one of the party of whom much is known, and he it was who probably gave the information about the region. He was, it is believed, a companion of Andrew Weston in the Charity, when she visited Boston Bay in the summer of 1622. He had seen America at the most beautiful season of the year and his glowing accounts led them hither. A season must have passed while they were building their houses and the winter which followed seemed to suffice for Captain Wollaston as it had for Robert Gorges. Consequently in 1626, he set sail for Virginia, leaving Rasdall in charge of the plantation. Wollaston soon sent for Rasdall to join him, leaving Fitcher in charge. At this time Morton's influence began to make itself felt. He had come with two distinct aims, pleasure and profit. Whatever may be said of his character, he was a close observer and a keen lover of nature, for his strange rambling book contains one of the best descriptions of Indian life, their traits and habits, and of the trees, products and animal life of New England, which have come down to us. He maintains a discreet silence as to his methods as a trader but he writes freely of his pleasures. His taste for boistrous enjoyment culminated in a proceeding which scandalized the sombre religious settlement at Plymouth. As Governor Bradford wrote: "They set up a May pole, drinking and dancing about it many days together, inviting the Indian women for their consorts, dancing and frisking together (like so many fairies or furies rather) and worse practices. As if they had anew revived and celebrated the feasts of the Roman Goddess Flora, or rather the beastly practises of the mad Bacchinalians."

Between 1625 and 1627 two new settlements had been effected in Boston Bay, one at Nantasket, the other at Thompson's

Island and Squantum. It would seem that a sort of trading-post had been established at Nantasket as early as 1622. Thomas Gray is said to have purchased this place of the Indian Sachem, Chikataubut, in this year. He, with others who favored the established church, finding Plymouth inhospitable, removed his residence to this place, John Gray and Walter Knight going with him. John Oldham and John Lyford had stirred up such strife and discord at Plymouth that the General Court was summoned in 1623 and these two men were arraigned on general charges of conspiracy, civil and spiritual, with intent to disturb the peace. Both were ordered to leave Plymouth but while Oldham was ordered to go at once, Lyford was allowed to remain six months. Roger Conant left Plymouth and came to Nantucket at the same time. In 1625 this settlement was broken up, and Roger Conant, Thomas Gray, Walter Knight and John Oldham joined the settlement of the Dorchester Company at Cape Ann.

(*To be continued*)

GARDNER FAMILY ASSOCIATION.

The third reunion of the Gardner Family Association will be held at the Salem Willows, on Wednesday, June 23, 1909. A pilgrimage about Salem will occupy the morning, the party starting from the Boston and Maine station at 10 A.M. Trolley cars will then be taken to the Willows, the beautiful shore resort opposite the residence which is to be occupied by President Taft this summer. A basket lunch will be eaten in the covered pavilion at noon, and following this, addresses will be given by members of the family. At the close of the exercises, a motor boat trip will be provided for those who desire, along the beautiful North Shore and among the islands of the harbor. A cordial invitation is extended to all who are descendants of Thomas Gardner the Planter, or are interested in the family through marriage. All members of the Old Planters Society and their friends will be gladly welcomed.

THE OLD PLANTERS SOCIETY.

The Annual meeting of the Old Planters Society was held according to the constitution, Wednesday, March 24th, at 3 P. M. Formal adjournment was made to March 25th at three o'clock in the parlors of the Salem Young Men's Christian Association in Salem. In the absence of the President, Colonel Thomas Wentworth Higginson, the Vice-President, Dr. Frank A. Gardner presided. The annual report of the secretary was read and accepted. Dr. Gardner reviewed the work of the year and congratulated the members upon the good fortune of the society in perfecting arrangements whereby The Massachusetts Magazine had been made the official organ, so that copies would be sent regularly to each member. The work for the coming year was outlined, especial emphasis being placed on the Gardner family reunion in June and the summer meeting at Plymouth.

Officers for the ensuing year were elected as follows:

PRESIDENT—COL. THOMAS WENTWORTH HIGGINSON, CAMBRIDGE
VICE PRES.—FRANK A. GARDNER, M. D., SALEM.
SECRETARY—LUCIE M. GARDNER, SALEM.
TREASURER—FRANK V. WRIGHT, SALEM.
REGISTRAR—MRS. LORA A. W. UNDERHILL, BRIGHTON.
COUNCILLORS—WM. PRESCOTT GREENLAW, BOSTON.
R. W. SPRAGUE, M. D., BOSTON.
HON. A. P. GARDNER, HAMILTON.
NATHANIEL CONANT, BROOKLINE.
FRANCIS H. LEE, SALEM.
COL. J. GRANVILLE LEACH, PHILA.
FRANCIS N. BALCH, JAMAICA PLAIN.
JOSEPH A. TORREY, MANCHESTER.
EDWARD O. SKELTON, ROXBURY.

Announcement was made that the society had adopted as its official hymn, "The Pilgrim and Puritan," written by Hon. John J. Loud, of Weymouth, and it was sung by the audience. Reverend Peter H. Goldsmith, D. D., pastor of the historic First Church of Salem, was then introduced and he delivered the annual address "The New England Minister in Early Puritan Communities." The descriptions of the various phases of life in the colonies were most vivid and interesting. The address was instructive and was lightened by many amusing incidents and extracts from letters and records which seemed to bring those early days very close to the present. At the close of the address, Dr. Goldsmith was given a very hearty vote of thanks.

The audience lingered for a social hour and enjoyed the dainty refreshments which had been provided. Owing to the very severe storm (one of the worst of the season) the audience was not large, but what was lacking in numbers was compensated for in enthusiasm.

Our Editorial Pages

REV. THOMAS FRANKLIN WATERS.

A VERY sensible and happy idea is gaining ground in our High Schools. Instead of indulging in the usual elaborate graduating exercises, which often involve a burdensome expense for appropriate dress, and cause much secret bitterness, many classes are agreeing to make their graduation simple and inexpensive and then devoting their energies to provide for a class excurison. The popular trip is a week's outing in Washington, and a better choice could not be made. The Journey thither is probably the first experience in travel to many and the night spent on one of the beautiful Sound boats, the early approach to New York, the glimpses of the huge bridges and the great buildings, the crossing of the Hudson and the swift run to the Capital are things to be long remembered.

The educational possibilities of such a pilgrimage are unlimited. A few days spent as busily as these young pilgrims rejoice in doing, will make them measurably familiar with the great public buildings, the Capitol, the Library of Congress, the Mint, the collections of the Smithsonian Institution and museums and collections of a hundred sorts. They are sure to see many eminent men. Mr. Roosevelt was always very gracious to the school boys and girls, and the young travellers invariably enjoyed the privilege of meeting him at the White House. No doubt the genial Mr. Taft is equally kind and approachable. They attain a new and keen interest in Congress. The whole history of the nation is seen in kaleidoscopic fashion. A proud and patriotic admiration of their country, and a deep and enduring appreciation of the privileges and responsibilities of citizenship, fill their minds and hearts. Such an excursion is a liberal education in itself.

WE have just enjoyed a brief visit to the battle fields of Antietam and Gettysburg, and we are impressed with the desirability of extending these school excursions so that they may include these famous localities. The trip could be made with facility and the slight additional expense could be met with no great self-denial.

The history of the war of the Rebellion is studied with ease and clearness, when we stand on the ground that felt the tread and was wet with the blood of our soldiers. The confused jumble of dates and events, the nebulous conception of campaigns and their issue, the vague location of battlefields, which most of us acknowledge, yield with surprising facility to an orderly idea of the general course of the War, a clear understanding of the strategy of a great campaign, and a precise location of the field of conflict, when we see the field with our own eyes.

Antietam is so near Washington that the roar of the guns was heard distinctly. Few realize that the danger line came so close to the Capital. It was a day of dreadful slaughter. The narrow sunken lane, the approaches to Burnside bridge, and the open fields where the clash of

battle came, were the scenes of awful carnage. In a few hours, by the help of the skilful guides, whose services are always available, the tour of the field can be made. Our government has erected tablets everywhere, marking the disposition of the forces, Confederate and Union, and describing the movements of the troops. Fine macadam roads have been constructed along the battle line, and approach is easy to every point of especial interest. Massachusetts men did their part nobly and our Commonwealth has erected a monument of chaste and beautiful design.

A few hours ride up the long slopes of the Blue Ridge mountains with ever widening views of the beautiful Cumberland valley, through the gap into the valley of the Susquehanna, brings one to Gettysburg. Only by a visit to the spot can the magnitude of that battle and the critical issues at stake for both armies be fully appreciated. General Lee had crossed the Potomac and was well on his way across Maryland and into Pennsylvania, before the Northern army was aware of his movements. Advancing rapidly, he was within sound of the bells of Harrisburg. Had he occupied this city, and it was wholly defenceless, he would have been within easy striking distance by railroad of Philadelphia and New York. It is said that England had given assurances of intervention, if the Confederate army should gain one substantial victory north of Mason and Dixon's line.

But before Lee could reap the fruit of his advance, the army of the North approached, threatening his line of communication with the South. He withdrew his forces, and planned to crush Gen. Meade's army. If he succeeded in this, Washington and the great cities of the North would be at his mercy and with the help of Great Britain, a victorious completion of the war was in sight. The stakes were tremendous. It was a death grapple for two mighty armies.

IT would be a thrilling and invaluable experience to young students of American history to go from point to point, see the fields where the first day's battle was fought, to the discomfiture of our forces, greatly outnumbered by their enemy, and then pass on to the south of the little town, where the deadly struggles of the second and third day occurred. Standing on Cemetery Ridge, where batteries still occupy the earthworks thrown up in those days, the charge of the Louisiana Tigers up the rugged slope, and the hand to hand fight on the crest, with clubbed muskets cannon rammers and stones and bare fists becomes a vivid experience. On Little Round Top, which commands a view of extraordinary breadth and beauty, we realize the seemingly impossible feat of arms involved in dragging batteries up through the woods to the summit and look down upon the Devil's Den and the Wheat Field, where thousands of brave men fell.

At the Bloody Angle, the ridge occupied by the Confederate batteries is a mile away over the sloping fields of grain. After an artillery fire of unparalleled fierceness, from out the woods yonder, came the solid ranks of infantry, marching as if for review, a sight of terrible magnificence, as they advanced deliberately into the jaws of death. A half mile from where we stand, the Northern batteries opened with solid shot and ploughed great lanes through that dense line. Grape and cannister did

their deadly work at shorter range. But that irresistible line, shattered and torn, but pressing on with quenchless enthusiasm, rushed up against the firing line, broke it for a moment, and then was overwhelmed. Pickett's Charge, the most dramatic and dreadful event of Gettysburg, will have a place in the memory of those who stand there today, with the defence of Thermopylae by Leonidas and his brave three hundred. Had General Lee's plan of an attack in the rear by his cavalry at the same moment that this desperate charge reached the Union line, been carried out successfully, the whole Northern army might have been vanquished.

The Roll of Honor reared at this point, the high water mark of the invading army, the six hundred monuments that dot the great battle fields, the Cemetery, hallowed by the thousands of graves and the glorious Dedication address of Abraham Lincoln, kindle patriotism and rouse sympathetic admiration for the courage and devotion of the thousands who laid down their young lives upon the field of blood.

But our boys and girls will learn here a better lesson, than this clear comprehension of great historic events, in their proper setting and full significance. They will realize the awfulness of War, the horrid sacrifice of precious lives and the measureless woe and misery, which it entails upon myriads of happy homes and millions of peaceful people. Military glory will always appeal to young men. To die for fatherland is sweet and glorious. Despite our Hague Conferences, nations fall quickly into thought and talk of war, when complications arise, and the mad rush to excel each other in building Dreadnoughts is unsettling to stable and unbroken peace. What better antidote to the War spirit in the minds of the coming generation can be conceived, than a visit to a great battlefield like this, where, under the solemn and sorrowful influence of the memories of suffering and death, there comes to every open mind, the vision of the higher glories of Peace, radiant in Light and Beauty, the friend of Life and Joy and all fruitful prosperity!

BUT apart from the more expensive school excursions, the historical pilgrimage to points of interest near at hand is an educational device, well worth the trying. Boston can be reached easily from a large proportion of the cities and towns of the Commonwealth and in case of the more remote towns and villages of western Massachusetts, the very difficulty of access may invite such a stay-at-home and stagnant habit, that a graduating class might be greatly profited by the broadening and stimulating effect of a few days' visit to Boston and its suburbs. Twice, recently, we have spent a few spare hours in the Old State house, and we have found it marvellously rich in its historic associations. The Council Chamber of the Royal Government is intact and the great round table about which the Council sat was witness of many thrilling scenes. Here Otis and Adams and Hancock spoke and the war of the Revolution had its birth. Here the printing press of Benjamin Franklin is preserved and many relics of years ago. Admission to this ancient building and to Faneuil Hall is free to all, and a slight fee admits to the Old South Church. The State House, the Public Library, the Navy Yard and Bunker Hill, the great Ocean steam ships, the bridges and parks, Harvard College close at hand with its wonderful museums, are all easily and cheaply reached. Why not economize in gowns and ribbons, flowers and music, and new graduating suits, and indulge in a class excursion to Boston, or Salem or Plymouth, or Lexington and Concord?

THE MASSACHVSETTS MAGAZINE

George Draper,
Governor Draper's Father

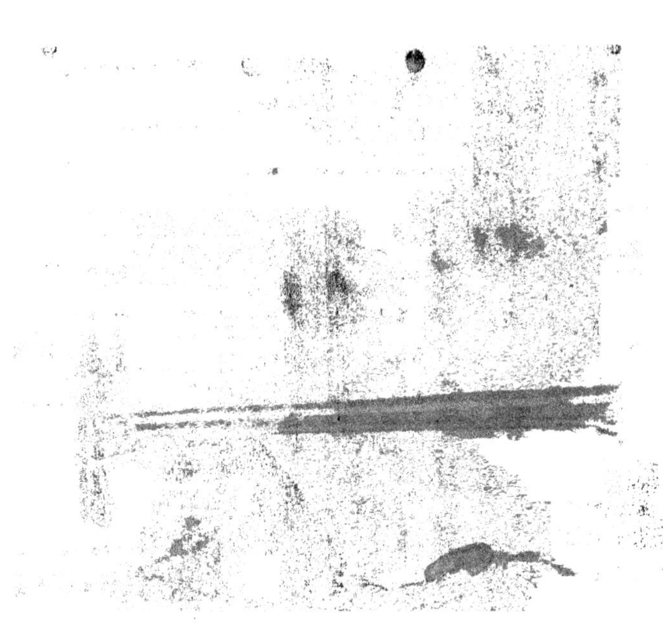

...rte y Magazine Devoted to History, Genealogy and Biography

THOMAS FRANKLIN WATERS, *Editor*. IPSWICH, MASS.

— *ASSOCIATE AND ADVISORY EDITORS* —

FRANK A. GARDNER, M.D. SALEM, MASS. CHARLES A. FLAGG WASHINGTON, D. C. JOHN N. MCCLINTOCK DORCHESTER, MASS. ALBERT W. DENNIS SALEM, MASS.

Issued in January, April, July and October. Subscription, $2.50 per year, Single copies 75c.

VOL. II JULY, 1909 NO. 3

Contents of this Issue.

ANCESTRY OF GOVERNOR EBEN S. DRAPER . *T. W.-M. Draper* . 123

WESTON . . . . *Colonel Daniel S. Lamson, John N. McClintock*. 129

COLONEL JOHN FELLOWS'S REGIMENT . . . *F. A. Gardner, M.D.* 141

SOME ARTICLES CONCERNING MASSACHUSETTS IN RECENT MAGAZINES . . . . *Charles A. Flagg* . 162

THE OLD RAND HOUSE . . . . *Caroline Rogers Hill* 165

DEPARTMENT OF THE AMERICAN REVOLUTION *F. A. Gardner, M. D.* 168

CRITICISM AND COMMENT 174

PILGRIMS AND PLANTERS . . . . *Lucie M. Gardner* . 176

OUR EDITORIAL PAGES . . . . *Thomas F. Waters* . 186

CORRESPONDENCE of a business nature should be sent to THE MASSACHUSETTS MAGAZINE, Salem, Mass.

CORRESPONDENCE in regard to contributions to the MAGAZINE may be sent to the editor, Rev. T. F. Waters, Ipswich, Mass., or to the office of publication, in Salem.

BOOKS for review may be sent to the office of publication in Salem. Books should not be sent to individual editors of the magazine, unless by previous correspondence the editor consents to review the book.

SUBSCRIPTION should be sent to THE MASSACHUSETTS MAGAZINE, Salem, Mass. Subscriptions are $2.50 payable in advance, post-paid to any address in the United States or Canada. To foreign countries in the Postal Union $2.75. Single copies of back numbers 75 cents each.

REMITTANCES may be made in currency or two cent postage stamps; many subscriptions are sent through the mail in this way, and they are seldom lost, but such remittances must be at the risk of the sender. To avoid all danger of loss send by post-office money order, bank check, or express money order.

CHANGES OF ADDRESS. When a subscriber makes a change of address he should notify the publishers, giving both his old and new addresses. The publishers cannot be responsible for lost copies, if they are not notified of such changes.

ON SALE. Copies of this magazine are on sale in *Boston*, at W. B. Clark's & Co., 26 Tremont Street, Old Corner Book Store, 29 Bromfield Street. Geo. E. Littlefield, 67 Cornhill, Smith & McCance, 38 Bromfield Street; in *New York*, at John Wanamaker's, Broadway 4th, 9th and 10th Streets; in *Philadelphia*, Am. Baptist Pub. Society, 1630 Chestnut Street; in *Washington*, at Brentanos, F & 13th St.; in *Chicago*, at A. C. McClurg's & Co., 221 Wabash Ave.; in *London*, at B. F. Stevens & Brown, 4 Trafalgar Sq. Also on sale at principal stands of N. E. News Co.

Entered as second-class matter March 13, 1908, at the post-office at Salem, Mass., under the act of Congress of March 3, 1879. Office of publication, 4 Central Street, Salem, Mass.

Contents of this Issue

Ancestry of Governor Eben S. Draper . . T

Weston . . . . Colonel Daniel S. Lamson, Jr.

Colonel John Fellows's Regiment . . . .

Articles Concerning Massachusetts

Recent Magazines C

The Old Rand House C

Department of the American Revolution F

Critici and Comment . . . . . .

Pilg and L

Our es . . . . . T

Correspondence of a business nature should be sent to The Mass

Correspondence in regard to contributions to the Magazine ma Waters, Ipswich, Mass., or to the office of publication, in Salem.

Books for review may be sent to the office of publication in Salem. B editors of the magazine, unless by previous correspondence the editor consen

Subscription should be sent to The Massachusetts Magazine. Sa payable in advance, post-paid to any address in the United States or Union \$2.25. Single copies of back . . . . ers 75 cents each.

Remittances may be made . . . . urrency or two cent postage stamps; the money this way, and they are a . . . . m lost, but such remittances must be a danger of loss send by post-office . . . . y order, bank check, or express money

Change of Address. When a subscriber makes a change of a giving both his old and new addr . . . The publishers cannot be respons lied of such change.

ANCESTRY OF GOVERNOR EBEN S. DRAPER

BY T. WALN-MORGAN DRAPER

JAMES DRAPER was the fourth son and fourth child of Thomas Draper of the Priory of Hepstonstall, Vicarage of Halifax, Yorkshire County, England; born Heptonstall 1618, died Roxbury July 1694; married Heptonstall, Apr. 21, 1646, Miriam, daughter of Gideon Stansfield and Grace Eastwood of Wadsworth, Yorkshire, who was born Heptonstall Nov. 27, 1625, died Roxbury, Mass., Jan. 1697.

Although James Draper is found in history as one of the original proprietors of the Town of Lancaster, there is no evidence that he ever lived there. His first residence was in Roxbury, and there Sarah, Susanna and James were born. He then moved into the adjoining town of Dedham, where his sons John, Moses and Daniel were born, but after some years, returned to his first home in Roxbury, where his youngest children, Patience and Jonathan were born, and where he and his wife died and are buried. In 1690, he was made a Freeman of Roxbury, which is now included within the corporate limits of the City of Boston, yet still preserves its rural aspect, and many of its old landmarks. James was also for a short time in Charlestown, Mass., where he sold to Jonathan Carey part of an orchard in 1672. (Deed recorded 1684), and he was notified there in 1676.

The following official records, bearing upon James Draper's career and the final settlement and division of his estate, are of great interest to his descendants.

Petition of Widow Miriam to Judge of Probate Court Suffolk Co. Mass. No. 2387.

"As the Honorable Wm. Houghton Esq. Judge of Probate is informed that I am leaft a widow throu God's providence therefore I do desire that my youngest son Jonathan Draper with my Eldest son James Draper may have adminestraytion granted unto them one the Estate of my deseased Husbands Estate I being agad and Crosey and not able to forto undertack a invuny.

Miriam Draper. M
her mark

John Alldis.
Jonathan Whiting.

Administration Bond of James Draper. Aug. 19, 1697. Know all men by these presents That We, James Draper, Jonathan Draper, John Davis. Yeoman, and Joseph Warren, Carpenter, all of Roxbury within the County of Suffolk—within his Majestys Province of the Massachusetts Bay in New England and holden and stand firmly bound and obliged unto William Houghton Esq. Judge of the Probate of Wills and Granting Administration within the said County of Suffolk, in the full sum of Four Hundred pounds currant money in New England. To be paid unto the said William Houghton his successors in the said Office or Assignes. To the true payment whereof, we do bind ourselves, our heirs, Executors and Administrators jointly and severally firmly by these presents. Sealed with our Seals. Dated the nineteenth day of August Anno Domini 1697.

Children

6. Miriam, born Heptonstall, Eng. Feb. 7, 1646–7, died England in infancy.
7. Susanna, born Roxbury, Mass., about 1650, married Charlestown, Mass., John Bacon, 1668.
8. Sarah, born Roxbury, Mass., 1652, married May 19, 1669, James Hadlock. Child:—1. Sarah, born Roxbury Dec. 16, 1670. Baptized as an adult Oct. 24, 1686, married about 1686, John Marcy. They had 8 sons and 3 daughters.
9. James, born Roxbury, Mass. 1564, died Roxbury, Apr. 30, 1698.
10. John, born Dedham 24th day of 4th month, 1656, died Dedham, Apr. 5, 1749.
11. Moses, born Dedham, Sept. 26, 1663, died Boston, Aug. 14, 1693.
12. Daniel born Dedham, May 30, 1665, died Dedham.
13. Patience, born Roxbury Mass. Aug. 17, 1668. married Mar. 13, 1689, Ebenezer Cass of Boston.
14. Jonathan, born Roxbury, Mass. Mar. 10, 1670, died Roxbury. Feb. 28, 1746–7.

9. James, fourth child, eldest son of James Draper and Miriam Stansfield, of Roxbury, Mass., married by Rev. Mr. Walter Feb 18, 1681, to Abigail, daughter of Nathaniel Whiting and Hannah Dwight, of Dedham. She was born Roxbury, June 7, 1663, and died there, Oct. 25, 1721. She was a granddaughter of John Dwight, from whom President Timothy Dwight of Yale and other prominent men are descended.

He was a soldier in the King Philip War during the year 1675. James had received from his father part of his farm at Roxbury. This he subsequently sold to John Aldis.

Children

15. Abigail, born Roxbury, Mass. Dec. 29, 1681, married James Griggs.
17. Nathaniel, born Roxbury, Mass. Apr. 2 1684, died Dec. 30, 1721.
17. William, born Roxbury, Mass. May 15, 1686, died young
18. Eunice, born Roxbury, Mass. June 5, 1689, married Nathaniel Aldis, June 24, 1708. She died June 13, 1714.
19. James, born 1691, died Apr. 24, 1768.
20. Gideon, born Roxbury, Mass. 1694
21. Ebenezer, born Roxbury, Mass. Apr. 27, 1698, died Attleboro June 3. 1784.

19. James, fifth child, third son of James Draper and Abigail Whiting, married 1st: May 2, 1716, Rachel, daughter of John and Mary Aldis. She was born Mar. 15, 1690, died May 16, 1717. He married 2dly: Nov. 12, 1719, Abigail, daughter of Joshua Child and Elizabeth Morris of Brookline, Mass. She was born 1698, died Nov. 23, 1767. She was a sister of Dorothy who married Ebenezer Draper.

James Draper was a Captain in the Trained Bands; was elected a Selectman in 1746 to serve one year, and again in 1756, to serve two years. He was a prosperous man, a large land owner, prominent in the affairs of the town of Dedham, and highly respected.

Child by first wife

22. John, born Jan. 29, 1716, baptized Mar 10, 1717, died Mar. 10, 1717.

Children by 2nd wife

23. James, born Stoughton, Sept. 22, 1720, died Spencer, Mar. 2, 1781.
24. Abigail, born Stoughton, Dec. 12, 1721, died Spencer, Nov. 3, 1817.
25. John 2d, born Stoughton, June 16, 1723, died Dedham, Nov. 8, 1745.

15. Abigail, born Roxbury, Dec. 29, 1

17. Nathaniel, born Roxbury, Mass. Apr. 2

17. William born oxbury May 15, 1

18. Eunice, born Roxbury, Mass. June 5, 1
June 24, 1708. She died June 18, 171

19. James, born 1691 died Apr. 24, 1708.

20. Gideon, born Roxbury, Mass. 1

21. Ebenezer, born Roxbury, Apr. 27,

1784.

19. James, fifth child, third son of James married 1st: May 2, 1716, Rachel, daughter o was born Mar. 15, 1690, died May 16, 1717. He Abigail, daughter of Joshua Child and Elizabe She was born 1698, died Nov. 28, 1767. She married Ebenezer Draper.

| James Draper was Capta n in the d man n 1746 to serve and again in 1 was a prosperous man, a large land owner, prom of Dedham, and highly respected.

Child by first wife

22. John, born Jan. 29, 1716, baptized Mar. 1

Children by 2nd wi

23. James, born Stoughton, Sept. 22, 1720,

24. Abigail, born Stoughton, Dec. 12, 1721,

26. Joshua, born Stoughton, Dec. 25, 1724, died Spencer, Oct. 27, 1792.
27. Josiah, born Stoughton, Apr. 3, 1726, died Aug. 18, 1726.
27a. Josiah 2d, born Stoughton, Sept. 12, 1727 (no record of his death.)
28. Rebecca, born Stoughton, June 30, 1729, died Spencer, Jan. 30, 1820.
29. Mary, born Stoughton, Sept. 24, 1731.
30. Abijah, born Dedham, July 13, 1734, died Nov. 18, 1734.
31. Abijah 2d, born Dedham, July 11, 1735, died Feb. 13, 1737.
32. Abijah 3d, born Dedham, May 10, 1737, died Dedham, May 1, 1780.
33. Samuel, born Dedham, Dec. 5, 1740, died Nov. 29, 1750.

32. Abijah, eleventh child, eighth son of James Draper and Abigail Child, of Dedham, married 1st: Alice, daughter of John Eaton and Elizabeth Lovering, of Purgatory, Dedham, Apr. 8, 1762. She was born Jan. 31, 1741, died Jan. 22, 1777. He married 2dly: Mar. 25, 1778, Desire, the widow of Nathaniel Metcalf. She was the daughter of Ebenezer Foster and Desire Cushman, born Attleboro, Aug. 12, 1746, died Dedham, Oct. 23, 1815.

Abijah Draper and both wives are buried in the cemetery in Dedham village.

He succeeded his father, Captain James Draper in his landed estate at Green Lodge, Dedham. He was an active and energetic man, of large executive ability, public spirited and always ready to take part in every public enterprise. He was one of three chosen by the citizens of Dedham to erect a monument to William Pitt, in 1766. The base of this monument still exists in Dedham village, and is called "Pillar of Liberty."

Mr. Draper held every office in the Militia up to that of Major, and commanded in the latter capacity, a body of minute men at Roxbury, under Washington. While on duty there he was exposed to the small-pox, and probably carried it to his home on one of his furloughs, as his first wife, Alice, died of that disease.

Children by Alice

34. Abijah, born June 11, 1763, died Dec. 1774.
35. Ira, born Dec. 24, 1764, died Jan. 22, 1848.
36. Rufus, born Nov. 27, 1766, died Nov. 18, 1788, at Norfolk, Va.
37. James, born Apr. 14, 1769, died Jan. 22, 1777.
38. Alice, born Apr. 13, 1771, died Jan. 27, 1852.
39. Abijah 2d, born September 22, 1775, died March 26, 1836.

Child by second wife

40. Lendamine, born Mar. 30, 1780, died Oct. 26, 1823.

35. Ira, second child and second son of Major Abijah Draper and Alice Eaton, married 1st: May 31, 1786, Lydia, daughter of Lemuel and Rebecca Richards. She was born Jan. 1768, died Sept. 18, 1811. He married 2dly: Mar. 9, 1812, Abigail, called Nabbie, his first wife's sister. She was born Sept. 12, 1783, died 1847.

In 1775, during the retreat of the British after the battle of Lexington and Concord Bridge, he was present with his father, who had taken part in the fighting. During the early part of the century, he removed from Dedham to Weston, Mass., and later to Saugus. Beginning life with a handsome property for the time, he expended most of it in the care and education of his sixteen children, and also in the development of his mechanical inventions, which proved more profitable to the community than to himself. He is said to have invented the first threshing machine of which there is any record, but it was never introduced extensively. He also invented the "fly shuttle hand loom," which possessed decided advantages it was believed, over those then in use. He invented the first machine for road scraping, and machines of this identical pattern were in use very recently in the vicinity of Boston. His invention which came into most general use, was the "revolving temple" for keeping cloth extended in weaving. This was adopted in the larger part of the looms both in this country and abroad, and formed the basis of a profitable business, which was carried on by himself, his sons, grandsons, and great-grandsons. Under the administration of John Quincy Adams he was a prominent candidate for U. S. Commissioner of Patents He was a man of large natural intelligence, mechanical ingenuity, and progressive thought. He was one of the early Unitarians and died in that faith

Children by first wife, all born in Dedham

41. James, born May 28, 1781, died Dec. 5, 1870.
42. Ira, born Jan. 4, 1789, died June 18, 1845.
43. Rufus, born Aug. 30, 1790, died in infancy.
44. A daughter born Aug. 7, 1791, died in infancy.
45. A son born Dec. 17, 1793, died in infancy.
46. Lucy Chickering born 1797, died Sept. 15, 1801.
47. Rufus Foster, born July 12, 1800, died 1841.
48. Abijah, born Jan. 5, 1802, died Oct. 4, 1802.
49. Abijah 2d, born Nov. 15, 1803, died Oct. 4, 1828, married Mary———; one child that died in infancy.

Children by second wife

50. Ebenezer Daggett, born June 13, 1813, died Oct. 20, 1887.
51. Lydia, born Mar. 31, 1815, died Apr. 3, 1847.
52. George, born Aug. 16, 1817, died June 7, 1887.
53. Abigail, born Oct. 24, 1819, died July 22, 1847, married William W. Cook, Feb. 2, 1842. Child: A son, born May 10, 1844, died June 9, 1846. Mr. Cook married 2dly: her niece, Nancy Marion.
54. Lemuel Richards, born Saugus, Dec. 1, 1823; die Jan. 10, 1891.
55. Lucy Rebecca, born Dec. 22, 1826; died July 1, 1827.

52. George, second son and third child of Ira Draper and his second wife, Nabby Richards, married Hannah, daughter of Benjamin and Anna Thwing of Uxbridge, Mar. 6 1839. She was born Jan. 1, 1817, died Dec. 30, 1883. He married 2dly: Mrs. Parmelia B. Blunt of Milford, Mass.

George Draper was born in Weston, Mass. Up to his 15th year he lived there, and in Saugus, Mass., on his father's farm, attending school winters and doing farm work summers. Though his years of schooling were brief, he acquired at school, and in later studies at home, a most excellent mathematical education, better than that possessed by most college graduates. At the age of fifteen he left home to take a position under his brother in the weaving department of the cotton mills at North Uxbridge, Mass. He remained there two years, and then was made superintendent and manager of a small cotton mill at Walpole, Mass. From there, he went to Three Rivers, Mass., becoming overseer of weaving in what was then one of the largest fine mills in the country. While there he devised an improvement in the temple for weaving, which had been invented by his father, and placed the same in the hands of his brother, Ebenezer D. Draper, who made a business of making and selling it. In 1839, owing to a general depression in manufacturing business, caused by a progressive reduction of the tariff, he was thrown out of employment, in common with a large part of the skilled operatives in New England.

He looked vainly for work as an overseer or superintendent, used up his small savings, ran into debt several hundred dollars, and finally accepted a position as an operator in the Massachusetts Cotton Mills of Lowell, at the remuneration of $5.00 per week. His experience at that time convinced him of the advantage to laboring men of a protective tariff, and he never forgot it.

In 1843 he accepted a position as designer of the celebrated Edward Harris cassimeres at Woonsocket, R. I. In 1845 he was appointed superintendent of one of the mills of the Otis Company, at Ware, Mass., and later had charge of the entire corporation. In 1853 he removed from Ware to Hopedale, Mass., forming a partnership with his brother, Ebenezer D. Draper, and soon after joined the Hopedale Community. In 1855, when the community broke up as a financial institution, he joined his brother, E. D. Draper, in guaranteeing and paying its debts. From this time his career was one of uninterrupted material prosperity. His business increased until it became one of the most important in the State. In 1868 his brother, E. D. Draper, retired, and he took into partnership his oldest son, William F. Draper, and later his sons, George A. and Eben S. Draper, and two of his grandsons.

Children

56. William F., born Apr. 9, 1842, at Lowell, Mass.
57. Georgiana T., born June 30, 1844, Lowell, Mass., died July 23, 1844.
58. Helen L., born July 11, 1845, Lowell, Mass., died Aug. 10, 1847.
59. Frances E., born July 26, 1847, Ware.
60. A son, born Dec. 15, 1850, died in infancy.
61. Hannah T., born Apr. 11, 1853, Ware.
62. George A., born Nov. 4, 1855, Hopedale.
63. Eben S., born June 17, 1858, Hopedale.

largest fine mills in the country. While there he devi
the temple for weaving, which had been invented b
the same in the hands of his brother, Ebenezer D
business of making and selling it. In 1839, owing to
manufacturing business caused by a progressive red
was thrown out of employment, in common with a l
operatives in New England.

He looked vainly for work as an overseer or supe
small savings ran into debt several hundred dollars,
position as an operator in the Massachusetts Cotton
remuneration of $5.00 per week. His experience at tl
of the advantage to laboring men of a protective t
got it.

In 1843 he accepted a position as designer of the cel
cassimeres at Woonsocket, R. I. In 1845 he was ap
of one of the mills of the Otis Company, at Ware, Mas
of the entire corporation. In 1853 he removed fro
Mass., forming a partnership with his brother, Ebene
after joined the Hopedale Community. In 1856, whe
up as a financial institution, he joined his brother, E.
teeing and paying its debts. From this time his car
rupted material prosperity. His business increased
the most important in the State. In 1868 his brother
and he took into partnership his oldest son, William
his sons, George A. and Eben S. Draper, and two of

Children

56. William F., born Apr. 9, 1842, at Lowell, Mass
57. Georgiana T., born June 30, 1844, Lowell, Mass.
58. Helen L., born July 11, 1845, Lowell, Mass., died
59. Frances E., born July 26, 1847, Ware.
60. A son, born Dec. 15, 1850, died in infancy
61. Hannah T., born Apr. 11, 1853, Ware.
62. George A., born Nov. 4, 1855, Hopedale.
63. Eben S., born June 17, 1858, Hopedale.

WESTON

By Colonel Daniel S. Lamson and John N. McClintock

Weston was a part of the ancient town of Watertown, and its history begins with the settlement of the Massachusetts Bay Colony in 1630, when Sir Richard Saltonstall, Mr. Phillips and their company located here. It is possible, however, that the Northmen may have attempted a settlement in this vicinity centuries before, and Spanish or French colonists or traders may have preceded the Puritans. The site of an ancient settlement at the former head of navigation on the Charles River has been marked by a massive and graceful tower, built by Professor Eben Norton Hosford.

For nearly a century after its first settlement the territory of Weston was referred to as the Farms; and with propriety it might be so called to this day, or even more appropriately the Park; for throughout the town the farms and the roads apparently form an ancient park of great beauty, where every prospect is pleasing. The old roads, laid out by the founders with good judgment, have been improved by labor and care extending over nearly three centuries; bordering walls are often works of art; concrete sidewalks through lonely reaches are surprises; groves of trees almost primeval are a delight; and broad fields without a stone in sight give evidence of years of loving toil.

The first allotment of farms in Weston was made in 1638, the year in which the bounds between Watertown and Dedham were established (the present line between Weston and Wellesley); and Jeremiah Norcross, Thomas Mayhew and John Whitney are the first recorded land-owners. In 1642 among the proprietors of Weston were Bryan Pendleton, Daniel Patrick, Simon Eire, John Stowers, Abraham Browne, John Whitney, Edward How, Jeremiah Norcross and Thomas Mayhew.

Weston was on the frontier of Watertown until 1651, when Sudbury was incorporated to the west, and the present line between Weston and Natick and between Weston and Wayland was established. In 1663 the so-called "Land of Contention," situated in the southwestern part of Weston, was resurveyed. In 1673 Lieut. Nathan Fiske bought 220 acres of land of Thomas Underwood in the northern part of Weston.

The Town was incorporated in 1712; and save for the set-off and incorporation of the northern part as a part of the Town of Lincoln, in 1754, the ancient boundaries of the town have remained practically unchanged. It has been in Middlesex County since the county was organized.

The oldest house in Weston, for many years the home of Oliver R. Robbins, now the home of William H. Hill, stands on Wellesley and Chestnut streets, and is said to have been built about 1690. The cellar of Herbert Seaverns house on Park street is said to have been built by his ancestor in 1695.

In 1695 the proprietors ordered the building of the first church in town, a building thirty feet square, on land given by Nathaniel Coolidge, Sr., and situated a few rods south and east of the corner of Central Avenue and School Street, where services were first held in 1700. In 1701 Rev. Joseph Morse, Harv. Coll. 1695, was called to preach, the precinct agreeing to build him a house; but difficulties arose, and Mr. Morse settled elsewhere. Rev. William Williams accepted a call to preach in town in 1709 and was settled the next year, when the church was organized.

The first members of the Weston church were:

Nathaniel Coolidge,	Thomas Flagg,	Joseph Lovell,
John Parkhurst,	John Livermore,	Francis Fullam,
Abel Allen,	Ebenezer Allen,	Francis Pierce,
Joseph Jones,	Thomas Wright,	Joseph Allen,
Josiah Jones, Jr.,	Joseph Woolson,	Joseph Livermore,
Joseph Allen, Jr.,	Josiah Livermore,	Samuel Seaverns,
George Robinson.		

The first book of Town records, covering a period of nearly sixty years (1695–1754), has disappeared; but the records of the church are very complete and of great value.

In 1721 Benjamin Brown, Benoni Garfield, Ebenezer Allen, Joseph Allen and James Jones were a committee to complete the new meeting-house. Rev. Samuel Woodward was minister from 1751 to 1782. Rev. Dr. Samuel Kendall was the minister from 1783 to 1814: Rev. Dr. Joseph Field from 1815 to 1869: Rev. Dr. Edmund H. Sears from 1869 to 1876: Rev. Charles F. Russell from 1882 to present time. The five, whose ministry covered a period of 167 years, died in town and were buried in the town cemetery.

In 1800 the meeting-house underwent thorough repairs, a steeple and two porches were added, and a new bell was bought of Paul Revere. In 1840 the second house was built. The present noble structure occupied by the ancient church was dedicated in 1888.

The first Baptists in Weston began to gather in 1776 under the lead of Deacon Oliver Hastings; the meeting-house was completed in 1788; and the church was organized in 1789. They had no settled minister until 1811, when they united with the church in Framingham and settled Rev. Charles Train as pastor. The union was severed in 1826 when the membership was about fifty. The present Baptist church building was built in 1828, Mr. Hews giving the land, and Mrs. Bryant contributing $1,000. Rev. Timothy P. Ropes (Waterville Coll.), was the first settled pastor, followed in 1835 by Rev. Joseph Hodges, Jr., in 1840 by Rev. Origen Cram, in 1854 by Rev. Calvin H. Topliff, in 1867 by Rev. Luther G. Barrett, in 1870 by Rev. Alonzo F. Benson, in 1875 by Rev. Amos Harris.

The Methodists of Weston began to gather about 1794, building a small chapel in the rear of present church. The first trustees were Abraham Bemis, Habbakuck Stearns, Jonas Bemis, John Viles and Daniel Stratton. The present church was erected in 1828, and in 1833 it became a regular station with a regularly appointed preacher.

Between 1893 and 1901 Weston published four volumes of the early records of the church and town, edited by Mary Frances Pierce, which gives all births, marriages and deaths from 1709 to a recent date, beside much other matter of historical interest. These records show that of the ancestors of present Weston families, other than the founders of the first church, John Warren was in Weston in 1709; Benjamin Brown, in 1711; Jonathan Bigelow, 1713; Benjamin Harrington, 1714; John Train, in 1715; Nathaniel Morse, in 1717; Thomas Upham, in 1722; Enock Stratton, in 1725; Isaac Hager, in 1726; Josiah Hobbs, in 1731; John Hastings, in 1735.

In 1700, the pioneer John Lamson came from Reading and settled in Weston, founding a family that for two centuries has been prominent in the military, civil and social history of the town, represented today by Colonel Daniel S. Lamson whose house, built during the War of the Revolution, was honored by a visit paid by President Washington to Mrs. Lamson, the wife of an officer in the Continental Army.

When the town was incorporated in 1712 it had a population of about 1,000. Next to the minister perhaps the most important man in town at the time was Honorable Francis Fullam, a judge from 1719 to 1755, who besides presiding as chief justice on the bench, served as a Colonel in the militia and a member of the Council. His son, Sergeant Jacob Fullam, was killed in 1725 in the expedition under command of Captain John Lovewell against the Indians of northern New England.

In 1675, John Parkkurst, Michael Flagg, John Whitney, Jr., George

Harrington, Jacob Ballard, Nathaniel Hely, and John Bigelow, all of "Weston Farms" served in King Philip's War. The Indians burned a barn in the northern part of the town in the following year, but did no further damage.

The men of Weston did their duty in the French and Indian War, 1735 to 1760, in camp and on the field of battle. Through the town led the thoroughfares to the frontiers over which went the soldiers and the munitions of warfare from the seaboard; and the Commonwealth then as now aided in maintaining highways of travel.

A hundred men from the town took up arms on the day of the Lexington alarm, and attacked the invading British force on their retreat from Concord. Many served until the close of the war, winning honor and renown. The roll of the Weston Company is as follows:

Captain, Samuel *Lamson;**
Lieutenants, *John Fiske,*
Matthew Hobbs;
Sergeants, Josiah Steadman,
Josiah Severn,
John Wright,
Abraham Hewes;
Corporals, Abijah Steadman,
Simon Smith,
Drummer, Samuel Nutting;
Privates, Nathan *Hager,*
John Allen, Jr.,
William Hobart,
Abijah *Warren,*
Isaac Cory,
David *Sanderson,*
Samuel Underwood,
Josiah Corey,
Thomas Rand, Jr.,
Nathl. Parkhurst,
Wm. Whitney,
Benjamin *Pierce,*
David *Livermore,*
Thomas Corey,
Jonas Underwood,
John Stimpson,
Jonathan *Stratton,*
John *Warren,* Jr.,
Micah *Warren*
Isaac *Flagg,*
James *Jones,*
Abraham *Harrington,*
Eben Brackett,
Reuben *Hobbs,*
Benjamin Dudley,
Samuel *Fiske,*
Abraham *Sanderson,*
David Fuller,
Jonas Harrington (3),
Roger *Bigelow,*
Converse *Bigelow,*
Thomas Williams,
Isaac Bullard,
Jonathan *Warren,*
John Frost,
Isaac Walker,
Amos *Jones,*
John Walker, Jr.,
Oliver Curtis,
Thomas Rand,
William Lawrence,
Elias *Bigelow,*
Benjamin *Rand,*
Saml. Child,
Jacob Parmenter,
Elijah Kingsbury,
William Pierce,
Increase *Leadbetter,*

* Family names italicized are borne by Weston families today.

[…] A hundred men from the town took up arms on the day of the Lexi[…]
[…]rm, and attacked the invading British force on their retreat from Con[…]
[…]any served until the close of the war, winning honor and renown.
[…]l of the Weston Company is as follows:

[…]ptain, Samuel Lamson;*
[…]eutenants, John Fiske,
Matthew Hobbs;
[…]rgeants, Josiah Steadman,
Josiah Severn,
John Wright,
Abraham Hews;
[…]porals, Abijah Steadman,
Simon Smith.
[…]ummer, Samuel Nutting[…]
[…]vates, Nathan Hager, Jonathan Stratton, Isaac Bullard
John Allen, Jr., John Warren, Jr., Jonat[…] Warren
William Hobbs, Micah Warren, John [illegible]t,
Abijah Warren, Isaac Flagg, Walker,
Isaac Cory, James Jones, Jones,
David Sanderson, Abraham Harrington, John [illegible]r, Jr.
Samuel Underwood, Eben Brackett, Oliver Curtis,
Josiah Corey, Reuben Hobbs, Thomas
Thomas Rand, Jr., Benjamin Dudley,
Nath'l Parkhurst, Samuel Fiske, Elias Bigelow,
Wm. Whitney, Abraham Sanderson, Benjamin R[illegible]d,
Benjamin Pierce, David Fuller, Saml. Child,
David Livermore, Jonas Harrington (3), Jacob Parmenter,
Thomas Corey, Roger Bigelow, Elijah Kingsbury,
Jonas Underwood, Converse Bigelow, William [illegible]erce,
John Stimpson, Thomas Williams

Elisha Stratton,	Isaac *Hobbs*,	Benjamin Bancroft,
Daniel Twitchel,	William Bond, Jr.,	John Flint,
John Norcross ,	William Carey,	John Bemis,
Daniel Lawrence,	Jedh. *Bemis*,	Lemuel Stimpson,
Samuel *Train*, Jr.,	Josiah Allen, Jr.,	Daniel Benjamin,
Joseph Whitney,	Josh. Steadman,	Jonas Pierce,
Nathl. Boynton,	Eben Phillips,	Jedh. Wheeler,
Benjamin *Pierce*, Jr.,	John *Pierce*,	William Jones,
John Gould,	John *Lamson*,	Soln. Jones,
Phineas Hager,	Paul Coolidge,	Samuel Taylor,
Josh. Lovewell,	Peter Carey,	Thadeus Fuller,
Joseph Pierce,	Saml. Woodward,	Elijah Allen,
Hezekh. Wyman,	Ebenr. Steadman,	William Bond,
Joel Smith,	Joseph Jennison,	Moses Pierce,
Daniel Bemis,	Benjamin Stratton,	Amos Parkhurst.

The Weston artillery company also served that day, comprising:

tain Israel Whitemore, Lieutenant Josiah Bigelow, Lieut. John George,

ates, John Whitehead,	John Pownell,	Nathan *Weston*,
Joseph Russell,	Nathan Smith,	John Flagg,
Jonathan Lawrence,	James Smith, Jr.,	Thaddeus Garfield,
Alpheus Bigelow, and Thomas Russell.		

The remarkable thing about this list of names is that it numbers about that of the voting population of Weston in 1775 and, so slow is the change wnership in town, it includes the ancestors of very many of the present ents in town.

s in the War of the Revolution, the men of Weston did their duty in Civil War. They numbered 126; of these, eight were killed, three died of nds, and one died at Andersonville prison. A tablet to perpetuate the ory of the dead heroes is erected in Weston's beautiful town library.

side from General Charles J. Paine, Colonel Daniel S. Lamson and Asses- orporal Henry L. Brown, Francis B. Ripley, Oliver L. Sherburne, Almon ht, Jason Wright, George E. Hobbs, John H. Stone, Chas. A. Deane, Hosea F. Traverse are the only veterans of the Union Army living in on in 1909.

he population of Weston in 1860 was 1,243; and the town raised about 00.00 as a war tax. The town debt was paid many years ago; and the nt tax rate is very low; while the present valuation is in excess of $6,000,- with a voting list of 410.

Benjamin Bancroft
John Flint,
John Bemis,
Lemuel Stimpson,
Daniel Benjamin,
Jonas Pierce,
Jedh. Wheeler,
William Jones,
Soln. Jones,
Samuel Taylor,
Thadeus Fuller,
Elijah Allen,
William d,
Moses Pi rce,

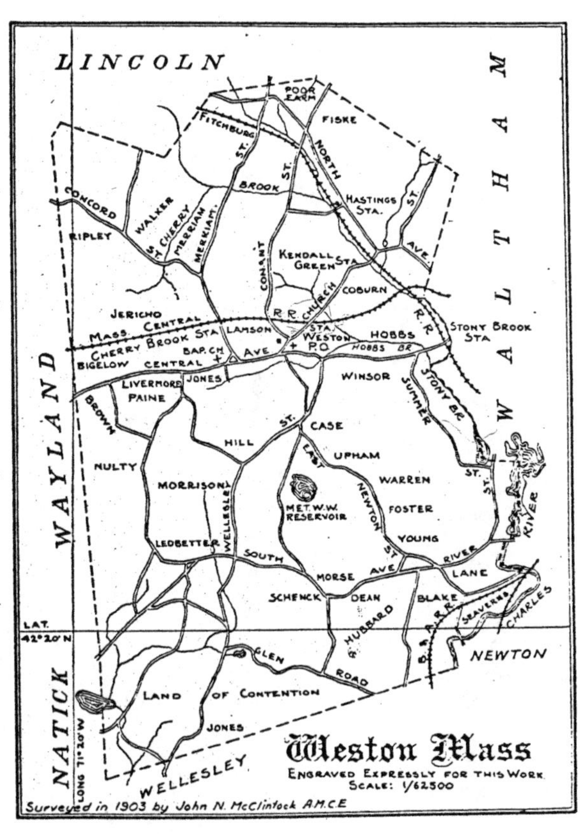
LINCOLN
WALTHAM
WAYLAND
NATICK
WELLESLEY
NEWTON
POOR FARM
FISKE
FITCHBURG
NORTH
ST.
BROOK
HASTINGS STA.
AVE
CONCORD
RIPLEY
WALKER
CHERRY
MERRIAM
CONANT
KENDALL GREEN STA.
COBURN
CHURCH
JERICHO
MASS. CENTRAL R.R.
CHERRY BROOK STA.
LAMSON
STA. WESTON
P.O.
HOBBS
HOBBS BR.
STONY BROOK STA
BAP. CH.
BIGELOW
CENTRAL
AVE
JONES
LIVERMORE
PAINE
BROWN
WINSOR
SUMMER
STONY BR.
CASE
HILL
NULTY
MORRISON
WELLESLEY
EAST
UPHAM
WARREN
NEWTON
FOSTER
MET. W.W. RESERVOIR
YOUNG
LEDBETTER
SOUTH
RIVER
CHARLES
MORSE
LANE
SCHENCK
DEAN
BLAKE
HUBBARD
SEAVERNS
B. & A. R.R.
LAT. 42°20′ N
LONG 71°20′ W
GLEN
ROAD
LAND OF CONTENTION
JONES
Weston Mass
Engraved Expressly for this Work
Scale: 1/62500
Surveyed in 1903 by John N. McClintock A.M.C.E

The Main Road or Central Avenue of Weston is of great antiquity. For many years it was a part of the post-road leading from Boston south and west, a thoroughfare of great importance, a county road, and finally a State highway. Many taverns along the way, some still standing, cared for the passing traveller and his horse, or the rattling stage-coach, in the eighteenth century and the early years of the nineteenth. At the sign of the Golden Ball, landlord Jones welcomed the officers of the British garrison stationed in Boston before the Revolution to overawe the American colonies, and won fame as a good provider. At Capt. John Flagg's tavern President Washington was entertained. Along the dusty way, Burgoyne's army marched as prisoners of war, and encamped one night by the wayside. The house later occupied by Mrs. A. H. Fiske was built in 1753 by the Rev. Samuel Woodward, who is said to have shouldered a gun and marched with the men of Weston to the aid of their Concord and Lexington neighbors, in 1775.

In 1765 Abraham Hews established a pottery in Weston, probably the first industry of its kind in New England, and the business was continued by several generations of the founder's descendants, until 1871, when the business was removed to Cambridge. Josiah Hobbs established a tannery in 1730, or later, which was maintained for many years. The waters of Stony Brook were utilized in 1679 by Richard Child for a grist-mill and later a saw-mill. The grist-mill stood until 1840. The property was bought in 1831 by Coolidge & Sibley, who erected a machine-shop for the manufacture of cotton machinery and looms and supplied the factories of Lowell, Lawrence, Clinton, Lancaster, and factories outside the state. The power was abandoned when Cambridge came to Weston for a water supply. The organ factory was established near Kendall Green by F. H. Hastings in 1888, the business having been begun in Salem in 1827 by Elias Hook. The Ralph Kenney chair factory for school goods is near the center of the town.

Weston has a system of graded schools, well maintained, and provides transportation for scholars to and from school from every section. The roads are lighted at night by electricity. Water from Clinton passes through the town to the Metropolitan District, being impounded in a large reservoir. There are two private water companies in town, and Cambridge draws largely from the territory for her water supply.

The town has a perfect set of assessors' plans, showing every lot in town, a uniformed police force, a poor-house, where there is generally one wreck of humanity, no electric-car lines, and a body of sturdy yeomen ready, as were their ancestors in olden times, to defend their rights and to uphold the law.

entertaine ... usty way. Burgoyne's army
war, and encamped one night by the wayside. The
Mrs. A. H. Fiske was built in 1753 by the Rev. Sa
said to have shouldered a gun and marched with th
aid of Concord and ngton neighbors, in 1

In 1765 Abraham Hews established a pottery i
first industry of its kind New England, and the
by several generations of the founder's descendant
business was removed to Cambridge. Josiah Holt
in 1730, or later, which was maintained for many yea
Brook were utilized in 1670 by Richard Child for a g
mill. The grist-mill stood until 1840. The property
Coolidge & Sibley, who erected a machine shop for th
machinery and looms and supplied the factories of Lo
Lancaster, and factories outside the state. The pow
Cambridge came to Weston for a water supply. The
lished near Kendall Green by F. H. Hastings in 18
been begun in Salem in 1827 by Hook. Th
tory for school goods is near the center of the

Weston has a system of graded schools, well m
transportation for scholars to and from school fr
roads are lighted at night by electricity. Water fro
the town to the Metropolitan District, being impoun
There are two private water companies in town, and
from the territory for her water supply.

The town has a perfect set of assessors' plans, sho
a uniformed police force, a poor-house, where here
of humanity, no electric-car lines, and a body of s
were their ancestors in olden times, to defend their

As in the past the chief business carried on in Weston is agriculture at the present time, and the male population is composed for the most part of farmers, although many of the landowners are engaged in professional work or business elsewhere.

GENEALOGY AND BIOGRAPHY

In the history of a New England town, chief interest attaches to the record of individuals and families; and who at different epochs, have been conspicuous in public affairs. The present board of Town officials is especially interesting.

Francis Blake, Chairman of the Board of Selectmen, has been elected continuously to the Board since 1890 and since 1900, he has been Chairman. He was born in 1850 in Needham, near Newton Lower Falls, the son of Francis and Caroline Burling (Trumbull) Blake; the grandson of the Hon. Francis Blake, of Worcester, an eminent lawyer, and also the grandson of George Augustus Trumbull, of Worcester; and a descendant in the eighth generation from William and Agnes Blake, who came from Somersetshire, England, in 1636, and settled in Milton, becoming prominent in colonial affairs.

In 1866 his uncle, Commodore George Smith Blake, secured for him an appointment in the service of the United States Coast Survey, in which he acquired the scientific education that has led to his membership in later years in many learned societies. His ability was recognized in his early promotion to the rank of Assistant.

In 1873 he married Elizabeth L., daughter of Charles T. Hubbard, and became a resident of Weston, settling and building on his estate, "Keewaydin." In April, 1878, he resigned from the Coast Survey; and in the following November he disclosed to the world the "Blake Transmitter," an invention that perfected the Bell Telephone and made it of great commercial value and of unbounded usefulness. In 1902 he received the honorary degree of A.M. from Harv. Coll. His children are:

Agnes Blake, born 1876; married 1906, Stephen Salisbury Fitz Gerald.

Benjamin Sewall Blake, born 1877; Harv. Coll. 1901; married 1908, Ruth Field.

Nathan S. Fiske, selectman and assessor, lives on the farm bought by his ancestor, Lieut. Nathan Fiske, in 1673.

CUTTING FAMILY

George Warren Cutting, son of Ephraim (b. East Sudbury, 1774; m. 1802; d. 1866) and Theoda (Pratt) Cutting, born 1805, in Roxbury; settled in Weston in 1822; bought the Jonathan P. Stearns grocery business in 1833; married 1830, Elizabeth Lord, of Medford (b. 1807; d. 1893); was postmaster from 1859 to 1885; for 52 years conducted the only grocery in Weston; held many offices within the gift of the people; was highly esteemed by the community for his great amiability and strict integrity; died 1885. Children:

Caroline Elizabeth Cutting, born 1831; married George Willis; died 1888.

Sarah Lord Cutting, born 1833; married Theodore Jones, died 1833.

George Warren Cutting, born 1834; married Josephine M. Brown.

Harriet Fenno Cutting, born 1838; married William C. Stimpson, killed at Poplar Spring, Va., Sept. 30, 1864, 35 Reg. Mass. Vol.

Margaret Lord Cutting, born 1842; married Isaac E. Coburn; died 1907.

Emma Louisa Cutting, born 1844.

Ellen Marion Cutting, born 1846; died 1849.

Edward L. Cutting, born 1850; married Caroline Augusta Keniston.

George Warren Cutting, Jr., born 1834; married 1865, Josephine M. Brown; became associated with his father in business. In 1875 the firm bought the Lamson store, property that had been in the Lamson family for 150 years. In 1864 upon the death of Nathan Hagar (died Nov. 14, 1863), he was chosen town clerk, and has served continuously in office since. He was representative in 1889, and assessor for a number of years, a trustee of of the Merriam Fund; a highly esteemed citizen, and is now postmaster. His children are:

Sarah Lillian Cutting, born 1866; married Arthur B. Nims.
Alfred Leslie Cutting, born 1868; married May C. Livermore.
Bessie Brown Cutting born 1874; died 1876.
George Warren Cutting (2d) born 1877.
Eleanor Mabel Cutting born 1880.
Edmund Eugene Cutting born 1882; died 1882.

Alfred Leslie Cutting, born 1868; opened a grocery store on North Ave., in 1888 and was appointed postmaster at Kendal Green when he was 21. He married 1890, May C., daughter of Charles H. and Almira (Child) Livermore, and became associated with his father and brother-in-law in business. He was elected a selectman in 1900 and continuously since; Representative in 1908 and re-elected for 1909. He is deservedly popular, trusted and esteemed.

Corporal Henry L. Brown, Assessor, was born in 1840.

David Weston Lane, Assessor, born in 1846, is Chairman of Park Commission.

Henry J. White, Town Treasurer and Collector, born in 1828, has served the town as representative, assessor and selectman. His father Henry J. White came to Weston from Hallowell, Maine.

HASTINGS FAMILY

I. Dea. Thomas Hastings migrated and settled in Watertown in 1634, with wife, Susanna (born 1609; died 1650); married 2, 1651, Margaret Cheney; died 1685.

II. Nathaniel Hastings, born 1661; married Mary—; died 1694.

III. John Hastings, born 1698; married 1726, Mercy Ward; lived in Weston. Children:

Elizabeth, born 1728; married 1750, James Livermore.
Esther, born 1730; married 1747, Ading Harrington.
Edward, born 1735; married 1758, Lydia Harrington.
John, born 1738; married 1, Elizabeth—; married 2, Esther Pierce, 1778.

HEWS FAMILY

Genealogies.

Abraham Hews of Weston established the first pottery business in New England in 1765.

Abraham Hews, his son, was appointed postmaster of Weston by President Madison in 1812 and held the office until his death in 1854.

Children:

George Hews, born 1806; married Caroline Pelletier, of Boston; died 1873.

Horace Hews, born 1815, was town treasurer 25 years, resigning office in 1889 on account of failing health.

HUBBARD FAMILY

William Hubbard, a graduate of Cambridge, England, came over to this country in 1632. His son, William, was graduated with the first class at Harvard College; afterward settled as a minister at Ipswich, Mass.; wrote the History of the Indian Wars.

The descendants are as follows:

John Hubbard,
John Hubbard,
Daniel Hubbard,
Daniel Hubbard,
Henry Hubbard,
Charles T. Hubbard,—the one who built in Weston.
Charles W. Hubbard,—the present owner.

The other children of Charles T. Hubbard are:

Louisa Sewall Hubbard, married 1st, John Cotton Jackson; 2nd, Ferdinand Canda.
Elizabeth L. Hubbard, married Francis Blake.
Charlotte W. Hubbard, married Benjamin Loring Young.
Charles Wells Hubbard, married Anne L. Swann.
Anne Hubbard, married Bancroft Chandler Davis.

LAMSON FAMILY

II. John Lamson, son of Joseph, I, or Samuel, I, settled in Weston in 1709; died 1757.

III. John Lamson, born in 1724, married Elizabeth Wesson in 1759.

III. Colonel Samuel Lamson, born in 1736; married Elizabeth Ball in 1759; married 2, Elizabeth Sanderson of Waltham in 1788. He was town treasurer and selectman of Weston many years, captain of Weston company at Concord, colonel of Third Middlesex regiment, active in town affairs.

Isaac Lamson third child of Samuel, married Abigail, daughter of Nathan Fiske in 1788; kept store in Weston from 1786 to 1806.

John Lamson, ninth child of Samuel, born 1791; married Elizabeth Turner Kendall of Boston in 1814; established the firm of Lane, Lamson & Co., with branches in Boston, New York, Paris and Lyons; retired in 1853; resided at homestead in Weston; died 1855.

Daniel S. Lamson, born 1793, tenth child of Samuel, married Patience, daughter of John Flagg, in 1822; kept the dry-goods store in Weston, was Lieut.-Colonel of 3rd Middlesex Regiment; died in 1824.

Daniel S. Lamson, grandson of Samuel, son of John, born in 1828; educated in France; studied law with Sohier & Welch and at Harv. Law School; was admitted to bar in 1854; commissioned Major of 16th Regt. Mass. Vols. (the old 3rd Middlesex Regt.) in 1861; Lieut.-Colonel in 1863; commanded regiment after death of Col. P. T. Wyman in battle; was discharged for disability in 1864; resides on old homestead.

John Lamson, son of John, was born in 1760; married Hannah Ayers. Their son, John A. Lamson, was a highly esteemed merchant of Boston.

Rev. Dr. Alvan Lamson, son of John (b. 1760), grandson of John (b. 1724), born 1792; Harv. Coll. 1814; tutor at Bowd. Coll.; Camb. Div. Sch. 1817; settled in Dedham in 1818; married Francis Fidelia Ward, daughter of Chief Justice Artemas Ward, in 1825; was a noted preacher, writer, antiquarian and historian; died in 1864.

SEARS FAMILY

Rev. Dr. Edmund Hamilton Sears, son of Joseph and Lucy (Smith) Sears, born in Standisfield in 1810; Union Coll. 1834; Harv. Div. Sch. 1837; settled in Wayland in 1839; married Ellen (who died 1897, aged 86), daughter of Hon. Ebenezer Bacon, of Barnstable; was called to Lancaster in 1840; returned to Wayland in 1848; was associated with Rev. Dr. Field at Weston in 1865; followed Dr. Field in 1869; was a preacher and writer of wide fame; died in 1876.

Children:

- Katharine, born 1843; died 1853.
- Francis Bacon, born 1849; married Mary E. Sparhawk.
- Edmund Hamilton, born 1852; married Hellen Clark Swazey of Springfield; lives in St. Louis, Mo.
- Horace Scudder, born 1855.

Francis Bacon Sears, son of Rev. Dr. Edmund H. and Ellen (Bacon) Sears, born in Wayland, 1849; passed his boyhood in Wayland; married in 1875 Mary E., daughter of George and Mary S. (Jackson) Sparhawk; settled finally in Weston in 1891.

Children:

1. Katharine, born 1876; married Henry Endicott, Jr., resides in Weston; has one daughter, Ellen Bacon Endicott.
2. Edmund Hamilton Sears, born 1878; Harv. Coll. 1899; married in 1904, Leslie Buckingham of Wayland; has children, Mary Sears, born 1905; Edmund Hamilton Sears, born 1907.
3. Jackson Knyvet Sears, born 1881; died 1905.
4. Francis Bacon Sears, Jr., born 1882; Harv. Coll. 1905; married Marian Buckingham; resides in Wayland; has one son, Francis Bacon Sears, born 1907.

WINSOR FAMILY.

Mrs. Anne Bent (Ware) Winsor, widow of Frederick Winsor of Winchester, settled in Weston in 1889, buying the Hager farm, corner of Central Ave. and Wellesley St.; she died in 1907. Her children were:

1. Robert Winsor, born 1858; Harv. Coll. 1880; banker (Kidder, Peabody & Co.) has farm of 300 acres; married Eleanor McGee of Winchester; has 4 children:
   Robert Winsor, Jr., Harv. Coll. 1905.
   Philip Winsor, Alexander Winsor, and Mary Winsor.
2. Mary Pickard Winsor.
3. Paul Winsor, born 1863; Chief Engineer Motive Power and Rolling Stock, Boston Elevated Railway Co.; married Jessie Baldwin of Winchester; has 2 sons, Paul Winsor, Jr., Felix Winsor.
4. Annie Ware Winsor, married Prof. Joseph Allen, of College of City of New York; has 3 children: Dorothea, Anne, Joseph.
5. Jane Loring Winsor, married Lyman W. Gale of Weston; has 3 children, Priscilla, Emma, Winsor Gale.
6. Elizabeth Ware Winsor, married Prof. Henry G. Pearson, of Mass. Inst. Tech.; has 1 child, Theodore Pearson.
7. Frederick Winsor, Jr., born 1872; Harv. Coll. 1893; resides in Concord; master, Middlesex School; married Mary A. Paine, daughter of Gen. Charles J. Paine; has 5 children: Charles Winsor, Dorothy Winsor, Frederick Winsor, John Winsor, and Theresa Winsor.

The genealogy of the other Weston families will appear in future numbers of this magazine.

[This is the fifth of a series of articles, giving the organization and history of all the Massachusetts regiments which took part in the war of the Revolution.]

COLONEL JOHN FELLOWS'S REGIMENT

COLONEL JOHN FELLOWS'S MINUTE MEN'S REGIMENT, 1775.
8TH REGIMENT ARMY OF THE UNITED COLONIES, 1775.

BY FRANK A. GARDNER, M. D.

North western Massachusetts contributed nearly all the men who composed this regiment, six companies being raised in Hampshire County, three in Berkshire and one in Worcester County.

Colonel Fellows's Minute Men's Regiment, which responded to the Lexington Alarm of April 19, 1775, was officered as follows:

Colonel, John Fellows, Sheffield.
Lieut. Colonel, Thomas Brown, Sandisfield.
Major, John Cotter, New Marlboro.
Adjutant, Ebenezer Bement, Great Barrington.

Company officers:

Lieutenant (commanding) Moses Soule.
Lieutenant Noah Allen.
Ensign Solomon Demming.

Captain William King.
Lieutenant Samuel Brewer.
Second Lieutenant Abijah Markham.

Captain William Bacon.
Lieutenant John Hubbard.
Ensign William Ashley.

Captain Caleb Wright.
No lieutenant.
Ensign Elisha Shelden.

Captain Jacob Brown.
Lieutenant Joel Smith.

Captain Israel Chapin.
Lieutenant Perez Bardwell.
Ensign William Watson.

Captain John Holmes
Lieutenant Michael Loomis.
Lieutenant David Tullar.

Lieutenant (commanding) John Hurlbut.
No other commissioned officer.

The regiment was reorganized April 25, 1775, and became the 17th Massachusetts Bay Regiment in the Provincial Army. The field and staff officers were as follows:

Colonel, John Fellows, Sheffield,	engaged	April	25,	1775.
Lieut. Colonel, Nahum Eagur, Worthington,	"	"	"	"
Major, Benjamin Tupper, Chesterfield,	"	"	"	"
Chaplain, Samuel Spring, Uxbridge,	"	May	10,	"
Adjutant, Ebenezer Bement, Great Barrington,	"	April	25,	"
Quartermaster, Seth Hunt, Northampton,	"	May	23,	"
Surgeon, Elihu Wright, New Marlboro,	"	April	25,	"
Surgeon, Samuel Adams, Truro,	"	June	28,	"
Surgeon's Mate, Josiah Harvey, Granville,	"	June	8,	"

Two letters connected with this period of the regiment explain themselves.

"In Com^tee^ of Safety, Cambridge May 11, 1775.

Sir The Capts Caleb Wright & John Holmes of the County of Berkshire, now report verbally, that your Excel^cy^ is willing that about 60 of Col^o^ Fellows's men, who have not enlisted, may have liberty to return home, they having first the consent of this Com^tee^ We have conferr'd with his Excellency Genl Ward upon the Subject, & are of Opinion, That no liberty ought to be granted to any, for that purpose, until the Camps are so far strengthened, as that all who were called in upon the late alarm, may have liberty to return. And as the Troops from Connecticut are very soon (in a few days) expected, we

Captain John Holmes.
Lieutenant Michael Loomis.
Lieutenant David Tullar.

Lieutenant (commanding) John Hurlbu
No other commissioned officer.

The regiment was reorganized April 23, 1775, and
chusetts Bay Regiment in the Provincial Army. Th
were as follows:

Colonel, John Fellows, Sheffield.
Lieut. Colonel, Nahum Eager, Worthington.
Major, Benjamin Tupper, Chesterfield.
Chaplain, Samuel Spring, Uxbridge.
Adjutant, Ebenezer Bement, Great Barrington.
Quartermaster, Seth Hunt, Northampton.
Surgeon, Elihu Wright, New Marlboro.
Surgeon, Samuel Adams, Truro.
Surgeon's Mate, Josiah Harvey, Granville.

Two letters connected with this period of the regi

"In Comm of Safety, Cambridge May 11, 17

Sir. The Capts Caleb Wright & John Holmes of t
Regiment verbally that, our Exigencies being that a
men, who have not enlisted, may have liberty to re
present consent of this Comm We have consider'd w
Want upon the Subject, & are of Opinion, That no libe
to any, for that purpose, until the Camps are so far
who were called in upon the late alarm, may have

think that these, with others which are daily coming in, will strengthen our hands so far as to relieve those who want to return to their homes.

We have the honor to be Sir, with great respect,

Yr Excelnys' most humble Servt

Pr order of the Committee

Richd Deven Chairman."

"The council of war having recommended that forty persons of the regiment commanded by Col. Fellows have liberty to return to their several homes. Resolved, that they be dismissed accordingly, and that the commissary general be directed to supply said persons with six days provisions to serve them on their return home."

Committee of Safety, May 15, 1775.

A return of the regiment made at Roxbury Camp, May 23, 1775, gave the the total enrollment of privates as 526.

We read in the records of the Committee of Safety, May 29, 1775, that "Col. Fellows having satisfied this committee that his regiment is full, we had a certificate thereof, and a recommendation that said regiment be commissioned accordingly, was given him for the honorable Congress."

"A true Return According to the Returns from every Company" dated Roxbury Camp, May 31, 1775, showed that the regiment numbered 548, 35 of whom were officers.

A resolve passed in the Provincial Congress June 4, 1775, directed "That Col. Lemuel Robinson. . . . pay the advance pay of the three companies of Col. [Fellows'] regiment, which came from the county of Berkshire, out of the first money he may receive from the receiver general."

"Roxbury Camp, June 10, 1775.

A return of Colo Fellows Regiment of the Names of Officers and Number of Men.

Capt. Robert Webster
Lt. Christopher Banester — 49
Ensg Everton Bosweck

Capt. Abner Pemroy
Lt. Jonathan Wales — 45
Ensg Daniel Kirtland

Capt. Ebenezer Webber Lieut Samll Bartlett Lieut Samll Allen	66
Capt Abel Shaw* Lieut Joseph Warner	39
Capt. William Bacon Lt John Hubbard Ensg Michel Loomis	57
Capt. William King Lt Sam[ll] Brewer Ensg Gamaliel Whiting	55
Capt. Jonathan Allen Lieut Oliver Lyman Ensg Jonathan Stearns	64
Capt. Moses Soul Lt Noah Allen Ensg Solomon Duning	55
Capt Israel Chapin Lieut Perez Bardwell Ensg William Watson	54
Capt Simeon Hazeltine Lieut George Blake Ensg Steward Blake	45

*Although this name is given as Shaw in the manuscript record it is a mistake. His name was Thayer as proven by other original records.

Elihu Wright Scurgeon
Sam[ll] Spring Chaplin
Eben[r] Bement Adj't
W[m] Bement Armerer
Seth Hunt Quartermaster

Field Officers
Colo John Fellows
Lt Col. Nahum Eager
Maj[r] Benjamin Tupper

N. B. 14 of the above soldiers have enlisted in the train of artillery 3 not joined 1 Deferted

		567
Colon & other officers of Commifiond Staff		37
	Total	564

Ebenezer Bement Adjt pr order of the Colo."

Commissions were ordered to be delivered to Colonel Fellows and the officers of his regiment, "agreeable to a list exhibited by the Lt. Col." June 7, 1775.

The following list shows the names of the company commanders about July 1, 1775, with the names of towns:

Captains.

William King, Great Barrington, Tyringham, Alford, etc.
Jonathan Allen, Northampton, Dorchester.
William Bacon, Sheffield, Egremont, Alford.
Robert Webster, Chesterfield, Bridgewater, Northampton, Pelham.
Israel Chapin, Hatfield, Whately, Chesterfield, Enfield, Williamsburg.
Ebenezer Webber, Ashfield, Worthington, Deerfield, Dorchester.
Simeon Hazeltine, Hardwick, Oakham, Rutland, Ashfield.
Abel Thayer, Williamsburg, No. 5. etc. etc.
Moses Soule, Sandisfield, New Marlboro, Egremont, Spencer.
Abner Pomroy, Southampton, Northampton, Norwich etc.

A return of company commanders for provisions made July 3, 1775, showed that the regiment contained at that time 539 men, each of whom had a pound of beef, a pound of pork, two pounds of bread, two (pints prob-

ably) of beer, a quarter of a pound of both rice and peas, and about 1-9 of a pound of butter, for the daily ration.

The regiment was assigned Brigadier General Thomas's Brigade. July 22, 1775, and served through the year in the fortifications at Roxbury. We have already given the strength of the regiment at various times up to August, 1775. The following shows the number of men each month through the remainder of the year.

Date.	Com. Off.	Staff.	Non Com.*	Rank and file.
Aug. 18.	33	5	56	460
Sept. 23.	33	5	59	470
Oct. 17.	33	5	59	468
Nov. 18.	31	5	59	466
Dec. 30.	31	5	59	453

Many of the officers of this regiment served in other organizations in later years of the war. Two attained the rank of brigadier general, one became a colonel, four, majors and others, company commanders.

COLONEL JOHN FELLOWS of Sheffield, was born in Pomfret, Connecticut, in 1733. He was in Sheffield in 1758 and was an Ensign in Colonel William Williams's Regiment from March 13 to November 1, of that year. He served as Captain in 1759, 60 and 61, and again in 1764. In 1771 he was 1st Major in Colonel John Ashley's South Regiment of Berkshire.

He was a member of the First Provincial Congress from Sheffield, Great Barrington, Egremont and Alford, in October 1774. On the 19th of the month he was appointed on a committee "to make as minute an inquiry into the present state and operations of the army as may be, and report." He was also to "consider what is necessary to be now done for the defence and safety of the province." December 7, 1774 he was appointed on a committee "to prepare . . . . a true statement of the number of the inhabitants and of the quantities of exports and imports of goods . . . . of all kinds, within the colony, [to] be used by our delegates in the Continental Congress." He represented Sheffield and Great Barrington in the Second Provincial Congress, February, 1775.

He organized a regiment of minute men and marched them from the hills and vales of Berkshire County upon the alarm of April 19th 1775. On the 25th of that month the reorganization took place and this regiment be-

* Sergeants, fifers and drummers.

came the 17th. Massachusetts Bay regiment in the Provincial Army. In the Army of the United Colonies, June–December, it was known as the 8th Regiment.

In the Provincial Congress, June 7, 1775, it was "Ordered, That commissions be delivered to Col. Fellows and officers of his regiment, agreeably to the list exhibited by his lieutenant colonel." Colonel Fellows received his commission on the following day. He served through the year 1775 with his regiment in the fortifications at Roxbury.

In January, 1776, he was raising a regiment in the County of Berkshire but on the 30th of that month was chosen Brigadier General for that county, and was commissioned February 8th. June 26, 1776, he was chosen to command a brigade of militia to reinforce General Washington at New York. This brigade was composed of three regiments, Colonel Simeon Cary's, Colonel Jonathan Holman's and Colonel Isaac Smith's. August 5th the brigade was assigned "to take the place of Gen. Scott's Brigade which was to move into the city." Unfortunately, the brigade was composed entirely of raw militiamen who had never been in action, and made a lamentable display in the retreat from New York. General Nathaniel Greene in a letter to Governor Cooke wrote: "We made a miserable, disorderly retreat from New York, owing to the disorderly conduct of the militia, who ran at the appearance of the enemy's advance guard; this was General Fellows's brigade. They struck a panick into the troops in the rear, and Fellows's and Parsons's whole brigade ran away from about fifty men, and left his Excellency on the ground within eighty yards of the enemy so vexed at the infamous conduct of the troops, that he sought death rather than life." General Washington did not consider that General Fellows was responsible for this stampede, as the following letter to the President of Congress makes evident.

"As soon as I heard the firing, I rode with all possible dispatch toward the place of landing, when, to my great surprise and mortification, I found the troops that had been posted in the lines retreating with the utmost precipitation, and those ordered to support them (Parsons' & Fellows's brigades) flying in every direction, and in the greatest confusion, *notwithstanding the exertion of their Generals to form them.* I used every means in my power to rally and get them in some order; but my attempts were fruitless and ineffectual; and on the appearance of a small party of the enemy, not more than sixty or seventy, their disorder increased, and they ran away in the greatest confusion, without firing a single shot. Finding that no confidence was to be placed in these brigades" etc. etc. Up to November 23, 1776, 17 members of the brigade had been killed, 4 taken prisoners and 11 missing.

General Fellows served later at Bemis Heights and Saratoga and was present at the surrender of Burgoyne. After the war he was made high sheriff of Berkshire County. He died at Sheffield, Massachusetts, August 1, 1808.

LIEUT. COLONEL THOMAS BROWN of Sandisfield was a Captain in Colonel John Ashley's South Berkshire Regiment, July, 1771. He was engaged April 21, 1775, as Lieutenant Colonel of Colonel John Fellows's Minute Men's Regiment and is credited with 18 days service.

LIEUT. COLONEL NAHUM EAGER of Brookfield "carried his own arms" as a private in Captain Asa Whitcomb's company February 5, 1756. In August of the following year he was a private in Captain Nathaniel Wolcott's Company, on the alarm at Fort William Henry. In 1758 he served in Captain Nathan Tyler's Company, Colonel William Williams's Regiment. He was a private in Captain Asa Whitcomb's Company in Colonel Jonathan Bayley's Regiment (year not given). From March 4 to November 27, 1762, he was a Lieutenant in Captain William Jones's Company. He was credited to Westboro at this time. He was engaged April 25, 1775, as Lieut. Colonel of Colonel John Fellows's Regiment of Minute Men and served through the the year under that commander. A list of officers of the Continental Army in 1776 credits him as Lieut. Colonel of Colonel Israel Hutchinson's Regiment, but this was either a mistake or he did substitute duty for a short time only, as Lieut. Colonel Benjamin Holden is given as second in command in that regiment throughout the year 1776.

MAJOR JOHN COTTER (COLLER or COLLAR), of New Marlboro, was a member of the Committee of Inspection of that town, January 24, 1775. He was Major of Colonel John Fellows's Minute Men's Regiment and was engaged for that service April 21, 1775. He was commissioned Captain in a Berkshire County regiment October 14, 1777, and in 1779 served in the same rank in Colonel John Ashley's 1st Berkshire County Regiment. He served six days in the same regiment in 1780. In 1784 he held the rank of Lieutenant Colonel.

MAJOR BENJAMIN TUPPER of Chesterfield was born in 1738 in that part of Stoughton now known as Sharon. He was the son of Thomas and —— (Perry) Tupper. His father died when he was quite young and he was apprenticed to a farmer in Dorchester by the name of Withington. At the age of sixteen he removed to Easton and kept a district school for several

winters. He was "centinel" in Captain Nathaniel Perry's Company in Colonel John Winslow's Regiment from June 13 to September 29, 1754. From April 1, to November 28, 1758, he was a Corporal in Captain James Andrews's Company in Colonel Thomas Doty's Regiment. March 25, 1759, he enlisted in Captain Josiah Thatcher's Company in Colonel Ephraim Leonard's Regiment. From November 1st of that year until January 11, 1761 he was a sergeant in Captain Samuel Glover's Company in Colonel Bayley's Regiment. He was a Lieutenant of militia at the breaking out of the revolution. He was engaged April 25, 1775, as Major in Colonel John Fellows's Provincial Regiment and as the efficient leader of several important expeditions during the year gained an enviable reputation for skill and valor. The first was on July 8, 1775, when a party of volunteers under Majors Tupper and Crane, at two o'clock in the morning attacked the advanced guard of the British at Brown's house on Boston Neck, within three hundred yards of their main works. They trained two field pieces on the guard house, fired two rounds, drove the guards back to their main lines and burned the house. The next of these expeditions is thus described by Frothingham in his "Siege of Boston."

"The enemy had commenced rebuilding the light-house, and this day, July 31, Major Tupper, with three hundred men, was detached with orders to disperse the working party. The enemy prepared to receive the Americans in a hostile manner. Major Tupper landed in good order on the island, marched up to the works, killed ten or twelve on the spot, and took the remainder prisoners. Having demolished the works, the party were ready to embark, but the tide leaving them, they were obliged to remain until its return. Meantime, a number of boats came up from the men-of-war to reinforce those at the island, and a smart firing from both parties took place. A field piece, under Major Crane, planted on Nantasket Point to cover a retreat, sunk one of the boats, and killed several of the crew. Major Tupper brought his party off with the loss of only one man killed, and two or three wounded. Washington, the next day, in general orders, thanked Major Tupper, and the officers and soldiers under his command, 'for their gallant and soldier-like behavior,' and remarked that he doubted not 'but the continental army would be as famous for their mercy as their valor.' " General Washington caused Jefferson to refer to it as an instance of "the adventurous genius and intrepidity of New Englanders." The British Admiral said that no one act of the siege caused as much chagrin in London as the destruction of the lighthouse.

In August, 1775, Major Tupper was sent to Martha's Vineyard to capture two vessels, and on the 27th of September, headed a party of two hundred

marching at the breaking

was engaged April 25, 1775, as Major in Colonel
Regiment and as the efficient leader of several in
the year gained an enviable reputation skill ar
July 8, 1775, when a party of under
at two o'clock in the morning attacked the adv
at Brown's house on Boston Neck, within three h
works. They trained two field pieces on the guar
drove the guards back to their main lines and bu
these expeditions is thus described by Frothingha

"The enemy had commenced rebuilding the
July 31 Major Tupper, with three hundred men,
to disperse the working party. The enemy prep
came in a hostile manner. Major Tupper landed
marched up to the works, killed ten or twelve on
mainder prisoners. Having demolished the wor
to embark, but the tide leaving them, they were
return. Meantime, a number of boats came up
reinforce those at the island smart firing fo
A field piece, under Major Crane, planted on Na
retreat, sunk one of the boats, and killed several of
brought his party off with the loss of only one ma
wounded. Washington, the next day, in gener
Tupper, and the officers and soldiers under his co
and soldier-like behavior, and remarked that he
tinental army would be as famous for their mercy
Washington caused Jefferson to refer to it as an ins
genius and intrepidity of New Englanders." The
no one act of the siege caused as much chagrin in
of the lighthouse.

men. This party "embarked in whale-boats at Dorchester, landed on Governor's Island and brought off twelve head of cattle, two fine horses, burnt a pleasure-boat just ready to be launched, and returned to camp without loss of life."

November 4, 1775, he was commissioned Lieut. Colonel of Colonel Ward's Regiment. He was Lieut. Colonel under the same commander in the 21st Regiment in the Continental Army, and did valiant service. January 15, 1776, he captured two vessels and carried them into Dartmouth. In May and June he commanded a fleet of whale-boats which cruised along the coast of Long Island, protecting "the western shore from Amboy Dam to Sandy Hook," and giving information about arrivals of the enemy's vessels at New York. He commanded a fleet of galleys about New York through the summer and was stationed at Dobbs Ferry in November. General Heath in a letter to General Washington, dated November 26, 1776, wrote that Col. Tupper brought over the Hudson, the stores at Tappan, Slot's Landing, etc. "although the ships fired a number of cannon shot at the boats."

From January 1, to July 7, 1777, he served in the Northern Army as Lieut. Colonel of the 2nd Regiment, Massachusetts Line, under Colonel John Bailey. On the latter date he was given command of the 11th Regiment, Massachusetts Line, after Colonel Ebenezer Francis had been killed at Hubbardton, Vermont. He commanded this regiment until January 1, 1781, when he was transferred to the 10th Regiment which he commanded until January 1, 1783. He was then appointed Colonel of the 6th Regiment and served until it disbanded June 12, 1783. He was at Valley Forge in the winter of 1777–8 and at the battle of Monmouth June 28, 1778, and had a horse killed under him during that engagement. He was appointed inspector in General Paterson's Brigade in September 1778 and served as aid to General Washington. In 1780 he superintended the stretching of a chain across the Hudson River at West Point. He was brevetted a Brigadier General toward the close of the war.

He represented Chesterfield in the Massachusetts Legislature after the war and was a justice of the peace. He was one of the signers of the petition of Continental officers for the laying out of a new state "westward of the Ohio" June 16, 1783, and in 1785 accepted the office of surveyor of the northwestern lands, which General Putnam had given up. March 1, 1786, he helped to organize the Ohio Company of Associates. He returned to Massachusetts and actively assisted General Shepard in suppressing Shay's rebellion. He removed with his family to Ohio arriving at Marietta August 9, 1788. He was justice of the quorum of the first civil court in the Northwest Territory Sep-

tember 9, 1788, and presided thereafter at every session but one or two until his death. His biographer in "Notable Americans" credits him with being the inventor of the screw propeller. He was a member of the Massachusetts Society of the Cincinnati. He died at Marietta, Ohio, June 1792.

ADJUTANT EBENEZER BEMENT of Great Barrington served in Colonel Fellows's Regiment and in the Provincial Regiment in May 1775.

CHAPLAIN SAMUEL SPRING of Uxbridge was engaged for service in Colonel Fellows's Provincial Regiment, May 10, 1775.

SURGEON SAMUEL ADAMS of Truro was engaged June 28, 1775, as Surgeon of the Provincial Regiment. In October he was credited to Captain William King's Company in Colonel Fellows's 8th Regiment, A. U. C.

SURGEON ELIHU WRIGHT of New Marlborough served as Clerk of Captain William Lyman's Company from September 13 to December 10, 1755. Later he was Captain of the New Marlborough Company in Colonel William Williams's Berkshire County Regiment. He was engaged April 25, 1775, as Surgeon of Colonel Fellows's Provincial Regiment.

SURGEON'S MATE JOSIAH HARVEY of Granville was engaged for service in Colonel Fellows's Provincial Regiment, June 8, 1775. He was examined and approved by the committee of Congress, at Watertown July 5, 1775.

QUARTERMASTER SETH HUNT of Northampton was engaged May 23, 1775, to serve in Colonel John Fellows's Provincial Regiment. His first service was as a private in Captain Jonathan Allen's Company in General Pomeroy's Regiment, which marched April 20, 1775, in response to the Lexington alarm. He was probably the same Seth Hunt, of Northampton, who was appointed a Captain in Colonel Henry Jackson's Regiment, September 6, 1777. He was not included in the arrangement for consolidation April 9, 1779, and was reported "never joined."

ARMORER WILLIAM BEMENT (or BEAMENT). The name appears in a list of officers to be commissioned dated Roxbury Camp, May 31, 1775; commissioned June 7, 1775. His name was crossed out of the list. It was voted in the Committee of Safety, May 15, 1775, that Mr. William "Beman" of Colonel Fellows's Regiment, be "appointed by this Committee to act as an armorer for the forces posted at Roxbury."

CAPTAIN JONATHAN ALLEN of Northampton, was in Colonel Jonathan Bayley's Regiment at Fort William Henry, March 23, 1756. He was a "Centinel" in Captain Israel Williams's Company from October 19, 1756? to January 19, 1757?*. He was a Captain in General Pomeroy's Regiment, April 20, 1775 and enlisted in Colonel John Fellows's Provincial Regiment seven days later. He served through the year, and through 1776 was a Captain in Colonel Jonathan Ward's 21st Continental Regiment. January 1, 1777, he began service in Colonel Rufus Putnam's 5th Regiment, Massachusetts Line, and on the 17th of the following May was promoted to the rank of Major. He died January 6, 1780.

CAPTAIN WILLIAM BACON of Sheffield was Captain of a company in Colonel John Fellows's Regiment of Minute Men, April 21, 1775. He enlisted in the Provincial Army and served through the year under the same commander.

CAPTAIN JACOB BROWN of Sandisfield served as an Ensign in Captain Jno. Chadwick's Tyringham Company, in Colonel William Williams's Regiment, in January 1764. He commanded a company in Colonel John Fellows's Minute Men's Regiment, April 21, 1775, and served for 1 month and 3 days. He was probably the Jacob Brown who was 2nd Major of Colonel Mark Hopkins's 1st Berkshire County Regiment, commissioned February 7, 1776.

CAPTAIN ISRAEL CHAPIN of Hatfield was a "centinel" in Captain Isaac Wyman's Company from April 15 to November 3, 1757. From November 13, 1758 to April 11, 1759, he was in the same officer's company at Fort Massachusetts and West Hoosack (Williamstown). Later in 1759, he was in Captain Selah Barnard's Company in Brigadier General Ruggles's Regiment. He was a Captain in Colonel John Fellows's Minute Men's Regiment, April 20, 1775, and served under him through the year. In 1777 he was a Major, probably serving as a volunteer in Captain Seth Murray's Company in Colonel Ezra May's Regiment. He was chosen Lieut. Colonel of the 2nd Hampshire County Regiment, October 6, 1777, in place of Lieut Colonel Dickinson, resigned. On the 16th of the following February he was chosen Colonel of the same regiment in place of Colonel Ezra May, deceased. In 1779 he was in command of the same regiment in General Timothy Danielson's Brigade.

CAPTAIN SIMEON HAZELTON of Hardwick was the son of Daniel Hazelton. He was in Hardwick as early as 1758, when we are told in the

*Year not given in the original manuscript record, but probably 1756 and 7.

"History of Hardwick" that he was a soldier in the French war although the writer has been unable to confirm this by the records in the Massachusetts archives. He commanded a company of Minute Men which marched on the alarm of April 19, 1775. He was engaged April 26, 1775 as a Captain in Colonel Fellows's Provincial Regiment and he was commissioned June 7th. He was a Captain serving as a Cadet in Captain Timothy Paige's Company in Colonel James Converse's 4th Worcester County Regiment, in August 1777, at the Bennington alarm. He became involved in Shay's rebellion and was obliged to leave the state. He settled at Sandgate, Vermont and represented that town in the legislature.

CAPTAIN JOHN HOLMES of Sheffield was a Sergeant in Captain John Fellows's Company from May 7 to December 5, 1759. He commanded a Company in Colonel John Fellows's Regiment of Minute Men, which marched April 19, 1775 and served until May 22nd. November 7, 1776, he was chosen by Massachusetts resolve, wagon-master for the southern army.

CAPTAIN WILLIAM KING of Great Barrington lived in Sheffield in 1755, and was a private in Captain Elisha Noble's Company from September 15 to December 5 of that year, in the expedition to Crown Point. In 1756 at the age of 24 he was a private under Colonel Dwight, having left Captain Burghert's Company in Colonel Worthington's Regiment. From March 3 to December 1, (probably 1760) he was an Ensign in Captain John Fellows's Company. He was a Captain in Colonel John Fellows's Regiment of Minute Men in April 1775, and he continued to serve in the Provincial Regiment in May, and in Colonel Fellows's 8th Regiment, Army of the United Colonies through the remainder of the year. Through 1776 he was a Captain in Colonel Jonathan Ward's 21st Continental Regiment. September 29, 1778, he was commissioned Brigade Major of Berkshire County Militia.

CAPTAIN ABNER POMEROY of Southampton was a Second Lieutenant in Captain Lemuel Pomeroy's Company which marched April 21, 1775, in response to the Lexington alarm. He was engaged April 27, 1775, as a Captain in Colonel John Fellows's Regiment and served through the year. August 16, 1777 he was engaged as First Lieutenant of Captain John Kirkland's Company, in Colonel B. Ruggles Woodbridge's Regiment. In 1778-9 he was a Captain in Colonel Ezra Wood's Regiment.

CAPTAIN ABEL SHAW. This name, appearing in a list dated May 23 1775, is evidently incorrect. Captain Abel "Thayer," as given in a list dated May 31, is the correct name.

CAPTAIN MOSES SOUL of New Marlborough was a Lieutenant in command of a Company in Colonel John Fellows's Minute Men's Regiment April 21, 1775. May 8, he was engaged as Captain in Colonel Fellows's Provincial Regiment and he continued to serve under the same commander through the year. January 1, 1776, he was appointed Captain of the 6th Company in Colonel Asa Whitcomb's 6th Continental Regiment. He was discharged (also given resigned) October 1, 1776.

CAPTAIN ABEL THAYER of Williamsburg was a Lieutenant in command of a detachment, in response to the Lexington alarm of April 19, 1775. April 28, he was engaged as a Captain in Colonel John Fellows's Provincial Regiment and he served through the year under him.

CAPTAIN EBENEZER WEBBER of Worthington was Captain of a Company of Minute Men which marched April 20, 1775, in response to the Lexington alarm. He was engaged April 27, as Captain in Colonel John Fellows's Regiment and served through the year. In April 1776, he was commissioned Captain in Colonel Seth Pomeroy's 2nd Hampshire County Regiment. From December 17, 1776, to March 20, 1777, he was Captain of a company in Lieut. Colonel Samuel Williams's Regiment. He was a Captain in Major Jonathan Clapp's Regiment from July 10, 1777 to August 12, 1777. He also served as Captain in Colonel Ezra May's Regiment in September-October 1777, and Colonel Israel Chapin's 2nd Hampshire County Regiment in 1778-80.

CAPTAIN ROBERT WEBSTER of Chesterfield was probably the man of that name who was a private in Captain Joshua Healy's Company in Colonel John Chandler Jr.'s Regiment, which marched to the relief of Fort William Henry in August, 1757. He was Captain of a Company of Minute Men in General Pomeroy's Regiment, April 21, 1775. April 27, he was engaged as Captain in Colonel John Fellows's Regiment, and he served in that command through the year.

CAPTAIN CALEB WRIGHT of New Marlborough was probably the man of that name who lived in Harvard (son or protege of Thomas Wright), who was in Captain Asa Whitcomb's Company in the French war. He was Ensign of Captain Elisha Noble's Company from September 12 to December 5, 1775, on the Crown Point expedition. He was Captain of a Company in Colonel John Fellows's Minute Men's Regiment, April 21, 1775, and served 1 month and 3 days.

LIEUTENANT NOAH ALLEN of Sandisfield held that rank in Lieutenant Moses Soul's Company in Colonel John Fellows's Minute Men's Regiment, April 21, 1775. He continued to serve under the same commander through the year with the rank of First Lieutenant according to the "Historical Register of the Officers of the Continental Army." January 1, 1776, he enlisted as First Lieutenant in Captain Moses Soul's Company, Colonel Asa Whitcomb's 6th Continental Regiment, and was promoted Captain, October 1 or 2, 1776. He was re-engaged in Colonel Smith's (late Wigglesworth's) 13th Regiment, Massachusetts Line, November 14, 1776, and served in that command as late as April 1779, and in the same regiment under Major John Porter in August of that year. His name also appears in a list of men in the 13th Regiment, dated December 14, 1780. He was transferred to the 1st Regiment, Massachusetts Line, commanded by Colonel Joseph Vose, January 1, 1781. In May 1781, he was in command of the regiment temporarily at West Point. He was wounded at Robinson's house and was retired August 1, 1782, according to the Historical Register of the officers of the Continental Army," but returns dated from November 8 to December 6, 1782, show that he was sick at New Marlborough by leave of General Washington.

FIRST LIEUTENANT CHRISTOPHER BANESTER (or BANNISTER) of Chesterfield was a private in Captain Obediah Cooley's Company in 1756. He was commissioned June 7, 1775, First Lieutenant in Captain Robert Webster's Company in Colonel John Fellows's Regiment. He served in that command through the year. April 5, 1776, he was commissioned Captain in the 2nd Hampshire County Regiment. He marched to Bennington with the regiment in August 1777, and was commissioned 2nd Major of the same command, May 30, 1778.

LIEUTENANT PEREZ BARDWELL of Whately (of Hatfield in 1755) was a centinel in Captain Moses Porter's Company from April 1 to September 8, 1755; and in Captain Hezekiah Smith's Company from September 9 to December 25 of the same year. From March 5 to April 2, 1757* he held the same rank in Captain John Burk's Company. April 13, 1758* he enlisted in Captain Salah Barnard's Company, Colonel William Williams's Regiment. He enlisted in Colonel Israel William Williams's Regiment, April 6, 1759, and was a private in Captain William Shepard's Company from June 24 to December 4, 1761. He was a Lieutenant in Captain Israel Chapin's Company, in Colonel John Fellows's Minute Men's Regiment, April 20, 1775, and served through the year under the same Colonel.

---

*

LIEUTENANT SAMUEL BARTLET of Ashfield may have been the man of that name who enlisted April 6, 1759 from Shirley, at the age of 19, in Colonel William Lawrence's Regiment. He was a Lieutenant in command of a company which marched April 22, 1775, in response to the Lexington alarm. He enlisted April 27, 1775, as a Lieutenant in Captain Ebenezer Webber's Company, in Colonel John Fellows's Regiment and served through the year. From January 1 to December 31, 1776, he was a Captain in Colonel Jonathan Ward's 21st Continental Regiment, and January 1st 1777, he became a Captain in Colonel James Wesson's 9th Regiment, Massachusetts Line. He resigned March 6, 1778.

LIEUTENANT GEORGE BLAKE of Oakham entered Captain Simeon Hazelton's Company in Colonel John Fellows's Regiment, May 1, 1775, and served through the year.

FIRST LIEUTENANT SAMUEL BREWER of Great Barrington (probably) may have been the man bearing that name who enlisted from Rutland in 1759, in Captain John Phelp's Company, Colonel Ruggles's Regiment, for the relief of Fort William Henry. He was First Lieutenant of Captain William King's Company, in Colonel John Fellows's Minute Men's Regiment, which marched April 21, 1775, in response to the Lexington alarm. He enlisted into the army later and was commissioned June 7, 1775. He served through the year in Colonel Fellows's Regiment.

FIRST LIEUTENANT JOHN HUBBARD of Sheffield was an Ensign in Captain Lemuel Barnard's North Sheffield Company, in Colonel John Ashley's Regiment, in July 1771. He was a Lieutenant in Captain William Bacon's Company of Minute Men in Colonel John Fellows's Regiment, April 21, 1775. He was engaged May 8, 1775, for service under the same commanders and continued in the same regiment through the year. According to family tradition, he was wounded in the knee and applied for a pension.

LIEUTENANT JOHN HURLBUT of Alford was Captain in the Alford Company in Colonel John Ashley's South Regiment of Berkshire County in July 1771. He was Lieutenant in command, and the only commissioned officer in a company in Colonel John Fellows's Minute Men's Regiment, April 21, 1775. A part of this company did not engage in the service but returned home after the enlistment of the army. He was probably the John "Hulburt" who was First Lieutenant in Captain Benjamin Bonney's Company, in the 2nd Hampshire County Regiment, in March and April 1776. May 8, 1777, he was engaged in the same rank in Captain Christopher Banis-

ter's Company, Colonel David Wells's Regiment, and marched to Ticonderoga. August 17, 1777, he was engaged as Lieutenant of Captain Benjamin Bonney's Company in Colonel Dickinson's Regiment (Lieut. Colonel John Dickinson, in the 2nd Hampshire County Regiment) which marched to Bennington on the alarm. He was again commissioned the same rank in tne same company and regiment, under Colonel Israel Chapin, July 6, 1778.

FIRST LIEUTENANT OLIVER LYMAN of Northampton held that rank in Captain Jonathan Allen's Company of Minute Men, General Pomeroy's Regiment, April 20, 1775. He was engaged April 27, 1775, to serve in the same rank under the same company commander in Colonel John Fellows's Regiment and served through the year. In March 1776, he was chosen Captain in the 2nd Hampshire County Regiment. September 12, 1776, his name appears on a warrant for pay as a Captain in Colonel Nicholas Dike's Regiment. He was commissioned December 1, 1776, and served until March 1, 1777. He marched from Northampton to East Hoosick, on the alarm of August 17, 1777, in command of a company, "probably made up of three companies." From September 20, to October 14, 1777, he served as Captain in Colonel Ezra May's 2nd Hampshire County Regiment, on an expedition to Stillwater and Saratoga. October 7, 1777, he was commissioned 1st Major of the 2nd Hampshire County Regiment. On account of certain dishonorable reports concerning his conduct at the time of the alarm of September 20, 1777, he was asked to resign, and complied at once. On July 6, 1778, he was commissioned Captain in the same regiment, under the command of Colonel Israel Chapin.

LIEUTENANT JOEL SMITH of Sandisfield served in that rank in Captain Jacob Brown's Company, in Colonel John Fellows's Regiment from April 21, to May 7, 1775.

LIEUTENANT JONATHAN WALES of Northampton was engaged May 3, 1775, for service in Captain Abner Pomeroy's Company in Colonel John Fellows's Regiment, and continued in that command through the year. In April 1776, he was commissioned Captain in the 2nd Hampshire County Regiment. December 20, 1776, he was engaged to serve as Captain in a regiment commanded by Lieut. Colonel S. Williams. He marched August 17, 1777, to East Hoosick on the alarm of that date, thence to Pittsfield and thence guarded Hessian prisoners to Springfield. On this tour of duty he was a Captain in Colonel Dickinson's (2nd) Hampshire County Regiment. September 22, 1777, he was engaged as a Captain in Colonel Ezra May's Regiment. He was commissioned July 6, 1778, a Captain in the same regiment under Colonel Israel Chapin.

LIEUTENANT JOSEPH WARNER of Number 5 (township) commanded a Company of Minute Men, which marched April 21, 1775. He was engaged April 28, as a Lieutenant in Captain Abel Thayer's Company, in Colonel John Fellows's Regiment. In April 1776, he was commissioned a Captain in Colonel Seth Pomeroy's 2nd Hampshire County Regiment. He was engaged August 16, 1777, as a Captain in Colonel B. Ruggles Woodbridge's Regiment on an expedition to the Northern department, and served until December 7, 1777.

LIEUTENANT GAMALIEL WHITING of Great Barrington was engaged as an Ensign in Captain William King's Company, Colonel John Fellows's Regiment, May 8, 1775. He was later promoted to the rank of Lieutenant and served through the year

SECOND LIEUTENANT SAMUEL ALLEN of Ashfield was probably the man of that name of Deerfield in 1759, who was a Corporal in Captain Salah Barnard's Company from March 29 to December 29 of that year. He was an Ensign in Lieutenant Samuel Bartlet's Company, which marched from Ashfield, April 22, in response to the Lexington alarm. April 27, he enlisted as a Second Lieutenant in Captain Ebenezer Webber's Company, in Colonel John Fellows's Regiment, and served through the year. He was a First Lieutenant in Colonel Jonathan Ward's 21st Continental Regiment through 1776. January 1, 1777, he entered Captain Bartlett's Company in Colonel James Wesson's 9th Regiment Massachusetts Line, and served until he resigned April 12, 1778.

SECOND LIEUTENANT EVERTON BESWICK of Chesterfield was a private in Captain Robert Webster's Company, General Pomeroy's Regiment, which marched April 21, 1775, in response to the Lexington alarm. He was called a Lieutenant in a list of the officers of Captain Robert Webster's Company, Colonel John Fellows's Regiment, dated May 23, 1775, and as Ensign in lists dated June 10, August 1 and October 8, 1775. He first enlisted in this regiment April 27, 1775, as a private. April 5, 1776, he was commissioned Second Lieutenant in Captain Benjamin Bonney's Company in the 2nd Hampshire County Regiment. He held the same rank under Captain Bonney in the same regiment, under Colonel Ezra May in September-October 1777, and under Colonel Israel Chapin in July, 1778. He was also in Captain William White's Company in the same regiment (year not given).

SECOND LIEUTENANT STEWARD (or STEWART) BLAKE of Oakham was a private in Captain John Crawford's Company, Colonel Jonathan Warner's Regiment, which marched on the alarm of April 19, 1775.

May 27, 1775, he enlisted as an Ensign in Captain Simeon Hazelton's Company, Colonel John Fellows's Regiment, and served through the year.

SECOND LIEUTENANT MICHAEL LOOMIS of Egremont held that rank in Captain John Holmes' Company, in Colonel John Fellows's Minute Men's Regiment, April 21, 1775. He was Ensign of Captain William Bacon's Company, in Colonel John Fellows's Regiment in the Provincial army, as early as May 23, 1775 and served in that rank in the same command through the year.

SECOND LIEUTENANT ABIJAH MARKHAM of Tyringham marched in Captain William King's Company, in Colonel John Fellows's Regiment of Minute Men, April 21, 1775. He is credited in the records with a service of one month and three days, but his name does not appear in a list of the officers of the regiment, dated May 23, 1775. September 19, 1777, he enlisted as a Sergeant in Captain Noah Lankton's Company, Colonel John Ashley's 1st Berkshire County Regiment, on the expedition to Stillwater.

SECOND LIEUTENANT JAMES SHEPARD of Northampton served in that rank in Captain Jonathan Allen's Company of Minute Men in General Pomeroy's Regiment, April 20, 1775. He was reported as having returned home, May 3d, but his name appears in a list made up on the 23d of that month, as a Lieutenant in Captain Jonathan Allen's Company, Colonel John Fellows's Regiment. June 5, 1776, he was chosen Adjutant of the 2nd Hampshire County Regiment. He was engaged July 20, 1779, as Adjutant of Colonel Elisha Porter's 4th Hampshire County Regiment, to serve at New London, Connecticut; service one month twelve days.

SECOND LIEUTENANT JONATHAN STEARNS of Northampton was probably the man of that name who served as a private in Captain Phineas Lovett's Company in Colonel Abraham Williams's Regiment in 1759, and in Captain William Shepard's Company from June 27 to November 29, 1761. He was a Sergeant in Captain Jonathan Allen's Company, General Pomeroy's Regiment, which marched April 20, 1775. Seven days later he was engaged as Second Lieutenant of Captain Jonathan Allen's Company, Colonel John Fellows's Regiment, and served at least to August 1, 1775.

LIEUTENANT DAVID TULLAR of Sheffield was in Captain John Holme's Company, Colonel John Fellows's Regiment of Minute Men, which marched April 21, 1775. As his name appears second in the list of lieutenants of the company, he is placed in the list of second lieutenants in this article although the title was not qualified in the original.

ENSIGN NATHANIEL CRITTENTON of Great Barrington was a Sergeant in Captain William King's Company, Colonel John Fellows's Regiment of Minute Men, which marched April 21, 1775. He served under the same officers through the year, and through 1776 was Second Lieutenant in Captain Joseph Thompson's Company, in Colonel Nixon's 4th Continental Regiment. His name appears in a return of men enlisted for the month of January 1777, dated January 25, that year.

ENSIGN SOLOMON DEMING (or DEMMING) of Sandisfield was engaged April 21, 1775, to serve in that rank in Captain Moses Soul's Company, Colonel John Fellows's Regiment of Minute Men. May 6, 1776, he was commissioned First Lieutenant in Captain Samuel Wolcott's Company, Colonel Mark Hopkins's 1st Berkshire County Regiment. December 16, 1776, he entered Colonel Benjamin Symonds's detachment of Berkshire County Militia, as First Lieutenant in Captain George King's Company and served at Ticonderoga. This engagement ended March 15, 1777. In September-October 1777, he served as Lieutenant in Captain Samuel Wolcott's Company, Colonel John Ashley's 1st Berkshire County Regiment, serving under Brigadier General John Fellows, to reinforce the Northern army.

ENSIGN STEPHEN FITCH of Worthington was a Lieutenant in Captain Ebenezer Webber's Company of Minute Men which marched April 20, 1775, in response to the Lexington alarm. His name appears as Ensign in the same Captain's Company, in Colonel John Fellows's Regiment, in a list of officers dated May 23, 1775, but it was crossed out of the list dated eight days later. July 20, 1777, he enlisted as a private in Lieutenant Abner Dwellee's Company, on an expedition to Manchester. He also served twelve days in August 1777 in Lieutenant Constant Webster's Company, on an expedition to Bennington to reinforce the army under General Stark. He returned home via Northampton, conducting prisoners fron Bennington.

ENSIGN DANIEL KIRTLAND of Norwich was a Sergeant in Captain Lemuel Pomeroy's Company which marched April 21, 1775 in response to the Lexington alarm. April 27, 1775, he was engaged as Ensign in Captain Abner Pomeroy's Company, Colonel John Fellows's Regiment. His commission was ordered in the Council April 8, 1776, as Second Lieutenant in Captain John Kirkland's Company, in the 2nd Hampshire County Regiment and he marched with this company to Bennington in 1777. For the next three years at least, he served in the same regiment; in Captain Bonney's Company as First Lieutenant under Colonel Ezra May in 1777, at Stillwater

ENSIGN NATHANIEL CRITTENTON of Great Barrington was a Sergeant in Captain William King's Company, Colonel John Fellows's Regiment of Minute Men, which marched April 21, 1775. He served under the same officers through the year, and through 1776 was Second Lieutenant in Captain Joseph Thompson's Company, in Colonel Nixon's 4th Continental Regiment. His name appears in a return of men enlisted for the month of January 1777, dated January 25, that year.

ENSIGN SOLOMON DEMING (or DEMMING) of Sandisfield was engaged April 21, 1775, to serve in that rank in Captain Moses Soul's Company, Colonel John Fellows's Regiment of Minute Men. May 6, 1776, he was commissioned First Lieutenant in Captain Samuel Wolcott's Company, Colonel Mark Hopkins's 1st Berkshire County Regiment. December 16, 1776, he entered Colonel Benjamin Symonds's detachment of Berkshire County Militia, as First Lieutenant in Captain George King's Company and served at Ticonderoga. This engagement ended March 18, 1777. In September-October 1777, he served as Lieutenant in Captain Samuel Wolcott's Company, Colonel John Ashley's 1st Berkshire County Regiment, serving under Brigadier General John Fellows, to reinforce the Northern army.

ENSIGN STEPHEN FITCH of Worthington was a Lieutenant in Captain

etc., and in Captain John Kirtland's Company as Second Lieutenant under Colonel Israel Chapin, in 1778–9.

ENSIGN WILLIAM WATSON of Hatfield held that rank in Captain Israel Chapin's Company, Colonel John Fellows's Regiment of Minute Men, which marched April 20, 1775, in response to the Lexington alarm. April 27, 1775, he was engaged to serve in the same rank and under the same officers in the Provincial army. He served at least as late as August, and in all probability through the year. Through 1776 he was a Second Lieutenant in Colonel Jonathan Ward's 21st Continental Regiment. From January 1, 1777, until February or March 1778, he was a Lieutenant in Colonel James Wesson's 9th Regiment, Massachusetts Line, and from that date on, he served as Captain. His commission as Captain was later made to date from October 27, 1777. He continued to serve in this command until taken prisoner at Young's House, February 3, 1780. He was exchanged in December 1782, and was transferred to the 3d Regiment, Massachusetts Line, commanded by Lieut. Colonel James Millen. He was on furlough in January-February 1783, but remained an officer in the regiment until June 1783.

SOME ARTICLES CONCERNING MASSACHUSETTS IN RECENT MAGAZINES

By Charles A. Flagg

General. D. A. R. Mass. Report to 18th Continental Congress, D. A. R. (American historical magazine, July, 1909. v. 35, p. 340-348).

—— Recent Mass. labor legislation. By F. S. Baldwin. (Annals of the American Academy of Political and Social Science, Mar., 1909. v. 33, p. 63-66).

Barnstable. Barnstable vital records. Transcribed by G. E. Bowman. (Mayflower descendant, Apr., 1909. v. 11, p. 95-100).

Part 13; began in Oct., 1900. v. 2, p. 212.

Barnstable County. Abstracts from the Barnstable County probate records. (Mayflower descendant, Jan., 1909. v. 11, p. 26-28).

Part 7; series began July, 1900. v. 2 p. 176.

Boston. Experiments in fellowship: Work with Italians in Boston. By Vida D. Scudder. (The Survey, 3 Apr., 1909. v. 22, p. 47-51).

—— The new charter for Boston. (The Nation, 11 Feb., 1909. v. 88, p. 131-132).

—— Old South Chapter, D. A. R. Report by Sarah R. Sturgis, historian. (American historical magazine, July, 1909. v. 35, p. 37-39).

—— The regeneration of Beacon Hill: how Boston goes about civic improvement. (The Craftsman, Apr., 1909. v. 16, p. 92-95).

—— A study of Boston. By a Boston woman. (Outlook, 1 May, 1909. v. 92, p. 42-44).

Bristol County. Abstracts from the first book of Bristol County probate records. Copied by Mrs. L H. Greenlaw. (New England historical and genealogical register, Apr.-July, 1909. v. 63, p. ——-133, 227-233).

Parts 7-8 (1696-1697); First three instalments appeared in the Genealogical advertiser, Dec., 1900-Dec., 1901, — later parts in the Register.

Chatham. Chatham vital records. Transcribed by G. E. Bowman. (Mayflower descendant, Jan.-Apr., 1909. v. 11, p. 39-42, 119-121).

Parts 10-11; series began in July, 1902. v. 4, p. 182.

Chelsea. District nursing after the Chelsea fire. By Katharine B. Codman. (Charities and The commons, 11 Feb., 1909. v. 21, p. 970-973).

Deerfield. Great fights in early New England history, III. The battle of Bloody Brook By H. A. Bruce. (New England magazine, May, 1909. v. 40, p. 299-305).

Dennis. Records in the cemetery near the railroad station at South Dennis. Communicated by Miss Mary A. Baker. (Mayflower descendant, Jan., 1909. v. 11, p. 11-15).

Duxbury. Duxbury vital records. Transcribed by G. E. Bowman. (Mayflower descendant, Jan.-Apr., 1909. v. 11, p. 22-25, 77-82).

Parts 7-8; series began Oct., 1906. v. 8, p. 23.

—— Gravestone records in the Cemetery on Keene street, Ashdod. Inscriptions prior to 1851. Copied by S. W. Smith and J. W. Willard. (Mayflower descendant, Apr., 1909. v. 11, p. 104-106).

DUXBURY. Records from the Dingley cemetery, North Duxbury. Inscriptions prior to 1851. Communicated by Mrs. T. W. Thacher. (Mayflower descendant, Jan., 1909. v. 11, p. 55-58).

EASTHAM. The records of Wellfleet, formerly the North precinct of Eastham. (Mayflower descendant, 1909. v. 11, p. 73-78).

Part 8 (1745-1750); series began Oct., 1902. v. 4, p. 27.

ESSEX COUNTY. Custom House records of the Annapolis district, Md., relating to shipping from the ports of Essex Co., 1756-1775. (Essex Institute, Historical collections, July, 1909. v. 45, p. 256-282).

——. Essex County notarial records, 1697-1768. (Essex Institute, Historical collections, July, 1909. v. 45, p. 212-220).

Part 12 (1732-1736); series began Apr., 1905. v. 41, p. 183.

—— The prehistoric relics of Essex County. By John Robinson. (Essex antiquarian, July, 1909. v. 13, p. 97-101).

—— Soldiers and sailors of the Revolution. Essex antiquarian, July, 1909. v. 13, p. 126-131).

Names Broughton to Brown. From state records. Began in v. 1, Jan., 1897.

—— Suffolk County deeds. Volume IX. (Essex antiquarian, July, 1909. v. 13, p. 112-113).

Abstracts of all records in "Suffolk deeds" liber IX, relating to Essex County. Part 8; series began with liber I in July, 1905. v. 9, p 97.

HAMPSHIRE COUNTY. Letter from Hampshire County to Connecticut Colony, Sept. 28, 1693. Signed by Rev. Solomon Stoddard and 13 others. (New England historical and genealogical record, July, 1909. v. 63, p. 299).

IPSWICH. Ipswich inscriptions before 1800. Old Linebrook parish cemetery. (Essex antiquarian, July, 1909. v. 13, p. 114-116).

LOWELL. The Whistler memorial. (The Outlook, 9 Jan., 1909. v. 91, p. 53).

MARBLEHEAD. Parts of Salem and Marblehead in 1700. By Sidney Perley. (Essex antiquarian, July, 1909. v. 13, p. 132-138).

A continuation of his "Salem in 1700," of which 35 nos. appeared in the "Antiquarian" from Nov., 1898 to Apr., 1909.

MARLBOROUGH. Colonial records of Marlborough. Copied by Miss M. E. Spalding and communicated by F. P. Rice. (New England historical and genealogical register, Apr.-July, 1909. v. 63, p. —— 126, 217-226).

Parts 4-5; series began July, 1908. v. 62, p. 220.

MARSHFIELD. Records from the "Little" cemetery at Sea View. By J. W. Willard, S. W. Smith and E. H. Whorf. (Mayflower descendant, Apr., 1909 v. 11, p. 70-73).

—— Records of the First church in Marshfield. Transcribed from the original records by G. E. Bowman. (Mayflower descendant, Jan.-Apr., 1909. v. 11, p. 36-39, 121-123).

Parts 1-2 (1696-1704).

MEDFORD. A Medford incident. Rev. Mr. Ames' prayer in the M. E. Church, Apr., 1861. (Medford historical register, Apr., 1909. v. 12, p. 42-43).

—— The pump in the market place; and other water supplies of Medford, old and modern. By Eliza M. Gill. (Medford historical register, Apr., 1909, v. 12, p. 25-41).

MENDON. Ahaz Allen's record of marriages, 1819-1831. Communicated by L. A. Cook. (New England historical and genealogical register, July, 1909. v. 63, p. 273-276).

NORFOLK COUNTY, OLD. Old Norfolk County records. (Essex antiquarian, July, 1909. v. 13, p. 105-110).

Began in v. 1, Feb., 1897 Not the present Norfolk County, but a county organized in 1643, to include the towns north of Merrimack River.

NORWOOD. Norwood. By C. M. Rockwood. (New England magazine, Jan., 1909. v. 39, p. 606-613).

OXFORD. General Ebenezer Larned chapter, D. A. R. Report by Mrs. Sarah L. Bartlett, historian. (American monthly magazine, July, 1909. v. 35, p. 37).

PEMBROKE. "Friends" burying ground, Washington street, North Pembroke. Gravestone records before 1851, copied by J. W. Willard, S. W. Smith, E. H. Whorf and A. M. Jones. (Mayflower descendant, Apr., 1909. v. 11, p. 128.

—— Gravestone records from the cemetery at Pembroke Centre. Communicated by J. W. Willard. (Mayflower descendant, Jan., 1909. v. 11, p. 28–31).

Part 7 (Taylor–Witherell); series began in Jan., 1907. v. 9, p. 3.

—— Inscriptions prior to 1851 in Pine Grove cemetery, East Pembroke. Copied by J. W. Willard and S. W. Smith. (Mayflower descendant, Jan., 1909. v. 11, p. 63–64).

—— Records from the Cemetery at the corner of Water and Church streets, North Pembroke. Inscriptions prior to 1851. Copied by S. W. Smith, E. H. Whorf and A. M. Jones. (Mayflower descendant, Apr., 1909. v. 11, p. 86–87.)

PLYMOUTH COLONY. Plymouth Colony deeds. Transcribed by G. E. Bowman. (Mayflower descendant, Jan., 1909. v. 11. p. 15–18.)

Part 28 (1656–1657); series began in Apr., 1899. v. 1, p. 91.

—— Plymouth Colony wills and inventories. Transcribed by G. E. Bowman. (Mayflower descendant, Jan.–Apr., 1909. v. 11, p. 6–11, 87–95).

Parts 27–28 (1651–1652); series began in Jan., 1899. v. 1, p. 23.

PLYMPTON. Cemetery back of Congregational church, Plympton centre. Gravestone records before 1851, copied by S. W. Smith, E. H. Whorf, J. W. Willard and W. J. Ham. (Mayflower descendant, Apr., 1909. v. 11, p. 127–128).

—— Gravestone records in the Old cemetery at Plympton. Communicated by J. W. Willard. (Mayflower descendant, Apr., 1909. v. 11, p. 115–119).

Part 7 (Randall–Samson); series began in July, 1906. v. 8, p. 50.

—— Inscriptions in Small pox cemetery, Plympton Centre. Copied by S. W. Smith, E. H. Whorf, J. W. Willard and W. J. Ham. (Mayflower descendant, Jan., 1909. v. 11, p. 64).

PROVINCETOWN. Provincetown vital records. Transcribed by G. E. Bowman. (Mayflower descendant, Jan., 1909. v. 11, p. 47–49).

Part 2; began in Apr., 1907. v. 9. p. 100.

SALEM. Parts of Salem and Marblehead in 1700. By Sidney Perley. Essex antiquarian, July, 1909. v. 13, p. 132–138.

A continuation of his "Salem in 1700," of which 35 nos. appeared in the "Antiquarian from Nov., 1898 to Apr., 1909.

—— Revolutionary letters written to Col. Timothy Pickering. By George Williams of Salem. (Essex Institute. Historical collections, July, 1909. v. 45, p. 286–292).

Part 6 (conclusion); series began in Oct., 1906. v. 42, p. 313.

SCITUATE. Records of the First Church of Scituate. (Mayflower descendant, Jan, 1909. v. 11, p. 44–46).

Part 3 (Marriages by Rev. N. Pitcher, 1707–1723); series began in Apr., 1908. v. 10, p. 90.

SPRINGFIELD. An American holiday. By William Orr. (Atlantic monthly, June, 1909. v. 103, p. 782–789).

July 4th as observed in Springfield.

TRURO. Truro church records. Transcribed by G. E. Bowman. (Mayflower descendant, Jan., 1909. v. 11, p. 19–22).

Part 7; series began Jan., 1907. v. 9. p. 53.

WELLFLEET see EASTHAM.

WORCESTER. Results of a dry year. (The Survey, 29 Mar., 1909. v. 22, p. 301–302).

YARMOUTH. Yarmouth vital records. Transcribed by G. E. Bowman. (Mayflower descendant, Apr., 1909. v. 11, p. 111–114).

Part 10; series began in Oct., 1900. v. 2. p. 207.

General Ebenezer Larned chap... A. R. Report by Mrs. Sarah L. ..., historian. (American monthly ..., July, 1909. v. 35, p. 37).

... "Friends" burying ground, ...ton street, North Pembroke. ...one records before 1851; copied ... Willard, S. W. Smith, E. H. ... and A. M. Jones (Mayflower descendant, Apr. 1909. v. 11, p. 128).

...vestone records from the cemetery ... Pembroke Centre. Communicated by J. W. Willard. (Mayflower descendant, Jan., 1909. v. 11, p. 28–31).
...Taylor–Witherell); series began in Jan., ...

...riptions prior to 1851 in Pine ... cemetery, East Pembroke. Copied ... Willard and S. W. Smith (Mayflower descendant, Jan., 1909. v. 11, ...).

...ords from the Cemetery at the ... of Water and Church streets, ...mbroke. Inscriptions prior to ... J. W. Willard. (Mayflower descendant, Apr., 1909. v. 11, p. 115–119).
Part 7 (Randall–Samson); series began July, 1908, v. 8, p. 30.

—— Inscriptions in Small pox cemetery, Plympton Centre. Copied by S. W. Smith, E. H. Whorf, J. W. Willard and W. J. Ham. (Mayflower descendant, Jan., 1909. v. 11, p. 64).

Provincetown. Provincetown vital records. Transcribed by G. E. Bowman (Mayflower descendant, Jan., 1909. v. 11, p. 47–49).
Part 2; began in Apr., 1907, v. 9, p. 100.

Salem. Parts of Salem and Marblehead in 1700. By Sidney Perley. Essex antiquarian, July, 1908. v. 12, p. 132–138.
A continuation of his "Salem in 1700," of which 33 nos. appeared in the Antiquarian from Nov., 1898 to Apr., 1909.

—— Revolutionary letters written to Timothy Pickering. By George Williams of Salem. (Essex ... Hist... ical collections, July, 19... 5, 209–232).

THE OLD RAND HOUSE.

BY MRS. CAROLINE ROGERS HILL

At the corner of Wellesley and Chestnut streets in the town of Weston, stands a little, old gray house. It was built and occupied in 1696 or 1698 by Thomas Allen, but Thomas Rand is the first dweller, whose history is known to us. On the day of the Lexington alarm, he, then a man of forty-eight years, and his sons, were engaged in building the barn, which still stands.* His son, Thomas, Jr., succeeded him.

The daughter of Thomas, Jr., Clarissa by name, married a Mr. Henry Robbins, a market gardener. They were living on the old Warren place in Roxbury, when Mr. Rand found that the place required more care than he was able to give. Accordingly, he sent for his daughter and son-in-law, who then came to make their home there, probably in 1832. The children were Sarah, Oliver J., and "Grandma Hastings." The latter died in 1908, at eighty-one years of age, and was six when she went to live there. Neither Oliver J. Robbins nor Sarah were married, and they lived together in the old house until the death of Oliver J. in 1903, when the place was sold to William H. Hill of Brookline, the present owner.

The exterior of the old mansion is simplicity itself. It is needless to say that the house has never been painted and that the clapboards, which the present owner has been strenuously attempting to preserve, have for many years been offering wood fibre to the hornets for their domiciles, and have been wearing away from long exposure to wind, sunshine and rain. The guardian trumpet vine relieves the severity of form and color, tempts the graceful humming-bird to its bright blossoms, and later the young orioles, destructive creatures, which snap off the blossoms and buds to get at the deeply hidden honey.

---

* In "Lexington Alarms," Vol. 12, page 170, the names of Thomas Rand and Thomas Rand, Jr. appear as among those who marched from Weston in "Capt. Samuel Lamson's Militia Company on ye 19th of April, 1775, for the Defence of the Colony against the Ministerial Forces"—and fought during the "Revolution."

Entering the house one comes into a little hallway only deep enough to allow the door to swing back. At the right-hand a door opens into a good sized closet; a narrow door on the left, into a smaller one. Directly facing one, looking into the small closet, is a blind door, opening into the unique feature of the house, a large dark compartment of the chimney. This is coated with soot and redolent with the odor of hams smoked there many, many years ago. The beams in this smoke-room are now coated with a tarry-like substance. Upon looking up, daylight is visible through a small flue in the chimney.

Before going further with the arrangement of the rooms it may be well to explain the necessarily small space available for the front hallway. The house is veritably built about its chimney, for there is but one, but this is very large. Owing to its size, and therefore its weight, it is built on a rock foundation level with the surface of the ground, thus dividing the cellar into two parts, oblong in shape and not large. In the cellar nearest the barn are several deep niches, faced with flat stones. I am told that these were receptacles of barrels cf the favorite beverage of the New England farmer. At the head of the stone stairs leading down to the cellar on the opposite side of the house is a large iron staple, to which a tackle was fastened, for lowering kegs or barrels to the cellar below.

A peculiar feature of the house is a little room, a sort of half cellar, which leads off from the stone stairway half way between the ground floor and the cellar. Its floor is lined with flat stones and the walls are fitted with shelves. It was the old time milk room. Air from outside was let in through a grated window. It is hardly necessary to comment upon the disfavor with which such surroundings for milk would be met today.

From the front hallway a door on the left opens into the dining-room. This is by far the largest room in the house. Two windows on the front and two on the southwest side let in abundant air and sunshine. The fireplace measured six and one-half feet across, originally, but this has been reduced in size and a Franklin frame set in. The kitchen is fairly narrow, but occupies the entire rear side of the house, excepting the space occupied by the small side-hallway. Here the busy housewife, with her many labors was busy. Here the men of the family discussed the stirring questions of the day: fit candidates to represent them in the Great and General Court, Taxation without Representation, the Declaration of Independence, and the various phases of the War of the Revolution. Here Thomas Rand melted, trimmed and boxed bullets before the fire. The fireplace originally was ten feet in length and five feet in height with the inevitable brick oven on the

left. Over the door, which leads to the cellar, a long and narrow door opens into a box-like closet which projects into the cellar directly over the stairway.

A narrow passageway, lighted by three panes of glass set in a frame, one directly above the other, opens from the kitchen and from this the stairs lead to the floor above, a very narrow door opens into the parlor. This is on the northeast side of the house, and is less cheerful than the large dining-room and also smaller. The most interesting feature of this room is the shutters which push back into the wall and were discovered by accident. Their existence was unknown to one of the previous occupants who had lived there from 1837 until 1902.

Passing up a few stairs of the hallway one comes upon a little room directly over the milk room mentioned before. This was undoubtedly the cheese room, and above this is a little room six feet by six, exactly the size of the cheese room and the milk room underneath. One of the steps leading up to it has received the name of "The Secret Stairs," as the tread may be removed and replaced, and the hollow space of the stairway used for secreting articles of value. An early resident affirms that this was the purpose of this stair.

Over the parlor is a large bed-room in which is a fireplace, as there is in the parlor below, and over the front hallway is another little box of a room used for a bed-room. The space over the dining-room has been divided into two rooms. In these rooms, underneath many thicknesses of wall paper, newspaper, silk and calico, a wide beveled panelling of richly colored pine was discovered by the present occupants. The rest of the room upstairs is unfinished, so that a generous amount of space on the second floor and at the top of the house makes a typical attic.

The names of members of the Rand Family appear in the town records as serving on the Board of Selectmen, as making repairs on the meeting house and school buildings, serving on committees to examine the War Committee's accounts, and being active in all the affairs of the day.

Thus the old house is closely associated with generations of this family and with earlier generations of the Puritan settlers. Its ancient rooms have witnessed much joy and sorrow. Its dwellers have looked out upon many thrilling scenes. Its builders and many who have made their home under its roof, have long since gone to their rest, but the old mansion binds them all together, and links them with the present. Its simple lines and enduring strength fitly commemorate the strong and simple lives of the Past.

Department of the American Revolution

1775-1782

FRANK A. GARDNER, M. D. Editor.

State Sloop Republic.

The "Republic" was one of the five vessels authorized in February, 1776. Her name was reported by a committee appointed for that purpose and was accepted, April 19, 1776. She was a sister vessel of the "Freedom" and was built at Swanzey at the same time.

Her first officers were the following:

Captain, John Foster Williams, entered service, May 14, 1776.

First Lieutenant, Samuel Laha, entered service, May 28, 1776.

Second Lieutenant, Joseph Smith, entered service, June 12, 1776.

Master, Isaiah Studson, entered service, June 12, 1776.

Surgeon, Moses Barnard, entered service, August 20, 1776.

CAPTAIN JOHN FOSTER WILLIAMS was a noted commander in the war and this was the first vessel assigned him. A full account of him with the record of his service in State vessels and privateers, has already been given in this magazine in the article upon the State brigantine "Hazard" in v. I, p. 199,

FIRST LIEUTENANT SAMUEL LAHA so far as the records show had seen no naval service previous to being engaged for the "Republic." He was engaged May 28 and commissioned June 12, 1776.

SECOND LIEUTENANT JOSEPH SMITH was engaged and commissioned on the same day, June 12, 1776.

MASTER ISAIAH STUDSON (or Stutson) was also engaged on that date.

SURGEON MOSES BARNARD of Lancaster, served first as Surgeon's Mate to Dr. Dinsmore, in Colonel Asa Whitcomb's Regiment, entering that regiment May 22, 1775. He was examined and approved by a committee July 7, 1775. His name appears in a receipt for wages in Captain Fuller's Company, Colonel Whitcomb's Regiment, for August-September, 1775, dated Prospect Hill. He was engaged as Surgeon of the sloop "Republic" August 20, 1776.

The following document relating to the fitting-out of this vessel is of interest:

"In Council, September 19, 1776.

Ordered, That Benjamin Austin, Esq. be, and hereby is appointed and empowered to provide the vessels of war commanded by Captain Williams and Captain Clouston with such stores, cannon, and other articles, as may be necessary to equip for sea; and the Commissary-General is hereby directed to supply the said vessels, out of the publick store, with such things as by said Austin, shall be required of him and William Watson, Esq., of Plimouth, who has been appointed agent to take care of the stores belonging to the Rising-Empire. Captain Walden, late Master is hereby directed to furnish the said vessels with such articles out of the stores of Brig Rising Empire as he may be directed to supply by the said Austin.

And it is further Ordered, That Benjamin Austin be and is empowered to order either of the above-named vessels to sail to Plymouth, and take on board and transport such stores and other necessary articles there, to the Harbour of Boston."

Captain Williams was ordered on September 19th to sail from Dartmouth to Boston, accompanying the State sloop

"Freedom," Captain John Clouston, "and there to wait for the further orders of the Council."

The following record explains itself:

"In Council, Oct. 1, 1776.

Whereas Captain John Foster Williams of the Sloop Republick and Captain John Clouston of the Sloop Freedom, both belonging to this State, are in want of some iron ballast that they may immediately proceed on their intended cruise; therefore the Committee for fortifying the Harbour of Boston be, and they are hereby directed to deliver the said Williams and Clouston, out of the row-galley lying in Boston harbour, so much iron ballast as they may stand in need of at this time for their several sloops."

During this month Richard Devens delivered to Captain John Foster Williams's order, "six Cannon, 6-pound £50 each, £300,00:00."

October 5, 1776, Captain Williams was ordered to cruise oft Nantucket in search of a fleet of about 20 topsail vessels. Shortly after this he captured the British armed ship "Julius Caesar" with a valuable cargo.

Reference to this ship and her crew was made in the following order:

"In Council Chamber, November, 5, 1776

Ordered, That Captain Jno Foster Williams be directed to discharge from on board the privateer sloop Republick, under his command, as many of those Seamen taken in the ship Julius Caesar as incline and shall in fact enter on board any armed vessel in this or any of the United States, and those of them who incline to go to Halifax be retained on board the said sloop till further orders."

The value of the prize and her cargo is shown by the following extract from the records:

"By N[t] proceeds Ship Julius Caesar,
Sloop Republick, Williams, £24581:17:1."

CAPTAIN JOHN FOSTER WILLIAMS commanded the "Republic" until December 5, 1776. From the 16th of that month until February 17, 1777, he commanded the State brigantine "Massachusetts." He was in command of the privateers "Active" and "Wilkes" in 1777, the State brigantine "Hazard" in 1778, the State ship "Protector" in 1779 and the ship "Alexander" in 1783. His full record has been given in the "Massachusetts Magazine," v. I, p. 199.

The remaining officers of the 'Republic received their discharge from her, November 18, 1776.

FIRST LIEUTENANT SAMUEL LAHA (or LAYHA) was commissioned to serve in that rank in the privateer brigantine "Hancock," Captain Daniel McNeil, November 30, 1776. Later he saw service in the same rank in the privateer brig "Active" under Captain John Foster Williams. She was a vessel of 85 tons, fitted out at Boston, in October, 1777. He was captured in her and his name appears in a list of prisoners sent from Newport, R. I., in prison ship "Lord Sandwich." He landed at Bristol, R. I., March 7, 1778. In the following year he was Master of the schooner "Hannah," according to a list of transports laden with provisions for the troops at Penobscot, as returned by John Lucas, Commissary, dated, Boston, July 12, 1779.

SECOND LIEUTENANT JOSEPH SMITH after leaving the "Republic" saw no further service so far as the records show.

MASTER ISAIAH STUDSON served as First Lieutenant in the ship "Rattlesnake," in 1781, under Captain Mark Clark.

SURGEON MOSES BARNARD'S name does not appear in the records after

his service in the "Republic" was completed.

The "Republic" was fitted out in December for a cruise to the West Indies, with the following officers according to a list in the State archives:

Captain, Allen Hallet, engaged December 5, 1776.

Master's Mate, Charles Hallet, engaged December 6, 1776.

CAPTAIN ALLEN HALLET had served in August 1776, as commander of the privateer "Sturdy Beggar" of Salem. He was engaged as Master of the State sloop "Republic," December 5, 1776.

MATE CHARLES HALLET was the only other officer mentioned in a list of the officers on this cruise, in the archives. October 6, 1776, he was engaged as Quarter master of the State sloop "Republic" under Captain John Foster Williams, and served until November 18, 1776. He was engaged as Master's Mate of the same vessel under Captain Allen Hallet, December 6, 1776.

Details about this cruise are given in the following documents:

"To the Hon[ble] the Council,

The Board of War Having fitted out the Sloop Republic Allen Hallet Master, navigated with ten hands, for the West Indies, mounting two 4 pd Cannon & ten Swivel Guns, & apprehending it may be of Service if the Master be furnished with a Commifsion for a Letter of Marque, do desire a Commifsion for him as such.

By Order of the Board

Sam Phps Savage Prest.

The vefsell will have 10 bbs provisions & 20 0 of Bread.

In Council Jan. 16, 1777.

Read & Ordered That a Commifsion be ifsued out to Allen Hallet Comoft he above mentianed Sloop, he complying with the Refolves of Congrefs.

Jno Avery, Dpy Secy.

Jan. 15, 1777."

A note in the records shows that supplies, not specified, were furnished the "Republic," January 16, 1777.

CAPTAIN ALLEN HALLET was commissioned September 12, 1777, commander of the privateer brigantine "Starks," and commander of the privateer brigantine "America," December 24th of the same year. He was Captain of the famous State brigantine "Tyrannicide" from July 6, 1778, to April 30, 1779. May 1, 1779, he was engaged as Captain of the State brig "Active," and commanded her until she was burned off Brigadier's Island, Penobscot, August 14, 1779, to prevent her falling into the hands of the enemy. February 16, 1780, he was commissioned commander of the privateer brigantine "Phoenix," and August 3d of that year was engaged as Captain of the State ship "Tartar." June 22, 1781, he was commissioned commander of the privateer ship "Franklin" and February 28. 1782, he received his commission as Captain of the privateer brigantine "Minerva."

MATE CHARLES HALLET has no further record of service. In the summer of 1777, the "Republic" went on a voyage under orders from the Board of War, to Martinique, with the following officers:

Master (in command) Isaac Bartlett, entry June 1, 1777.

Mate, Joseph Holmes, entry June 9, 1777.

Second Mate, Jeremiah Holmes, entry June 9, 1777.

Seventeen others made up the crew.

CAPTAIN ISAAC BARTLETT (or BARTLET) commanded first the State schooner "Plymouth."

MATE JOSEPH HOLMS (or HOLMES) and JEREMIAH (or JARNEAH) HOLMS had neither of them seen any service previous to this on the "Republic."

A letter is preserved in the Archives which was written from Port Royal, Mar-

tinique, November 25, 1777, by G. Hutchinson the agent, to S. A. Otis, President of the Board of War, announcing the arrival of the Sloop "Republic" and giving an account of the cargo and its condition. The salmon were mentioned as "exceedingly good" but unsalable there. "The Mackarel were quite spoiled" and the agent was glad to get rid of them at any price. "The Master being dead & the Mate confined to his Cabbin notwithstanding the care that was taken many more of the boards were used or wasted Headg Beds & Coins than were necefsary. Most part of the Staves were not merchantable; many of them and the Hoops thrown overboard on ye pafsage when they were chaced. But as they were sold here in Neat hundreds they fell but little short. The Ox Bows & yokes are very little used by ye French. There were but 12 Setts Trufs Hoops delivered me which the Mate says was all that were shipped altho' your Inv^o says 24 Setts. I saved as much as possible of the unreasonable Duties on Fish, Molafses & Rum. This Latter was obliged to clear out as the produce of this Island & pay the Duty on it altho' it is foreign rum. Capt Bartlett had employed a Cooper immediately on his arrival & Bought the Shook Hhds, & during his Illness, the Mate & all the other people were sick on board, except the Cooper who was employed in taking care of him, otherwise he would have been of more Service in making Casks for the Cargo. . . . As the Mate was so Dangerously ill that I was obliged to send him to ye Hospital & still continues in such an ill state of Health as to be incapable of taking the command of her to go on a winter's Coast I judged it prudent to put in another Master.

Capt. Carey the present Master, came to ye W. Indies about Nine months ago in ye employ of the State of Maryland, was taken by one of the non-commifsioned Priv^at and Carried into Antigua. He has ever Since Commanded a Priv^e out of this Island & has Distinguished himself & as he is now returning home, I thought I could not intrust your property in better hands." He wrote that he had taken care of Captain Bartlett's effects.

CAPTAIN CAREY is not mentioned elsewhere in regard to this service. He may have been the Captain John Carey who was commissioned commander of the privateer sloop, "Retaliation," March 18, 1778.

No record of the "Republic" has been found of a later date than the above named voyage from Martinique.

F. A. G.

Heroes and Monuments.

The oft repeated statement that "Republics are ungratefol" has been frequently reasserted and variously explained. One of the chief causes of this seeming ingratitude in the opinion of the writer, is the freedom of speech which we as sharers of the privileges of self-government all enjoy. This freedom of speech antedates our national life-span many years. The founders of these United States indulged in it vigorously, long before the Concord fight or the promulgation of the Declaration of Independence. All through our history it has been one of our most highly prized and frequently used privileges.

No man who has come prominently before the American people, has escaped its attacks. Washington is today honored by the entire civilized world, but no man in his life time suffered more from its open and often virulent onslaughts than the "Father of the Country."

Thinking men must certainly regret that indiscrete or misinformed public speakers so frequently attack the memories of deceased heroes, and obscure their deeds of

valor by their unjust accusations. A recent unfortunate instance of this is reported to have occurred in Boston on July 4th of this year when the Reverend Thomas Van Ness, according to the daily press, gave utterance to the following:

"Can it be true" he asked, "that instead of honoring today our revolutionary forefathers, we should abhor the names of those who brought on war and bloody battle? If war is so costly, why not save the many millions gained by peace and engage in industrial enterprises? Honor, justice and right cannot be measured in dollars and cents, nor in human lives." He described the type of man in whose memory he would erect a monument, and deplored the present position of some of the statues, especially that of General Hooker, "standing in the grounds of the State House, overshadowing as it does all other statues in Boston by its commanding location and expensiveness. . . . Boston is not alone in this placing of the crown of enduring honor upon certain insignificant and unheroic men," he said. He deplored the condition in the national capital where "the statues of the war heroes are given the places that should be given to hero patriots, and where the man on horseback does not bring to consciousness some struggle of an oppressed people, as would the statues of Washington, Wayne and Starke, but does recall a fratricidal war. . . . This is the standard I would have for our monuments," he said, "if they are to mean anything worth while. If a monument was to be put up to a soldier, I would ask, first of all, 'Was there an ideal element in the man,' as in the case of Colonel Shaw leading the black regiment, or was he simply a profane talker a rough, ungentlemanly type of fighter like 'Phil' Sheridan or 'Joe' Hooker?"

The writer upon reading this attack upon General Sheridan, felt compelled to make answer. Having met the general socially, and given much study to the Shenandoah valley campaign, he felt that such unjust words should not go unchallenged. General Sheridan personally, was an affable, courteous gentleman, who deeply impressed those with whom he came in contact. If as a great leader of men in a campaign, he appeared to our clerical friend "rough and ungentlemanly," it was because he believed that his country needed vigorous and aggressive warfare, and the results of his forced fighting amply justified him in the eyes of his fellow countrymen.

Once before we have read derogatory words against "Little Phil," as his men loved to call him. General Jubal A. Early, his opponent in the Shenandoah valley, in his "Own Story," also declaimed against him, and thought that Sheridan should have been cashiered instead of promoted. Sheridan had defeated him and laid waste the fertile valley which had been Early's base of supplies, thus stopping the disastrous raids, upon the National capital and outlying towns. The term "ungentlemanly" is puerile and effeminate in any such connection. The bone which he had to pick with Early was not a disagreement between members of a club at a smoke talk, but a bitter, aggressive campaign, upon which depended the safety of the city of Washington and the integrity of the nation.

Sheridan saw that the only way to check Early was to turn the fertile valley into a desert and he did it and put an end to the raids. We can well imagine what the effect would have been of a polite ("gentlemanly" if you please) request forwarded to General Early, requesting him to desist from raiding, in the name of humanity. Sheridan was successful because he "knew his man" and had the courage to go ahead and crush him in the only way possible.

The whole country in the Spanish-American war, united in honoring General Joseph Wheeler, the gallant leader who had won renown in the Confederate army by similar vigorous and energetic fighting.

War is to be deplored and avoided whenever the honor and integrity of the nation can be maintained without open conflict. When, however, other means fail and war actually begins, the men who earn the nation's gratitude, are the leaders who, by their courage, skill and aggressiveness, bring the conflict to an end as soon as possible. Such men were Greene and Morgan and Wayne in the Revolution, and Grant and Sherman and Sheridan in the war of the Rebellion, and such deserve the stately monuments of a grateful people.

F. A. G.

The Dedication of the Massachusetts Bay at Valley Forge.

All loyal sons of the old Bay State will rejoice in the completion and appropriate dedication of the Massachusetts Bay in the Cloister of Colonies of the Washington Memorial Chapel at Valley Forge. The members of the Massachusetts Society, Sons of the American Revolution, have honored themselves and the noble state which they represent in carrying on this work to a successful termination. The Bay was dedicated on Evacuation Day, June 19, 1909, the orator of the day being the Reverend Lewis Wilder Hicks, A. M., Chaplain of the society. In his very eloquent address he said: "Massachusetts, with the record made by her sons at Lexington, Concord and Bunker Hill, has reason to be more proud of none of her sons than of those soldiers of her eleven regiments who faithfully stood by the colors during that fateful winter at Valley Forge. The spirit shown in the writings of Col. Brooks and Surgeon Waldo,—the spirit that rose superior to adverse circumstances, that denied itself, that was unfalteringly loyal, that emerged from trial triumphant, is something that should be forever commemorated. If valor which has had but an hour to display itself is worthy of monumental recognition, how much more worthy to be remembered is that valor which holds out through weeks and months of privation and suffering! How eminently fitting, then, it was that the Massachusetts Society, Sons of the American Revolution, should embrace this opportunity that was graciously offered to them to join with the representatives of the other of the thirteen original states in paying honor here to her sons, and to the soldiers from the other colonies, who, on this holy ground, proved of what stuff heroes are made; and who by their fidelity to principle, made possible the independence of the United States! By erecting this Bay in the Cloister of Colonies we would testify both to the heroism of those brave men and to the gratitude in which the old state of Massachusetts would forever enshrine their memory."

The Reverend W. Herbert Burk, rector in charge, is doing a grand work in arousing enthusiastic interest in this chapel and it is hoped that before many years have elapsed he will see the completion not only of the "Cloister of Colonies" but also the Chapel and Patriots' Hall, "Porch of the Allies" and Thanksgiving Tower. Many officers of the state society were present including President E. C. Battis, Secretary Herbert W. Kimball, Chaplain Rev. L. W. Hicks, Dr. Charles M. Green, Mr. Charles F. Reed, Mr. William W. Pearson and many others. The local committee was a strong and representative one and their entertainment of the guests was greatly appreciated by all. F. A. G.

Fall Field Day, Massachusetts Society, S. A. R.

The fall field day of this society will be held at Salem on Wednesday, September 25th, 1909, at which time it is hoped that the tablet to be erected upon the Jonathan Haraden House will be unveiled with appropriate ceremonies. The plans for the day's celebration have not been completed as yet but they will probably include a pilgrimage about the city in the morning, a banquet in Ames Memorial Hall, to be followed by the formal exercises in the afternoon with an address upon Captain Jonathan Haraden by the president of Old Salem Chapter, Dr. Frank A. Gardner. Is is a matter of sincere congratulation that the distinguished services of this hero of the war for the independence of America, are to receive proper and enduring recognition. F. A. G.

Criticism & Comment

on Books and Other Subjects

Tenth Annual Reunion of the Chase–Chase Family Association.

A very successful reunion was held at the Vendome in Boston on June 30, 1909. Among the many good things upon the programme was a valuable paper by William E. Gould of Brookline, Mass., upon the "Early History of Aquila Chase; Emigrant." He said that Aquila and his brother Thomas, came to Hampton, N. H., in 1639, in a vessel whose name is not known. In 1640 he received a grant of 6 acres and 4 years later 6 acres more. This land was near the marsh where the fishermen drew up their boats near the Deacon Perkins place, and the location of Aquila's house is known by an old man still living at the age of 90 years. Aquila was a fisherman and this was probably the reason of his removal to Newbury. In 1646 Newbury gave him 4 acres for a house lot and a farm lot of 6 acres if he would go fishing for four years. This lot was on what is now the corner of Federal and Water Streets in Newburyport. He lived here until 1658, when he sold the place to one Moody, a maltster. It has been stated that Aquila was a sea captain going on foreign voyages, but he was a shore fisherman and pilot. The story of the pea-picking episode "on ye Lord's day" has been variously embellished. The facts are that Aquila was served with a writ for so doing and smiled. As the writ called him "of Hampton" a new one was made out and he paid the fine. He moved about 1646 to Sawyer's Lane and lived until 1670.

The Reverend James DeNormandie, D.D. spoke in his usual pleasing vein and told many amusing stories about the candor of his noble predecessor in the Roxbury Church, the Apostle John Eliot, in his notes and comments in the church records. Other addresses were delivered by the President of the association John C. Chase of Derry Village, N. H. and the Reverend Dr. George A. Crawford, U. S. N. Retired. Several excellent musical numbers and a poem "The Pioneer" by Mrs. Clara Ross Dudley of Somerville, Mass., completed the programme.

William Abbatt's "Magazine of History."

In the old days before historical periodicals in this country were as numerous or as highly specialized as they have since become, Dawson's "Historical Magazine" came pretty near occupying the entire field; from 1857 to 1875. Then came the "Magazine of American History" which flourished from 1877 to 1893 and was frequently known by the name of Mrs. Martha J. Lamb, who was its editor during the greater part of its life. Since the decease of the latter periodical there have been many magazines attempting to cover our country's history, and some of them are with us today. Perhaps it is not generally known that after the lapse of nearly a quarter of a century, Mrs. Lamb's magazine has a namesake continuing the voluming of the original. This periodical, however, is of slight importance: scarcely more than notes and queries. But the old "Magazine of American History" has a real successor in William Abbatt's "Magazine of History" which began publication in 1905 in New York. Valuable as it is in

the chosen field, probably New England receives less than its fair share of attention owing to the multiplicity of historical serials in one section. It is rather the "Extra numbers" issued by the magazine that are of peculiar interest to us: one of the several agencies now at the work of reprinting old and valuable Americana.

No. 4 contains a reprint of "A plain narrativ of the uncommon sufferings and remarkable deliverance of Thomas Brown of Charlestown in New England." Two editions were printed in Boston in 1760; this is a reprint of the second.

No. 5 is entirely devoted to reprints of matter on the Pigwacket fight. This Indian skirmish took place near Fryeburg, Me., in 1725, but not only was the region at that time in Mass., but the men engaged, Lovewell's company, came from Dunstable, Groton, Lancaster, Billerica and Haverhill. The reprints include "The expedition of Capt. John Lovewell. . . By Frederic Kidder 1865;" "Historical Memoirs of the late fight at Piggwacket, with a sermon . . . By Thomas Symmes. 2d ed. 1725;" "John Chamberlain, the Indian fighter at Pigwacket. By G. W. Chamberlain, 1898;" also a collection of contemporary and other illustrative material. C. A. F.

Pilgrims and Planters
1620–1630

LUCIE M. GARDNER, A. B., Editor.

Settlers About Boston Bay Prior to 1630.

(Continued from Vol. II, No. 2.)

About this time Blackstone moved across to the north side of Boston Bay. David Thompson seems to have come over to New England early in 1623, bringing with him his wife and a number of servants. He (according to Samuel Maverick) settled on a point of land near the entrance of the Piscataqua River. In 1626 he moved down to Boston Bay and established himself on the island which still bears his name. Of the number of dwellings in the settlements, except in the case of Merry Mount, we have no definite knowledge. At that place there were seven, all men, and at Hull there were several families. Thompson, Maverick and Walford were married and all had children. We have no means of knowing the number of servants, but there may have been in 1627 somewhere in the neighborhood of fifty whites of all ages and both sexes, dwelling in seven separate settlements on the shores of Boston Bay, according to the estimate made by General Charles Francis Adams.

As long as Morton, "mine host of Merre Mount" as he chose to style himself, was content with amusements, there was little but the verbal remonstrance of his scandalized Plymouth neighbors, to disturb him. He was here, however, for trade as well as pleasure and he adopted a fatal policy. As General Adams says, "he provided the Indians with the two things they most craved, fire-arms and fire-water." The disfavor of his neighbors soon deepened into alarm. The planters saw plainly that either this illicit trade must be stopped or the straggling settlers must leave the country. Accordingly the heads of the various plantations arranged a meeting to take counsel for the common safety. This meeting took place early in 1628, and included the Hiltons from Dover, Conant, Balch and Palfrey from Salem, as well as those about Boston Bay. A messenger was sent to Morton asking him to desist from his dangerous practises, but he answered unsatisfactorily, and undertook to carry things with a high hand. They decided to send Miles Standish with a sufficient force to arrest him. He was taken prisoner to the Isle of Shoals, whence a month later he was sent to England. Three months after this, September 6, 1628, Governor John Endicott landed in Salem. The patent under which he came, plainly included the whole region in which Wessagusset, Mount Wollaston, Thompson's Island and Shawmut were situated, as the boundary was three miles south of the shore of Boston Bay. John Endicott, that typical Puritan magistrate, immediately gave violent expression to his disapproval of Morton and his followers. He crossed the Bay, hewed down the Maypole and rebuked Morton's terrified followers.

After this visit of Endicott, no mention is made of these settlers about Boston Harbour until the summer of 1629. On the ship George, which reached Salem on the 20th of June in that year, came the Reverends Francis Higginson, and Samuel Skelton, and several men who had emigrated at their own expense. Among these were the three brothers named Sprague, sons of a Dorsetshire fuller. Instead of settling in Salem, they pushed on through the woods to a spot on the north side of the Charles River, where they obtained from Sagamore John, a son of Nanepashemet, permission to establish themselves on a hill in the place called Mishawum, where lived Thomas Walford, a smith. The Spragues were soon followed by a larger party from Salem under the charge of Thomas Graves, an engineer, who was to "survey and set forth lands" and "to fortify and build a town." In the course of the summer at the mouth of the Mystic, a place was laid out on a plan approved by Governor Endicott and a large house built. This was Charlestown and it was intended to be the seat of govern ment of Massachusetts Bay. The large house, intended for the many who were soon to come, became the Charlestown

meeting house. In the autumn of 1629, about 100 persons are supposed to have been living near it.

In the latter part of 1629, Endicott, in pursuance of instructions from England, summoned the settlers to meet in a General Court in Salem. He informed them of the general policy to be followed and presented certain articles which he and Rev. Samuel Skelton had drawn up. Morton, who had returned to New England, alone refused to sign. He openly defied Endicott and did all he could to breed discontent among the old planters. Morton had profited by past experiences and when a party was sent across to seize him, they found that he had escaped. He would have been dealt with in summary fashion if Endicott's men had caught him then, but the winter of 1629–30 demanded all the Governor's care and thought. On the 30th of May, 1630, the much longed for relief came, when the "Mary and John," under Captain Squib, cast anchor off Hull. There were on board 120 passengers, the advance of that larger body of emigrants who had embarked with Winthrop on the fleet at Southampton, only two days after Captain Squib sailed from Plymouth. Captain Squib doubtless knew that in landing them at Hull he was not fulfilling his contract, but land them he did and they were obliged to shift for themselves. They rowed along the shore and encamped at the spot since occupied as the U. S. Arsenal at Watertown and long known as Dorchester fields. They soon removed from there and finally settled on Dorchester Heights, now better known as South Boston. June 12, 1630, Winthrop's company sailed into Salem harbor and soon after went on to Boston bay, where they landed and "began to build their houses against winter; and this place was called Boston."

JOHN BAKER, Charlestown 1629–30, number 12 on the first list of inhabitants. He and his wife Charity were admitted to the church, March 3, 1633. The General Court allowed him 38 shill. from Mr. Clerk, 7 Sept., 1630, for damages in a bargain of cloth.

JOHN BALCH came from Somerset Co., England. He was born about 1579 and came to New England with the Robert Gorges Company in 1623. After Gorges left he went in 1624 to Cape Ann, removing to Naumkeag (now Salem) in 1626. He was one of the five overseers in 1635, and on Nov. 25th of the same year was one of the five old planters, who received a grant of 200 acres each at the head of Bass River. He lived in Beverly near the present Kittredge Crossing, where the house built by him in 1638 is still standing. This is the only original house of a Cape Ann planter still in existence. He died in May, 1648. His descendants have been numerous and many of them prominent.

WILLIAM BLACKSTONE was one of the first to come to Boston Bay. Governor Hopkins in his "History of Providence" says that he had been at Boston long enough, before the company of settlers came "to raise apple trees and plant an orchard." He lived as we have already stated on the western slope of the peninsula of Shawmut, opposite the mouth of the Charles River. He subscribed toward the expense of returning Thomas Morton to England in 1628. He was appointed one of the attorneys of the Council of New England to put Mr. Oldham in possession of his grant and to transfer the Council grant to Thomas Lewis, gentleman, and Captain Richard Boynthon. The document signed by Warwick and Gorges was endorsed by the attorneys, June 28, 1631. Cotton Mather refers to him as a "goodly Episcopalian." He was granted 50 acres of land near his home in Boston, April 1, 1630.

He removed from Boston in 1635, and began a settlement in that part of the town of Rehoboth which is now Cumberland, R. I., on the banks of the river which bears his name. Mr. Leonard Bliss in his "History of Rehoboth," writes as follows: "The character of Blackstone so far as developed to us is one of peculiar interest and singular eccentricity. He was one of the few whose spirits are centuries in advance of the age in which they are sent as though by mistake to take up their abode on earth. Born at a time when religion formed the whole business instead of the mere pastime of life and finding the freedom of conscience so necessary to the enjoyment of that religion whose native air is liberty, untrammelled by the shackles of ignorance and bigotry, inseparable companions, he left the land of his fathers, the friends of his youth and the scenes of his boyhood and sought an asylum on the stern and rock-bound shores of New Eng-

land. Here he found with the untutored savage that right which the polished Christian had denied him, 'Freedom to worship God,' and when this far off retreat was invaded by men stern and intolerant and inheriting much of the bigotry of the mother country, he uttered no complaints, he provoked no quarrels, but quietly sold his lands and again retired from the face of civilization and again took up his solitary abode in the wilderness, and luckily for his peace, the tide of civilization had but just reached him at the period of his death." It was on the occasion of his leaving Boston that he made the celebrated speech, which tradition has preserved and handed down to us: "I came from England because I did not like the Lord Bishops, but I cannot join with you because I would not be under the Lord Brethren." Jameson states that he died in 1675.

WILLIAM BRACKENBURY, planter, was in Charlestown, according to Pope, in 1630. As Putnam in his list states that he was there in 1629, we include him in this list. He applied to be made a freeman in October 19, 1630 and was admitted March 4, 1632. He was a town officer. November 1, 1639 he sold his house and later resided at Malden.

REV. FRANCIS BRIGHT was trained under Mr. Davenport and came from Rayleigh, County Essex, England. He was engaged by the Massachusetts Bay Company, Feb. 2, 1628–9, to come over to New England and preach to the company's servants, to remian three years, and to be free to return at that time, transportation both ways, maintenance and a salary of twenty pounds per annum to be provided. They voted in April, 1629, to give him five pounds toward his loss of wages in England, his charge being in London. He came over in the Lion's Whelp, arriving May 11, 1629. He preached to the settlers and workmen at Charlestown, returning to England in the summer of 1630. He was the first person engaged for clerical service in New England. Morton states that he was a conformist, not agreeing with those that were for reformation.

JOHN BURSLEY is said to have been at Wessagusset in 1623. He was admitted as a freeman from Dorchester, May 18, 1631. He was a deputy from Weymouth, to which place he had evidently returned, in 1636.

CAPTAIN ROGER CLAPP was born at Salcombe Regis, England, April 6, 1609. Pope tells us that he joined in the Church-Colony organized at Plymouth, England, in March, 1629, and came in the Mary and John, May 30, 1630, settling at Dorchester. He was a proprietor and town officer in 1634. He was a Captain of militia, was authorzied to join persons in marriage aad was appointed, August 10, 1665, Captain of the Castle, where he remained 21 years. He removed to Boston, 1686. He died February 2, 1690–1 and was buried in the old burying-place now called King's Chapel burying ground. He left an autobiography which has been printed and constitutes one of the most valuable memorials of the founders of New England.

ROGER CONANT was born at Budleigh, England, and baptized April 9, 1592. He came to Plymouth about 1622 and of his own free will left Plymouth, when Oldham and Lyford were expelled, going to Nantasket. He went from that place to Cape Ann in 1625, having been invited to take charge of the plantation of the Dorchester Company at that place. In 1626 he led the colonists to Naumkeag and founded Salem. The full account of his great service to that community, and the neighboring town of Beverly, which he also founded, has already been given by the writer in the Massachusetts Magazine, Vol. I, page 177. Few men have done greter service to New England than this calm, persevering, God-fearing Puritan leader.

EDWARD CONVERSE came to Charlestown according to Wyman in 1629. His name is 4th on the list of 13. He was a juryman, 1630, and set up a ferry between Boston and Charlestown, June 14, 1631. He removed to Woburn and was a proprietor there in 1640, a deacon and town officer later. He died August, 10 1663, aged about 75.

FITCHER, LIEUTENANT, was one of the colony at Mount Wollaston about 1623. He was left in charge by Rasdell and was ejected by Morton, returning to England.

MR. HUMPHREY GALLUP was one of the first company at Dorchester in the

spring of 1630 and was a proprietor there in 1633.

WILLIAM GAYLORD, Planter, is believed to have been a member of the first church company which came to Dorchester in the Mary and John in 1629–30. He was one of the deacons of the church there. His signature, together with those of the minister and Mr. Rockwell can be found on the earliest land grants. He was a juryman in 1630, and later a town officer and deputy. In 1636 he removed with Mr. and Mrs. Warham to Windsor, Conn.

CAPTAIN ROBERT GORGES came "about ye midle of September (1623) in ye Bay of Massachusetts, with sundrie passengers and families, intending ther to begine a plantation; and pitched upon the place Mr. Weston's people had forsaken. He had a commission from ye Counsell of New-England, to be generall Gover of ye cuntrie." He had a council and assistants and was invested with power to appoint others. Bradford tells us that "The Govr and some yt depended upon him returned for England, havinge scarcly saluted ye cuntrie in his Govermente, not finding the state of things hear to answer his quallitie & condition. The peopl dispersed themselves, some went for England, others for Virginia, some few remained, and were helped with supplies from thence." Bradford then relates what we have stated about Mr. Morrell, whose going away he says was "in effect ye end of a plantation in that place."

MATTHEW GRANT was born in England, October 27, 1601, and came to Dorchester, probably as a member of the original Church Colony, in the Mary and John in 1629–30. He was a made freeman May 18, 1631. He removed to Windsor, Conn., in 1635–6, and was clerk of the church there.

MR. THOMAS GRAVES, Gentleman, of Gravesend, England, was an expert surveyor and engineer who was engaged to come to New England in the employ of the Massachusetts Bay Company. He came to Salem with Governor Endicott in 1628 and removed to Charlestown in the following year. He surveyed and laid out that town in that year. He was made a freeman May 18, 1631, and later served on a committee to lay out the town of Woburn, where he was one of the first town officers.

THOMAS GRAY came very early and is said to have purchased Nantasket of the Indian sachem, Chicataubut, about 1622. The persecuted Episcopalians of Plymouth found refuge at this place. When this settlement broke up he went with Roger Conant to Cape Ann and Naumkeag. He may have been the Thomas Gray who was living at Marblehead as early as 1631.

JOHN GRENAWAY, a millwright at Dorchester, probably came in 1629–30 in the Mary and John He was a town officer. His death occurred about 1652 or 3.

SIMON HOYTE, according to Frothingham, was in Charlestown in 1628–9. He was made a freeman in May, 1631. He removed first to Dorchester and later to Windsor, Conn.

WILLIAM JEFFREY or Jefferies was born at Chuddington Manor, County Sussex, England. He was a Master of Arts of Cambridge University. He came first with the Robert Gorges Company to Weymouth and when that settlement broke up, went with John Balch to Cape Ann. In 1626 he went with Conant and his party to Salem, a letter dated April 21, 1629, being sent to him at that place. While there he resided at Jeffrey's Creek, or Manchester. He also gained possession of the Great Neck in Ipswich, still known as Jefferies Neck, prior to 1633. As late as 1666, he claimed ownership and the General Court voted him 500 acres elsewhere, "to be a final issue of all claims by virtue of any grant, heretofore made by any Indians, whatsoever." After stable government was established at Weymouth, he returned there, but later, went to Newport, R. I., and was resident there as early as 1654. He died January 2, 1675. His tombstone is still standing in the Newport cemetery.

WALTER KNIGHT was one of the Episcopalians with Thomas Gray at Nantasket, and removed with Conant and the others to Cape Ann in 1625. He went with them to Salem and was living there when Endicott came in 1628, according to the deposition of Richard Brackenbury. He had suits in the Essex and General Courts in 1640 and 41.

WILLIAM LOVELL, Captain, of Dorchester, was one of the original church company which came in 1629–30. He had a suit before the Salem Court in 1637.

REV. JOHN LYFORD went from England to Ireland about 1620. He came to Plymouth about 1624 and evidently stirred up discord at that place. Bradford tells us that, "Lyford with his complices, without ever speaking one word either to ye Govr., Church, or Elder, withdrewe them selves & set up a publick meeting aparte, on ye Lord's day; with sundry such insolent cariages, too long here to relate, beginning now publickly to acte what privately they had been long plotting." He was tried and sentenced to be expelled, being given six months to prepare to go "with some eye to his release, if he caried him selfe well in the meane time, and that his repentence proved sound." Bradford tells us that he "acknowledged his censure was farr less than he deserved," and that he "confest his sin publicly in ye church," but when the time had expired he was "so farre from answering their hopes by amendmente in ye time, as he had dubled his evill." Serious charges were brought against him and the edict of expulsion was carried out. He went to Nantasket, thence with Conant, to Cape Ann. From there he went to Virignia, where he died before Oct. 10, 1634.

REV. JOHN MAVERICK of Devon, England, M. A. Oxford, 1603, was chosen one of the ministers of the church-colony which came to Dorchester, May 30, 1630. He was one of the signers in the distribution of lands. When the colony divided, half of the settlers going to Windsor, Conn., he remained at Dorchester. Winthrop states that he was "near 60, years of age; a man of humble spirit and faithful in furthering the work of the Lord here, both in the churches and civil state."

MR. SAMUEL MAVERICK settled in Winnissemet or Chelsea in or prior to 1625. He removed later to Noddle's Island, where he carried on fishing, trading and farming. He was made a freeman in 1632. When the Indians were afflicted with smallpox he did much good in caring for them. He sold his land at Winnisimmet in 1634 and the mill, bakehouse and land on Noddle's Island in 1649. He removed to New York and became one of the commissioners of King Charles II in 1664. He took strong ground against the Mass. Bay Company. Jocelyn states that he was the son of Rev. John Maverick, and calls him the only hospitable man in the colony. Captain Edward Johnson speaks of him as "a man of very loving and courteous behaviour, ever ready to entertain strangers yet an enemy to the Reformations in hand being strong in the Lordly Prelatial power." He built a fort to protect him from the Indians. In 1632 his pinnace was used in the hunt for Dixey Bull a pirate of the Piscataqua. Drake writes: "It may seem strange that Mr. Maverick should submit to so many indignities as from time to time it has been seen that he did, a man that Boston could not do without." He was a gentleman of wealth and great liberality. He wrote a description of New England about 1660.

JOHN MEECH was in Charlestown, according to Frothingham, in 1628–9. We know nothing further about him.

THOMAS MORTON, Gentleman, came in 1622 with Captain Wollaston and about 30 servants and settled at a place on the south shore of Boston Bay which they called Mount Wollaston. After Wollaston and Rasdell went to Virginia with many of the employed men, Morton drove Lieutenant Fitcher out and took the remianing men under his own charge. They drank to excess, scandalized the honest planters by their misconduct with the Indian women, sold liquor and firearms to the Indians and lived a riotous life generally. The settlers became so fearful of the consequences of this matter of arming the natives that they called a general council at which representatives were present from many of the settlements. As a result, Captain Miles Standish was sent against Morton and his followers. Morton was captured and taken to the Isle of Shoals until he could be carried to England. He was taken to England, but Bradford tells us that "he foold of ye messenger, after he was gone from hence, and though he wente for England, yet nothing was done to him, not so much as rebukte, for ought was heard: but returned ye nexte year." Bradford tells us that Mr. Allerton brought him back "and lodged him in his owne house, and for a while used him as a scribe to doe his business till he was caused to pack him away. So he went to his old

nest in ye Massachusetts, wher it was not long but by his miscarriage he gave them just occasion to lay hands on him; and he was by them againe sent prisoner into England, wher he lay a good while in Exeter Jeole." He wrote a book which was hostile to New England. When he returned to Boston about 1644 he was tried but allowed to go on account of his age. He removed to Agamenticus and died there about 1646.

MR. MORRELL, a minister, came with the Robert Gorges company in 1623. Pope tells us that he had been appointed by the Council Governor for New England. "He had power and authority of superintendencies over other churches, but made no use of it; only spoke of it as he was about to return, a year after the governor." He resided at Wessagusset.

MR. JOHN OLDHAM came to Plymouth in 1623. He was implicated with Lyford in an attempt to establish episcopal rule in place of the government at Plymouth. Bradford writes that Oldham and Lyford drew "as many into faction as they could; were they never so vile or profane, they did nourish & back them in all their doings; so they would but cleave to them and speak against ye church hear." Various charges against them were proved by means of intercepted letters. Oldham was banished and went to Nantasket. In 1625 he returned to Plymouth for a brief time according to Bradford. He went to Cape Ann in the same year and later went to England. Upon his return he resided at Watertown. He had grants there and also grants from the Indians of islands in Narragansett Bay. While on a trading trip to the latter place in 1636, he was murdered by the Indians. Bradford tells us that his death was "one ground for the Pequente warr which followed."

ABRAHAM PALMER came to Charlestown, Frothingham tells us, in 1628–9. He was admitted to the church in 1630, freeman in 1631 and later served as town clerk and deputy. He sent trading vessels to the West Indies, and died at Barbadoes about 1653.

WALTER PALMER is also listed by Frothingham at Charlestown in 1628–9. He was a constable there from 1633 to 1636. He removed to Seakonk where he held several offices. He died at Souther-towne in the County of Suffolk, about 1662, according to Pope.

HUMPHREY PENN came in the original company to Dorchester in the Mary and John in 1629–30. He removed to Windsor, Conn., where he died August 20, 1683.

WILLIAM ROCKWELL of Dorchester was probably another member of the church colony in 1629–30. He was a juryman and deacon. In 1636–7 he went with the large number who moved to Windsor, Conn.

REV. RALPH SMITH, a Puritan minister of a less rigid type than the promoters of the colony, was permitted to come on his own request. Pope tells us that "he was allowed to come, on the consideration that he would submit to such orders as should be established, and that he would not exercise the ministry within the limits of their patent." He landed with his wife and family at Nantasket in 1628. Bradford narrates "here being a boat of this place putting in ther on some occasion, he ernestly desired that they would give him & his passage for Plimouth, and some such things as they could carrie; having before heard yt ther was liklyhood he might procure houseroome for some time, till he should resolve to setle ther, if he might, or els-wher as God should dispose: for he was werie of being in yt uncoth place & in a poore house yt would neither keep him nor his goods drie. So, seeing him to be a grave man, & understood he had been a minister, though they had no orders for any such thing, yet they presumed and brought him. He was here accordingly kindly entertained & housed, & had ye rest of his goods & servants sente for and exercised his gifts amongst them, and afterwards was chosen into ye ministrie, and so remained for sundrie years." The same authority writing in 1637, tells us that "This year Mr. Smith layed downe his place of ministrie, partly by his owne willingness, as thinking it too heavie a burthen, and partly at the desire, and by ye perswasion, of others." He continued to live in Plymouth for some time, and was called about 1645 to take charge of the church at Jeffrey's Creek (Manchester). He became a member of the church at Salem in 1647, and died in Boston, March 1, 1660–1.

CAPTAIN SOUTHCOAT came with the church-colony to Dorchester in 1629–30 and led the exploring party which went up Charles River in search of a location for the colony. He had been a soldier in the low Country. He was either the Mr. Richard or Mr. Thomas Southcoat who applied to be made freeman May 18, 1631. Both removed when the colony divided.

The three SPRAGUE brothers, came to Salem in the Abigail with John Endicott in 1628. Endicott sent them in the spring of 1629, to explore the country to the westward, and they made their way to the site of Charlestown. RALPH SPRAGUE was a lieutenant, and a husbandman and fuller by occupation. He was made a freeman, May 18, 1631. In 1630 he was appointed constable of Watertown. He served as deputy in 1635. He removed later to what is now Malden, and his descendants have always been prominent there. He died in 1650. RICHARD SPRAGUE was in Charlestown with his brothers in 1629. He was a Lieutenant, was made a freeman in 1631 and a town officer. He and his wife were members of the church in Boston in 1630, and the Charlestown church at the time of its organization in 1632. He died November 25, 1668, aged 63. In addition to the bequests to his wife and relatives, he left money to Harvard College and the church at Charlestown. He had no children. WILLIAM SPRAGUE the third brother came to Charlestown and later removed to Hingham. He was a proprietor and town officer. His death occurred October 26, 1675.

NICHOLAS STOWERS, according to Frothingham, was in Charlestown in 1628–9. He was a member of the church in Boston in 1630, residing at Charlestown, and an original member of the Charlestown church in 1632. He died 17(3) 1646.

JOHN STRICKLAND, STICKLAND or STICKLING was in Charlestown in 1629–30. He removed to Watertown in 1630. He served on the jury and was made a freeman in 1631. He removed to Wethersfield, Conn.

JOHN STRONG, a tanner, was a member of the church-colony at Dorchester in 1629–30, coming over in the Mary and John. He removed to Taunton, where he was a constable in 1638 and a juryman in 1640. He removed to Windsor, Conn., and about 1659 moved to Northampton. He served the church here as ruling elder. He died 14 April, 1699.

MR. STEPHEN TERRE came in the Mary and John to Dorchester in 1629–30. He was a freeman in 1631 and a constable in 1635. He removed to Windsor, Conn., and later to Hadley.

MR. DAVID THOMPSON, according to Hubbard, was a fish-monger of London who came over in 1623 to begin a plantation at the mouth of the Piscataqua River. In 1626 he came to Boston Bay and took possession of Trevour's Island. He did not live long and in 1648 upon presentation of the facts to the general Court, the island was granted to his son John.

MR. JOHN TILLIE came to Dorchester in the first company in 1629–30. Pope states that he evidently died soon, and the house which had been his was ordered to be repaired.

WILLIAM TREVOUR (TREVORE) came in the Mayflower and visited Boston Bay with an exploring party from Plymouth as already related. Bradford in his list of the Mayflower passengers writes of him as "a seaman hired to stay a year here in this country" and states that when his time was up he returned to England

THOMAS WALFORD came to Charlestown in 1628 or before, and Pope tells us that he was living in a thatched and palisadoed house on the arrival of the Spragues. He incurred the displeasure of the authorities in some way and was ordered to pay a fine which he did by killing a wolf. His offence was described as "contempt of authority and for confronting officers." His goods were sequestrated for debts, Sept. 3, 1633. He died in New Hampshire.

REV. JOHN WARHAM was ordained at Silferton, Devon, May 23, 1619. He was one of the two ministers who came with the colony to Dorchester in the Mary and John in May, 1630. He settled at Mattapan, soon after this called Dorchester. He was made a freeman in 1631. In 1635–6 he removed with half of the colony to Windsor, Conn. Pope writes of him that he was "a man of great strength of character, and deserves much praise for his con-

secration and service in laying the foundations of two commonwealths." He died April 1, 1670.

MR. THOMAS WESTON, a citizen and merchant of London, who assisted the Pilgrims of Plymouth at first but in 1622 became a rival and sent over a company to Wessagussus (Weymouth), consisting of about 60 men and 19 women. It resulted in a miserable failure and according to Morton was entirely abandonned after a year. He came over again in the following year. and got into difficulties with Robert Gorges, who regarded Weston as a interloper. Weston later went to Virginia and later "dyed at Bristoll, in ye time of the warrs, of ye sicknes in yt place." (Bradford.)

CAPTAIN WOLLASTON, the founder of the colony at Mount Wollaston, came about 1623. He was called a "man of pretie parts" by Bradford. When the colony failed, he took many of the servants and went to Virginia. He evidently returned and had a conditional grant of land at Scituate in 1640.

In closing we may profitably make a general review of these settlements in eight distinct localities by these nearly fifty men whom we have named, all of whom came before Winthrop in 1630.

They were divided in localities as follows:

Charlestown, 15.
Wessagusset or Weymouth, 5.
Shawmut, 1.
Dorchester, 15.
Nantasket, 6.
Mount Wollaston, 4.
Winnisimmet, 1.
Trevore's or Thompson's Island, 2.

Deducted for a name counted twice, 1, as Simon Hoyte was at both Charlestown and Dorchester.

We have already shown in the biographical sketches, that many of these men were here in Boston Bay for a short time only, and that upon the breaking up of the particular settlement with which they were connected, they either removed to Plymouth, Salem or Virginia, where they believed that they would have larger opportunities for success, or returned to England. Of those who did remain we are able to name 32 whose records we have given, and who were distributed as follows: 14 men at Charlestown; 1 at Shawmut; 15 at Dorchester; 1 at either Winnisimmet or Noddle's Island; and 1 at Thompson's Island. Many of these men had families, and some of them many servants, so that Governor Winthrop, when he sailed into Boston Bay in 1630, came not to the howling wilderness which some have pictured but to a comparatively sizeable colony under a competent Governor, John Endicott, who from the seat of government at Salem, had exercised the authority which had been given to him by the officers of the company in England, over this entire territory. This authority he abundantly demonstrated when he visited Merry Mount and hewed down the May pole, and when he approved of the plan of Graves in laying out Charlestown.

It is indeed fitting that we should honor today these men, who coming to a wilderness inhabited by savages, had prepared a place for the large company who were to lay the substantial foundation for the noble metropolis of New England.

Gardner Family Reunion.

The third reunion of this association was held at Salem, June 23d, 1909. Owing to the excessive heat is was decided to omit the pilgrimage about the city and cars were taken to the Willows. Basket lunch was served at noon, followed by the business meeting of the association. The officers were reelected for the ensuing year and the annual reports were read and accepted.

The address of the afternoon was delivered by the president of the association, Dr. Frank A. Gardner, upon the "Gardner Families of New England, Prior to 1720." An account of the original emigrant ancestor in each of nine separate families was given, together with important facts about each of the families, such as their geographical distribution, names and records of prominent descendants and other interesting facts. As the address will be published in full in a later number of this magazine, no extended notes from it will be given at this time. Other speakers were Sergeant John P. Hodgkins, of Winthrop; Mr. Howard P. Gardner, of Marblehead and Mr. Stephen W. Gardner of Salem. Letters were read from many Gardners who were unable to be present. After the meeting many of those present went on a sail about the harbor in a large motor boat, passing

the summer home of President Taft, skirting the North Shore to Manchester and then across the harbor to the beautiful inner harbor of Marblehead. The party then returned to the Willows and took cars for home.

Gloucester Day, 1909.

The reproduction in the near future of the Old Planters House upon the original site at Stage Fort Park, Gloucester, is, we are pleased to note, practically assured. The Gloucester Day Committee have voted to devote the proceeds of the pageant to that praiseworthy object. It is the plan of those interested to have a meeting place in the building for historical societies and to have various memorial rooms furnished by the Conants, Woodburys, Balches, Gardners and descendants of the old planters.

Great praise is due the committee having this celebration in charge for the magnificent pageant which they produced on the 4th of August in honor of President Taft. Owing to the delayed passage of the tariff bill, the President was unfortunately detained in Washington, but otherwise the celebration was a marked success. A large military, naval and civic parade was held in the afternoon and the beautiful harbor was made attractive by the presence of a large fleet of naval vessels, including the famous flagships of Admirals Farragut and Dewey, the "Hartford" and the "Olympia." The new scout ships "Salem" and "Chester" were also there with the "Chicago" and the "Tonopah."

The great feature of the celebration was the evening pageant at Stage Fort Park. The Coburn players assisted by a very large company of adults and children of Gloucester produced "The Canterbury Pilgrims," under the direction of Mr. Eric Pape. The whole conception of this out door spectacle was grand and it was produced with the accuracy of detail in the matter of costumes and scenery so characteristic of Mr. Pape. The vast audience of nearly 20,000 people was a wonderful sight in itself and the display of fireworks was especially pleasing to the eye.

A motor boat party under the auspices of the Old Planters Society left Salem at noon returning at midnight, giving the members an excellent opportunity of viewing both the war ships and the pageant.

The Roger Conant Monument.

An effort is being made by Gloucester people to have the statue of Roger Conant which is being executed by Kitson, erected in Stage Fort Park, Gloucester, instead of at Salem as originally planned, notwithstanding the fact that they already have the tablet which was placed on the boulder in 1907 and are to erect in the park, a facsimile of the original Planters House. There can be no doubt as to the appropriateness of that site for the house, but many of the descendants of the upright and peaceful leader believe that the proper place for the statue is Salem, and give the following reasons for their belief:

1. Salem was a place of his own selection and he obtained permission to transfer the colony there. He himself bargained with the Indians for the land and chose a place on the southern side of the Naumkeag river for the purpose of avoiding complications on account of the Gorges claims. In contrast with the above; he did not select the site at Stage Fort Point in Gloucester. He was invited to come there and take charge, after they had been there a year or more. We know that he was greatly dissatisfied with the place and personally chose the site in Salem to which he led the planters.

2. He spent most of the years of a very long life within the original borders of the town which he founded, while he was at the Gloucester site only one brief year. He was very prominent in Salem and was honored with all the emoluments of office which his appreciative associates could give him.

3. The magnitude of his work should be kept constantly before the people of Salem, as there has always been a tendency to extol the work of the able and energetic Puritan-militant — John Endicott — who came in 1628, and to overlook the invaluable labors of the equally able but conciliatory leader—Roger Conant—who led the planters to Salem in 1626 and was their mainstay during the following hard years. If our object is to emphazise his work, Salem is in the opinion of the writer by far the better site.

4. Memorials should be distributed to accomplish their design of disseminating knowledge. There is no lesson of the life of Roger Conant which could not be brought out in the memorial reproduction of the

Old Planters House which is to be erected at Gloucester, and the tablet which is already there, while as stated above there is a great need of bringing before the public the great work which he did at Salem.

5. If three memorials are to be erected, all of which will bring prominently before the people, the work which Roger Conant did, at least one of them should be set up in a public place in Salem, a city visited every year by thousands who come from all over the world. The number of such pilgrims is increasing each year, making the educational advantage of such a statue, enormous. By all means let it be placed near the scene of his great work that all men may know what he accomplished and how much we owe to his memory.

Meeting of Descendants of Robert Bartlett, First, at Plymouth, Mass., in August.

The second annual reunion of the Descendants of Robert Bartlett, First, will be held at White Horse Beach, Manomet, Plymouth, Mass., August 27, 1909. Manomet is a charming section of the historic old town of Plymouth, and White Horse Beach is the finest of Plymouth's fine beaches and only a minute's walk from Hotel Crescent where the meeting will be held.

Robert Bartlett came to Plymouth in the ship Ann in 1623, He married in 1628, Mary, a daughter of Richard Warren, one of the Mayflower Pilgrims who came in 1620, and lived and died in Manomet, where his possessions were. The estate has been known as the Bartlett farm from that time and has been in possession of the Bartlett family continuously to the present. The house built in 1680 is still standing.

All persons who can trace their ancestry to Robert Bartlett, First, are cordially invited to be present and assist in making the occasion interesting and profitable. It is hoped that many will attend and remain over Saturday to visit points of historic interest in the town. The morning of Friday, August 27, will be devoted to the reception of members, registration and social reunion. Dinner will be served at the headquarters, Hotel Crescent, at 1.30, after which the exercises and business meeting will follow.

The officers are; President, Luicus W. Bartlett, Hartford, Conn.; first Vice president, David L. Bodfish, Palmer, Mass.; second vice president, John A. Bartlet, Brockton, Mass., secretary and treasurer, Mrs. Edith I. Cushing, Middleboro, Mass.; historian, Mrs. Sarah S. Bartlet, 617 Warren st.; Roxbury.

Putnam Reunion.

The seventh annual reunion of the Putnam Association of Western New York was held at Seneca Park, Rochester, Aug. 12, about eighty being present from various parts of the state.

After a bounteous dinner the assembly resolved itself into a more social affair than usual, omitting a part of the program, which consisted of papers by Miss Cornelia Moore of Erie, Penn., Mrs. Erastus Putnam of Elizabeth, New Jersey, Mrs. Mae Holland of Rochester, N. Y., and one from Eben Putnam of Boston, the historian of the family in England and America.

H. W. Putnam of Rochester showed a document, yellow with age, which was a commission to Joshua Putnam of Danvers, Mass., in 1808, appointing him ensign in the Militia of Massachusetts, also a letter written to Deacon Daniel Putnam in 1769 by his brother Aaron. It was sealed with wafers, there having been no envelopes in those days, and bore the words, "postage clear," which meant it was prepaid, as there were also no stamps at that early date.

Letters of regret were received from Massachusetts, New Hampshire, New Jersey, Pennsylvania, Illinois, Montana, Colorado, Michigan and Vermont.

Officers for the coming year were elected as follows: Pres., D. C. Putnam, Lyons; V. Pres., L. D. Pollock, Newark; Treas., Daniel Phillips, Sodus Point; Sec., Sarah J. Higgins, Sodus Point; Hist., Ophelia M. Cogswell, Williamson.

Next meeting at the home of the president, D. C. Putnam, in Lyons, on the second Thursday in August, 1910.

Meeting of the Old Planters Society.

The Annual Fall outing of the Old Planters Society will be held in Marblehead on Thursday, September 16. The formal exercises will be held at the new headquarters of the Marblehead Historical Society in the Lee Mansion at three-thirty when an address will be given by Mr. Nathan P. Sanborn, president of the local society, on Col. Jeremiah Lee. At the conclusion of the meeting, the party will enjoy a basket lunch at Castle Rock, Marblehead Neck.

Our Editorial Pages

Rev. Thomas Franklin Waters.

IN my summer rambles, a few years ago, I came to the town of Henniker, New Hampshire, on the afternoon of Old Home Week, when the public exercises were held. A large and enthusiastic gathering crowded the Hall, felicitous addresses were made, the songs of the old time were sung, and a fine spirit of love and loyalty to the old home town pervaded the whole exercise. In the evening, other public festivities found place, and the groups of old friends on the hotel piazza were in a quandary as to whether the prospective pleasure of the larger gathering would exceed the delight of the present moment.

Walking up the pleasant street, I found that Henniker had been generously remembered with a library and other public institutions by those who had gone out from the quiet town to make elsewhere their home and fortune, and it seemed a very natural sequence of events. The generous remembrance of the public needs of the town by these broad minded and devoted individuals must have inspired the general enthusiasm, which brought many of the sons and daughters from distant homes and gave such unction to their gatherings; and the Old Home celebrations in turn were likely to bring forth in the future further gifts for the general good.

It would be of exceeding profit to all our Massachusetts towns and villages, if the natural affection of multitudes for their old home were touched and appealed to, by the regular observance of Old Home Week. Every town rejoices in the careers of her fortunate and successful sons and daughters. The return of these favored ones to the homes and haunts of their childhood, the renewing of the old friendships, their sincere and unaffected delight in the reunion, is a bright and stimulating event in the quiet lives of those who have stayed at home. But the stimulating influence of these gatherings is not limited to those who are bodily present. Many, who do not return, are reminded very tenderly of their childhood and youth in the old town, and far and wide, as the call goes out to the widely scattered ones, there is a genial awakening of the home feeling. A quickened home feeling is likely to reveal itself in a new interest in the affairs of the early home, and many a generous gift may result. To be sure, the securing of such public benefactions would be a very mercenary motive, and the true sentimental observance of Old Home Week would lose its finest flavor, if it were celebrated in the hope of touching the fat money bags of her old residents. But it remains true

that many of the smaller towns and villages are in need of public benefactions of various kinds, and those, who are able to be of service, in meeting these needs, should be reminded of their privilege and duty in this regard.

HITHERTO the favorite gift of the wealthy friend has been the erection of a public library building, with a generous endowment to ensure its usefulness; and whichever way we journey, we find these substantial edifices, many of them costly and elegant, in towns and villages alike. Sometimes a school building has been erected, and again the old church has been helped in the days of her decline by the establishment of a fund for her maintenance. Public benefactions of this kind require large means, and the question may well be asked, Are there not many, who have only moderate means, who desire to show their regard for their birth-place, and would make a helpful gift if they could be sure that a small contribution would be really valuable?

I AM convinced that two benefactions, which are fresh in mind, are practically suggestive. In the one case, the testator, imagining himself to be the possessor of millions, planned a grand Institute for the technical education of the youth of his town and elsewhere. The erection of buildings, and the creation of a learned faculty were provided for, and vast sums would necessarily be spent for the plant and its equipment before a single boy could be educated. The estate has been found to be so heavily encumbered, that many years must elapse before even a beginning of this scheme can be realized, and the commendable and wise desire of the donor to benefit the rising generation will fail utterly for long years, and perhaps forever, because his bequest is bound hard and fast by the limitations he has imposed upon it. Had he realized that the precise lines of education that he had in mind are already being taught with great success in famous institutions near at hand, and had he been willing to deny himself the posthumous honor of creating a new school, and devised his fortune as a trust-fund, which should be used directly in providing for the higher technical education of those he wished to benefit, his trustees might have been enabled to begin in a modest way, at an early date, to carry out his laudable and generous desires.

THE moral is obvious. In this and many other bequests for educational purposes, the use of the gift has been so rigidly defined that its usefulness is greatly curtailed. A fund, intended for the help of deserving youth in securing an education, administered by Trustees, who have large discretionary power in its use, would be of great benefit to any community, however large, however small. A gift of a few hundred dollars might become the nucleus of a gradually enlarging

Educational Fund, which would secure great advantage to many needy students.

The other benefaction was primarily for a Home for Old People, but incidentally provision was made for a visiting nurse. A trained nurse, of broad experience and very sympathetic nature, has been installed in the Home. She is open to call for any and every service by any person. A nominal fee is asked of those who are able to pay, to save it from being a charity, but practically, it puts no bar in the way of her service. Physicians call upon her in critical cases and whenever a skilled attendant is necessary. She finds her way to the humblest homes, and ministers to many who are stricken with fatal illness, or helpless cripples, or bed ridden invalids, as well as those, who need only a few visits for temporary ailments. Her salary and living expense are very moderate. A comparatively small endowment would establish such a nurse in any community.

BUT why not invent a Public Utility Fund, which may be used for a score of purposes, which would never be included in any specific bequest? Every community has one or more individuals, level headed but tender hearted, gifted pre-eminently with common sense, competent to take and use such a fund for the common good; for enhancing the outward beauty, or the moral tone of the town, or for relieving the desperate need of an individual, as he requires; for loans, or for gifts. The scheme sounds Quixotic but is it so? Every person of mature age has had a variety of experiences, which suggest a multitude of uses which might arise for a fund of such broad scope. A single gift might begin this Public Utility Fund, its success in small ways would encourage other contributions, and eventually a large and elastic fund might accumulate for a great variety of wise and helpful purposes.

THE SSACHVSETTS MAGAZINE

Old Haraden House,
Salem.

The Massachusett

The Massachusetts Magazine.

A Quarterly Magazine Devoted to History, Genealogy and Biography

THOMAS FRANKLIN WATERS, *Editor.* IPSWICH, MASS.

— *ASSOCIATE AND ADVISORY EDITORS* —

THOMAS WENTWORTH HIGGINSON, CAMBRIDGE, MASS. GEORGE SHELDON, DEERFIELD, MASS. DR. FRANK A. GARDNER, SALEM, MASS.

LUCIE M. GARDNER, SALEM, MASS. CHARLES A. FLAGG, WASHINGTON, D. C. JOHN N. MCCLINTOCK, DORCHESTER, MASS. ALBERT W. DENNIS, SALEM, MASS.

Issued in January, April, July and October. Subscription, $2.50 per year, Single copies 75c.

VOL. II — OCTOBER, 1909 — NO. 4

Contents of this Issue.

CAPTAIN JONATHAN HARADEN	*F. A. Gardner, M.D.*	191
MASSACHUSETTS PIONEERS IN MICHIGAN	*Charles A. Flagg*	200
COLONEL EBENEZER BRIDGE'S REGIMENT	*F. A. Gardner, M.D.*	203
SOME ARTICLES CONCERNING MASSACHUSETTS IN RECENT MAGAZINES	*Charles A. Flagg*	228
THE GEORGE GARDNER HOUSE	*F. A. Gardner, M.D.*	230
DEPARTMENT OF THE AMERICAN REVOLUTION	*F. A. Gardner, M.D.*	234
PILGRIMS AND PLANTERS	*Lucie M. Gardner*	239
FAMILY GENEALOGIES	*Lucie M. Gardner*	240
CRITICISM AND COMMENT		254
OUR EDITORIAL PAGES	*Thomas F. Waters*	255

CORRESPONDENCE of a business nature should be sent to THE MASSACHUSETTS MAGAZINE, Salem, Mass.

CORRESPONDENCE in regard to contributions to the MAGAZINE may be sent to the editor, Rev. T. F. Waters, Ipswich, Mass., or to the office of publication, in Salem.

BOOKS for review may be sent to the office of publication in Salem. Books should not be sent to individual editors of the magazine, unless by previous correspondence the editor consents to review the book.

SUBSCRIPTION should be sent to THE MASSACHUSETTS MAGAZINE, Salem, Mass. Subscriptions are $2.50 payable in advance, post-paid to any address in the United States or Canada. To foreign countries in the Postal Union $2.75. Single copies of back numbers 75 cents each.

REMITTANCES may be made in currency or two cent postage stamps; many subscriptions are sent through the mail in this way, and they are seldom lost, but such remittances must be at the risk of the sender. To avoid all danger of loss send by post-office money order, bank check, or express money order.

CHANGES OF ADDRESS. When a subscriber makes a change of address he should notify the publishers giving both his old and new addresses. The publishers cannot be responsible for lost copies, if they are not notified of such changes.

ON SALE. Copies of this magazine are on sale in *Boston*, at W. B. Clark's & Co., 26 Tremont Street, Old Corner Book Store, 29 Bromfield Street. Geo. E. Littlefield, 67 Cornhill, Smith & McCance, 38 Bromfield Street. *New York*, at John Wanamaker's, Broadway 4th, 9th and 10th Streets; in *Philadelphia*, Am. Baptist Pub. Society, 1630 Chestnut Street; in *Washington*, at Brentanos, F & 13th St.; in *Chicago*, at A. C. McClurg's & Co., 221 Wabash Ave.; in *London*, at B. F. Stevens & Brown, 4 Trafalgar Sq. Also on sale at principal stands of N. E. News Co.

191

CAPTAIN JONATHAN HARADEN*

By Frank A. Gardner, M. D.

The annals of the War for the Independence of America contain the names of many heroes, who rose from private life to places of marked eminence in the service of their country. Very few of these had a more striking career in the naval service than the honored subject of our sketch, Captain Jonathan Haraden.

"Soldier and sailor too" like Kipling's marine, he served as a Lieutenant of infantry before he walked the quarter deck. Records of such dual service are not uncommon in the revolutionary annals of Massachusetts, where so many citizens were sea-faring men. Colonel John Glover's Marblehead command became known as the "amphibious" or "web-footed regiment", as they were detailed so frequently to man ships or boats. In April, 1776, "near fifty" men of Glover's 14th Continental Regiment were "absent on board Continental privateers." Two of the captains of this regiment, Nicholson Broughton and John Selman, sailed from Beverly in September 1775, in command of vessels sent out by the United Colonies and both subsequently held the rank of Major in Essex County Regiments. Captain Haraden, therefore, was not alone in his role of "soldier on the sea," but his naval victories won for him a place in history above that of any other patriot who served on both land and ocean.

* This paper in somewhat modified form was delivered as an address before the Massachusetts Society, Sons of the American Revolution, at their Annual Field Day, at Salem, Sept. 25, 1909. On that occasion a memorial tablet was placed upon Captain Haraden's house on Essex street, and a wreath of laurel with flags and the colors of the society were deposited upon his grave in the Broad Street Burying ground.

Born in Gloucester in 1745, the son of Joseph and Joanna (Emerson) Haraden he removed to Salem and made that thriving commercial town his home through life. July 11, 1775, he enlisted as a Second Lieutenant in Captain Benjamin Ward's Company, stationed at Salem for the defence of the seacoast. This seacoast service was of great importance during the Revolution. Very little has been written about it but every important seaport from Dartmouth (now New Bedford) on the south to Newburyport on the north, and all along the coast of the present state of Maine, had its coast defence corps of one or more companies. As a large proportion of the able bodied men of these seaports were absent through the year 1775, with the army at the siege of Boston and later in the Continental and militia regiments, the constant danger of attack from British vessels made it necessary to protect these towns by fortifications, garrisoned by seacoast companies, as they were called. The burning of Falmouth (now Portland, Maine) made this necessity more apparent and the strength of these garrisons and fortifications was increased. The ports of Salem, Beverly and Marblehead were protected in this way early in the war on account of their commercial importance.

Jonathan Haraden held the rank of Second Lieutenant in the Salem Company until January 16, 1776, when he was chosen First Lieutenant in the same organization. This higher rank he held until June 3d 1776, when he was commissioned First Lieutenant on the newly built State sloop "Tyrannicide," commanded by Captain John Fiske of Salem. This vessel, built at Salisbury was one of five constructed for the Massachusetts Navy in the Spring of 1776. Captain Fiske was the son of Reverend Samuel Fisk of the historic old First Church in Salem, and was commissioned April 20, 1776. He was ordered to cruise from "Harbour to Harbour in the same colony and Newhampshire," June 13th, and on the same day captured the British packet schooner "Despatch" with 8 guns, 12 swivels and 31 men, under command of Capt. Gutteridge. At this time the Tyrannicide had 14 guns and 100 men. On the 4th of July (the first Independence day) he was ordered to sail again and cruise between Cape Sable and Nantucket. He soon captured the armed ship "Glasgow." The officers among the Tyrannicide's prisoners at Salem were ordered to be removed to Topsfield, July 24, 1776. In August she captured the brig St. John and the schooner Three Brothers. Captain Fisk petitioned that she be rigged as a brigantine and the change was ordered on the 13th of September.

The Tyrannicide was again ordered to sea, Oct. 22, 1776, and additional instructions were issued to Capt. Fisk, Dec. 13 On the 31st of the month he captured the scow "John," 140 tons, Capt. Barrass. Jan. 1, 1777, Richard

later in the Continental and militia regiments, c
from British vessels made it necessary to protect
garrisoned by seacoast companies, as they were
mouth (now Portland, Maine) made this neces
strength of these garrisons and fortifications w
Salem, Beverly and Marblehead were protected i
account of their commercial importance.

Jonathan Haraden held the rank of Second Li
pany until January 16, 1776, when he was chosen
organization. This higher rank he held until Ju
missioned First Lieutenant on the newly built
commanded by Captain John Fiske of Salem.
was one of five constructed for the Massachusetts
Captain Fiske was the son of Reverend Samue
Church in Salem, and commissioned April
cruise from "Harbour to Harbour in the
June 13th, and on the same day captured
patch" with 8 guns, 12 swivels 31 men, under c
At this time the Tyrannicide 14 guns and 1
(the first Independence day) he was ordered to
Cape Sable and Nantucket. He soon captured
The officers among the Tyrannicide's prisoners at
moved to Topsfield, July 24, 1776. In August sh
and the schooner Three Brothers. Captain Fisk
as a brigantine and the change was ordered on th
The Tyrannicide was again ordered to sea, O
instructions were issued to Capt. Fisk, Dec. 1
[illegible] the scow "John," 4-6 men, Capt.

Derby, Jun., Agent of the "Tyrannicide" and the "Massachusetts, petitioned for the settlement of the sale of their prizes; the schooner "Despatch," snow "Ann," and brigantine "Henry & Ann." The value of the vessels was as follows: "Despatch" £1802:16:10, "Ann" £857:5:4, "Henry & Ann" £5685: 7:11¼ and the net proceeds of the sale to the state was £5103:11:3. On the 27th of January or the 3d of Feb. (two dates given in the archives) Capt Fisk captured the brig "Three Friends," 100 tons, Capt. Holms, and she was brought into Salem, Feb. 23d. Her cargo was appraised at £4269:3:7½ and that of the "John" previously mentioned, at £9029:2:0.

On the 20th of February, 1777, Jonathan Haraden was made Commander and Israel Thorndike of Beverly, who had commanded the schooner "Warren," was his first Lieutenant. A few days later Benjamin Moses of Salem was made Second Lieutenant and Benjamin Lovett of Beverly, Master. Thomas Hunt was engaged as Master's Mate. Capt. John Fisk was given command the ship "Massachusetts," Dec. 10, 1777. After the war he engaged in commerce and became very wealthy. He was commissioned a Major General of Militia in 1792.

A resolve was passed in the Council, March 26, 1777, that the "Hebrew Books, Sabbath Lamp & the pontifical Cup etc. captured by the brigantine Tyrannicide and now in the State Store be sent to the Library of Harvard College for the use of the same." April 27, Capt. Haraden, on board the brig, wrote a letter to the Board of war, informing them that he had that day captured the snow "Sally," Capt. Stephen Jones, from London to Quebec, with a cargo of English goods. He also stated that he would soon be obliged to make a port to procure water, and that he had captured a transport brigantine with sixty-three Hessians on board. The "Sally" arrived in Salem, June 6. Capt. Haraden wrote a letter in May stating that he had taken the ship "Chalkley," Capt. James "hines"? from Honduras, bound to Bristol, with a cargo of mahogany, logwood, etc. Another letter from him the same month contained an inventory of goods taken from the brig "Eagle." May 10, he captured the ship "Lonsdale," 500 tons, Captain James Grayson, which was taken into Boston, on the 20th. At this period the "Tyrannicide" was sailing in company with the brigantine "Massachusetts." Littlefield Sibley, prizemaster of the barque "WhiteHaven," in a letter to the Board of War May 13, announced his arrival at Piscataway, the barque having been captured by the Tyrannicide on her way to Quebec.

Capt. Haraden captured May 31, brigantine "Trepassy," 160 tons, Capt. Isaac Follett, and she arrived in Boston, June 25th. On June 20 James Miller,

who had been captured on the "Lonsdale," was allowed to go to Rhode Island as he was only a passenger on board the ship. A memorandum is on file in the State archives, which shows that the rations issued to this ship from June 25 to Sept. 1, amounted to £114:2:1. A receipt was given to Capt. Haraden Oct. 21, 1777, for "five hundred three Quarters of Ship Bread (7 barrels)" for the "Guard Ship Rifing Empire."

Capt. Haraden in the "Tyrannicide" and Captain Sampson in the "Hazard" were ordered, November 16, 1777, to sail to the coast of Spain and Portugal, thence to the southward of Madeira and home by the West Indies. Definite instructions were given regarding the various ports to which the different classes of cargoes were to be sent. Before they got away they were ordered to sail to Townsend and capture, if possible, two schooners, one commanded by Capt. Callahan of Halifax and another the "Halifax," supposed to be coasting for the purpose of capturing "two ships now laden and ready to sail for France." Dec. 2nd Capt. Haraden, in a letter to the Board of War, wrote that he had lost his grip and had put into the harbor or Falmouth to refit. While at the wharf four of his men deserted. He soon got to sea however and in company with the sister ship captured on Dec. 13, the brigantine "Alexander," Capt. James Waddie, bound from Halifax to Jamaica with a cargo of shooks and fish. On the 22nd they captured the schooner "Good Intent," Capt. William Dashpar, bound from "Harbor Grafs, N. F. to Dominco," laden with fish and hoops. They made another capture on the following day, the "Polly," Capt. Walter Stevens, from St. John's, N. F., bound for Barbadoes, loaded with fish, hoops and feathers. Capt. Haraden announced in a letter written February 17, 1778, that they had taken two vessels, one of which had arrived at Antigua and the other having mistaken Dominica for St. Pierre, had been recaptured. A letter written four days later from St. Pierre, Martinique, announced their arrival there and stated that they had received all needful assistance.

Captains Haraden and Sampson sent a petition to the authorities that they be allowed eight full shares of prizes like other officers of their rank, instead of six as granted by the Council. A letter written at St. Pierre, Mar. 10, stated that the Tyrannicide would be ready to sail in five or six days. Another letter dated the 15th from the same port, gave the net proceeds of the sale of the brig "Polly" above mentioned as 74,257 livres, 2 sols. The "Tyrannicide" and "Hazard" in company with the brig "Lion" of Salem, sailed from St. Pierre Mar. 30, 1778. We next hear from Capt. Haraden in a letter written from Squam Harbor, where he had run in after seeing a British frigate off Thatchers'

Island. He mentioned ill luck and stated that some of the men were sick with small pox. The announcement was also made that he had captured the snow "Swift" from Bristol, loaded with flour. As the cargo was of a perishable nature, the Maritime Court authorized "Samuel Philips Savage of Westown and George Williams of Salem" to make immediate sale of the same. The First Lieutenant, John Bray, received his discharge from the Tyrannicide May 8. He became First Lieutenant of the ship "Franklin" in 1780, and commander of the ship "Oliver Cromwell," Apr. 19, 1781.

In a letter from the Board of war dated May 15, 1778, Capt. Haraden was mentioned as having arrived a few days before and as soon "going out again." The letters on file in the archives reveal the fact that the agents at St. Pierre had protested to the authorities at Boston on account of the large amount of money advanced in refitting the "Tyrannicide" and "Hazard" for the return voyage. They found fault especially in regard to the matter of rations, and as a result the Secretary of the board wrote, expressing surprise that the commanders had applied for funds for rations and requesting that in the future no such requisitions be complied with. These agents wrote May 24 that the last of the "Tyrannicide's" men had left the hospital. A bill was enclosed for the care of three men. Supplies for the "Tyrannicide" were delivered to Capt. Waters at St. Pierre, May 28th. An account of rations to June 25, shows that triple rations were given to Jonathan Haraden, double to Israel Thorndike (who had returned to the brig) Benjamin Moses, Benjamin Lovett, William Coffin, James Grayson, Christopher Asbridge, Stephen Jones and Capt. Coombs. At least two of these had been captains of captured vessels, James Grayson of the "Lonsdale" and Stephen Jones of the snow "Sally."

A letter from the Board of War to the Council, dated June 25, 1778 announced the determination of Capt. Haraden to resign his commission. The document read as follows: "The Board most sincerely laments ye Lofs of so brave an officer and deserving a man, who has been in the Service of his Country from the beginning of the war in which he hath always acquitted himself wt spirits & honor. This step Capt. Haraden declares he takes with the greatest reluctance but the late difsarrangements of Commanders as he apprehends oblige him to it. The officers and men entering into their Captains motives have one & all left the vessel & represent to your Honor that the Tyrannicide is now ready for sea and that the season most favourable . . . request your Honor to appoint some person Commander of said Brigt that she may proceed on her voyage without further loss of time."

Captain Haraden was commissioned September 30, 1778, commander of

the privateer "General Pickering" of Salem, of 180 tons with 16 guns and a crew of 106 men. She was described as a brigantine at this period, but her rig was changed in the spring of 1779 to that of a ship and after that date she was so called repeatedly in the records of the Continental Congress and the Massachusetts State Archives. She was owned by George Williams and others or Salem. John Bray, his First Lieutenant on the "Tyrannicide" held the same rank under him in this ship. Captain Haraden made a famous record in her. Only a few of these sea fights can be mentioned at this time.

In October 1779, off Sandy Hook, he fought at the same time and captured after an engagement of thirty minutes, the ship "Hope," reported to have been armed with 14 guns, the brig "Pomona," said to have had 12 guns and the cutter "Royal George" also with 12 guns. The "Pomona" was brought to Salem and sold Oct. 23, 1779, to Jonathan Grafton for £8,900. About a month prior to this date the agents of the ship sold another prize, the brigantine "True Briton," 70 tons, to George Dodge for £4,100. It is narrated that in one of the cruises in this ship "he fell in with a king's mail packet from one of the West India isles, homeward bound, which gave him a very warm reception. After an action which lasted four hours, Captain Haraden found it necessary to haul off and repair damages. Having done so, he went alongside the packet with all the powder he had left in his cannon. He then hailed the enemy, and told him he would give him five minutes to haul down his colors, and if they were not down at the expiration of that time he would sink him. At the end of three minutes the colors came down. The boat, on going alongside the prize, found the blood running from her scuppers, while the deck appeared more like the floor of a slaughter house than the deck of a ship. The fight depicted upon the tablet which was unveiled in Salem in September, 1909, is thus described in the "Sketch of Salem."

"He sailed from this port in the Spring of 1780 with a cargo of sugar for Bilboa, then a famous resort for American privateers. On his passage, May 29, 1780, he was attacked by a British cutter of twenty-one guns and beat her off after a contest of about two hours. Upon entering the Bay of Biscay, he fell in with a British privateer of twenty-two guns and sixty men. Having approached in the night unobserved, he ran alongside and commanded her through his trumpet to strike to an American frigate or he would sink her. The privateer struck her flag and the captain when he came on board the "General Pickering" was mortified to think that he had submitted to such inferior force. Mr. John Carnes was put in charge of the prize. As the vessels approached Bilboa they met a sail coming out, which the captured captain said

was the "Achilles", a privateer from London of forty-two guns aand 140 men and added that he knew her force.

Captain Haraden coolly replied; "I sha'n't run from her." The British ship first retook the prize and placed a crew on board, and night coming on, deferred his attack on Captain Haraden till morning. As the day dawned, June 4, 1780, the "Achilles" bore down upon the "General Pickering" and Captain Haraden placed his vessel in condition for action. After a desperate contest of about three hours duration, the British ship was obliged to seek safety in flight, notwithstanding his greatly superior force. Captain Haraden gave chase, but the "Achilles" was light, outsailed the "General Pickering" and escaped. He then returned, coolly recaptured the prize and carried her in safety into Bilboa.

The battle was fought so near the Spanish coast that an immense concourse of spectators amounting, as was supposed, to nearly one hundred thousand, assembled along the shore, in boats, and on the hillsides, during the action and before the Captain with his prize had been at anchor half an hour, one could walk a mile from his ship by stepping from one boat to another. So great was the admiration with which the battle and victory were witnessed, that when the captain landed he was surrounded by this vast throng of strangers and borne in triumph into the city where he was welcomed with public and unbounded honors. The late venerable Robert Cowan who was with him in this action, said that the "General Pickering" in comparison with her antagonist "looked like a long-boat by the side of a ship," and "that he fought with a determination that seemed superhuman," and that although in the most exposed positions, "where the shot flew around him in thousands, he was all the while as calm and steady as amidst a shower of snowflakes."

Later in 1780, while still in the "General Pickering" he captured many other vessels, including the ship "Rodney," 120 tons, which was sold in Salem by the agents of the owners to George Williams for £90,000; the brigantine "Myrrh" sold on the same date for £25,000 and the brigantine "Venus" sold, October 13, 1780, for £24,000. On the 10th of November, 1780, he started on another cruise in the "General Pickering" to the West Indies. He was captured in the harbor of Saint Eustatius, when Rodney made his descent upon it, February 3, 1781. This capture by the British Admiral was one of the richest of the war, the value of the loot being estimated at over $15,-000,000

We do not know how long he remained a prisoner, but May 3, 1782, he

was commissioned Captain of the letter of marque ship "Julius Caesar," 200 tons, 14 carriage guns and 40 men. She hailed from Salem and was owned by Joshua Ward and others.

On July 18th, 1782, off Bermuda, in sight of two English brigs, one of 20 guns and another of 16, he took a schooner which was a prize to one of them, but they both declined to attack him. During this cruise he fell in with two British vessels, a ship of 18 guns and a brig of 16 guns, both of which he fought 5 glasses and got clear of them. The enemy's ship was much shattered and so was the Caesar, but the men of the latter were unharmed. Captain Haraden was subsequently presented with a silver plate by the owners of the ship, as commemorative of his skill and bravery. Before he reached Martinique he had a severe battle with another English vessel, which he carried thither with him as a prize. He arrived in Salem from the cruise, December 31, 1782, having captured a ship of 400 tons which had been a store ship for Lord Howe. This ended Captain Haraden's active service as a commander of armed vessels, as on the next voyage of the "Julius Caesar," he as one of the owners petitioned that his former First Lieutenant, Thomas Benson, be commissioned Captain.

His record on the sea was certainly remarkable. One writer affirms with justice that he is entitled to a "place in history by the side of Paul Jones, Decatur, and Farragut and Cushing." Maclay says of him he "was one of the most daring and skillful navigators that ever sailed from Salem, and that is saying a great deal when we come to consider the long list of successful commanders who have hailed from that port." He goes on to say further, "Haraden had a reputation of being one of the most intrepid commanders known to Salem ship lore. It has been said of him that, amid the din of battle he was calm and self-possessed. The more deadly the strife, the more imminent the peril, the more terrific the scene, the more perfect seemed his self-command and serene intrepidity, He was a hero among heroes and his name should live in honored and affectionate remembrance'." Maclay acknowledges that this is lavish praise but declares that the man deserved it. Captain Haraden is said to have taken nearly a thousand cannon from the British during the war.

Time forbids our considering the life of Captain Haraden as a citizen of Salem during the years following the war of the Revolution. The house which was adorned with the tablet was purchased by him May 4, 1801, and he lived there until his death which occurred November 23, 1803. He was married three times and had several children, but none of his descendants are known

to be living at the present time. Most of the inhabitants of Salem who have borne the name in the past hundred years have been the descendants of Captain Haraden's nephew, whom the Captain brought up and who bore his honored name through life.

It seems appropriate to present in closing this necessarily brief address, the review of his life which appeared as an obituary notice in the Salem Gazette of November 25, 1803,

"On Wednesday last, departed this life, in the 59th year of his age, Captain Jonathan Haraden, whose funeral will be at 3 o'clock this afternoon from his house in Essex Street, which his friends are requested to attend. This gentleman having been for several years a prey to a disorder which has finally consigned him to death, he has been in a great measure secluded from society but still it is impossible to forget one who was so much its ornament and benefactor. Captain Haraden was a native of Gloucester but came to this town when a lad where he learnt a mechanical trade. Early in the contest between this Country and Great Britain, he engaged in that species of warfare which was carried on from this town with so much spirit and success, and was employed either in the public or private ships of war till the establishment of our independence; and he will be recollected by those who know the history of that eventful period, as one of the most able and valiant naval commanders that the war produced. He never rashly sought danger nor did he shrink from duty. It was remarkably his fortune to meet with enemies of superior force and numbers; yet he had always the address to conquer or to clear himself of them. On one occasion in a small ship of 10 guns he fought and beat off a lugger of 40 guns, and wrested a prize out of her hands. When a battle was inevitable, he deliberately prepared for it, and was as cool and calm in the combat, as on the most common business. Of the perfect obedience of his men he was sure; for he always attended to their wants, their comforts and convenience, as a father to those of his children, and they loved and obeyed him as a parent; and he knew how to inspire them with courage, or fire them with rage, as should best second his own valorous deeds. As he was intrepid, so was he modest, as he was brave, so was he just; as he was terrible to his enemies, so was he the best of friends. His manners were the most gentle, his disposition the most kind, and his heart the most tender. With these qualities, it is superfluous to add, he has left numerous friends, we believe, no enemies."

200

[This is the sixth instalment of a series of articles on Massachusetts Pi neers to other states, to be published by The Massachusetts Magazine.]

MASSACHUSETTS PIONEERS. MICHIGAN SERIES.

By Charles A. Flagg

Besides the abbreviations of book titles, (explained on pages 76, 77' 78 and 79 of April issue) the following are used: b. for born; d. for died; m. for married; set. for settled in.

Converse, James, of Northampton; set. Mich., 1840. Lenawee Hist. I, 513.

—— Maria L., b. Northampton, 1832, m. 1854 George T. McKenzie of Mich. Lenawee Hist. I, 513.

Cook, Amelia, m. 1825 Justin Cook of Mich. Washtenaw Hist., 1307.

—— Edwin, b. Hadley, 1812; set. N. Y., 1834, Mich. Lenawee Port., 353.

—— George, b. Hampshire Co., 1828; set. Mich., 1845. Washtenaw Hist., 1307.

—— Justin, b. Hampshire Co., 1802; set. Mich., 1845. Washtenaw Hist., 1307.

—— Levi, b. Bellingham, 1792; set. Mich., 1815. Detroit, 1033.

—— Martin E., b. Shelburne Falls; set. N. Y., 1820? Jackson Hist., 791.

—— Randolph, b. 1831; set. Mich., 1845. Washtenaw Hist., 1307.

—— Samuel, set. Vt., N. Y., 1800? Calhoun, 75.

—— Vienna, b. Bellingham, 1795; m. 1820 Benjamin Taft of Mass. Oakland Port., 225.

Cooley, Chester, b. Berkshire, 1790? set. N. Y., O., Mich., 1850. Kalamazoo Port., 888.

—— Dennis, b. Deerfield, 1789; set. Ga., Mich., 1827. Macomb Hist., 817.

—— George, b. Deerfield, 1819; set. Mich., 1830. Ionia Hist., 290.

—— George N., b. Conn. Valley, 1810; set. N. Y., Mich. Kent, 653.

—— Jerusha M., b. S. Deerfield, 1810; m. 1840 Philip Reeve of Mich. Washtenaw Past, 219.

Cooley, Joanna, b. Lowell. 1825; m. Solon T. Hutchins of Mich. Midland, 288.

—— Leonard, set. N.Y., 1800? Mich., 1842. Lenawee Port., 594.

—— Orsimus, set. Mich., 1830; Genesee Hist., 410.

—— Reuben, set. N. Y., 1811. Kalamazoo Hist., 433.

—— Russell, b. Deerfield; set. Mich., 1830. Ionia Hist., 290; Washtenaw Hist., 689.

—— Sally, m. 1800? Lemon Copley of O. and Mich. Genesee Port., 620.

—— Smith, set. N. Y., 1840? Huron, 287.

—— Sophronia, b. 1811; m. Sylvester Scott of Mich. Clinton Port., 666, 912.

—— Thomas, set. N. Y., 1804. Washtenaw Port., 235.

—— Zadoc, b. 1793; set. O. 1825, Mich., 1833. Oakland Biog., 367.

Coolidge, Henry H., b. Leominster, 1805 or 11; set. Mich., 1836. Berrien Hist., 146; Berrien Port., 213; Berrien Twent., 154, 286; Cass Hist., 90.

Coon, Huldah, m. 1800? Elijah Knox of Mass. and N. Y. Kalamazoo Port., 983.

Cooper, Jeremiah, set. N. Y., 1810. Lenawee Illus., 90.

—— John, b. Plymouth; set. Me., 1820? Mich., 1865. Ionia Port., 746.

—— Sarah, b. Cheshire, 1803; m. 1821 Edmund B. Dewey of N. Y. Lenawee Illus., 90

Copeland, Emeline, m. 1835? David Burton of Me. and Mich. Midland, 240.

Cossett, Isabinda, m. 1810? Asaph Robinson of O. Branch Port., 556.

Cotrell, Lucy, b. Worthington, 1817; m. 1837 James Rogers of Mass., Mich. and O. Lenawee Port., 915.

Cotton, Otis W., set. N. Y., 1808; La., 1818, Mich., 1828. Macomb Past., 168.

Coulson, Lovina, m. 1815? William Pratt of Mass. and O. Hillsdale Port., 827.

Courtis, William M., b. Boston, 1842; set. Mich., 1883. Wayne Land. Appendix 28.

Covey, Hiram, b. Mt. Washington, 1802; set. N. Y., 1814, Mich., 1837. Oakland Hist., facing 218.

Cowan, N. B., b. 1810; set. Mich., 1840. Clinton Port., 456.

—— Sally, m. 1805? Elkanah Ring. Saginaw Hist., 757.

Cowles, Horace, see Coles.

—— Israel T., b. Belchertown, 1854; set. Mich., 1878. Wayne Land. Appendix, 119.

—— Proctor P., b. Amherst, 1818; set. Mich., 1858. Upper P., 277.

—— Shepard B., b. Amherst, 1826; set. N. Y., 1830? Mich., 1836. Grand Rapids City, 622; Kent, 1354.

—— Sylvester, b. Amherst, 1795; set. N. Y., 1830? O., 1836. Grand Rapids City, 622.

Cowls, Samuel, b. Hatfield, 1766; set. O. Lenawee Hist. II, 116.

—— Sophia, b. Williamsburg, 1796; m. 1821 John Wilson of N. Y. and Mich. Lenawee Hist. II, 116.

—— Sophia, m. 1825? George H. Smith of Mass. and Mich. Jackson Port., 451.

Cox, James N., b. Fairhaven, 1844; set. Mich. 1869. Houghton, 213; Northern P., 400; Upper P., 303.

Crafts, Frances, m. 1832 Warren Pease of Mich. Washtenaw Hist., 1348.

—— Solomon C., set. Mich., 1842. Jackson Hist., 881.

Crandell, Edgar B., b. Cheshire; set. N.Y., Mich., 1878. Grand Rapids City, 119.

—— Stephen R., b. W. Stockbridge, 1836; set. N. Y., Mich., 1878. Grand Rapids City, 119; Mecosta, 491.

Crandle, Betsey, b. 1787; m. 1802 Jacob Hoadley of Mass., N. Y. and Mich. Lenawee Hist. II, 94.

Crane, Abraham, 1812 soldier, set. N. Y., 1825? Allegan Twent., 170.

Crane, Albert, b. Taunton, 1815; set. Mich. 1832. Hillsdale Port., 842, 845.

—— George, b. Norton, 1783; set. N. Y., 1804, Mich., 1833. Lenawee Hist. I, 252, 509; II, 466; Lenawee Port., 371.

—— Hannah, m. 1835 Sylvanus Kennedy of Mich. Lenawee Port., 223.

—— John, set. Ct. Hillsdale Port., 223.

—— Samuel, set. Ct., N. Y., 1810. Hillsdale Port., 223.

—— Turner, b. Norton, 1789; set. N. H., N. Y., 1816, Mich., 1833. Hillsdale Port 845; Lenawee Hist. II, 102 483; Lenawee Illus., 87; Lenawee Port., 569.

Cranson, Elisha, b. near Boston, 1782; set. N. Y., 1815? Mich., 1830. Washtenaw Port., 419.

—— John, set. N. Y., 1825? Mich., 1832. Clinton Port., 987.

Crapo, David, b. Dartmouth; set. O., Mich., 1854. Ionia Port., 736.

—— Henry H., b. Dartmouth, 1804; set. Mich., 1856. Branch Port., 149; Genesee Hist., 179.

Craw, Farley, b. Cheshire, 1824; set. N.Y., 1827, Mich., 1845. Genesee Port., 303.

Cressy, Erastus, of Rowe; set. Mich., 1842. Allegan Hist., 472.

Crissey, William S., b. 1806; set. N. Y., 1811, Mich., 1855. Kent. 533.

Crittenden, Chauncy, set. N. Y., 1830? Kalamazoo Port., 825.

—— John, b. Conway, 1796; set. R. I., N. Y., 1816, Mich., 1831. Macomb Hist., 577, 906; Macomb Past, 146.

—— Levi, set. Mich., 1835. Macomb Hist., 794.

—— Orris, set. Mich., 1834. Hillsdale Port., 375.

Crocker, Joseph, b. Cape Cod, 1801; set. N. Y., 1830? Osceola, 249.

Crofoot, Joseph, b. 1811? set. N. Y. Berrien Hist., 405.

Crosby, Hale E., b. Ashburnham, 1816; set. Mich., 1844. Berrien Port., 900.

—— Warren, set. N. Y., 1840? Mich. Muskegon Port., 276.

Cross, Darius, b. Rowe or Buckland, 1814; set. Mich., 1837. Lenawee Hist. II, 309; Lenawee Illus., 383; Lenawee Port., 1025.

CROSS, Eunice, m. 1785? David Peabody of N. H. Calhoun, facing 112.

—— Prudence, b. Rowe, 1807; m. 1828 Aaron S. Baker of Mich. Lenawee Hist. II, 109.

CROSSMAN, Nathaniel, b. Taunton; set. N. Y., 1805? Calhoun, 133.

CROVER, Amanda, of Worcester, m. 1853? Dennis Wakefield of Mich. Lenawee Illus., 284.

CUDWORTH, Mrs. A. L., set. Mich., 1828. Wayne Chron., 74.

CULVER, Martin, b. Chester; set. N. Y., 1826, Mich., 1837. Jackson Port., 296.

—— Marvin, b. Chester, 1807; set., N. Y. 1828, Mich., 1837. Jackson Port., 296.

CUMMINGS, Elvira, m. 1840? John Bonner of Pa. and Mich. Newaygo, 445.

—— Mary A., b. Royalston, 1805? m. Samuel S. Burpee of Mich. Calhoun, 76.

CURRIER, Hannah; m. 1820? Hugh Tolford of N. H. and Mich. Lenawee Port., 683.

—— Jacob, set. Mich., 1836. Berrien Hist., 402.

CURTIS, Hannah, m. 1805? Jonathan E. Davis of N. Y. Washtenaw Hist., 979.

—— Jeremiah, set. N. Y., 1800? Saginaw Hist., 729.

—— Moses, of Dudley, set. N. Y., 1800? Kalamazoo Hist., facing 476.

CURTISS, Waterman F., b. 1806; set. N.Y., Mich., 1859. Gratiot, 266.

CUSHING, James H., set. N. Y., 1825? Mich., 1851. Cass Twent., 687.

CUTLER, Dexter, b. 1811; (name changed from Shepherd) set. Mich., 1838. Northern M., 343.

—— Dwight, b. Amherst, 1830; set. Mich., 1848. Muskegon Port., 142; Ottawa Hist., 49.

CUTTER, Catharine, m. 1830? Peter Bradt of N. Y. Saginaw Hist., 908.

—— E. B., set. Ill., 1852, Mich., 1880. Saginaw Hist., 551.

DALRYMPLE, James, of Colerain, set. N. Y., 1018. Oakland Biog., 113.

—— Polly, b Colerain, m. 1815? Joseph Bancroft of N. Y. and Mich. Oakland Biog., 113.

DAMON, I. B. T., b. Hampshire Co., 1826; set. Mich., 1850? Saginaw Hist., 821.

DANA, Edmund, b. Cambridge, 1739; set. England. Bay Gansser, 374.

—— Mary, m. 1850? James H. Clapp of N. Y. and O. Grand Rapids City, 438.

DANIELS, David H., of Brimfield; set. Mich., 1832. Kalamazoo Hist., 383.

—— Elijah, b. 1793; set. N. Y.; d. 1839. Ingham Port., 733.

—— Elizabeth, m. 1805? Zenus Roberts of Mass. and Pa. Lenawee Port., 601.

—— Tamer, b. Hingham; m. 1810? Thaddeus Hopper of N. Y. and Mich. Berrien Twent., 338.

DARLING, Ephraim, b. 1791; set. Mich. Washtenaw Hist., 593.

—— Joseph, set. N. Y., 1804, Mich., 1844. Jackson Port., 324, 824.

—— Lewis, b. 1812; set. N. Y., Mich., 1836. Jackson Port., 545.

—— Matilda A., b. Mendon, 1820; m. 1840 Stephen T. Hardy of Mich. Monroe, 587.

—— Pascal, set. N. Y., 1804, Mich., 1834. Jackson Port., 824.

—— Reed, b. Springfield, 1785; set. N. Y., Mich., 1834. Kalamazoo Hist., 309.

—— Simon, set. Mich., 1829. Ingham Hist., 463.

DARWIN, S. A., b. Pittsfield, 1813; set. Mich., 1836. Ingham Port., 221.

—— Seth C., set. N. Y., 1817, Mich., 1835. Ingham Port., 221.

DAUBY, Alexander J., b. near Springfield; set. N. Y., 1820. Jackson Port., 243.

DAVIS, Asa, set. N. Y., 1802. Lenawee Port., 232.

—— Bela, set. Vt., 1795? Macomb Past, 167.

—— Calvin, b. Hubbardston, 1793; set. N. Y., 1804, Mich., 1824. Macomb Hist., 726, 773; Macomb Past, 355.

—— Dolly, m. 1790? Lemuel Foster of Mass. and Mich. Jackson Port., 745.

—— Ebenezer, b. Conway, 1800; set. N. Y., 1827, Mich., 1831. Lenawee Hist. II, 130.

—— Jehiel, b. Wilbraham, 1787; set. Mich. 1831. Oakland Port., 612.

(To be continued.)

This is the sixth of a series of articles, giving the organization and history of all the Massachusetts regiments which took part in the war of the Revolution.]

COLONEL EBENEZER BRIDGE'S REGIMENT

COLONEL EBENEZER BRIDGE'S MINUTE MEN'S REGIMENT, 1775.
27TH REGIMENT ARMY OF THE UNITED COLONIES, 1775.

BY FRANK A. GARDNER, M. D.

Middlesex County furnished a majority of the companies of which this regiment was composed. Of the seven companies in the Minute Men's Regiment six were from Middlesex County and one from New Hampshire, and of the ten companies in the 27th Regiment, Army of the United Colonies, seven were from Middlesex, two from Essex and one from New Hampshire.

We may properly consider that the nucleus of this regiment was formed in March, 1775, when Ebenezer Bridge was chosen Captain of a company of fifty Minute Men in Billerica. When the Lexington Alarm was sounded, April 19, 1775, Colonel Bridge responded at the head of a regiment composed of seven companies. The officers of this Minute Men's Regiment were as follows:—

Colonel, Ebenezer Bridge of Billerica.
Lieut. Colonel, Moses Parker of Chelmsford.
Major, John Brooks of Reading.
Adjutant, Joseph Fox of Billerica.
Surgeon, Walter Hasting of Chelmsford.

Reading Company.

Captain, John Bacheller.
First Lieutenant, Ebenezer Damon.
Second Lieutenant, James Bancroft.
58 non-commissioned officers and men.

Tewksbury Company.

Captain, John Trull.
First Lieutenant, John Flint.
Second Lieutenant, Luke Swett.
30 non-commissioned officers and men.

Billerica Company.

Captain, Jonathan Stickney.
First Lieutenant, James Lewis.
Second Lieutenant, John Lewis.
51 non-commissioned officers and men.

Dunstable Company.

Captain, Leonard Butterfield.
First Lieutenant, Nathaniel Holden.
Second Lieutenant, Lemuel Perham.
35 non-commissioned officers and men.

Dracut Company.

Captain, Peter Coburn.
First Lieutenant, Josiah Foster.
Second Lieutenant, Ebenezer Varnum.
36 non-commissioned officers and men.

New Hampshire Company.

Captain, Archelaus Towne of Amherst, N. H.
First Lieutenant, James Ford of Nottingham, N. H.
Second Lieutenant, David Wallingford of Hollis, N. H.
54 non-commissioned officers and men.

Wilmington Company.

Captain, Cadwallader Ford.
First Lieutenant, John Harnden.
Second Lieutenant, (wanting.)
25 non-commissioned officers and men.

April 24, 1775, this regiment was reorganized as a regiment in the Provincial Army and when a little later the regiments in that army were numbered, it became the 11th Massachusetts Bay Regiment. He reported that his regiment was full and the officers were recommended for commissions; these were granted to the officers of the regiment in the session of the Second Provincial Congress, May 23–29, 1775.

The following interesting return of the regiment at this period is preserved in the Massachusetts Archives:—

"Coll° Bridge's Return.
Moses Parker Lt Col°
John Brooks Major

Capt Jonathan Stickney	66	men
Capt Benj Walker	73	
Capt John Batcheller	69	
Capt Ebenezer Bancroft	50	
Capt Peter Coburn	51	
Capt Eben^r Harnden	47	
Capt John Ford	59	
Capt Oliver Will Lane	recruiting	
Capt John Row	40	
Capt Jacob Tyler	recruiting	
	455	

May 26, 1775. Eben^r Bridge."

A general return of the army dated June 9, 1775, credited Colonel Bridge with 3 field officers, 7 captains, 14 subalterns, 28 sergeants, 24 corporals, 7 drummers, 7 fifers and 315 privates, making a total of 405. He had at that time arms sufficient for all of the privates and 3,195 rounds of ammunition.

This regiment played an important part in the battle of Bunker Hill, June 17, 1775. It was one of the three infantry regiments from Massachusetts in that memorable conflict. Frothingham tells us that "Though the whole regiment was ordered to parade on the 16th of June, yet it is stated that three of its companies did not go on under Colonel Prescott. Ford's Company reached the field just before the action began, and a portion of this regiment—two companies under Major Brooks—were on the way to the hill when the Americans were retreating." Many of the men in this regiment were in the redoubt with Colonel Prescott and fought valiantly as shown by the account of the battle written by Captain (afterwards Lieut. Colonel) Ebenezer Bancroft and proven by the records of the killed and wounded. Captain Bancroft in his account of the battle states that Colonel Prescott came to him and said; "If you can do anything with the cannon I wish you would, I give (you) the charge of them." Accordingly he directed the men

to dig down the bank in order to form an embrasure, which they were forced to do with their hands as the intrenching tools had been carried off. Captain Bancroft further states that he fired a cannon twice to loosen up the earth and he learned later that both of these balls fell in Boston, one in Brattle Square and the other in Cornhill. The account of the casualties to the officers of this regiment will be given in their records in the biographical section of this article. A newspaper printed in Providence, Rhode Island, July 15, 1775, stated that sixteen members of this regiment were killed in the battle and twenty-nine wounded. An account published in Force's American Archives, (v. 4–II, p. 1628,) gives the numbers as seventeen killed and twenty-five wounded. In the general accusation which followed the battle, Colonel Bridge was included in the list of those who were blamed for not being sufficiently aggressive. In the court martial which followed he was acquitted on account of his wounds and the indisposition of body resulting therefrom.

The following list of officers of the regiment is preserved in the State Archives;

"Ebenezer Bridge, Colonel.
Moses Parker, Lieut. Col° Prisoner in Boston.
John Brooks, Major.

Captains.	Lieutenants.	Ensigns.
Jona Stickney	Elijah Danforth	John Lewis
Benj[a] Walker	John Flint	Ebenezer Fitch
John Batchelor	Eben[r] Damon	James Bancroft
Eben[r] Bancroft	Nath'l Holden	Samuel Brown
Peter Coburn	Josiah Foster	Ebenezer Varnum
John Ford	Isaac Parker	Jonas Parker
John Harnden	Will[m] Blanchard	Eleazer Stickney
John Row	Mark Pool	Ebenez[r] Cleveland
Jacob Tyler	Charles Forbush	

Joseph Fox, Adjutant
John Bridge, Quarter Master
Walter Hastings, Chirurgeon.

Captain Walker missing
supposed killed.

June 23, 1775."

Fourteen cartridge boxes were ordered June 24, 1775, by Colonel Bridge for his men and they were received by them later.

The following list of companies with the names of the towns represented is from the State Archives:

"Col. Eben[r] Bridge's Reg't

Captains

Benj. Walker, Tewksbury, Chelmsford, Bedford, An lover &c.
John Ford, Chelmsford, Tewksbury, &c,
Jona. Stickney, Billerica, &c.
John Row, Cape Ann.
Peter Coburn, Dracut, Methuen, Tewksbury &c.
John Harnden, Wilmington, Billerica, Tewksbury, Reading &c.
John Bacheller, Reading &c.
Eben Bancroft, Dunstable, Derry, &c.
Archulaus Towne, Hollis, N. H.
Charles Furbush, Andover."

In the records of the Third Provincial Congress, June 28, 1775, mention is made of a petition of the officers of this regiment relating to organization and the rank of officers. The committee to whom it was referred reported on the following day.

In the records of the Committee of Safety in the Journal of the Provincial Congress, July 7, 1775, we read;

"Eight small arms were delivered Col. Ebenezer Bridge, for the use of his regiment, amounting, as by appraisement to seventeen pounds, six shillings, for which receipt was taken in the minute book."

A list of the field and staff officers of the regiment dated August 1, 1775, is like those given with the exception of the name of John Sprague, Surgeon's Mate, which is added. Another similar list bears the date of September 30. The regiment was stationed at or near Cambridge through the year. November 23, 1775, Colonel Bridge with his regiment was ordered at the foot of Cobble Hill (the hill between Somerville and Cambridge on which the McLean Asylum formerly stood) to patrol towards the bay and neck during the night as a strong detachment under General Putnam was throwing up fortifications there.

When the regiments were reorganized for the Continental Army service

a letter from the officers of this regiment was sent to General Washington. This was acknowledged as follows:

"Head-Quarters, Cambridge, December 10, 1775.

(Parole, Burke.) (Countersign, Barre.)

The General has great pleasure in thanking Colonel Bridges, and the officers of the Twenty-seventh Regiment, (who, from a peculiarity of circumstances, or want of vacancies, have no appointment in the new established army,) for their polite address to him. He considers the assurances which they have given, of their determination to continue in service, (if required) until the new regiments are completed, in a very favorable light, especially as it is accompanied with further assurances that the men of the Twenty-seventh Regiment are consenting thereto. Such a conduct at this important crisis cannot fail of giving pleasure to every well-wisher of his country; and next to engaging for another year, is the highest proof they can give of their attachment to the noble cause of liberty. At the same time that it reflects honor upon themselves, it may, under Providence, give posterity reason to bless them as the happy instruments of their delivery from those chains which were actually forging for them."

The strength of the regiment each month is shown in the following table:

Date.	Com. off.	Staff.	Non-Coms.	Rank & File	Total.
June 9,	24	–	66	315	405
July –	19	3	53	406	481
Aug. 18,	26	3	50	468	547
Sept. 23,	26	4	55	472	557
Oct, 17,	30	4	49	464	547
Nov. 18,	24	4	42	460	530
Dec.	25	3	50	455	533

COLONEL EBENEZER BRIDGE of Billerica was the son of Reverend Ebenezer Bridge of Chelmsford. He went to Billerica a few years before the war and engaged in business as a "merchant," living at the Farmer place nearly opposite the (Colonel) Stickney house. He was chairman of a committee of the town which reported resolutions protesting against the acts of the "British Ministry and Parliament against the colonies" June 4, 1774. He was

a letter from the officers of this regiment was sent to General Wa
This was acknowledged as follows:

"Head-Quarters, Cambridge, December 10, 1775.

(Parole, Burke.) (Countersign, Barre.)

The General has great pleasure in thanking Colonel Bridges and
cers of the Twenty-seventh Regiment, who, from a peculiarity of
stances, or want of vacancies, have no appointment in the new est
army) for their polite address to him. He considers the assuranc
they have given, of their determination to continue in service, (if
until the new regiments are completed, in a very favorable light,
as it is accompanied with further assurances that the men of the
seventh Regiment are consenting thereto. Such a conduct at this in
crisis cannot fail of giving pleasure to every well-wisher of his
and next to engaging for another year, is the highest proof they ca
their attachment to the noble cause of liberty. At the same time th
flects honor upon themselves, it may, under Providence, give posterit
to bless them as the happy instruments of their delivery from those
were actually forging for them."

The strength of the regiment each month shown in the followin

Date.	Com'd off.	Staff.	Non-Coms.	Rank & F
June 9,	24	—	66	316
July —	19	2	53	406
Aug. 18,		3	50	408
Sept. 28,		4	56	472
Oct,		4	49	464

also chosen chairman of the "committee of Correspondence." He was a member of the Middlesex Convention August 30–31, 1774, and served as its clerk. He was appointed on a committee of the convention to take into consideration "an act for the better regulating the government of the province of Massachusetts Bay in New England," and was chosen representative to the First Provincial Congress, in October 1774.—December 5, 1774, he was appointed on a committee "to prepare an address to the clergy of this province desiring them to exhort to carry into execution the resolves of the Continental Congress." Two days later he was appointed on a committee "to collect the several expenses that have accrued to the Congress in this and the former session thereof, and they are directed to sit forthwith." He was chosen chairman of the "committee of Inspection" of Billerica in December, 1774.

In March, 1775, he was chosen captain of a company of fifty minute men, and this we have reason to believe was his first military service, as we can find no French war record, and he was always called "Mr" Bridge in the records prior to this date. He evidently developed considerable military ability for when the call came April 19th, he responded as Colonel in command of a Regiment of Minute Men composed of seven companies. When the Provincial Army was organized a few days later he was continued as regimental commander and the regiment was stationed at Cambridge. He was "Field Officer of the Day" May 17, "Officer of the Main Guard" May 22, and "Field officer" May 30–31, 1775. The account of the service of his regiment at Bunker Hill has been given in the records of the organization. He was wounded "on the head and neck by a sword cut" and is said by the historian of Billerica to have been one of the last to leave. Later in the year he rendered the following:

"An account of what I loft in the Battle at Bunker's Hill.

Viz 1 new Beaver Hat	£1:10:00
1 Silver Hilted Hanger	4:16:00
	£6:06:00

A true Account

Attest

Eben[r] Bridg Col[o] 27th Regiment.

Camp at Cambridge, Nov. 30, 1775."

He was tried for "misbehaviour & neglect of duty in action at Bunker's Hill," and the following verdict was rendered:

"The Court are of opinion that indisposition of body rendered the prisoner incapable of action and do therefore acquit him." He commanded the regiment through the year and on January 1, 1776, returned "one firelock" to the State authorities. He was one of the corporators of the Middlesex turnpike which was chartered in 1804. He did not return to Billerica after the war. At the time of his marriage, September 17, 1817, he lived in the town of Harvard.

LIEUT. COLONEL MOSES PARKER of Chelmsford was a Sergeant in the Company commanded by Captains John Reed and Benaiah Young, in the late Colonel Titcomb's Regiment, from April 7 to September 8, 1755 (probably). He served as Ensign of the same Company from the last named date to December 15, of that year. From March 31, 1759 to August 6, 1760, he was Captain of a company at "Saint Johns." This was evidently St. John, (now New Brunswick) for another record shows that he was a Captain in Colonel Frye's Regiment at "Nova Scotia" during this period. From a list dated July 22, 1761, we learn that he served three months as a Captain in Colonel Nathaniel Thyng's Regiment. Two other undated records of service are also to be found in the archives. When the Lexington Alarm was sounded April 19, 1775, he marched as Lieut. Colonel of Colonel Ebenezer Bridge's Regiment and the independant company of Minute Men of which Lieut. Colonel Parker was the commander was led by his Lieutenants, Benjamin Walker and Isaac Parker. April 24, he was engaged in the same rank in the Provincial Regiment under the same commander. He was field Officer of the Main Guard" May 8 and June 5, "Field Officer of Fatigue," May 11, and June 3, and Officer of the Main Guard" June 4, 1775. He marched with the regiment from Cambridge to Breed's Hill on the night of June 16, in the body of men under Colonel William Prescott, consisting of Prescott's Regiment, a part of Colonel Frye's, part of Colonel Bridge's with the artillery and about 200 Connecticut troops. He fought valiantly on the following day and was desperately wounded and taken prisoner. He died of his wounds July 4, 1775.

MAJOR JOHN BROOKS of Reading was the son of Caleb and Ruth (Albree) Brooks. He was born in Medford May 31, 1752. He worked on his father's farm and when fourteen years old was taken into the home of the family physician, Dr. Simon Tufts, to study medicine. He began to practice at Reading in 1773. In response to the Lexington Alarm, April 19, 1775, he marched as Major of Colonel Ebenezer Bridge's Regiment of Minute Men, and he held the same rank under that commander through the year. January 1,

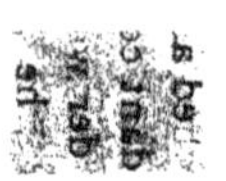

1776, he became Major of Colonel Charles Webb's 19th Regiment in the Continental Army, and served through the year. January 1, 1777 he was made Lieut. Colonel of Colonel Michael Jackson's 8th Regiment, Massachusetts Line. He was appointed Lieut. Colonel Commanding the 7th Regiment Massachusetts Line, (formerly Alden's) November 11, 1778 and served until June 12, 1783. A portion of this time he was called "Acting Colonel." He made a distinguished record for himself during these years of conflict. One writer states that, "The capture of General Burgoyne and his army may de attributed in no small degree to the gallant conduct of Colonel Brooks and his regiment, on the 7th of October in the battle of Saratoga." Hon. Roger Walcott Williams of Connecticut described Colonel Brooks conduct on that day as follows: "When the Colonel saw that the decisive moment had come, he lifted his sword in air and cried 'Follow your Colonel at double quick.' He immediately led the way to the top of the entrenchments, crying 'come on, come on.' They did come on, and the most violent and bloody conflict ensued, in which they decided the fate of the day." He was with Washington during the memorable winter at Valley Forge, and in June, 1778, distinguished himself at the battle of Monmouth. As a tactician he has been considered second only to Baron Steuben, and after that officer was made Inspector General, Colonel Brooks was associated with him in establishing a uniform system of drill and exercise. A writer in the New England Historic Genealogical Register states that, "When in March, 1783, the officers had planned a conspiracy causing Washington the most anxious moments of his life, the Commander-in-Chief went to Colonel Brooks to ascertain how the officers stood, and finding him sound asked him to keep his officers in quarters. Colonel Brooks replied, 'Sir, I have anticipated your wishes,' to which Washington replied with tears in his eyes, 'Colonel Brooks, this is just what I expected from you.' "

At the close of the war he was invited by his old family physician and preceptor to take his place in Medford and the offer was accepted. One of his biographers has said of him that, "As a physician he ranked in the first class of practitioners, possessing in an eminent degree those qualities which were calculated to render him the most useful in his professional labors, and the delight of those to whom he administered relief."

In 1786, he was made Major General of the 3d Division, Massachusetts Militia and April 11' 1792, was given the rank of Brigadier General in the United States Army. He was honorably discharged November 1, 1796. In 1788, he was a member of the Convention by which the Constitution of the

United States was adopted. He represented the county of Middlesex for several years in the Massachusetts Senate and served as a member of the executive council. He was United States Marshall of the district of Massachusetts, 1791-96, and was appointed, December 20, 1796, Inspector of the Revenue for Survey No. 2, in the district of Massachusetts. Governor Strong appointed him Adjutant General of the State, in 1812, and he served in that responsible office during the second war with England until 1815. In 1816 he was elected Governor and served seven consecutive years. He declined to be a candidate again and, retiring to his Medford home, resumed practice. Chief Justice Parker said of him that, "he maintained the dignity of his office, and thereby honored the people who bestowed it. . . . Bred in the best school of manners, — a military association of high-minded, accomplished officers, — his deportment, though grave and dignified like Washington's was nevertheless warm and affectionate. . . . He was one of the last and best samples of that old school of manners."

He was President of the Massachusetts Medical Society for many years, continuing so to the time of his death. He was Secretary of the Massachusetts Society of the Cincinnati in 1783-6 and President from 1810 until 1825. Harvard College conferred upon him the degree of A.M. in 1787, that of M.D. in 1810 and LL.D. in 1817. He also held many other positions of honor and trust. He died March 1, 1825, at the age of 73 years.

ADJUTANT JOSEPH FOX of Billerica. His name appeared on the tax lists of that town from 1769 to 1776. He served as Adjutant under Colonel Bridge in the Minute Men's Regiment and later in the Provincial and United Colonies' Regiments through the year. January 23, 1776, he was appointed Ensign in Colonel Burrill's Connecticut State Regiment, and promoted to Second Lieutenant, September 19, of that year. January 11, 1777, he became a first Lieutenant in Colonel William R. Lee's Additional Regiment and a Captain in Colonel Henry Jackson's Regiment on June 23d of that year. In October, 1778, he was in Colonel David Henley's Regiment and served as Paymaster of that command from October 30, 1778, to April 1, 1779. He was transferred to Colonel Henry Jackson's Regiment April 22, 1779. This regiment was designated the 16th Continental, July 23, 1780. He was a Captain in the 9th Massachusetts Regiment January 1, 1782, and retired just a year later. He died March 24, 1820.

QUARTERMASTER JOHN BRIDGE of Chelmsford may have been and probably was the man of that name who held the rank of First Lieutenant

in Captain John Tapley's Company from February 12, to October 23, 1757. This company was evidently in Colonel Joseph Frye's Regiment and was present at the capitulation of Fort William Henry, August 9, 1757. His name appears as Lieutenant in the same company in a roll dated March 7, 1758. He was engaged April 24, 1775, as a "Captain acting as Quartermaster" and he served under Colonel Bridge through the year.

SURGEON WALTER HASTINGS held that rank in Colonel Ebenezer Bridge's Minute Mens Regiment, April 19, 1775. His name appears in a list of Surgeons and Surgeon's Mates, examined and approved at Watertown, July 5, 1775. He served through the year. January 1, 1777, he was appointed Surgeon in Colonel Michael Jackson's 8th Regiment Massachusetts Line and served until retired January 1, 1781.

SURGEON'S MATE JOHN SPRAGUE was probably the John Sprague who was credited with £8:03:00 for Medical attendance on Moses Bennet, pilot of the ship "Massachusetts," June 20, 1759. He held the above rank in Colonel Ebenezer Bridge's Regiment from May 1, 1775, through the year. January 1, 1776, he was appointed Surgeon's Mate of Colonel Edmund Phinney's 18th Continental Regiment and served through the year. He was reported sick at Fort George, December 8, 1776. October 6, 1778, he was Surgeon of the privateer schooner "Active," Captain Andrew Gardner. He was engaged as Surgeon of the State sloop, "Winthrop," Captain George Little, May 4, 1782, and served through two cruises until March 17, 1783.

CAPTAIN JOHN BACHELLER of Reading was one of the company commanders in Colonel Ebenezer Bridge's Minute Mens Regiment, April 19, 1775. He enlisted in the same rank in the provincial Army under Colonel Bridge and served at least as late as August 1st, as shown by his company pay rolls, preserved in the Military Manuscripts in the Essex Institute.

CAPTAIN EBENEZER BANCROFT of Dunstable was the son of Timothy and Elizabeth (Farwell) Bancroft. He was born April 1, 1738, in that part of Dunstable, which later became Tyngsborough. From September 15 to December 14, (endorsed 1755) he was a Corporal in Captain Jonathan Butterfield's Company and marched from Albany to Dunstable. He was a Sergeant in the same company from March 29 to December 4, (endorsed 1756). From March 31 to April 30, (probably 1759) he served as a second Lieutanant in the same company, and from February 14 to December 4 (endorsed 1760) he was a Lieutenant in Captain Silas Brown's Company. In 1771, he served

as a Selectman of Dunstable and later was chosen on a committee to divide the town into "districts for schooling." He marched on the Lexington Alarm April 19, 1775, and was described asta "Captain serving as a volunteer" in Captain Reuben Butterfield's Company, Colonel David Green's Regiment. He overtook the British at West Cambridge and did effective work with his gun. April 24, 1775, he was engaged as a Captain in Colonel Ebenezer Bridge's Regiment and served until June 17th, when he was severely wounded at Bunker Hill. On the evening of June 16, 1775, he was on a court martial and was not able therefore to march with his command. He obtained permission from General Ward on the morning of the 17th and hastening to Charlestown, joined his regiment. While standing by the redoubt before the action began, a ball from the "Somerset" passed within a few inches of his head and affected his left eye so that he ultimately became totally blind. His effective management of the artillery pieces and the making of the embrasures have already been described in the record of the achievements of the regiment. Captain Bancroft stated that he fired twenty-seven musket shots during the fight at the redoubt. Nason, the author of the "History of Dunstable " states that he "fought nobly in the redoubt and was the last to leave it. He used a musket in the melee and being a man of remarkable strength, knocked down several British soldiers. He had his musket wrenched from him, his hat knocked off, his shoulder injured and his forefinger shot away." He wrote an account of the battle which is a valuable addition to our original records of that important event. The "Historical Register of the Officers of the Continental Army" states that he did not return to the army, but we have an abundance of proof from the records in the Massachusetts Archives that he saw much service and rose rapidly in rank.

He was commissioned February 8, 1776, 2nd Major of Colonel Simeon Spaulding's 7th Middlesex County Regiment. From September 27 to November 16, 1776, he served as Major in Colonel Ebenezer Brooks's 3d Middlesex County Regiment. June 20, 1778, he was chosen 1st Major in the 7th Middlesex County Regiment, and April 21, 1780, he was commissioned Lieut. Colonel in the same regiment, at that time commanded by Colonel Jonathan Brown. He also served in the same rank in Colonel Cyprian How's 4th Middlesex county Regiment from June 28 to October 30, 1780, to reinforce the Continental Army in Rhode Island. He evidently was at his home in Dunstable much of the time through 1776 and 7 for he was chosen on the "Committee of Correspondence" March 4, 1776, and as "Major" Ebenezer Bancroft, was chosen on a committee to "prepare y^{e} Draft of a vote," June 8, 1776.

He served as a Selectman February 17, 1777, and was the Representative of his town to the General Court in that year. This absence from the army was evidently due to his wounds, for a resolve entitling him to quarter pay was passed January 26, 1778, to commence from January 1, 1776, as he was wounded at Bunker Hill. Later his name was transferred to the United States Pension Rolls. The author of "Old Dunstable," however, states that he was at the battle of Bennington, and that he commanded a guard which conducted the Hessians to Cambridge, after the battle of Saratoga. He lived the remainder of his life in Dunstable, purchasing the house once owned by Henry Farwell and in 1877, occupied by his grandson Ebenezer Bancroft, Esq. In September, 1827, Colonel Bancroft met with an accident by a fall and broke the thigh bone in the socket. He lingered several days in great pain and died September 22, 1727, in the 90th year of his age. He was buried under arms, the band playing "Blue-Eyed Susan" on the way to the grave as it was the only tune they all could play. He was, buried with Masonic rites as he had become a member of a travelling lodge in the French and Indian war in 1755.

CAPTAIN LEONARD BUTTERFIELD of Dunstable was a private in Captain Leonard Whitney's Company, from March 31 to November 15 (endorsed 1760). He was reported sick and was allowed "90 miles travel home." From May 1 to January 10 (endorsed 1761–2), at that time called a resident of Chelsmford, he was a Corporal in Captain Moses Parker's Company. January 23, 1775, he was chosen on a committee of Dunstable "to carry into execution the agreement of the Continental Congress." He commanded a company in Colonel Ebenezer Bridge's Minute Mens Regiment on the Lexington alarm, April 19, 1775, and served five days. A bounty of £5 per month was voted him later for "Service on Guards att Cambridge." No further service is on records in the Massachusetts Archives. Nason, the historian of Dunstable, however, states that he is given as Captain in the "Alarm List," May 1776; that he was drafted for the third time June 3, 1777, and that he was in Captain Oliver Cummings's Campany in 1777–8. He died November 17, 1800, aged 60.

CAPTAIN PETER COBURN of Dracut marched in command of a company in Colonel Ebenezer Bridge's Minute Mens Regiment, April 19, 1775. He was engaged for service in the Provincial Regiment under Colonel Bridge, April 26, 1775. He fought in the battle of Bunker Hill and was re-

imbursed for losses in the battle. The nature and amount of the losses were not specified however in the records. He served through the year.

CAPTAIN CADWALLADER FORD, JR., of Wilmington, was the son of Cadwallader and Mary Ford, born November 27, 1743. As commander of one of the companies in Colonel Ebenezer Regiment of Minute Men, he marched on the Lexington alarm, April 19, 1775 and served twenty-one days. The records state that he enlisted March 9, 1775, to "be ready at a minute's warning till the last of June, 1775, and trained 10 half days." He died at Wilmington October 15, 1804, aged sixty-one years.

CAPTAIN JOHN FORD of Chelmsford, may have been the man of that name who enlisted April 11, 1758, as a member of Captain Angier's Company in Colonel Joseph Williams's Regiment. He was a Captain in Colonel Ebenezer Bridge Minute Mens Regiment April 19, 1775. Six days later he was engaged for service in Colonel Bridge's Regiment in the Provincial Army and served under that commander through the year. He was in the battle of Bunker Hill and lost articles there. February 5, 1776, he was commissioned a Captain in Colonel John Robinson's Regiment to serve until April 1, 1776. May 31, 1776, he was commissioned Captain in the 7th Middlesex County Regiment. From July 11, to November 30, 1776, he was a Captain in Colonel Jonathan Reed's 6th Middlesex County Regiment. He was engaged September 27, 1777, as Captain of a volunteer company in the same regiment and served until November 8, 1777.

CAPTAIN CHARLES FURBUSH of Andover, served in the French and Indian war. Several terms of service are credited in 1756–8 to men of this name, but as his father, Charles also served it is impossible to separate their records. The following extract from Bailey's "History of Andover" gives a part of his record:

"Charles Furbush (Sr) had a son of the same name. Charles the son, as soon as he was of age was called to serve in the French and Indian war at the forts on Lake George and Champlain. He was so young that his father chose to enlist with him. Father and son camped and bivouacked together and they were sleeping under the same blanket upon the ground one night, when Charles awoke and found by the light of the moon shining in his father's face that he was dead." According to family tradition he was in the battle of Bunker Hill and was disabled in action and carried to the rear. He served through the year in Colonel Bridge's Regiment and was first engaged for that

service April 25, 1775. An interesting family relic was the following invitation: "General Washington's Compliments to Captain Furbush and requests his company to dinner today."

CAPTAIN JOHN HARNDEN, of Wilmington, enlisted March 9, 1775, as First Lieutenant of Captain Cadwallader Ford's Company, Colonel Ebenezer Bridge's Minute Mens Regiment. He was engaged as a Captain in Colonel Bridge's Provincial Regiment, April 24, 1775, and probably served through the year.

CAPTAIN OLIVER WILL LANE is included in a list of the Officers of Colonel Bridge's Regiment, dated May 26, 1775, with the word "recruiting" following it. No further record of the man has been found in the Massachusetts archives.

CAPTAIN JOHN ROWE, (also called JR), was the son of Lieutenant John and Mary (Baker) Rowe, born in 1737. In a return dated at the camp at Lake George, November 22, 1755, giving a list of invalids belonging to Colonel Ichabod Plaisted's Regiment, is written against his name; "Judged unfit for service." He was a private in Captain Samuel Glover's Company, Colonel Joseph William's Regiment, from May 15 to October 10, (endorsed1758). Babson in his "History of Gloucester" states that he was a Sergeant in his father's company but as the records in the Massachusetts archives show the presence of Sergeant John Row and Private John Row both in the army in 1755, it is probable that the senior John Row was a Sergeant at that time, being promoted to the rank of Lieutenant later. The son was engaged as Captain in Colonel Ebenezer Bridge's Regiment May 19, 1775. Babson states that he was at Bunker Hill with his company, June 17, 1775. He served through the year in this regiment. An account dated Gloucester, January 16, 1776, shows that stores and money were given to Captain Rowe's Company when it departed for headquarters. An official record of a ballot by the house of Representatives, April 24, 1777, shows that he was chosen 1st Major in Colonel James Collins's 6th Essex County Militia Regiment. He received his commission the same day. Babson tells us in his "History of Gloucester," that while at home on a furlough in 1776, he engaged in an attack upon a British vessel off the Cape and was taken and carried a prisoner to New York. He died on his farm at Pigeon Hill, about 1800.

CAPTAIN JONATHAN STICKNEY of Billerica was the son of Captain Daniel and Mary (Hill) Stickney of Billerica. He was born in that town Au-

gust 17, 1736. The author of the "History of Billerica" states that Jonathan enlisted for the invasion of Canada in 1759, but no record of such service by a man of that name and town is given in the Massachusetts Archives. He was chosen Lieutenant of Captain Ebenezer Bridge's Company of Minute Men of Billerica in March 1775, and was Captain of the Billerica Company in Colonel Ebenezer Bridge's Minute Mens Regiment, April 19, 1775. Six days later he was engaged for service in Colonel Bridge's Provincial Regiment and he served under that commander through the year. He was with his company at the battle of Bunker Hill. March 10, 1777, he was one of a committee of five chosen in Billerica "to Indent with persons to Inlist into the Continental Service." He was a Selectman in Billerica in 1777 and 1787. In 1785, he was Major and led the Billerica Artillery in a snowstorm to Cambridge to guard the Supreme Judicial Court in Shay's Rebellion.

CAPTAIN ARCHELAUS TOWNE (or TOWN) of Amherst, N.H., was the son of Israel and Grace (Gardner) Towne of Middleton, Mass. He was born in the last named town in 1734 and went with his father at the age of six to Narraganset (now Amherst, N.H.) He was a man of remarkable strength and endurance. He marched on the Lexington alarm, April 19, 1775, in command of a New Hampshire Company in Colonel Ebenezer Bridge's Minute Mens Regiment. Through May and June this company was one of the thirteen composing Colonel John Stark's New Hampshire Regiment and did valiant service at the battle of Bunker Hill. In the first week in July the company numbered about fifty men. Between the 3d and 7th of that month he had been transferred to Colonel Ebenezer Bridge's 27th Regiment, Army of the United Colonies. He presented a petition to the House of Representatives (of N.H.), in which he stated that he and his son, Archelaus Towne, Jr., did on the 24th day of July 1777, "set out from Amherst, and marched and joined the Continental army, commanded by Gen. Gates; served as scout and did duty as other soldiers; were in the battle on the 19th of September near Stillwater, and continued in the service until four days before Gen. Burgoyne surrendered, when being taken very sick, he was obliged to return home. That neither himself nor his son had received any recompense for their services from any person whatever; wherefore he prayed that the same allowance might be made to himself and son that others had received for similar services." He died at Fishkill, New York, November, 1779.

CAPTAIN JOHN TRULL of Tewksbury may have been the John Trull whose name appears on the muster roll of Captain John Wright's Company,

dated Boston, January 1, 1756. It states that he was a sentinel and that he entered service November 22, 1754 and served until August 3, 1755. An endorsement shows that the company was at Fort Halifax. The name also is found in a list of men under His Excellency John, Earl of Loudon, out of Colonel Ezekiel Cushings' Regiment. He was reported as entitled to a bounty of $10 and to have received therefor, £3. This was dated Falmouth, April 12, 1757. The name of John Trull appears on a card of David Trull of Tewksbury, as said Trull's father or master in 1761. Captain John Trull commanded a company in Colonel Ebenezer Bridge's Minute Mens Regiment, April 19, 1775, and served ten days. He was commissioned Captain of the 11th Company (West Company in Tewksbury) in Colonel Simeon Spaulding's 7th Middlesex County Regiment, May 31, 1776.

CAPTAIN JACOB TYLER was a member of the First Company of Andover, Lieut. Colonel John Osgood, Commander, April 18, 1757. He was an Ensign in Captain Peter Parker's Company from April 28 to December 11, 1760 and Lieutenant in the same company from December 12, 1760 to March 30, 1761. He was named as a Captain in Colonel Ebenezer Bridge's Regiment and was reported as "recruiting" in a regimental return dated May 26, 1775. No further record of his service is given.

CAPTAIN BENJAMIN WALKER of Chelmsford may have been the man of that name from Wilmington or Bradford, whose service is recorded in the French war records at the Archives. He was a Lieutenant in Colonel Moses Parker's Company of Minute Men which marched April 19, 1775. May 27th, he was commissioned Captain in Colonel Ebenezer Bridge's Regiment. He commanded his company at the battle of Bunker Hill and was wounded and taken prisoner. He died of his wounds in August.

FIRST LIEUTENANT JEREMIAH BLANCHARD of Andover was a member of Captain John Forster's 4th Company of Andover, which was in Lieut. Colonel John Osgood's Regiment. This service was attested to April 19, 1757. From March 19 to October 23, 1757, he was a Corporal in Captain Richard Saltonstall's command. A roll which included his name, was made of a part of the above company at the capitulation of fort William Henry, August 9, 1757. His name appears as Private in Captain Isaac Osgood's Company, Colonel Ebenezer Nichols's Regiment, from April 7 to November 12 (endorsed 1758.) He enlisted April 25, 1775, as a Lieutenant in Captain Charles Furbush's Company in Colonel Ebenezer Bridge's Regiment and served

through the year. He was commissioned a Second Lieutenant in Colonel Thomas Poor's Regiment, June 10, 1778. He is also described as a "Lieutenant acting as Captain" during this service which terminated February 17, 1779. During the early part of this service he was in Captain David Whittier's Company in this same regiment.

FIRST LIEUTENANT WILLIAM BLANCHARD of Wilmington was a Sergeant in Captain Cadwallader Ford Jr's Company in Colonel Ebenezer Bridge's Minute Mens Regiment. He enlisted in the company March 9, 1775, and responded with it to the Lexington alarm, April 19th. Five days later he enlisted as a Lieutenant in Captain John Harnden's Company in the same, regiment and served through the year. He probably was the Colonel William Blanchard who died in Wilmington, January 8, 1833, aged 82 years.

FIRST LIEUTENANT EBENEZER DAMON of Reading served as a Sergeant under Captain William Williams from June 26 to December 2, 1760. He was First Lieutenant of Captain John Bacheller's Company in Colonel Ebenezer Bridge's Regiment of Minute Men, April 19, 1775. He served through the year under the same officers.

FIRST LIEUTENANT ELIJAH DANFORTH of Billerica was the son of Thomas and Rebecca (Simonds) Danforth and was born in Billerica August 8, 1737. In 1757, he served as a private in Captain Thomas Flint's Company, Colonel Eleazer Tyng's Regiment, and marched for the relief of Fort William Henry. From March 28 to December 1, 1759, he was a private in Captain Jonathan Butterfield's Company, Colonel Eleazer Tyng's Regiment, at Crown Point. He served as a private in Captain Silas Brown's Company from November 18, 1761, to July 1, 1762. From the latter date to November 16, 1762, he was a private in Captain Gideon Parker's Company. April 25, 1775, he was engaged as a Lieutenant in Captain Jonathan Stickney's Company, Colonel Ebenezer Bridge's Regiment, and served through the year. In 1776 he served as First Lieutenant of Captain Abishai Brown's Company in Colonel Josiah Whitney's additional regiment for the defence of Boston. Jan. 1, 1777, he became a Captain in Colonel Thomas Nixon's 6th Regiment, Massachusetts Line. He served in that command until he was retired as a supernumerary February 1, 1779. March 24, 1777, he was added to the committee of five "to Indent with persons to Inlist." He died about November, 1792.

FIRST LIEUTENANT JOHN FLINT of Tewksbury marched on the Lexington alarm, April 19, 1775, as an officer of that rank in Captain John Trull's

Company, Colonel Ebenezer Bridge's Regiment of Minute Men. When the Provincial Regiment was formed he became Lieutenant of Captain Benjamin Walker's Company in Colonel Bridge's Regiment and served through the year. May 13, 1778, he was engaged as First Lieutenant in command of the company in Colonel Thomas Poor's Regiment, which was called the "late Capt. Lawrence's Co." The company was raised to fortify the passes on the North River.

FIRST LIEUTENANT JAMES FORD of Nottingham, N.H., held that rank in Captain Archelaus Towne's Company, in Colonel Ebenezer Bridge's Minute Mens Regiment, April 19' 1775. He served in the same company in the Provincial Army in May and June when it belonged to Colonel John Stark's N.H. Regiment, and was at the battle of Bunker Hill. Early in July he returned with the company to Colonel Bridge's Regiment and served through the year. In 1776, we are told by the compiler of the New Hampshire Revolutionary Rolls, that he was in Colonel "Lutwych's" Regiment. In 1777 he commanded a company from Nottinham West, N.H., in Colonel Moses Nichols's Regiment of New Hampshire, and had a hard experience at Bennington as the following certificate shows:

State of New Hampshire } This may certify that James Ford Esq being a Captain in ye Detachment Commanded by Me upon the Right wing of Gen[l] Stark's Brigade in the Battle of Walloonsuck Hill (so called) near Bennington on the 16th day of August 1777 was very badly wounded by two Musket Balls which pass[d] through his two thighs.

Moses Nichols Col[o]"

He was paid September 19, 1777, for four months service in full, £24:00:00. His pension commenced on that date and he was paid on account of it £24:00:00 in February, 1778. He recovered from his wounds sufficiently to re-enter the service and in 1781 was Second Major of Lieut. Colonel Daniel Reynolds' New Hampshire Regiment at West Point.

FIRST LIEUTENANT JOSIAH FOSTER (or FORSTER) of Dracut was probably the man of that name who was a centinel in Captain William Lyman's Company, from September 15, to December 10, 1755; Sergeant in Captain John Burk's Company June 23– October 22, 1758; and Second Lieutenant in Captain Moses Parker's Company, Colonel Frye's Regiment at St. John, Nova Scotia (now N.B.) from March 31, 1759, to July 23, 1760. He marched on the Lexington alarm as First Lieutenant of Captain Peter Coburn's Company,

Colonel Ebenezer Bridge's Minute Mens Regiment. He served under the same commanders through the year. At the battle of Bunker Hill he lost articles and was allowed 4 shillings for the following:

"To one ftrait bodied Coat	£1:00:00
To one fword and belt	0:18:00
To one Cartridge Box	0:04:00
	Josiah Fofter."

He was a Lieutenant in Captain Joseph B. Varnum's Company, Colonel Simeon Spaulding's Regiment. Endorsed "1777".

FIRST LIEUTENANT NATHANIEL HOLDEN of Dunstable was a Selectman of the town in 1772 and a member of the committee of inspection January 23, 1775. He marched as a Lieutenant in Captain Leonard Butterfield's Company, Colonel Ebenezer Bridge's Minute Mens Regiment, April 19, 1775. He was engaged April 24, 1775, as First Lieutenant in Captain Ebenezer Bancroft's Company, Colonel Bridge's Regiment, and served through the year. From September 27 to November 16, 1776, he was a First Lieutenant in Captain Zaccheus Wright's Company, Colonel Eleazer Brooks's 3d Middlesex County Regiment. He was a member of the committee of correspondence in Dunstable March 4, 1776, and a member of the committee of assessors for the First Precinct (now Tyngsborough) in the same year. In 1783, he was on a committee to divide the town into school districts and served as a Selectman in 1787. He lived in that part of Dunstable which is now Tyngsborough, on the margin of Howard's Brook, and bore the name of "Peacemaker."

FIRST LIEUTENANT JAMES LEWIS of Billerica was probably the son of Benjamin Lewis of Billerica, who was born September 25, 1735. He was chosen Second Lieutenant of Captain Ebenezer Bridge's Minute Mens Company, in March, 1775, and was First Lieutenant in Captain John Stickney's Company, Colonel Ebenezer Bridge's Minute Mens Regiment, April 19, 1775. He removed to Groton in 1796 and died there June 12, 1810.

FIRST LIEUTENANT ISAAC PARKER of Chelmsford was a Lieutenant in Lieut. Colonel Moses Parker's Independent Company of Minute Men April 19, 1775. This company was led by Lieutenant in command, Benjamin Walker. He enlisted April 25, 1775, as Lieutenant of Captain John Ford's Company and was called First Lieutenant in a return dated September 25, 1775. December 13, 1776, he was engaged to serve as Second Lieutenant in Captain

[illegible]

FIRST [illegible]

[illegible] le[illegible]man [illegible]

January 2[illegible] He [illegible]

[illegible]ield Com[illegible] Colonel [illegible]

[illegible]775. He [illegible]

[illegible] Company [illegible]

[illegible] From September [illegible]

in [illegible] Zacheus Wright [illegible]

[illegible] Young [illegible] He [illegible]

in Dunstable March 4, 17[illegible]

the First Precinct (now Ty[illegible]

on a committee to divide the [illegible]

[illegible] He [illegible]

[illegible]

[illegible]

[illegible] Company, Colonel [illegible]

removed to [illegible]

LIEUTENANT ISAAC P[illegible]

in [illegible] Colonel Moses Parker's [illegible]

[illegible] company was led by [illegible]

[illegible] April 5, 1776, [illegible]

[illegible] killed [illegible]

[illegible]

John Minott's Company, Colonel Nicholas Dike's Regiment, for the defence of Boston, stationed at Dorchester Heights. His commission for this service was to date from December 1, 1776. He was First Lieutenant in Colonel Michael Jackson's 8th Massachusetts Regiment from January 1, 1777, to October, 1778, when he was honorably discharged. A certificate dated Medford, February 15, 1779, signed by Lieut. Colonel John Brooks, showed that when in service he was not absent except on furlough or on command. A gratuity of £36, dated February 15, 1779, was drawn in his favor, allowed by resolve of May 1, 1778.

FIRST LIEUTENANT MARK POOL of Gloucester was the son of Joshua and Deliverance (Giddings) Pool. He was born after his father's death, which occurred June 27, 1739. He was a private in Captain William Thompson's Company, Colonel Ichabod Plaisted's Regiment, from March 30 to December 3, 1756, at Fort William Henry and Crown Point. From March 20 to November 20, 1758, he was a private in Captain Andrew Gidding's Company, Colonel Jonathan Bagley's Regiment. He held the rank of Sergeant in Captain Nathaniel Bayley's Company, from April 24 to November 14, 1759. May 19, 1775, he was engaged as a Lieutenant in Captain John Rowe's Company, Colonel Ebenezer Bridge's Provincial Regiment, and served under the same officers through the year. December 24, 1776, he was a Captain in Colonel Timothy Pickering Jr's 1st Essex County Regiment. His name as Captain appears in a list of officers appointed to command men drawn from the brigade of General Farley in April, 1777. These troops were to reinforce General Spencer at Rhode Island. He was Captain of a Company in Colonel Jonathan Titcombs' Regiment for Rhode Island service in 1777 (May and June), and held the same rank in Colonel Jacob Gerrish's Regiment of Guards from November 13, 1777 to April 5, 1778. After the war he held the rank of Major in the Militia. He died February 11, 1815, aged 76, "having been always held in high esteem for the undaunted bravery of his military career."

SECOND LIEUTENANT JAMES BANCROFT of Reading was a Sergeant in Captain Thomas Eaton's train band (year not given.) He was Second Lieutenant of Captain John Bacheller's Company, Colonel Ebenezer Bridge's Minute Mens Regiment, April 19, 1775. On the 24th of that month, he enlisted as Ensign under the same officers and served through the year. He was commissioned May 6, 1776, Captain in Colonel Jonathan Fox's 2nd Middlesex County Regiment, and held the same rank in September-November of the same year in Colonel Jonathan Reed's 6th Middlesex County Regiment,

at Ticonderoga. January 1, 1777, he was made Captain in Colonel Michael Jackson's Regiment and served until December 31, 1779. He is also credited with service in 1780 to May 12th, when he was reported as resigned. The Historical Register of the Officers of the Continental Army calls him a Sergeant and later a Lieutenant in Colonel Jackson's Regiment, but the records in the Massachusetts Archives and his company rolls in the Essex Institute give an abundance of proof that he held the rank of Captain. The Historical Register above cited states that he served to June, 1783, and that he died April 2, 1803. He was a member of the Massachusetts Society of the Cincinnati.

SECOND LIEUTENANT SAMUEL BROWN of Dunstable was probably the man of that name who was a private in Captain Moses Parker's Company at St. John, March 27 to September 7, 1759, and Corporal from September 8, 1759, to July 23, 1760. He was a Sergeant in Captain Reuben Butterfield's Company, Colonel David Green's Regiment, which marched on the Lexington alarm, April 19, 1775. May 27, 1775, he was commissioned an Ensign, also called Second Lieutenant, in Captain Ebenezer Bancroft's Company, Colonel Ebenezer Bridge's Regiment. He was wounded in the left shoulder at the Battle of Bunker Hill, June 17, 1775. His name was on the Dunstable alarm list in 1776.

SECOND LIEUTENANT EBENEZER FITCH of Bedford was a Sergeant in Lieutenant Moses Abbott's Company, which marched from Bedford on the Lexington alarm, April 19, 1775. May 27, 1775, his commission was ordered as Ensign in Captain Benjamin Walker's Company, Colonel Ebenezer Bridge's Regiment. He served through the year and was called Second Lieutenant in a muster roll dated October, 1775. From January 1, to December 31, 1776, he was a First Lieutenant in the 11th Continental Regiment. He died March 21, 1833.

SECOND LIEUTENANT JOHN LEWIS of Billerica was a Corporal in Captain Isaac Osgood's Company, Colonel Ebenezer Nichols's Regiment, from April 1, to July 20, 1758, and a Sergeant in the same command, to November 4, 1758. He was Lieutenant of Captain Jonathan Stickney's Company, Colonel Ebenezer Bridge's Regiment of Minute Men, April 19, 1775. April 25, he was engaged as Second Lieutenant under the same officers and served through the year. He was engaged as Lieutenant in Captain Solomon Pollard's Company, Colonel Samuel Denny's Regiment, October 23, 1779. The regiment was detached to march to Claverickand join the Continental Army for three months.

He was probably the John Lewis, born August 5, 1737, who was the son of Benjamin Lewis of Billerica.

SECOND LIEUTENANT JONAS or JAMES PARKER of Acton (also given Chelmsford) may have been the James Parker who was a private in Captain Benjamin Milliken's Company, Colonel Richard Saltonstall's Regiment, enlisting April 22, 1756. April 25, 1775, he became an Ensign in Captain John Ford's Company, Colonel Ebenezer Bridge's Provincial Regiment and served through the year. He was also called Second Lieuetnant in a return made September 25, 1775. He served through 1776 as Second Lieutenant of Captain W.H.Ballard's Company, Colonel Asa Whitcomb's 6th Continental Regiment, until August and First Lieutenant during the rest of the year. January 1, 1777, he was commissioned a Lieutenant in Colonel Alden's 7th Regiment, Massachusetts Line, promoted to Captain Lieutenant October 1, 1778, and to Captain June 5, 1779. During the latter part of this service the 7th regiment was commanded by Lieut. Colonel John Brooks. Captain Parker was reported "absent without leave from October 18, 1780" and was dismissed from service January 24, 1781.

SECOND LIEUTENANT LEMUEL PERHAM of Dunstable was chosen committee man of the Second Parish in that town in 1763-4. On the Lexington alarm, April 19, 1775, he marched as Second Lieutenant of Captain Leonard Butterfield's Company, Colonel Ebenezer Bridge's Minute Mens Regiment, and served ten days. June 12, 1775, he was a member of the committee of Correspondence of Dunstable. February, 1776, he was commissioned First Lieutenant of Captain John Ford's Company, Colonel John Robinson's Regiment, to serve until April 1st. He was on the Dunstable alarm list in 1776, and later in the year was given a bounty for six months service at Rhode Island in 1777, although the record of this last named service has not been found in the Massachusetts Archives. He served again as a member of the Committee of Correspondence in 1781.

SECOND LIEUTENANT JAMES SILVER of Methuen was a Sergeant in Captain James Parker's Company, Colonel Ichabod Plaisted's Regiment (Endorsed July 26, 1756). The record of this service shows that he was born in Haverhill and resided in Methuen. He was 33 years of age and a cordwainer by trade. April 25, 1775, he was engaged as Lieutenant in Captain Charles Furbush's Company, Colonel Ebenezer Bridge's Regiment, and served in that command through the year. He was called Ensign in some returns and his

LIEUTENANT JAMES PARKER ... (also spelled) may have been the James Parker who was a private in Benjamin Milliken's Company, Colonel Richard Saltonstall's Regiment, April 22, 1756. April 25, 1775, he became an Ensign in Captain ...'s Company, Colonel Ebenezer Bridge's Provincial Regiment and ... the year. He was also called Second Lieutenant in a return ... ber 25, 1775. He served through 1776 as Second Lieutenant ... H. Ballard's Company, Colonel ... Whitcomb's ... until August ... Lieutenant ... during the rest of the ... 1777, he was commissioned a Lieutenant in Colonel ... to Captain Lieutenant ... the latter part of this ... Colonel John Brooks' ... 18, ... since January ...

LIEUTENANT ... of the Second ... 10, 1775 he ... Company ... days. June ... of ... Captain ... until ...

commission as Second Lieutenant was recommended October 26, 1775. From August 3 to September 30, 1779, he was First Lieutenant in Captain John Kettell's Company, Major Nathaniel Heath's detachment of guards, and Lieutenant in Captain Caleb Champney's Company in the same detachment during the rest of the year.

SECOND LIEUTENANT ELEAZER STICKNEY of Tewksbury was the son of William and Anne (Whiting) Stickney. He was born in Billerica August 30, 1740 and was admitted a member of the church there, June 5, 1763. He marched in Captain Jonathan Brown's Company, Colonel David Green's Regiment, on the Lexington alarm, April 19, 1775. May 24, 1775, he was engaged as Second Lieutenant of Captain John Harnden's Company, Colonel Ebenezer Bridge's Regiment, and served through the year. He died in Tewksbury, January 5, 1824.

SECOND LIEUTENANT LUKE SWETT of Tewksbury held that rank in Captain John Trull's Company, Colonel Ebenezer Bridge's Regiment of Minute Men, April 19, 1775. April 28, he was engaged as Sergeant in Captain Benjamin Walker's Company, Colonel Bridge's Regiment, and served through the year.

SECOND LIEUTENANT EBENEZER VARNUM of Dracut was a private in Captain Moses Parker's Company from June 1, 1761, to January 10, 1762, at Ticonderoga and Crown Point. He was Second Lieutenant of Captain Peter Coburn's Company, Colonel Ebenezer Bridge's Minute Mens Regiment, April 19, 1775, and served in the same rank during the year. In some returns he was called Ensign. He was at the battle of Bunker Hill and sent the following account of losses:

"To one great Coat	£1:00:00
To one filk Handkerchief	0:06:00
To one Knap fack	0:03:00
	1:13:00

Eben[r] Varnum."

He was a Lieutenant in Captain Joseph B. Varnum's Company, Colonel Simeon Spaulding's 7th Middlesex County Regiment, endorsed 1777. He lived in the upper part of Dracut, near Pelham, and was a farmer by occupation. He was an own cousin of Colonel William Prescott. According to the Varnum Genealogy he was over "six feet tall, very heavy with huge legs, and

up to the time of his death wore stockings and small knee breeches. He had a stentorian voice and a powerful will." He left a large property when he died March 13, 1813.

SECOND LIEUTENANT DAVID WALLINGFORD (or WALLINGSFORD) of Hollis, N. H., was the son of Jonathan Wallingford of Bradford, and was born in that town, Sept. 25, 1744. His name was first on the Hollis, N.H., tax list in 1770. He enlisted April 19, 1775, as a private in Captain Reuben Davis's Company of Minute Men. He was engaged April 25, 1775, as Second Lieutenant of Captain Archelaus Towne's Company, Colonel Ebenezer Bridge's Regiment. He served as a private in Captain McDuffie's Company in the 2nd New Hampshire Regiment which marched to join the Continental Army at New York in September, 1776. In the summer of 1777, he was Second Lieutenant of Captain Daniel Emerson's Company, Colonel Nichols's New Hampshire Regiment, which marched on the Ticonderoga alarm. He was discharged September 28, having served 71 days. He died at Hollis, N.H., march 12, 1791, "aged 45."

ENSIGN EBENEZER CLEAVELAND was the son of Reverend Ebenezer and Abigail (Stevens) Cleaveland. The father was a Chaplain in Colonel Jonathan Ward's Regiment in 1775, and Colonel Paul Dudley Sargent's Regiment, later in the war. May 19, 1775, he was engaged as Ensign in Captain John Rowe's Company, Colonel Ebenezer Bridge's Regiment, and served through the year. January 1, 1776, he became First Lieutenant of Captain Josiah Fay's Company, Colonel Jonathan Ward's 21st Regiment in the Continental Army, and July 12th, was promoted to the rank of Captain. He served as a Captain in Colonel Michael Jackson's 8th Regiment, Massachusetts Line, from January 1, 1777 until he resigned, October 3, 1778. He died November 26, 1822.

SOME ARTICLES CONCERNING MASSACHUSETTS IN RECENT MAGAZINES

By Charles A. Flagg

General. The Red and Blue war of 1909. By Lieut. W. M. Pratt. (New England magazine, Sept., 1909. v. 41, p. 777–787.)

Barnstable. Barnstable vital records. Transcribed by G. E. Bowman. (Mayflower descendant, July, 1909. v. 11, p. 130–132.)

Part 14; series began Oct., 1900. v. 2, p. 212.

Dedham. Diary of John Whiting of Dedham, 1743–1784. Communicated by J. F. Whiting. (New England historical and genealogical register, Apr.–July, 1909. v. 63, p. —— - 192, 261–265.)

Duxbury. Duxbury vital records. Transcribed by G. E. Bowman. (Mayflower descendant, July, 1909. v. 11, p. 148–151.)

Part 9; series began Oct., 1906. v. 8, p. 23.

Essex County. Essex County notarial records, 1697–1763. (Essex Institute. Historical collections, Oct., 1909. v. 45, p. 333–340.)

Part 12; series began Apr., 1905. v. 41, p. 183.

—— The French Canadians in Essex County and their life in exile. By G. F. Dow. (Essex Institute. Historical collections, Oct., 1909. v. 45, p. 293–307.)

—— Newspaper items relating to Essex County. (Essex Institute. Historical collections. Oct., 1909. v. 45, p. 341–349.)

Part 7 (1758–1759); series began Apr., 1906. v. 42, p. 214.

Gloucester. Revolutionary prisoners at Gloucester, 1782. By G. E. Merchant. (Essex Institute. Historical collections, Oct., 1909. v. 45, p. 350–352.)

From "Gloucester daily times," Jan. 11, 1907.

Hadley. The original settlers of Hadley, and the lots of land granted them. By Dr. Franklin Bonney and Elbridge Kingsley. (Grafton magazine of history and genealogy, Aug., 1909. v. 2, p. 3–37.)

—— The tombstone inscriptions in the old part of the Center cemetery at Hadley. By Dr. Franklin Bonney and Elbridge Kingsley. (Grafton magazine of history and genealogy, Aug., 1909. v. 2, p. 38–55.)

Harwich. Harwich vital records. Transcribed by G. E. Bowman. (Mayflower descendant, July, 1909. v. 11, p. 173–176.)

Part 13; series began July, 1901. v. 3, p. 174.

Ipswich. Ipswich voters in 1673. (Essex Institute. Historical collections, Oct., 1909. v. 45, p. 355–356.)

From Ipswich MSS. in Essex Institute.

Lawrence. A little Italy along the banks of the Merrimac. By Joseph McCarthy. (New England magazine, Sept., 1909. v. 41, p. 832–835.)

Middlesex County. The development of Middlesex Fells. By F. W. Coburn. (New England magazine, Sept., 1909. v. 41, p. 813–817.)

NEW BEDFORD. New Bedford. The wonderful growth of a Massachusetts cotton manufacturing city. By W. H. B. Remington. (New England magazine, Sept., 1909. v. 41, p. 819–831.)

PEMBROKE. Gravestone records in the Briggs burial ground, North Pembroke. Inscriptions prior to 1851. Copied by J. W. Willard, S. W. Smith, A. M. Jones and E. H. Whorf. (Mayflower descendant, July, 1909. v. 11, p. 168–170.)

PLYMOUTH COLONY. Plymouth Colony deeds. Transcribed by G. E. Bowman. (Mayflower descendant, July, 1909. v. 11, p. 165–168.)

Part 29 (1657); series began in Apr., 1899. v. 1. p. 91.

—— Plymouth Colony wills and inventories. Transcribed by G. E. Bowman. (Mayflower descendant, July, 1909. v. 11, p. 152–161.)

Part 29 (1652–1653); series began in Jan., 1899. v. 1, p. 23.

PLYMPTON. Gravestone records in a small cemetery in the north village of Plympton. Inscriptions prior to 1851. Copied by S. W. Smith, J. W. Willard, E. H. Whorf and W. J. Ham. (Mayflower descendant, July, 1909. v. 11, p. 176–177.)

—— Gravestone records in the Old cemetery at Plympton. Inscriptions prior to 1851. Copied by J. W. Willard, S. W. Smith, E. H. Whorf and W. J. Ham. (Mayflower descendant, July. 1909. v. 11, p. 161–165.)

Part 8 (Shaw–Virgin): series began in July 1906. v. 8. p. 50.

PROVINCETOWN. The birthplace of American liberty. By Henry Waterman. (Americana, New York, Aug., 1909. v. 4, p. 498–502.)

—— Provincetown vital records. Transcribed by G. E. Bowman. (Mayflower descendant, July, 1909. v. 11, p. 187–188.)

Part 3, series began in Apr., 1907. v. 9, p. 100.

SCITUATE. Records of the First church of Scituate. Transcribed by G. E. Bowman. (Mayflower descendant, July, 1909. v. 11, p. 138–142.)

Part 4 (Admissions by Rev. S. Bowen); series began in Apr., 1908. v. 10, p. 90.

UXBRIDGE. Deborah Wheelock chapter, D. A. R. By marcia P. Griswold, historian. (American monthly magazine, Aug., 1909. v. 35, p. 419–420.)

WELLFLEET. Records from the Duck Creek cemetery, Wellfleet. Inscriptions prior to 1851. Copied by S. W. Smith and J. W. Willard. (Mayflower descendant, July, 1909. v. 11, p. 142–145.)

Part 3 (Gill–Hinckley); series began July, 1908. v. 10. p. 180.

THE GEORGE GARDNER HOUSE

Frank A. Gardner, M. D.

Old Salem is visited each year by many thousands of pilgrims who in their mad rush to "do" the place, have little conception of the size of the original township or of the great wealth of early colonial houses still standing within those bounds. One of the many interesting groups of such houses can be seen in West Peabody along what is known as the "Old Lowell Road." The first of this trio as one journeys out from Salem is the Anthony Needham house, at the crossroads formed by the modern Newburyport turnpike and the Lowell road. This is a picturesque white leanto house nestled beneath the trees of a fine old orchard. A half mile further along we came to the Joseph Flint house and a mile beyond this, out toward the "Seven Men's Bounds" we find the third house in our group, the Lieutenant George Gardner house.

This last named house, the subject of our sketch is the original domicile erected on the George Gardner farm. George was the second son of Thomas Gardner, Planter, who came to Cape Ann as overseer of the plantation in 1623–4 and moved with Roger Conant and the other "Old Planters" to what is now Salem in 1626. Thomas Gardner the father was granted a farm lot of 100 acres on this same highway on the 20th of the 12th month in 1636. This tract was just east of the Anthony Needham house above mentioned. Thomas erected a house of the leanto type like the Needham and George Gardner houses and it remained standing until October 1854, when it was set on fire by a man who had formerly worked there as a farm hand.

In 1649 (25th of the 2nd mo.) George Gardner and his brothers Thomas, Samuel and Joseph, were ordered to survey land, "for wch they shall haue allowance in ꝑte of the medow for theire paynes." On the "30th day" of the following month, he was granted "4 acres of medow . . . at the 7 mens bounds," and forty acres of upland to be laid out near his meadow. The "7 mens bounds" referred to was the line laid out between what is now West Peabody and Lynnfield, the original bounds in that section between Salem and Lynn. An interesting reminder of this old line still stands in the woods

THE GEORGE GARDNER HOUSE, WEST PEABODY.

By courtesy of the Essex Institute.

a short distance to the south of the road, in the shape of a heap of stones, piled up there to mark an angle in the line.

The land which was granted to George Gardner at that time lies between the present Phelps' Mill station on the Salem and Lowell branch railroad and the Lynnfield line. His holdings in this section were greatly increased in a few years by additional grants as the following extracts from the town records will show;

"27th 2° m° 1654. Vpon the request of Sergeant Georg Gardner for a small playne of vpland contayning about six acres lying and scituate neare to Robert Moultons Jun' his medow & to the round hill neare mr Humfres ffarme and soe to that land that is graunted to ffrances Perries: Accordingly it is graunted."

13, 11mo, 1662. "Granted to Sergeant George Gardner that he ſhall haue a lott next to the land that runeth to his house by those lotts alredie laide out and of the same size he payinge five pounds as others have done."

The following entry is made in the Book of Grants, p. 155: "By virtue of an order from the Selectmen of Salem, directed unto Jeffrey Maſsey, Lit George Gardner and myself or unto any two of us to lay out unto Seueral persons seueral parcells of land between Humphries Farm & the farm formerly belonging to Phelps on this side Ipswich River so called near the seven mens bounds:—We accordingly laid out unto Lt. George Gardner One hundred & ninety acres of said lande which was for seueral grants, which he bought of seueral persons amounting unto soe much adjoining unto his own land, and is bounded as followeth viz: to the widow Pope, Geoyles Corey, Humphres Farm, and to Lynn bounds, and the Seven Men's bounds a little pine [tree] by Boston path, . . . Goodman Buxton's land on the west, lying unto Lynn bounds; Lt. Gardner Forty poles by the river unto Samuel Gardner's bounds; Sam'l Gardner and John Robinson s land and a little red oak & a great White Oak, between John Rubton & John Robinson & Lt Gardner's a little walnut, John Rubton on the East, an oak standing near Lt. Gardner's meadow.

The return of the laying out of this land I formerly gave in unto the Selectmen of Salem.

Attest Nathl Putnam,

Salem 24th. of Sept. 1697."

The above record was certified to by John Croade, Clerk, as being a copy of an original entry made in the year 1665.

Lieut. George Gardner, the grantee, soon after he became possessed of the

property, erected the house which is the subject of this sketch. He was born in England and is first mentioned in the Salem Records in 1637 at which time he received a grant of ten acres of land. In 1641 he became a member of the First Church. He frequently served on juries and in September, 1663, was appointed Lieutenant of the foot company. He also served as selectman. He had large financial interests, trading with the West Indies and the other colonies. In 1660 he set up the business of baking at his house on the eastern side of Daniels Street, near the water, and in the following year went to Barbadoes.

In 1663 or earlier he leased his farm to Thomas Gould, who remained on it as a tenant through Lieut. George Gardner's life. About 1673, Lieut. Gardner went to Hartford, Connecticut, and he was a prosperous merchant there until his death, August 20, 1679. He left a large estate in Salem and his Connecticut possessions amounted to over £3000. This farm was described in the inventory as containing "about 400 acres of upland & meddow with the dwelling houfe & outhousing upon it now in poffeffion of Thomas Goold." This was valued at £320:00:00. In his will he left this farm to his son Samuel Gardner, but specified that his son Ebenezer should have the income from the rental of it during his mother's life. We know from the records that Thomas Gould was a tenant as late as 1684–5. Other land adjoining was allowed him in 1796–7 making about four hundred and fifty acres in all.

Captain Samuel Gardner the second owner of this farm was one of the leading citizens of Salem during his long life. He held many town offices and was a representative and deputy to the General Court. He was a successful merchant and left a large estate when he died, in February, 1724.

A part of this farm was left to his grandson, John Higginson; another portion to the five daughters of his deceased son John Gardner, and the remainder, including the portion with the farmhouse on it to the three sons of John: — John, Daniel and Samuel. This property was distributed to the heirs in 1733, and John and Samuel sold their shares in the farm to their brother Daniel. The farm at this time was known as the Walden farm receiving that name from a lessee.

Daniel Gardner, called in the records "gentleman" lived most of his life in this old farmhouse. He held many town offices in Salem and in the new town of Danvers, after the division in 1752. He also represented Salem in the General Court in 1750. He died September 15, 1759, and left his estate to his two sons Samuel and John. The farm is described in the inventory as

"220 Acres of Upland and Meadow with the buildings ftanding on the same fcituate in sd Danvers; £8 pr. £1760." John Gardner died before July 9, 1768 and Samuel purchased of the other heirs, their interest in his brothers half of the farm. Samuel lived on the farm during his life. He held various town offices and served on several patriotic committees during the revolution.

Samuel Gardner sold forty-eight acres of the farm to Ezra Upton, July 9, 1768. April 14, 1808, he sold the remainder of the farm, amounting at that time to 150 acres, to his sons Asa and George Gardner, for $4,200, retaining a mortgage for that amount on the same. These sons divided the farm between themselves, October 14th of the same year, Asa retaining the western portion containing the old farmhouse. Asa lived in the house during his life. He was chosen surveyor of highways in 1818 and field-driver in 1812 and 1819. In the latter year he also served on the jury. He increased the size of his land holdings by the purchase of forty-eight acres from his sister Sally Walcott, July 22, 1835. He died March 9, 1858. He had no children, and his widow, conveyed the homestead to Bowman Viles, October 18, 1871.

The house has been well cared for and is in an excellent state of preservation. The first reunion of the Gardner Family Association was held there August 14, 1907, when the old doors, projecting timbers and ancient panellings were inspected and admired by all. The present occupants of the farm Mr. George D. Viles and his wife gave the guests a hearty welcome and well maintained the old time reputation of the house for its hospitality.

2 J T

Department of the American Revolution
1775-1782
FRANK A. GARDNER, M. D. Editor.

State Brigantine Active.

In the spring of 1779, Captain John Foster Williams in the "Hazard" captured the brigantine "Active", Captain William Simm (or Sims,) off St. Thomas, West Indies, after an action lasting thirty-seven minutes, in which the American vessel lost three killed and five wounded. The prize arrived safely in Boston, as the following extract from the records of the Board of War will show:

"Ordered That m^r Ivers pay Samuel Stibbens for piloting Brig Active to boston Prize to the Hazard & gates.
April 14, 1779. £2–00–00"

"In the House of Representatives
Resolved that this state will and hereby do renounce all Claim to the British Privateer called the Active, William Simm, late Commander, in favor of John Foster Williams, Commander of the Brig Hazard and the Officers and Seamen thereof; and all Claim to the Privateer Brig Revenge, Edward Thompson late Master, in favor of Capt. Allen Hallet, Commander of the Brig Tyrannicide, the Officers and Seamen thereof, in testimony of their approbation of the spirit and good conduct of the said John Foster Williams and Allen Hallet Esq^rs Commanders of the said Briggs Hazard and Tyrannicide, the Officers and Seamen thereof, in Capturing the said British Privateers and all persons concerned are directed to take notice of this Resolve and govern themselves accordingly.

In Council Read and Concurred
April 23, 1779.
Confented to by Fifteen of the Council."

An inventory of the "Active" was taken April 24, 1779.

"Ordered, That Captain Hopkins receive from Captain Gustavus Fellows & Capt Martin the Brig^a Active, with her Boats Guns and all their appurtenances & Stores agreable to Inventory."

"Ordered That Mr Ivers receive from Capt Daniel Martin being so much paid Samuel Stibbings through mistake ye 14th inftant for Piloting the Brig Active a prize to the Hazard and Gates. Board of War, April 29, 1779. 12:00:00."

"In the House of Representatives.
The House made choice by Ballot of Capt Allen Hallet to Command the Armed Brigantine called the Active, lately purchased by the Board of War.
In Council Read and Concurred.
Friday April 30, 1779.
Confented to by Fifteen of the Council"

May 1, 1779, the Board of War, "Ordered That Mr Ivers . . . pay Labourers removing the Brig Active from Rowe's to Grey Wharf &c. 10:00:00."

The records of the Board of War for May 7 1779, state that, "Allen Hallet Esqr This day produced a Commifsion from the Honorable Council appointing him to the Command of the Armed Brig: Active."

Captain Hopkins was ordered to deliver to Charles Willis for the Brig "Active."

Duck to the value of	£615:00:00
Twine " " " "	48:00:00
1 Cod line " " "	2:02:00
	£665:02:00

"We the fubfcribers do severally engage and Inlist ourfelves as Officers Seamen &

Marines on Board the Brig "Active" under the Command of Allen Hallet Esq[r] in the Service in the State of Mafsachufetts Bay, for the defence and protection of Said State to serve faithfully on board said Brig and her Boats, and on board Such Vefsel or Vefsels as may be made prizes by said Brig for & during the term of Four Months from the day of our Inlistment and until our return to and proper discharge at Boston if the fervice should require it, on the Establishment made for that purpofe.

And we do hereby bind ourselves to Submit to all orders and regulations of the Navy of the United States of North America and this State and faithfully to observe and obey all such orders and Commands as we Shall receive from time to time from our Superior Officers on board or belonging to the faid Brig Active and on board any Such Boats or Vefsel or Vefsels as aforesaid. And it is on the part of the State that such perfons as by land or fea fhall Loofe a Limb in any Engagement with the Enemies of these United States of America or be otherwife incapable of gitting a Lively Hood, Shall be intitled to the fame Provifions as the disabled Perfons in the Continental Service. And it is further agreed that there Shall be fix dead Shares, to be distributed by the Commifsion Officers of the said Brig to Such non Commifsioned officers and Seamen as shall honorably distinguish themfelves on the Courfe of the Cruise against the Enemies of these United States.

		Entered
Allen Hallet	Captain	May 23,
Solomon Hallet		" "
Ifaiah Hallet		" "
Georg Hallett		" "
Enoch Hallet Junr		" "
Ebenezer Sears		" "
William Warren		" "
Samuel Chafe		May 27,
Josiah Gage		" "
James Gage		" "
James Rallosom		May 28,"

The "Active's complement in May, 1779, was as follows:

Captain, Allen Hallet.
First Lieutenant, Roger Haddock.
Second Lieutenant, Peter Pollard.
Master, Cleaves Bean.
Lieutenant of Marines, Wm. Thompson.
Surgeon, Henry Stephens.
Surgeon's Mate, Gideon Frost.
21 other officers, 61 men and 11 boys.

CAPTAIN ALLEN HALLET had previously commanded the State sloop "Republic" and the privateer "Sturdy Beggar" in 1776, the privateers "Starke" and "America" in 1777, and the State brigantine "Tyrannicide" in 1779. A full account of his naval career has already been given in the Massachusetts Magazine, v.1, pages 106-7.

FIRST LIEUTENANT ROGER HADDOCK was Prize Master of the State Brigantine "Hazard", Captain John Foster Williams, from March 1, 1779, to April 20, 1779. He was engaged June 2, commissioned June 2, 1779, First Lieutenant of the State brig "Active."

SECOND LIEUTENANT PETER POLLARD was commissioned December 21, 1777, commander of the privateer sloop "Independence." July 20, 1778, he was engaged as Prize Master of the State Brigantine "Tyrannicide", Captain John Allen Hallet. He was engaged May 4, 1779, Second Lieutenant of the State Brig "Active" and was commissioned June 2nd.

MASTER CLEAVES BEAN was engaged in that rank on the "Active" May 4, and commissioned June 2, 1779.

LIEUTENANT OF MARINES WILLIAM THOMPSON (also called JR.) held that rank on the State brigantine "Tyrannicide", Captain Allen Hallet, from July 15, 1778 to December 18, 1778. He was en-

gaged for the same service on the State brig "Active", May 10, 1779.

SURGEON HENRY STEPHEN was engaged for service on the "Active" May 12, and a warrant for service was issued June 25, 1779.

SURGEON'S MATE GIDEON FROST was engaged to serve on the "Active" May 10, 1779.

"State of Mafsachufetts Bay,
Council Chamber, May 18, 1779.

Whereas information has been given to this Board that there are five negroes lately captured & Carried into Plymouth who are willing to serve this State in some one of the State vefsels as also a Negro Man called Jack now on board the Guard Ship in the Harbour therefore

Ordered that Cap[t] Hallet Commander of the Brigan[t] Active be & he hereby is directed to send some Officer to Plymouth for the purpose of enlisting those five negroes provided s[d] Negroes are yet free & willing to enlist on board said Brig[t] as Seamen as also the Negro Man Jack a prisoner on board the Guard Ship provided he is also willing to serve on board s[d] Brig[t] and if he shall so incline the Commifsary of Prisoners is hereby directed to liberate him.

True Copy
Atteft
John Avery D. Secy."

"Brigantine Active to Allen Hallet, Dr.
To cash disbursted at Portsmouth as per following Acctt.
June 30th 1779.

To Mr Haddock's Bill for felf & horse Exprefs to Boston	£52–09–00
To hire of a horse & Sulkey for above Express	46–16–00
To Elisha Hill's Bill for Smith's Work	207–04–00
To John Marshall's Bill for Carpenter's Work	93–19 06
To Joel Leighton's Bill of Sundries as pr Bill	57–02–00
To John Gooch's Bill for Sundries as pr Bill	4–16–00
To one pair Steelyards for Ships Use	8–00–00
	470–06–06
To Commifsions for advancing the above Cash a 5 p.c.	23–10–00
	£493–16–06"

The following order was presented in payment of this bill and honored:

"Portsmouth, June 29, 1779.

At Sight
Gentlemen

Please to pay to M[r] Neal McIntyer or Order the fum of Four Hundred & Ninety three pounds twelve shillings & six pence Value received on acct Brigt[n] Active in fo doing you will oblige

Your Humble Serv[t]
£493:12:06 A. Hallet.
The Hon[l] Board of War, Boston
Pay it."

"Brig Active Dr to Account of Prizes

14 Six pound Cannon at 610 per pair	4270:00:00
209 Pound Six pound Shott att 24—	130:16:00
226 dobble h[d] do 30—	339:00:00
280 Clusters Grape do for 6 pounders 30—	420:00:00
	£5159:16:00

"Bill to Board of War to Thos Knox Jun 17, 1778 To piloting the Brig Active and tendance to Sea 25:00:00"

The "Active was one of the vessels in Commodore Saltonstall's Squadron on the Penobscot expedition and had 16 guns and 100 men. She was burned off Brigadier's Island August 14, 1779 to prevent her falling into the hands of the enemy.

Announcement for 1910.

The general plan followed during the past two years will be continued and each quarterly number of the magazine will contain, as heretofore, a historical review of one of the Massachusetts regiments which served in 1775 and the record of one of the vessels in the Massachusetts State Navy in the Revolution. The following ist shows the regiments and ships which will be presented during the year:

January. Colonel Timothy Walker's Regiment, composed of companies raised in the County of Bristol.

April. Colonel Theophilus Cotton's Regiment of Plymouth County men.

July. Colonel James Frye's Regiment, made up of men from the County of Essex.

October. Colonel Benjamin Ruggles Woodbridge's Regiment, containing six companies from Hampshire County, two from Berkshire County, one made up of men from both Hampshire and Worcester Counties and one company from Essex County.

January. State schooner "Diligent," Captain John Lambert.

April. State sloop "Machias Liberty," Captain Jeremiah O'Brien.

July. State sloop "Defence," Captain Seth Harding.

October. State ship "Mars," Captain John Lambert.

In addition to the above, various short articles of interest to students of that period will appear together with reports of the doings of the various patriotic societies. Further installments of the Ashley Bowen diary will be presented, the notes therein increasing in interest and value as the per od of the American Revolution is approached. Patriotic movements will receive the cordial support of this department, notably the one looking to a saner and more dignified celebration of Independence Day and the one having for its object the placing of memorial tablets upon sites and buildings of historic interest. The frightful loss of life and limb annually recorded makes the former change imperative, while the educational value of the latter movement is apparent to all.

Field Day, Massachusetts Society, S. A. R.

The annual Field day of the Society was held at Salem, on Saturday, September 25, 1909. The members and their friends met in the parlors of the Salem Young Men's Christian Association at 10 A.M. where they were recieved by the local committee. At 10.45, line was formed and the members, headed by the color guard of the Salem Cadets under Sergeant Clay, proceeded to the Broad Street Burying Ground, where simple but impressive services were held at the grave of Captain Jonathan Haraden. Dr. Hicks, State Chaplain, offered prayer, following which a large laurel wreath bearing the colors of the Society was placed upon the gravestone by State President E. C. Battis. The colors were dipped by the bearers and taps sounded by cornetist Bernier of the Salem Cadet Band. The line was re-formed and the members returned to the hall, passing the house of the distinguished patriot, General Timothy Pickering. The compatriots and their friends then started out in groups under competent guides and visited the many places of historic interest in the Puritan city. At 12.30 they re-assembled in the Y. M. C. A. parlors and marched behind the colors to Ames Memorial Hall where the dinner call was sounded, after Chaplain Hicks had asked the Divine blessing and the company was seated. The hall was decorated with national flags and the colors of the society, while bouquets of the dark purple New England asters were on every table.

After dinner had been served, Honorable E. C. Battis, President of the Massachusetts Society, welcomed the compatriots with a few well chosen words and turned the meeting over to Dr. Gardner, President of Old Salem Chapter, S. A. R. An address upon Captain John Haraden was then delivered, a copy of which will be found in this number of the Massachusetts Magazine. In the introduction of the next speaker, Mr. William C. Greene, President of the Rhode Island Society, S. A. R., reference was made to the invaluable service in the revolution, rendered by his distinguished kinsmen, Major General Nathaniel Greene. Mr. Greene referred in a pleasing manner to the historical ties binding Old Salem to Rhode Island and showed that when Salem lost Roger Williams, Rhode Island made a great gain. The next speaker was Brigadier General Phillip Reade, U. S. Army Retired, a kinsman of Colonel Jonathan Reed who commanded the 6th Middlesex County Regiment in the Revolution. He spoke of his early ancestors in Salem, making especial mention of the saintly Rebecca Nourse. The last speaker of the afternoon was Rev. Howard F. Hill D. D., President of the New Hampshire Society, S.A.R. At intervals during the afternoon the Salem Cadet Orchestra played patriotic selections, the audience rising during the rendering of "The Star Spangled Banner" and the closing hymn "America."

539

Pilgrims and Planters
1620–1630
LUCIE M. GARDNER, A. B., Editor.

Societies

MAYFLOWER SOCIETY.

Membership, Confined to Descendants of the Mayflower Passengers.

GOVERNOR—ASA P. FRENCH.
DEPUTY GOVERNOR—JOHN MASON LITTLE.
CAPTAIN—EDWIN S. CRANDON.
ELDER—REV. GEORGE HODGES, D. D.
SECRETARY—GEORGE ERNEST BOWMAN.
TREASURER—ARTHUR I. NASH.
HISTORIAN—STANLEY W. SMITH.
SURGEON—WILLIAM H. PRESCOTT, M. D.
ASSISTANTS—EDWARD H. WHORF.
MRS. LESLIE C. WEAD.
HENRY D. FORBES.
MRS. ANNIE QUINCY EMERY.
LORENZO D. BAKER, JR.
MISS MARY E. WOOD.
MISS MARY F. EDSON.

THE OLD PLANTERS SOCIETY.

INCORPORATED.

Membership Confined to Descendants of Settlers in New England prior to the Transfer of the Charter to New England in 1630.

PRESIDENT—COL. THOMAS WENTWORTH HIGGINSON, CAMBRIDGE
VICE PRES.—FRANK A. GARDNER, M. D., SALEM.
SECRETARY—LUCIE M. GARDNER, SALEM.
TREASURER—FRANK V. WRIGHT, SALEM.
REGISTRAR—MRS. LORA A. W. UNDERHILL, BRIGHTON.
COUNCILLORS—WM. PRESCOTT GREENLAW, BOSTON.
R. W. SPRAGUE, M. D., BOSTON.
HON. A. P. GARDNER, HAMILTON.
NATHANIEL CONANT, BROOKLINE.
FRANCIS H. LEE, SALEM.
COL. J. GRANVILLE LEACH, PHILA.
FRANCIS N. BALCH, JAMAICA PLAIN.
JOSEPH A. TORREY, MANCHESTER.
EDWARD O. SKELTON, ROXBURY.

The Fall meeting of The Old Planters Society was held Thursday, Sept. 16, in the historic town of Marblehead. Members and friends had opportunity to visit many of the places of interest about town, gathering for the formal exercises at three-thirty o'clock at the Lee Mansion, which has recently become the headquarters of the Marblehead Historical Society. After a few words of cordial greeting Mr. Nathan P. Sanborn, president of the local society, gave a most interesting account of the life of Col. Jeremiah Lee, builder and owner of the famous old house.

Col. Jeremiah Lee was born at Manchester, Massachusetts, in 1721. As a young man he came to Marblehead, went into the shipping business and early identified himself with the interests of the town. He held a commission as Colonel in the Marblehead Regiment, was one of the firewards, was one of the committee appointed to draw up opposition to the Stamp Act, was appointed a delegate to the first Continental Congress, and was on the Committee of Safety. He was wealthy, but as his wealth was in shipping, his estate became poor. His beautiful house, built in 1768, was the resort of many famous people, including General Washington and the Marquis de Lafayette. He died on May 10, 1775, leaving a widow, two daughters and one son. On the death of his widow in 1791, the house became the property of Judge Sewall who sold it in 1804 to the Marblehead Bank in whose hands it has remained until this summer. The house has much that attracts more than a passing glance, especially the hand carving, which at the present day, would command a prohibitive price.

Mr. Sanborn was followed by Dr. Frank A. Gardner, vice-president of the Old Planters Society who read the entries of the month of June, 1775, from the diary of Ashley Bowen, a quaint character of old Marblehead. The diary furnished interesting contemporary comment on the stirring events of the early days of the Revolutionary War.

At the close of the meeting many of the party went by ferry to the Neck, where a basket lunch was enjoyed at Castle Rock. The meeting was well attended and attested to the attractiveness of the field meeting which has become an annual feature of the society's program.

A Continuation of the Genealogical Dictionary of Essex County Families, compiled until Oct., 1909, by Sidney Perley, Esq., in The Essex Antiquarian.

Family Genealogies

LUCIE MARION GARDNER, A.B., Editor

Essex was the first county settled in the Massachusetts Bay Colony, and all the records of early Massachusetts families found in the probate court and town records of this county prior to the year 1800 are gathered and published here in alphabetical form, and arranged genealogically when possible.

BROWNING NOTES

Thomas Browning, born about 1587, lived in Salem as early as 1636, and had a house there as early as 1645. He lived in Topsfield, 1659–1661 and subsequently in Salem, where he died Feb. —, 1670–1. His wife Mary survived him. His daughter Sarah married Joseph Williams in Salem 20:9:1661: and she was living in Salem in 1719. Mr. Browning's daughter Elizabeth married James Symonds of Salem 20:9:1661, lived in Salem and died before 1725. Mr. Browning's daughter Deborah married, first, John Perkins of Topsfield Nov. 28, 1666; and he died there May 19, 1668. She married, second, Isaac Meachum of Salem, yeoman, Dec. 28, 1669; and after 1682 removed to Enfield, Conn. where they were living in 1696. Mr. Browning had another daughter who married —— Towne of Topsfield, and they were living in 1671. The estate of Mr. Browning was appraised at £444:1s.

George Bruce of Marblehead, mariner, married Hannah Hanover Sept. 21, 1773 in Marblehead; he died before April 1, 1776, when administration was granted upon his estate: she survived him and married, secondly George Tishue, April 8, 1776 in Marblehead.

Reynold (Roland or Ronald) Bruce[1] of Marblehead married Miss Hannah Blaney Oct. 28, 1756, in Marblehead. She died in Marblehead, his widow Oct. 9, 1811, at the age of eighty.

Chidren born in Marblehead:

1. Jonathan,[2] baptized July 22, 1759.
2. Hannah,[2] baptized Sept. 13, 1761.
3. William,[2] baptized April 29, 1764; died young.
4. David,[2] born Jan. 18, 1768: master mariner; lived in Marblehead m. Sarah Chapman July 4, 1790, in Marblehead; she was his wife in 1809; he died Nov. 7, 1828, aged sixty; children born in Marblehead; David born Nov. 4, 1191, captain, married Alice Nutting Feb. 14, 1814; died suddenly of fever and ague Dec, 21, 1822, aged thirty-one; 2. Sally,[3] born June 21, 1794: 3. Eliza,[3] born May 24, 1797; married Ambrose Gregory, March 6, 1821; 4. William,[3] born Oct. 1, 1799; died at Batavia (received the news Dec. 23, 1821); 5. Mary Grant,[3] born June 2, 1802; 6. Clarissa,[3] born May 21, 1805; married Zephaniah Bassett of Boston, March 24, 1833; 7. Daniel,[3] born Aug. 13, 1807; married Mary J. Shirly, June 20, 1830; 8. Maria,[3] born Oct. 15, 1809;* 9. Elizabeth Buffinton,[3] baptized Oct. 22, 1809; married William Hart of Lynn Sept. 29,

*This is probably the record of Elizabeth's birth.

1833; 5. Jane,[2] baptized June 10, 1770; 6. William,[2] baptized March 1, 1772.

BRUCE NOTES

Mary Bruce married Edward Hiller in 1788. — *Private Record in Marblehead.*

Joseph Bruce married first, Mary Allen, Nov. 10, 1793 in Marblehead; and second, Elizabeth Main, June 10, 1804 in Marblehead. He lived in Marblehead, died at sea (news was received April 3) 1822, aged forty-nine. Children, born in Marblehead 1. John Trefry, baptized May 11, 1794; 2. Joseph, baptized Dec. 25, 1796; lost overboard at sea (news received Dec. 17, 1819; 3. Mary, baptized Feb. 3, 1799; 4. William Allen, baptized Oct. 31, 1802; 5. Thomas Maine baptized Nov. 9, 1806; "drowned siting a Net at Cape Ann" Nov. 13, 1823 aged seventeen. — *Marblehead records.*

Lewis Bruce married Hannah Batt's (published March 8, 1784); Revolutionary soldier; died July 1, 1828, at the age of sixty-six; children: 1. Salley born June 10, 1784; married Nathaniel Richardson Dec. 31, 1806; 2. Lewis, born May 3, 1786; 3. Hannah, born Nov. 13, 1788; died Oct. 18, 1805; 4. William, born July 14, 1791; died Oct. 8, 1839; 5. Lot, born Oct. 7, 1793; died Sept. 25, 1813; 6. Harriet, born April 1, 1796; married Timothy Johnson, Jr., May 11, 1818; 7. George, born Sept. 13, 1798; died by accident Oct. 14, 1824; 8. Mary, born Nov. 29, 1801; married Jacob I. Johnson Nov. 5, 1820. —*Lynn Records.*

Administration upon the estate of Thomas Bruce of Marblehead. mariner, was granted Jan. 2, 1770. His estate was valued at £5 13*s.* 2*d*; and included one pair of silver buckles, clothing, wages due from Capt. Samuel Poate, "3 months & 20 days Hospatell money" etc. — *Probate records.*

Jonathan Bruce married Alice Utley, both of Salem Feb. 14 1782.— *Salem Town Records.*

George Bruce of Woburn, butcher was married out of Salem, May 30, 1791.—*Salem Town Records.*

George, Ester, William, Sarah, Francis, Lathe, John, and Polly, children of George and Ester Bruce, baptized Nov. 8, 1795.—*East church (Salem) records.*

BRUER NOTES

John Bruer of Rowley published to Hannah Dodge of Ipswich, June 3, 1789.—*Rowley town records.*

— Bruer married John Tomson about1690.—*Salisbury town records.*

Elizabeth Bruer married Samuell Ingolls Feb. 2, 1681.

Mary Bruer married John Richards Nov. 18, 1674

Sarah Bruer married Samuell Graves March 12, 1677-8.

Thomas Bruer married Elizabeth Graves Dec. 4, 1682.

BRUMAGIN NOTES

Katherin Brumagin married Jonathan Johnson June 11, 1745. —*Lynn town records.*

Richard Brummingham married Lydia Rhoades Jan. 11, 1757. —*Marblehead church records*

BRUNIER NOTE

Louis de la Brunier (Brunnier) married Lucy Challis March 12, 1789; children: Louis, born June 27, 1789; Gideon Challice, born April 13, 1802; Lucy Challice.

—Gloucester town records.

BRUNSON NOTE

Joanna Brunson married John Mare July 18, 1682.—*Salem town records.*

BRYANT NOTES

Benjamin Briant married Elizabeth Obear Nov. 21, 1790; she died Jan. 7, 1833, aged seventy-one; children: Betsey, born Sept. 5, 1791; Rebecca, born Oct. 19, 1793; James, born July 4, 1795; Benjamin, born Feb. 9, 1797; Anna, born May 26, 1799, died Aug. 23, 1800; John Graves, born Jan. 29, 1801; Jonathan, born Nov. 26, 1802; William, born Nov. 24, 1804.

Mary Bryant died in 1749.

John Bryant of Lynnfield married Anna Larcom, at Lynnfield, Aug. 4, 1761. *—Beverly records.*

Mrs. Elizabeth Bryant married Lt. James Andrews April 16, 1765.

—Boxford town records.

Andrew Bryant of Haverhill married Sally Endicott Dec. 23, 1798.

Lucy Bryant published to Joseph P. Morton June 30, 1798.

—Danvers town records.

Thomas Bryant married Mary Joslin Oct. 28, 1712; child: Elizabeth, born Sept. 24, 1713.

Mary Bryant married James Demerit March 7, 1727.

William Briant married Sarah Smallman April 2, 1734.

—Gloucester town records.

William Bryant of Plaistow married Anna Whittaeker of Haverhill Dec. 4, 1755; yeoman; lived in Haverhill; she was his widow in 1801, lame and infirm; his will, dated May 6, 1797, was proved Jan. 6, 1800; children, born in Haverhill: David, born Oct. 10, 1756; living in 1797; Anna, born Feb. 11, 1759; married Jonathan Johnson before 1797; Betsey, born Oct. 28, 1760; died May 19, 1764; James, born Feb. 23, 1763; not mentioned in his father's will in 1797; Betsey, born May 3, 1767; married in 1797; William, born April 14, 1770; living in 1797; Mary, born Sept. 26, 1773; unmarried in 1797; Andrew, born Jan. 15, 1776; living in 1797; Matthew, born Apr. 22, 1779; living in Haverhill, laborer, in 1800, and died before Apr. 1801; Hannah, living in 1797; Calvin, under twenty-one years old in 1797.

John Bryant, lived in Lynnfield, husbandman, as early as 1744; wife Anna, 1770–1792 (dau. of William Richardson of Lynn, yeoman?); he died Oct. 5, 1795, aged seventy-three; she died in Lynnfield Aug. 29, 1812, at the age of eighty; children, born in Lynn: 1. Mary[2], born May 12, 1746; married Jephthah Tyler of New Marlboro, Oct. 9, 1765; and was living in 1792; 2. Jonathan[2], born Jan. 13, 1748; lived in Lynn; married Sarah Norwood Dec 4, 1770; died in Lynn, "after a lingering and painful illness of about 3 months of something supposed to breed in his head," April 4, 1775, aged 27; children: 1. John[3], born April 14, 1771; lived in Lynnfield; yeoman; in 1796 he was weak and unable to travel; married Eunice Shelden Oct. 30, 1790; he died in Lynnfield Sept. 11, 1827, aged fifty-

six; 2. Anna[3], baptized Aug. 13, 1775; died in Lynnfield March 17, 1797 at the age of twenty-four; 3. Sarah[3], baptized Aug. 13, 1775; 4. Elizabeth[2], born Nov. 10, 1749; married Joseph Emerson of Chelmsford Sept. 20, 1768; 5. Sarah[2], born May 14, 1753; married Jacob Parker of Hopkinton May 28, 1771; 6. Lydia[2], born June 15, 1755; married —— Gowin before 1792; 7. Benjamin[2], born Oct. 6, 1757; living in 1792. —*Records.*

Margaret, wife of John Briant, died "of something supposed to breed in her brain," June 4, 1759.

John Briant, Jr., died "of fever and canker," March 7, 1766, aged twenty-one. —*Lynn church records.*

Elizabeth, daughter of Thadeus Brian, died Oct. 26, 1675.

Mary, daughter of Thadeus Brian, died Oct. 19, 1675.

Katherine Bryant of Andover published to Joshua Burnham June —, 1778. —*Lynn town records.*

Mehitable Bryant published to Samuel Starns of Middleton Oct. 4, 1761. —*Lynn town records.*

Peter Brian married Mary Jones Nov. 24, 1776,

George Briant married Mary Mackintire Nov. 10, 1767.

Mrs. Mary Briant married John Lasdel Sept. 27, 1778.

—*Marblehead town records.*

Hepzibah Briant married Samuel Stearns Dec. 2, 1761.*

—*Middletown town records.*

* Samuel Stearns of Middleton, husbandman, was appointed guardian of Tabitha Bryant, under fourteen years of age, daughter of Jeremiah Bryant of Reading Jan. 10, 1763.—*Essex County Probate records.*

Miss Patience Bryant of Newburyport, married Nathan Lunt of Newbury, Jan. 13, 1785.

—*Newburyport town records.*

Hannah (Joanna — *publishment*) Bryant married Jacob Averill, Jr., Nov. 23, 1752.—*Topsfield town records.*

Joanna Bryant, a young woman, daughter of Richard Bryant, baptized Oct. 28, 1744.

—*First church* (*Salem*) *records.*

Richard Bryant of Salem, mariner, married Sarah Flint Nov. 10, 1720; she was his wife in 1731; he was living in Salem in 1733; children, born in Salem: Richard, born June 11, 1721; Sarah, born Oct. 9, 1723.

—*Records.*

Daniel Flint of Wenham appointed guardian of Sarah Briant aged upward of fourteen years, minor, daughter of Daniel Briant of Salem, deceased, Jan. 1, 1738-9.—*Probate records.*

Job Bryant married Mary Dodd, both of Salem, May 2, 1792.—*Salem town records.*

Joseph Bryant of Salisbury, blacksmith, lived there 1751-1759; married Jedediah (Jedida, Zedidee) Wheeler April 14, 1753, in Salisbury; he died in the winter of 1758-9, administration being granted on his estate to his widow Jedida Briant of Salisbury Feb. 5, 1759; she married, secondly, —— Short before 1770; the children of Joseph and Jedida Bryant were born in Salisbury as follows; Sarah, born Jan. 31, 1755; living in 1770; Patience, born July 14, 1758; living in 1770.—*Records.*

John Bryant, Jr., of Lynnfield, yeoman, 1788-1794.

Timothy Bryant of Salem, mariner, 1796. —*Registry of deeds.*

Timothy Bryant of Reading, mariner, warned out of Salem May 30, 1791.—*Salem town records.*

Mary, Sarah and Samuel, children of Job and Mary Bryant, baptized April 24, 1796, in *East Church (Salem) records.*

Timothy Bryant's children, baptized Timothy, Mary ——, 1789; and Lydia, Aug. 9, 1795.—*North church (Salem) records.*

BRYERS NOTES

Jane Bryers married William Gilford Sept. 6, 1763.—*Danvers town records.*

Jacob Bryor, married Elizabeth Burne (published Jan. 25, 1766); son John, born April 27, 1777.

Jacob Bryor married Sarah Littlehale March 29, 1787.

—*Gloucester town records.*

Elias Brian also Bryer) married Mary Pitman, June 2, 1726. He was a fisherman, and they lived in Marblehead in 1748, 1761, and he was living there in 1788.—*Records.*

Elias Bryars married Elizabeth Gale April 21, 1799.—*Marblehead town records.*

Richard Bryer married Ellena Wright Dec. 21, 1665; and she died, his wife, Aug. 29, 1672.—*Newbury town records.*

Sally Briers published to Samuel Swasey, both of Salem, Dec. 7, 1793.

BRYSON NOTE

Sarah Bryson (?) published to Ebenezer Collins, both of Salem, Dec. 27, 1735. —*Salem town records.*

DESCENDANTS OF JOSEPH BUBIER OF MARBLEHEAD.

The name of BUBIER is variously spelled in the early records of Essex County, as *Boober, Boobier, Booby, Bubier,* etc. The first of the name in the country was

JOSEPH BUBIER[1]. He was a fisherman and lived in Marblehead. He married, first, Jane ——, who was called granddaughter of Richard Bennett. She was living in 1695, and was dead the next year. He married, second, Rebecca, widow of William Pinson (or Pinsent), of Salem, Jan. 1, 1696–7. Mr. Bubier died before Sept. 22, 1701, when administration was granted upon his estate, which was appraised at £320. His wife, Rebecca, survived him and married, thirdly, Robert Bartlett, Dec. 24, 1702.

Children:—

2—I. CHRISTOPHER[2], "eldest" son 1702. *See below* (2).

3—II. JANE[2], bapt. April 28, 1695, in Marblehead; m. Nicholas Pickett Oct. 28, 1703.

4—III. MARY[2], bapt. April 28, 1695 in Marblehead; "youngest daughter," 1707; was brought up by William Hemett of Marblehead, husbandman, to whom she was a maid, and in his will he gave her his house and land in Marblehead, goods, stock, etc. She married Francis Bouden, Sept. 22, 1707; and died in 1748.

2

CHRISTOPHER BUBIER[2] was a fisherman and mariner and lived in Marblehead. He married Miss Margaret Palmer of Marblehead, Aug. 11, 1700; and died before Oct. 11, 1706, when administration was granted upon his

Bryant of Salem, mariner
—*Registry of deeds.*

Timothy Bryant of Reading, mar-iner, warned out of Salem May 30, [illegible]791.—*Salem town records.*

Mary, Sarah and Samuel, children of [illegible] and Mary Bryant, baptized [illegible] 26, 1766 in *East Church* (Sa-[illegible] records.

Timothy Bryant's children, bap-tized Timothy, Mary ——, 1759; and Lydia, Aug. 9, 1761.—[illegible] church (Salem) records.

BRYERS NOTES

Jane Bryer married [illegible] Gil-ford Sept 6, [illegible]—Da[illegible] records.

Jacob Bryer married [illegible] Burne (published Jan. [illegible] 1769); son John born April 27, 1770.

Jacob Bryer married Sarah Little-hale March 29, 1782.
—*Gloucester town records.*

Elias Brian (also Bryer) married Mary Pitman, June [illegible] He was a fisherman, and [illegible] blehead in 171[illegible] living there in [illegible]

Elias Brya[illegible] Gale April [illegible] town records.

DESC[illegible] **D**[illegible]
BUBIER

[illegible] name of [illegible] in the early [illegible] Bubier, [illegible] The first of [illegible] the country was [illegible]

Joseph Bubier [illegible] erman and lived [illegible] married, first Jane [illegible]

estate which was appraised at £113, 14*s*. 7*d*. She survived him, and married, secondly —— Andrews.

Children (only one surviving Mr. Bubier) born in Marblehead:—

5—I. JOSEPH[3], bapt. Feb. 6, 1703-4. *See below* (5).
6—II. CHRISTOPHER[3], bapt. June 16, 1706. *See below* (6).

5

JOSEPH BUBIER[3], baptized in Marblehead Feb. 6, 1703-4. He was a fisherman and lived in Marblehead. He married Mary Stacy Feb. 8, 1724-5; and died before Dec. 30, 1741, when administration was granted on on his estate. She survived him.

Children, born in Marblehead:—

7—I. MARGARET[4], bapt. Oct. 2, 1726.
8—II. JOSEPH[4], died young, bapt. July 7, 1728.
9—III. JOHN[4], bapt. Oct. 26, 1729.
10—IV. MARY[4], bapt. June 13, 1731.
11—V. MARGARET[4], bapt. Aug. 26, 1733.
12—VI. CHRISTOPHER[4], bapt. Aug. 3, 1735.
13—VII. WILLIAM[4], bapt. June 26, 1737.
14—VIII. HANNAH[4], bapt. Sept. 3, 1738.

6

CHRISTOPHER BUBIER[3], baptized in Marblehead June 16, 1806. He was first a shoreman, then a coaster, then a merchant, and the last twenty-five years of his long life a yeoman. He married Margaret LeVallier Oct. 30, 1726; and she died Feb. 2, 1782, at the age of seventy-three. He died at the home of his daughter Sarah Besom, in Marblehead, June 30, 1789, at the age of eighty-three. His estate was valued at £758, 10*s*. 2*d*.

Children, born in Marblehead:—

15—I. MARY[4], m. John Bassett, Nov. 1, 1750; and d. before 1789.
16—II. JOHN[4], bapt. May 27, 1733. *See below* (16).
17—III. SARAH[4], bapt, Sept. 28, 1735; m. Philip Besom of Marblehead, mariner, Sept. 30. 1751; and was his widow in 1799.
18—IV. JOSEPH[4], bapt. Jan. 15, 1737-8. *See below* (18).
19—V. PETE[4], bapt. March 2, 1739-40. *See below* (19).
20—VI. MARGARET[4], bapt. Apr. 18, 1742; m. Capt. Thomas Grant of Marblehead, goldsmith. July 12, 1761, and d. before 1789.
21—VII. GRACE[4], bapt. Apr. 1, 1744; m. Joseph Prentiss of Marblehead. merchant, before 1789.
22—VIII. WILLIAM[4], bapt, March 30, 1746. *See below* (22).
23—IX. CHRISTOPHER[4], bapt. June. 17, 1750.

16

CAPT. JOHN BUBIER[4], baptized May 27, 1733. He was a mariner and lived in Marblehead. He married Ruth Darling May 23, 1754; and died before June 5, 1770; when administration was granted upon his estate. She survived him and died, his widow, in Marblehead, Jan. 13, 1791, at the age of fifty-six.

Children, born in Marblehead:—

24—I. CHRISTOPHER[5], bapt. Nov. 17, 1754.
25—II. JOHN[5], bapt Feb. 13, 1757.
26—III. BENJAMIN[5], bapt. Jan. 28, 1759. *See below* (26).
27—IV. JOSEPH[5], bapt. May 24, 1761.
28—V. PETER[5], bapt. Oct. 2, 1763; mariner; lived in Marblehead; m. Hannah Collyer Sept. 16, 1792; he d. before March 26, 1778, when administration was granted upon his estate and she was his widow of Marblehead in 1799.
29—VI. HENRY[5], bapt. Feb. 16, 1766; mariner; lived in Marblehead; and administration was granted upon his estate in 1799.

18

Capt. Joseph Bubier[4], baptized in Marblehead Jan 15, 1737-8. He was a mariner, and lived in Marblehead. He married Miss Mary Adams of Marblehead April 19, 1759; and died Dec. 20, 1783, at the age of forty-five years, eleven months and eighteen days. She survived him and was his widow in 1796.

Children, born in Marblehead:—

30—i. John[5], bapt. Nov. 4, 1759; living in 1789.

31—ii. Mary[5], bapt. March 28, 1762; m. John Curtis Aug. 4, 1782; and was living in 1789.

19

Capt. Peter Bubier[4], baptized in Marblehead, March 2, 1739-40. He was first, a mariner, and subsequently a shoreman, and lived in Marblehead, except in 1777 and 1778, when he lived in Lancaster. He married first, Mary Hooper, May 14, 1761; and she died Aug. 28, 1768, at the age of twenty-four years and seven months. He m. second, Miss Abigail Chipman, Jan. 29, 1769, and died before Nov. 11, 1790, when administration was granted on his estate. His wife, Abigail, survived him, and died in Marblehead, his widow, May 30, 1815. She was living in Sterling in 1793 and 1794.

Children, born in Marblehead:—

32—i. Sarah[5], bapt. Aug. 14, 1763; d. Aug. 8, 1781, at the age of eighteen.

33—ii. Mary[5], bapt. June 22, 1766; m. Joseph Barker, 3d, of Marblehead, coaster, July 24 (29?), 1784; and was living in 1789.

34—iii. Abigail[5], bapt. Nov. 12, 1769; unmarried in 1789.

35—iv. John[5], bapt. Sept. 8, 1771; d. Sept 6, 1772.

36—v. Peter[5], bapt. July 18, 1773; mariner; lived in Marblehead; died before July 13, 1793; when administration upon his estate was granted to his mother.

37—vi. John[5], d. Feb. 24, 1777.

38—vii. Sophia Mellen[5], d. Oct. 22, 1780.

39—viii. Elizabeth[5], bapt. Aug. 14, 1785; d. Aug. 13, 1786.

22

William Bubier[4], baptized in Marblehead March 30, 1746. He was a goldsmith and lived in Marblehead. He married Deborah Howard, June 19, 1770; and died before Sept. 4, 1792, when administration upon his estate was granted. She survived him and died, his widow, in Marblehead, Sept. 18, 1808, at the age of sixty-two.

Children, born in Marblehead:—

40—i. Elizabeth[5], bapt. Nov. 18, 1770; unmarried in 1789.

41—ii. Deborah[5], bapt. June 21, 1772; unmarried in 1789.

26

Benjamin Bubier[5], baptized in Marblehead Jan. 28, 1759. He was a mariner and lived in Marblehead. He married Jane Dixcey Nov. 15, 1779; and died before 1791. She survived him* and died in Marblehead of consumption Oet. 25, 1830, at the age of seventy.

Child, born in Marblehead:—

42—i. Ruth[6], bapt. May 2, 1779; of Marblehead; unmarried in 1797.

NOTES

John Bubier, mariner, lived in Marblehead, in 1805. Administration

* Jane, "spurious" dau. of Jane Bubier, bapt. Aug. 21, 1789.—*Marblehead Church Records.*

granted his widow, Hannah, Jan. 15, 1805, of Marblehead.

Child, born in Marblehead:—

1. Joseph, baptized May 30, 1784; lived in Marblehead; mariner in 1810. He married Mary Dodd Oct. 30, 1808. He died in Calcutta. Administration granted to his widow Mary Bubier of Marblehead July 18, 1810.

Christopher, son of Christopher Bubier, baptized Sept. 22, 1728.

John Bubier married Hannah Wadden Nov. 5, 1781.

John Bubier married Hannah Jarvis Jan. 1, 1784. Children of John and Hannah Bubier: Barbara, baptized May 11, 1783; Christopher, baptized March 26, 1786; Hannah, baptized Oct. 4, 1789; John, baptized Aug. 24, 1788; John, baptized Sept. 23, 1792; Mary, baptized Jan. 15, 1786; Sarah, baptized June 12, 1791.

Hannah, daughter of Joseph and Hannah Bubier, baptized Jan. 20, 1788.

Christopher Bubier married Elizabeth Laskey July 28, 1778.

Mrs. Elizabeth Bubier married Edward Grace Sept. 1, 1788.

Henry Bubier married Elizabeth Hooper Aug. 26, 1786.

—*Marblehead records.*

Mary Bubier married Thomas Oliver of Aronsick Feb. 28, 1742.

Peter Bubier published to Mary Martin Oct. 12, 1782. She died before marriage.

Sarah Bubier married Samuel Wormstead Dec. 27, 1762.

—*Marblehead records.*

Widow Elizabeth Bubier of Marblehead was appointed administratrix of estate of Christopher Bubier Jr. of Marblehead, fishermen, July 9, 1788.

—*Probate records.*

Mary daughter of Christopher Boober, baptized March 21, 1730–1

Gloucester church records.

Christopher Bubier lived in Marblehead. He married Sarah Horton Oct. 3, 1754 in Marblehead. She was appointed administratrix of his estate, Feb 2, 1761. She was living, his widow in 1762.

Children baptized in Marblehead:

1. Mary Oct. 19, 1755.
2. Christopher Aug. 11, 1757
3. John Horton Nov. 18, 1559.

DESCENDANTS OF EBENEZER BUCK OF HAVERHILL.

Ebenezer Buck[1], son of Ephraim and Sarah (Brooks) Buck, born in Woburn May 20, 1689; was a weaver, married (probably second wife) Miss Judith Weed of Amesbury Feb. 21, 1722–3; and came to Haverhill to live. He conveyed his homestead in Haverhill to his son Jacob in 1750, and died in 1752; his will, dated March 9 1752, being proved June 29, 1752. She survived him.

Children:—

2—i. Jonathan[2], eldest son, 1752. *See below* (2).

3—ii. Lydia[2], b. about 1715; d. Oct. 11, 1736, aged twenty-one years.

4—iii. Ebenezer[2], b. about 1717, d. May 14 (15?) 1736 aged nineteen.

5—iv. Mary[2], b. April 21, 1724, in Haverhill; m. Nathaniel Green July 16, 1741; and d. Oct. 8, 1741.

6—v. Asa[2]. b. June 23, 1726 in Haverhill; d. Oct. 28, 1741.

7—VI. JACOB[2], b. June 10, 1731 in Haverhill. *See below* (7).
8—VII. PHEBE[2], b. May 21, 1741; d. Feb. 2, 1741-2.

2

JONATHAN BUCK[2], a mariner along the coast, lived in Haverhill. He married Miss Lydia Morse of Newbury Oct. 19, 1742; and was living in Haverhill in 1771.

Children, born in Haverhill:—

9—I. EBENEZER[3], b. March 21, 1743; d. Sept. 21, 1744.
10—II. ASA[3], b. Aug. 29, 1744; d. Feb. 7, 1747-8.
11—III. LYDIA[3], b. April 20, 1746; d. Sept. 15, 1753.
12—IV. JONATHAN[3], b. April 3, 1748. *See below* (12).
13—V. MARY[3], b. Sept. 29, 1750.
14—VI. EBENEZER[3], b. April 25, 1752.
15—VII. AMOS[3], b. July 24, 1754; m. Lydia Chamberlain in Methuen, Oct. 14, 1778.
16—VIII. DANIEL[3], b. Sept. 2, 1756.
17—IX. LYDIA[3], b. Oct. 22, 1761; m. Joshua Treat March 5, 1780.

7

JACOB BUCK[2], born in Haverhill, June 10, 1731. He was a yeoman and lived in Haverhill upon the homestead of his father, which had been conveyed to him before he was of age. He married Hannah Ames of Boxford May 7, 1752. He was living in Haverhill in 1771; and she died in Chester, N. H., March 18, 1809, at the age of eighty-one.

Children, born in Haverhill:—

18—I. MOSES[3], b. March 3, 1754.
19—II. ASA[3], b. Dec. 18, 1755.
20—III. HANNAH[3],* probably m. William Davis June 25, 1780.
21—IV. SAMUEL[3], b. Feb. 26, 1759.
22—V. PHEBE[3], b. Sept. 11. 1760; m. Benjamin Chase of Newbury. (pub. May 13, 1781.)
23—VI. JACOB[3], b. July 27, 1762.
24—VII. ELIPHALET[3], b. Oct. 10, 1764. *See below* (24).
25—VIII. MARY[3], b. July 21, 1766.
26—IX. NATHAN[3], b. Dec. 19, 1768.

* Abraham Buck, son of Hannah Buck, singlewoman, born Dec. 11, 1776.—*Haverhill town records.*

12

JONATHAN BUCK[3], born in Haverhill April 3, 1748. He married Hannah Gale, and lived in Haverhill.

Children, born in Haverhill:—

27—I. BENJAMIN[4], b. Nov. 19, 1768.
28—II. JOHN[4], b. Oct. 27, 1771.
29—III. RUTH[4], b. Aug. 9, 1775.
30—IV. LYDIA[4], b. Oct. 25, 1777.

24

ELIPHALET BUCK[3], born in Haverhill Oct. 10, 1764. He married Sarah Cole Sept. 6, 1785; and lived in Haverhill.

Children, born in Haverhill:—

31—I. SAMUEL[4], b. April 21, 1786.
32—II. SARAH[4], b. Nov. 19, 1787.
33—III. JOHN[4], b, Sept. 27, 1789.
34—IV. SALLY[4], b. Oct. 14, 1791.
35—V. DEBORAH[4], b. Dec. 10, 1792.
36—VI. EBENEZER[4], b. Nov. 28, 1794.
37—VII. KATHERINE[4], b. April 18, 1797.
38—VIII. POLLY[4], b. Dec. 28, 1800.
39—IX. ABIAH[4], b. Nov. 26, 1802.

NOTES

Administration on the estate of John Buck of Marblehead was granted March 3, 1701. Credit was given for money received from the province treasurer.—*Probate records.*

Keziah Buck of Andover married James Marble (of Middleton?) March 17, 1742-3—*Andover town records.*

Ezra Buck married Hannah Jaques June 15, 1794.—*Bradford town records.*

William Buck of Newbury married Phillis Hooper of Newbury Oct. 10, 1783.

Capt. John Buck married Miss Elizabeth Bartlet, both of Newburyport, Dec. 28, 1784, and had a daughter Eliza, born July 23, 1796.

—*Newburyport town records.*

Polly Buck of Haverhill married Winthrop Flanders June 8, 1786.

—*Salisbury town records.*

BUCKHORN NOTE

Alexander Buckhorn published to Elizabeth Grealey, Aug. 6, 1774.

—*Marblehead town records.*

BUCKLER NOTES

Daniel Buckler married Ruth Picket Jan. 16, 1787; she was buried June 9, 1796; aged thirty-two. They lived in Beverly, where their children were born as follows; James, born June 27, 1787; Daniel, born Aug. 3, 1789; William, born Aug. 3, 1789; William born Sept. 20, 1791; Pegge, born April 11, 1794; Ruth, born May 25, 1796.—*Beverly records.*

William Buckley, a shoemaker, lived in Ipswich 1657-1674, and in Salem, 1681-1702; married Miss Sarah Smith of Ipswich. He was dead in 1705, administration being granted on his estate Feb. 8, 1714; she died before 1726. Children born in Ipswich; 1. William, born Dec. 8, 1657; died in 1659. 2. William, died Aug. 16, 1660. 3. John, born May 8, 1660. 4. Priscilla, married William Stacey 28: 9: 1697; and was his widow, of Salem, in 1726. 5. Mary, married —— Procter, and was his widow, of Salem, in 1727. 6. William, born Oct. 14, 1666; was a shoemaker or cordwainer; lived in Salem; married first, Abigail Caves of Topsfield Dec. 21, 1697; second, widow Dorcas Faulkner of Salem Feb. 20, 1734-5; he died; and she married, third, Joshua Felt of Lynn June 16, 1736. In 1714 and 1729, he was the only surviving son of William Buckley. 7. Elizabeth, born May — 1669.

—*Records.*

Children of Joseph Buckley: Elizabeth, born Feb. 12, 1772; Joseph, May 13, 1774; ——lly (daughter) born June 6, 1780.

—*Newbury town records.*

Mary Buckley, married Silvester Whitterage Nov. 17, 1684.

—*Marblehead town records.*

Mrs. Dorothy Buckley married Jonathan Wade Dec. 9, 1660 in Ipswich.—*Court records.*

BUCKMAN NOTES

Samuel Buckman, feltmaker of Amesbury, 1687-1689; of Newbury 1702-1734; wife Martha Harris 1687-89, wife Mary 1736-7; children of Samuel and Martha (Haines) Buckman; Samuel (first son) born Sept. 16, 1687; died Oct. 21, 1687; Samuel (second son), born Nov. 10, 1688; died Nov. 28, 1688; Sarah, born Nov. 26, 1689; married Abraham Colby of Rowley Nov. 21, 1712.

—*Amesbury town records.*

John Buckman married Elizabeth Woodberry April 5, 1772; she died in Beverly March 24, 1827, of dyspepsia, at the age of seventy-eight; children, born in Beverly; 1. Elizabeth, born March 6, 1773; married —— True; and she was his widow in 1827: 2.

John; born Sept. 21, 1775, living in 1819, married Miss Sarah Wood Oct. 4, 1798; she died Oct. 16, (18?) 1825, aged forty-nine; he died March 15, 1831; their children were born as follows; Sophia, born Nov. 21, 1778; ———; died Sept. 28, 1800, aged three days; Elizabeth, born March 11, 1802; Sally, born Nov. 26, 1804; Almira, born Sept. 20, 1807; married William H. Johnson Dec. 24, 1829; Mercy Wood, born Feb. 5, 1810; John James, baptized Oct. 23, 1813; John James, born Oct. 8, 1814; Mary Wood, born July 11, 1816; died Oct. 11, 1817.—*Beverly records.*

James Buckman of Salem, mariner, died on board the brig Ranger, and administration upon his estate was granted May 7, 1787.

Widow Sarah Buckman of Ipswich was appointed administratrix in the estate of her late husband John Buckman of Ipswich, fisherman, Feb. 24, 1724-5. Dr. Samuel Wallis of Ipswich attended him in his last sickness, before Nov. 19, 1723.

—*Probate records.*

Mary Buckman married William Collins, Sept. 10, 1769.

Sarah Buckman married Samuel Shattock, Jr. July 24, 1676.

Dr. David Buckman married Esther Sprague of Malden, March 4, 1745-6.

—*Salem records.*

Hannah Buckman married John Masters Feb. 12, 1729-30.

Sarah Buckman published to Samuel Whitaker of Concord, Sept. 4, 1731.

Children of Jeremy Buckman; ———, baptized April —, 1717; Stephen; baptized Oct. 7, 1722; Martha, baptized Aug. 16, 1724.

—*Ipswich records.*

Jose Buckman of Malden married Hannah Peabody of Boxford Feb. 24, 1690; her son Joses baptized Oct. 30, 1692.—*Topsfield church records.*

Children of Jeremiah and Hannah Buckman; Jeremiah, baptized June 29, 1729; Hannah, June 29, 1731.

David, son of Jeremiah Buckman, baptized June 19, 1726.

Betsey Buckman married Jacob Thomson, Jr. Jan. 24, 1793.

—*Beverly records.*

Elisha Buckman married Elizabeth Porter Aug. 1 (7——*church record.*) 1799.

Mary Buckman of Ipswich married William Handcock of Marblehead, Jan., 18 1719-20.

Sarah Buckman married John Perault July 12, 1725.

—*Marblehead records.*

Jeremiah Buckman* of Ipswich 1713–1731; laborer 1713, 1714; yeoman 1720, 1721; housewright 1730–31; son Jeremiah, lived in Beverly 1720-1731, cordwainer 1730-1731; married Hannah Lamson (published Dec. —, 1720.)

—*Records.*

Joseph Buckman married Judith Maddox Oct. 16, 1791.

—*Gloucester town records.*

Joseph Buckman of Ipswich married Mary Legro of Wenham Nov. 29, 1724; children, born in Ipswich; 1. John, baptized Nov. 14; 1725; 2. Joseph, baptized May 26, 1728; 3. Benjamin, baptized Aug. 30, 1730.

—*Ipswich records.*

Daniel Buckman of Ipswich married Elizabeth Edwards of Wenham

*Jeremiah Buckman of Lexington, carpenter and wife Hannah sold land in Hamlet parish, Ipswich in 1732.—*Essex Registry of Deeds.*

Dec. 7, 1720; lived in Wenham 1722-1724; and in Beverly 1725-1735; was a cordwainer and fisherman. He died in Ipswich of apoplexy, Aug. 3, 1773, aged seventy-one. Children born in Beverly: 1. —— died May 26, 1725; 2. —— d. in infancy Jan. 9, 1729-30; 3. Daniel, born Sept. 16, 1726; 4. Eleanour, baptized Sept. 8, 1728; 5. Edwarde, born July 31, 1730; Pelatiah, baptized Nov. 14, 1731.

—*Records*.

BUCKMASTER NOTES

Elizabeth Buckmaster married Moses Moody Sept. 10, 1785.

—*Haverhill town records*.

John Buckmaster married Deborah Wood Nov. 29, 1789.—*Boxford town records*.

BUCKMINISTER NOTES

Rachel Buckminster married Joshua Brown May 25, 1788.—*Boxford tow records*.

John Buckminster, resident in Ipswich, published to Hannah Butler of Ipswich Nov. 3, 1787.—*Ipswich town records*.

Judith, wife of Richard Buckminster of Newburyport, died, on a visit to his sister, Mrs. John Smith, Nov. 2, 1772, aged thirty-seven.

—*Rowley town records*.

BUDESART NOTE

John Griffin was appointed administrator of the estate of his mother, Agnes Budesart (also deceased 24: 9: 1682) April 10, 1683, by court at Ipswich. She was apparently of Newbury.—*Probate records*.

DESCENDANTS OF THOMAS BUFFINGTON OF SALEM.

THOMAS BUFFINGTON[1] lived in Salem 1671-1728; husbandman 1685-1726; married Miss Sarah Southwick of Salem, 30: 10 mo. 1670. Will dated Sept. 18, 1725, proved Aug. 28, 1728. Wife Sarah survived him and was his widow in 1733.

Children, born in Salem:—

2—I. THOMAS[2], b. March 1, 1671. *See below* (2).
3—II. BENJAMIN[2], b. July 24, 1675. *See below* (3).
4—III. ABIGAIL[2], b. July 25, 1695; married Samuel King, jr., husbandman, of Salem, Aug. 13, 1714.

2

THOMAS BUFFINGTON[2], born in Salem March 1, 1671; lived in Salem; married Hannah Ross Feb. 28, 1699. She was his wife in 1705 and he was dead in 1725.

Children*, born in Salem:—

5—I. HANNAH[3], b. May 11, 1701.
6—II. SARAH[3], b. Aug. 30, 1703.
7—II. THOMAS[3], b. June 25, 1705 of Killingsly Co., yeoman, 1749.
8—IV. JAMES. *See below* (8). It is not absolutely certain that James (8) was the son of Thomas (2), but evidences point that way and Thomas (3) mentions a brother or brothers.

3

BENJAMIN BUFFINGTON[2], born in Salem July 24, 1675; husbandman; lived in Salem in 1705, and in Swansey, Mass., 1725-1733.

Children, born in Salem:—

9—I. BENJAMIN[3], born May 4, 1699.
10—II. WILLIAM[3], b. Oct. 9, 1702.
11—III. Jo[3], b. March 25, 1704-5.

* There were sons other than Thomas.

8

JAMES BUFFINGTON, lived in Salem 1739–1773; cordwainer 1739–1773; wife Elizabeth 1740–1773. His will dated May 13, 1773, proved June 8, 1773; his estate being appraised at £631:1*s.*:8½*d.* Many shoes on hand at death.

Children:—

12—I. BETTY[2], baptized July 27, 1740, in middle precinct (Peabody); m. Nathan Putnam Aug. 2, 1752, and was living in 1773.

13—II. MARY[2], born Aug. 25, 1735, in Salem; m Thomas Gardner of Danvers, June 13, 1755, and was living in 1773.

14—III. HANNAH[2], baptized July 27, 1740, in middle precinct (Peabody).

15—IV. JAMES[2], baptized July 27, 1740, in middle precinct (Peabody). *See below* (5).

16—V. JOHN[2], b. about 1742. *See below* (6).

17—VI. SARAH[2], married Benjamin Chapman Nov. 24, 1762.

18—VII. NEHEMIAH[2], b. about 1745; mariner 1775–1799; merchant, 1789–1799; yeoman 1816–1832. Lived in Salem; married, first, Elizabeth Procter, Sept. 14, 1774; second, Elizabeth Ashton, Jan. 26, 1786. He died March 18, 1832. She survived him and died of palsy, his widow, April 4, 1845, aged eighty-eight.

19—VIII. ELIZABETH[2], married William Butman before 1773.

20—IX. LYDIA[2], married Robert Cook, jr., March 10, 1767, and was living in 1773.

21—X. JONATHAN[2], mariner, of Salem. 1775.

22—XI. ZADOCK[2]. *See below* (12).

15

JAMES BUFFINGTON[2], baptized middle precinct (Peabody) July 27, 1740. Lived in Salem and was a cordwainer in 1762 and 1772, and a mariner in 1776. He married Prudence Procter of Danvers Feb. 14, 1765. Administration was granted on his estate May 6, 1776. His estate was appraised at £494:5*s*:10*d*. She survived him, and married, secondly, Daniel Frye March 15, 1783.

Children:—

23—I. PRUDENCE[3], married Jacob Tucker Sept. 7, 1788, and was of Salem, his widow, in 1794.

24—II. HANNAH[3], b. in Salem Jan. 30, 1767; married Elijah Briggs of Scituate, ship-builder, Aug. 15, 1789, and returned to Salem to live in 1796.

25—III. BETSEY[3], married David Nichols Nov. 17, 1798.

26—IV. JAMES[3], mariner. lived in Salem; married Elizabeth Dennis Dec. 10, 1797. Administration was granted on his estate Aug. 28, 1805, and she survived him.

27—V. SARAH[3], born in Salem, Sept. 27, 1772, married Ebenezer Mann of Salem, ship-builder, Oct. 31, 1791.

16

CAPT. JOHN BUFFINGTON[2], born about 1742; mariner, 1775–1805; merchant 1779–1827. Lived in Salem; married Mary Pitman Aug. 18, 1767, and she was his wife in 1818. He died of old age Feb. 17, 1827, aged eighty-three.

Children (only heirs-at-law in 1827):—

28—I.— JOHN[3], b. about 1767; died of a rupture in Salem Nov. 5, 1818, aged fifty-one.

29—II. ELIZA[3], married Nathaniel Williams Crafts, before 1818.

30—III. POLLY[3], b about 1773; died Apr. 27, 1797.

22

CAPT. ZADOCK BUFFINGTON[2], cordwainer 1775; gentleman 1782–1793; esquire 1797–1799. Conducted tavern at the corner of Washington and

Church streets in 1793. He married, first, Miss Abigail Procter in Aug. or Sept., 1776, in Salem; and she was his wife in 1788. He married, second, Deborah Saltmarsh, June 7, 1789. His will dated March 15, 1799, was proved June 26, 1799, and his estate was valued at $8,483.50. His wife Deborah survived him and died, his widow, in the spring of 1815.

Children:—

31—I. JONATHAN[3], minor in 1799 and of Boston, merchant, in 1815.

32—II. LYDIA[3], aged under twenty-five years in 1799.

NOTES

Thomas Nehemiah Buffington, of Salem, laborer. 1797.—*Registry of deeds.*

Mary Buffington, baptized March 31, 1728.—*Middle precinct (Peabody) Salem church records.*

Children of James and Abigail Buffington:—

1. James, b. Dec. 12, 1798.
2. Mary, b. May 5, 1802.
3. Martha, b. July 1, 1805.
4. Abigail, b. Nov. 26, 1806.
5. Hannah, b. Dec. 4, 1808.

—*Danvers town records.*

Hannah Buffington married Jonathan Marsh, Sr., Oct. 7, 1725.

Hannah Buffington married Sylvester Procter Dec. 3, 1761.

Thomas Buffington married Mary Coffen, Aug. 22, 1758.

—*Salem town records.*

(*To be continued.*)

Criticism & Comment

on Books and Other Subjects

Randall Family

"A Biographical History of Robert Randall and his descendants 1608-1909. By William L. Chaffin. The Grafton Press genealogical publishers, New York MCMIX. xx. 247 pages. $5.00 from the compiler, Rev. W. L. Chaffin, North Easton, Mass.

From the admirable introductory essay on the Randall families of America by A. F. Randall, president of the "Randall Historical Association of America," it appears that there are no less than 25 distinct and, as far as known, unconnected Randall families in this country; and while several accounts of individual lines have appeared, this is "the first genealogy of all the descendants of an immigrant Randall ancestor."

The original Robert Randall settled in Weymouth about 1635, but his descendants for several generations centered at Easton, Mass., where they were at one time the largest family, and no less than 25 of the name enlisted in the Revolutionary army from that town.

The work is no mere genealogy, if by that term we understand a dreary succession of names and dates; perhaps its most notable feature is Mr. Chaffin's success in making the members of the family live before us, the little sketches or characterizations of individuals, which lend a touch of personal interest to its pages. Those of us who have tried, know how difficult an art this is.

The compiler, for forty years pastor at North Easton, and well known as author of the "History of the town of Easton", has been collecting data for twenty years, the last two or three since retirement from active professional work, being devoted to perfecting and completing this history. The volume concludes with an excellent index of nearly fifty pages.

Numbers of the Indian Tribes Overestimated.

R. A. Douglas-Lithgow, in his new work, "Dictionary of American Indian Place and Proper Names in New England," says of the Indian tribes occupying Massachusetts and the other New England states: "With regard to their aggregate tribal numbers many opinions have been expressed and many estimates given by some of the earlier writers, but most of them have been as rash as extravagant. More careful recent inquiry has elicited the fact that the number of Indians occupying New England, at any time subsequent to the year 1600, has been very much exaggerated, and the writer has been assured by two well-known modern anthropologists, who have made a special study of the matter, that the total number of Indians in New England about the year 1600 did not exceed 24, or 25,000. Their calculations, arrived at independently, are based upon an average of between 75 to 80 souls in each village, and the results are as follows:—

Pequots,	2000
Narragansetts,	5000
Massachusetts,	2500
Wampanoags,	3000
Pawtuckets,	2000
Mohegans,	2000
Maine Indians,	2500
All others,	2500
Total,	21,500

255

Our Editorial Pages

REV. THOMAS FRANKLIN WATERS.

WITH the completion of the work on the Rebecca Nourse house in Danvers, another has been added to the long list of ancient dwellings rescued from decay and preserved to future generations. It needs not be said that the work has been done with good judgment and fine sympathy. Restoration has become a fine art. Architect and amateur alike recognize that the cardinal principle is absolute adherence to the original architecture, wherever it can be determined.

The small casement windows, with diminutive panes have been wisely adhered to through the great rooms heavily beamed above and the side walls finished in matched boarding of an ancient style, are dark and gloomy, save when the sunlight or firelight bring good cheer. A single coat of whitewash was common in ancient times and a whitened ceiling would have relieved the depressing atmosphere of these shadowy, mysterious rooms. But no such light touch has found place here. The dark time-stained hue of the natural wood is its only adornment and it lends itself with peculiar fitness to a dwelling, filled with such solemn and pathetic memories. The cavernous fire places with the black mouth of the oven opening into unknown depths of darkness, are in fine harmony. Severe, homely simplicity is never departed from. This Puritan home breathes the spirit of the stern Puritan times, in every nook and corner.

The story of its restoration to its primal dignity is the old familiar one. It was in danger of destruction by an owner, who had no appreciation of sentimental values. A woman of fine historic sense, feeling keenly the shame that would be entailed by its loss, gave herself with wonderful patience to the task of raising funds for its purchase. She made appeal to a public, always generous and with its generosity unexhausted by the frequent demands upon it. The response was gratifying and adequate One princely gift came from a descendant of Governor Endicott, who was the original owner of the farm. Small contributions from many givers swelled the total sum to some seven thousand dollars. The house and twenty-five acres adjoining and surrounding the dwelling, were bought and the title was vested in an Association, organized to hold the property. The deed was done so quietly, so quickly, and apparently so easily, that any enthusiastic friend of any old dwelling in any part of our Commonwealth, which has reasonable claim for preservation, may proceed with confidence to raise a fund by public subscription.

Apart from its intrinsic value, as an excellent specimen of a seventeenth century home, peculiar personal associations hallow this ancient house. From this fireside, a woman of spotless character, well advanced in years, the mother of a goodly family was dragged to prison, to trial and to the scaffold in the summer of 1692. She was charged with the practise of witchcraft, and some frivolous girls accused her of tormenting them in supernatural fashion. When she was arraigned before the Justices, they uttered piercing shrieks and declared that she bit or stamped upon them. She protested her innocence and

made solemn appeal to God to help her but in the frenzied excitement of that dreadful time, calm judgment or natural sympathy was impossible

THOSE who were first accused may have been beldames of sharp tongue and persons of unsavory reputation. Robert Calef observes that among these were "Sarah Good, who had long been counted amel ancholy or distracted woman; and one Osborn, an old bedridden woman; which two were persons so ill thought of, that the accusation was the more readily believed." But the distracted victims of that extraordinary delusion soon brought charges against people of finest quality. Little Dorothy Good, the five year old daughter of Sarah, was charged with being a witch and was imprisoned with her mother. Mary Easty, the sister of Rebecca Nourse, was accused, acquitted, arrested again two days later and sentenced to death. She petitioned the Court: "the Lord above knows my innocence then and likewise doth now, as at the great day will be known by men and angels, I petition your honors not for my own life, for I know I must die, and my appointed time is set; but the Lord he knows if it be possible that no more innocent blood be shed, which undoubtedly cannot be avoided in the way and course you go in." When she bade farewell to her husband, children and friends, "she was, as is reported by them present, as serious, religious, distinct and affectionate as could well be exprest; drawing tears from the eyes of almost all present." The excellent Madame Hale of Beverly, wife of the minister, fell under suspicion; Rev. George Burroughs, the former minister of a Salem church, was condemned and executed.

The history of Salem witchcraft has been written again and again, wisely and well, and the innocence of the unfortunate victims has been abundantly proved, but a lingering suspicion abides in some minds that the condemned were at fault, and may have met a fate that was in some measure deserved. There is a popular misconception, that passes for truth with too many of careless mind, that the witch was an old hag, arrayed in conical hat and flowing cloak, who bestrode her broomstick and rode down the midnight wind, in quest of victims.

She is seized upon by tradesmen as a catchy advertisement of their wares. Thoughtless young men, innocent of any evil motive, taking their cue from the common error, parade the streets as political campaign clubs, wearing the accepted garb of the ancient witch. Thus in burlesque, with gibe and sneer, or silly grin, the saddest and most pitiful of all delusions is recalled, with monstrous falsity, and painful heartlessness.

NO more wise and weighty protest against the prevalent shallow thought, no more apt and suggestive portrayal of the Truth, no more befitting honor to those who died, can be conceived than this silent but eloquent memorial. It has seemed worth while that the home of one of those, who died so ignominiously, should be restored, and preserved to all time. It was dedicated with no labored eulogy of the good woman, who dwelt here. With a few well chosen words by broad minded and sympathetic men, it was opened to all who care to come. In the course of years, many will come and as they tarry a little in these old rooms, they will feel the spell of the Past. Rebecca Nourse, the wife and mother, the neighbor and friend, loyal, loving and tender, will live again. Her gentle presence will glorify her old home, and win the hearts of many to herself, and to her companions in sorrow and bitterness, in wiser and more just appreciation, in tender sympathy and enduring love.

INDEX OF AUTHORS AND SUBJECTS FOR VOLUME II, MASSACHUSETTS MAGAZINE

PREPARED BY CHARLES A. FLAGG

Authors' names italicized.

"Active," Mass. brigantine, 234.
Adultery, The "Scarlet letter," 3.
American Revolution, Department of the, 45, 101, 168, 234.
——— Lamson's Weston company, 132.
——— Mass. brigantine, "Active." 234.
——— Mass. brigantine, "Independence," 45.
——— Mass. naval legislation, 45.
——— Mass. officers, 18, 46, 72, 101, 146, 168, 191, 208, 235.
——— Mass. sloop, "Freedom," 101.
——— Mass. sloop, "Republic," 168.
——— Mass. sloop, "Tyrannicide," 192.
——— Negroes in naval service, 236.
——— Privateer, "General Pickering," 196.
——— Privateer, "Julius Caesar," 198.
——— Rations, Beer complained of, 17.
——— Regiments, Bridge's, 203.
——— " Danielson's, 69.
——— " Doolittle's, 11.
——— " Fellows', 141.
See also Bunker Hill; Haraden, Capt. J.; Lexington; Valley Forge.
Antietam battlefield, 118.
Army of the United colonies; *see* American Revolution, Regiments.
Bachiller, Mrs. Mary, of Kittery, the original of Hawthorne's Hester Prynne, 3.
Bartlett family gathering, 1909. 185.
Battlefields, High school trips to, 118.
" Bay State Monthly," 48.
Beer in rations, Complained of, 1775, 17.
Benefactions to towns, 187.
Berkshire County, Fellow's regiment, partly from, 141.
Bodge, George M., historian, 51.
Books reviewed
Chaffin, W. L. A biographical history of Robert Randall and his descendants, 254.
Fisher, S. G. The struggle for American independence, 105.
Pope, C. H. The pioneers of Maine and New Hampshire, 50.
Boston, Historical pilgrimages to, 120.
Boston Bay, Settlers before 1630, 115, 176.
Bowen, Ashley, Diary, 109.
Bridge's regiment, 1775, 203.
Browning family notes, Essex County, 240.
Bruce family notes, Essex County, 241.
Bruer family notes, Essex County, 241.
Brumagin family notes, Essex County, 241.
Brunier family notes, Essex County, 242.
Brunson family notes, Essex county, 242.
Bryant family notes, Essex County, 242.
Bryers family notes, Essex County, 244.
Bryson family notes, Essex County, 244.
Bubier family, Descendants of Joseph of Marblehead, 244.
Buck family, Descendants of Ebenezer of Haverhill, 247.
Buckhorn family notes, Essex County, 249.
Buckler family notes, Essex County, 249.
Buckman family notes, Essex County, 249.
Buckmaster family notes, Essex County, 251.
Buckminster family notes, Essex County, 251
Budesart family notes, Essex County, 251.

Buffington family, Descendants of Thomas of Salem, 251.
Bunker Hill, Bridge's regiment at, 205.
——— Doolittle's regiment at, 15.
Carnegie Institution. Failure to encourage art and literature, 56.
Chaffin, William L. Biographical history of Robert Randall and his descendants. Reviewed, 254.
Chase Family Association, 174.
Civil War, *see* Antietam, Gettysburg, Newbern, N. C.
Clemens family notes, Salem 107.
Conant, Roger, Monument in Salem, or Gloucester? 184.
Criticism and comment department, 48, 107, 174, 254.
Cutting family of Weston, 136.
Danielson's regiment, 1775, 69.
Danvers. Rebecca Nourse house restored, 255.
Deerfield, Williams house, 41.
Dennis Albert W. Some Massachusetts historical writers, 51.
Doolittle's regiment, 1775, 11.
Douglas-Lithgow, R. A. Indians in Mass, overestimated, 254.
Draper, Eben S. Ancestry of, 123.
Draper, T. W. M. Ancestry of Gov. Eben S. Draper, 123.
Editorial department, 55, 118, 186, 255.
Eliot, Charles W., 59.
Emigrants from Mass., Michigan series, 39, 66, 200.
"Essex Antiquarian" Genealogical department continued in Mass. Magazine, 240.
Essex County. Bridge's regiment, partly from, 203.
——— Genealogical Dictionary, 240.
Fellows' regiment, 1775, 141.
Fisher, Sidney G. The struggle for American independence. Reviewed, 105.
Flagg, Charles A. Dedication of Mass, monument at Newbern, N. C., 48.
——— Local historical societies in Mass., 84.
——— Mass. pioneers, Michigan series, 39, 66, 200.
——— Name "Massachusetts Magazine," 48.
Charles A. Flagg. Old Merriam house, Grafton, 98.
——— Review of Chaffin's Biographical history of Robert Randall, 254.
——— Review of Pope's Pioneers of Maine and New Hampshire, 50.
——— Some articles concerning Mass. in recent magazines, 42, 99, 162, 228.
——— Some Mass. books of 1908, 49.
——— William Abbatt's "Magazine of History," 174.
"Freedom," Mass. sloop and brigantine, 101.
Gardner, Frank A. Ancestors of Benjamin Clemens Witherell, 107.
——— Captain Jonathan Haraden, 191,
——— Colonel Ebenezer Bridge's regiment, 203.
——— Colonel Ephraim Doolittle's regiment, 11.
——— Colonel John Fellow's regiment, 141.
——— Colonel Timothy Danielson's regiment, 69,
——— Department of the American Revolution, 45, 101, 168, 234.
——— The George Gardner house, West Peabody, 230.
——— Heroes and monuments, 171.
——— Historical pageants, 107.
——— Review of Fisher's Struggle for American independence, 105.
Gardner, Lucie M. Family genealogies, Essex Co., 240.
——— Gloucester day, 1909. 184.
——— Pilgrims and planters department, 54, 115, 176, 239.
——— Settlers about Boston Bay prior to 1630, 115, 176.
Gardner Family Association, 117, 183.
Gardner house, West Peabody, 230.
Genealogists, Presumption of, 55.
"General Pickering," privateer, 196.
Gettysburg battlefield, 119.
Gloucester day, 1909, 184.
Grafton, Merriam house, 98.
Hampden County, *see* Hampshire County.

Hampshire County, Danielson's regiment from, 69.
Hampshire County, Fellow's regiment, partly from, 141.
Haraden, Capt. Jonathan, of Salem, 191.
Hastings family of Weston, 137.
Hawthorne, Nathaniel. The "Scarlet letter" and old Ketterie, 3.
Henniker, N. H. Old home week, 186.
Heroes and monuments, 171.
Hews family of Weston, 138.
High school trips to Washington and battlefields, 118.
Hill, Mrs. Caroline R. The old Rand house, 165.
Historic houses, Gardner house, West Peabody, 230.
——— Merriam house, Grafton, 98.
——— Nourse house, Danvers, 255.
——— Noyes house, Newbury, 30.
——— Rand house, Weston, 165.
——— Williams house, Deerfield, 41.
Historical investigation, Encouragement of, 56.
Historical magazines, Early American, 174.
Historical pageants in Mass. 1909, 107.
Historical societies in Mass., List of, 84.
Hubbard family of Weston, 138.
"Independence," Mass. brigantine, 45.
Indians in Mass. Numbers in colonial times, 254.
James, Edward J. Tribute to Pres. Eliot, 60.
Jordan, David S. Tribute to Pres. Eliot, 63.
"Julius Caesar," privateer, 198.
Kittery, Maine. The "Scarlet Letter," 3.
Lamson, Daniel S. Weston, 129.
Lamson family of Weston, 138.
Lamson's Weston company at Lexington, 132.
Lee, Col. Jeremiah, of Marblehead, 239.
Lexington, Battle of, Weston company at, 132.
Livermore, Mrs. Mary A. at Marietta, 1888, 33.
Local historical societies in Mass., 84.
Local history, Encouragement to students of, 56.
McClintock, John N., Weston, 129.
"Magazine of history," 174.
Marblehead, Bowen's diary, 109.
——— Col. Jeremiah Lee, 239.
——— Old Planters Society meeting, Sept. 1909, 239.
Marietta, O. Centennial of 1888. Mrs. Mary A. Livermore at, 33.
Massachusetts, Bibliography of historical writings. Books of 1908, 49.
——— ——— Magazine articles, etc., 1908–1909, 42, 99, 162, 228.
——— Historical pageants, 1909, 107.
——— Historical writers, 51.
——— Indian population overestimated, 254.
——— Local historical societies, List of, 84.
——— Monument at Newbern, N. C. dedicated, 48.
——— Naval legislation in Revolution, 45.
——— Navy *see* American Revolution; Haraden, Capt. J.
——— Pioneers, Michigan series, 39, 66, 200.
——— Privateer, "General Pickering," 196.
——— Privateer, "Julius Caesar," 198.
——— Regiments *see under* American Revolution.
——— Revolutionary officers, 18, 46, 72, 101, 146, 168, 191, 208, 235.
——— Settlers about Boston Bay before 1630, 115, 176.
"Massachusetts Magazine," Earlier periodicals of the name, 48.
Mayflower Society, 54, 239.
Merriam house, Grafton, 98.
Michigan, Pioneers from Mass., 39, 66, 200.
Middlesex County, Bridge's regiment partly from, 203.
Military heroes, Monuments to, 171.
Minute men, *see* American Revolution, Regiments.
Monuments to military heroes, 171.
Negroes in the Revolutionary navy, 236.
New Hampshire, Bridge's regiment partly from, 203.
Newbern, N. C. Dedication of Mass. monument, 48.

Newbury, Noyes house, 30.
Northrop, Cyrus, Tribute to Pres. Eliot, 65.
Northwest Territory. Centennial 1888, An incident, 33.
Nourse house, Danvers, restored, 255.
Noyes, Benjamin L., The Rev. James Noyes house in Newbury, 30.
Noyes house, Newbury, 30.
Old home week, 186.
Old planters, Boston, 115, 176.
Old Planters Society, 54, 117, 185, 239.
Our editorial page, 55, 118, 186, 255.
The Pathfinder (Mrs. Livermore) at Marietta, 33.
Peabody, Gardner house, 230.
Perley, Sidney, Genealogical dictionary of Essex County, Continuation of, 240.
Pilgrims and planters department, 54, 115, 176, 239.
Pope, Charles H., The pioneers of Maine and New Hampshire. Reviewed, 50.
Public utility funds, Plea for establishment, 187.
Punishments, The " Scarlet Letter," 3.
Putnam Association, 185.
Record officials, Unreasonable requests from, 55.
Regiments, *see under* American Revolution.
"Republic," Mass. sloop, 168.
Revolution, American, *see* American Revolution.
Salem, Capt. Jonathan Haraden, 191.
——— Field day, of Mass. S. A. R. Sept. 1909, 173, 237.
——— Privateers "General Pickering" and "Julius Caesar," 196.
——— Witchcraft, 255.
Sanborn, Nathan P., Sketch of Col. Jeremiah Lee, 239.
Sears family of Weston, 139.
Sectional feeling, Decline of, 48.
Sheldon, George, The Pathfinder at Marietta, O. in 1888, 33.
Sheridan, Philip H., Defence of, 172.
Society of Mayflower Descendants, 54, 239.
Sons of the American Revolution, Mass. Field day, 173, 237.
——— Mass. Bay cloister, at Valley Forge, 173.
Sylvester, Herbert M., The "Scarlet letter" and old Ketterie, 3.
Sylvester, Herbert M., historian, 52.
Town clerks, Unreasonable requests from, 55.
Towns, Benefactions to, 187.
"Tyrannicide," Mass. sloop, 192.
Valley Forge, Dedication of Mass. Bay cloister, in Memorial chapel, 173.
Van Ness, Thomas, Protest against monuments to military heroes, 172.
Washington, Booker T., Tribute to Pres. Eliot, 61.
Washington, D.C., High school trips to, 118.
Waters, Thomas F., Our editorial pages, 55, 118, 186, 255.
West Peabody, Gardner house, 230.
Weston, History and genealogy, 129.
——— Lamson's company at Lexington. 1775, 132.
——— Rand house, 165.
Williams house, Deerfield, 41.
Winsor family of Weston, 139.
Witchcraft delusion, 255.
Witherell, Benjamin C., Ancestors of, 107.
Witherell family of Salem, 107.
Worcester County, Doolittle's regiment from, 11.
——— Fellow's regiment partly from, 141.

The foregoing is *not* an index of personal names. Such an index covering every name found on the pages of the magazine will be issued at convenient periods, probably every five years; the theory being that for genealogical or general reference use such a consolidation will be more helpful than an annual issue

HOTEL ENDICOTT

Our Series of

Famous Old Houses

Nearly every town in the State has some old house, a historic land mark for generations, about which clusters some old legend or association that makes it celebrated in the neighborhood. We wish to get photographs of all such and will pay $1.00 apiece for all that we can use. Send with photograph a description of the house.

Settlers about Boston prior to

The Pilgrims and Planters Department magazine is devoted to the study of the sett made in Massachusetts before 1630 and t who made them. We have considered th Ann–Salem Planters in these pages and in tl issue we will publish a study of the settler Boston Bay. An endeavor will be made to complete a list as possible of the men w with an account of what they accomplishe

Communications to our Department of Comment and Criticism

In our department of "COMMENT AND CRITICISM ON BOOKS AND OTHER SUBJECTS" we invite communications from our readers on any subject of Massachusetts history. We will be glad to have important newspaper clippings submitted. In fact, we shall welcome anything of wide-spread interest concerning men, books, societies, or records associated with Massachusetts history.

Some Massachusetts Historical Writers

Suggestions from our readers of names for this department will be gladly received. We wish to print biographies of the town historians, compilers of family genealogies, and other historical writers. All over Massachusetts, we desire to know the historians of the small towns as well as the men who have written many books and pamphlets on a variety of historical subjects.

In recognition of Dr. Chas. W. Eliot's retirement from the presidency of Harvard University after 40 years of service, in May, the April number will contain an article, taking notice of the event.

A complete list of the active historical Societies in Massachusetts, with names of officers, etc., will be printed in the April number. It is now in preparation by Mr. Chas. A. Flagg, of the Library of Congress, who has conducted an extensive coresonpdence with all parts of the State, in order to locate the small societies, which have not appeared in previous lists.

N. E. N. C.

The Massach Historical Soc

A feature of o issue will be an a the historical soc the state, includi of such societie plete as near as to make it. wit particulars about

Weston

Owing to conge other material v been obliged t publication of ar on Weston by Clintock.

Membershi the Heredit Patriotic Sc

Dr. Gardner in partment of the A Revolution" will to answer quest supply any inform can regarding tionary matters, t persons to identi genealogical conr or to prove the tionary service o ancestors;as a pre to membership in A. R., S. A. R. a patriotic orders.

CPSIA information can be obtained
at www.ICGtesting.com
Printed in the USA
BVHW072127231118
533618BV00054B/1054/P

9 781527 867444